D0154078

DATE DUE

Q
127
.U6
H32
1998

Hart, David M.
Forged consensus

COGSWELL COLLEGE LIBRARY
1175 Bordeaux Drive
Sunnyvale, CA 94089
408/541-0100, Ext. 144

DEMCO

FORGED CONSENSUS

PRINCETON STUDIES IN AMERICAN POLITICS:
HISTORICAL, INTERNATIONAL, AND
COMPARATIVE PERSPECTIVES

SERIES EDITORS

IRA KATZNELSON, MARTIN SHEFTER, AND THEDA SKOCPOL

A list of titles

in this series appears

at the back of

the book

FORGED CONSENSUS

SCIENCE, TECHNOLOGY, AND ECONOMIC POLICY IN THE UNITED STATES, 1921–1953

David M. Hart

RECEIVED
APR 1 3 1999

PRINCETON UNIVERSITY PRESS   PRINCETON, NEW JERSEY

Copyright © 1998 by Princeton University Press
Published by Princeton University Press, 41 William Street,
Princeton, New Jersey 08540
In the United Kingdom: Princeton University Press, Chichester, West Sussex
All Rights Reserved

Library of Congress Cataloging-in-Publication Data
Hart, David M., 1961–
Forged consensus : science, technology, and economic policy in the
United States, 1921–1953 / David M. Hart.
p.   cm.
Includes bibliographical references and index.
ISBN 0-691-02667-X (cl : alk. paper)
1. Science and state—United States—History.   2. Technology and
state—United States—History.   3. United States—Economic policy—
History.   I. Title.
Q127.U6H32   1998
338.973′06—dc21   97-43913

This book has been composed in Times Roman

Princeton University Press books are printed
on acid-free paper, and meet the guidelines
for permanence and durability of the Committee
on Production Guidelines for Book Longevity
of the Council on Library Resources

http://pup.princeton.edu
Printed in the United States of America
1   3   5   7   9   10   8   6   4   2

For Lois

Contents

Preface

SCIENCE AND TECHNOLOGY policy is not very well understood. Policy-makers and scholars outside the field think it obscure and esoteric. For most within the field, it seems idiosyncratic, detached from the rest of American politics. These impressions need to be corrected. Science and technology impinge on almost every aspect of public life in the United States. And science and technology policy is not made in particularly strange ways. It is affected by many of the same ideas, institutions, and interests that affect other federal policies.

This book is my contribution to making the study of science and technology policy a normal part of the study of American politics, particularly of American political development, and vice versa. It aims to undermine the field's creation myth, which says that postwar science and technology policy sprang full-blown from the mind of Vannevar Bush, was written down in *Science, the Endless Frontier* in 1945, and that the past fifty-odd years have merely been implementation. Bush was brilliant, as an engineer and administrator—and politician. It is a mark of his success in this last role that the creation myth still holds practitioners and analysts in its grip. If we can let go of this myth and see Bush in the light of normalcy and the New Deal as well as of the war, of Robert Taft and Curtis LeMay as well as of Harley Kilgore, then we can make much better sense of what happened and why. Perhaps equally important, we can also understand better what might have happened but did not.

This project began as a dissertation in the MIT Political Science department. Each member of my dissertation committee, Ira Katznelson, Gene Skolnikoff, and Dick Samuels, provided a different expertise and a different form of encouragement to me, and each made a real difference. I owe special thanks for support and incisive criticism to two fellow graduate students, Brian Burgoon and Wade Jacoby. My work, like all work, builds on earlier scholarship; I have been particularly influenced by the work of Ellis W. Hawley and Daniel J. Kevles. I have benefited from comments by Daniel Bell, Bruce Bimber, Lewis Branscomb, Harvey Brooks, Owen Cote, Hunter Dupree, Henry Ergas, Richard Florida, Marshall Ganz, John Gerring, Eugene Gholz, David Guston, Peter Hall, Roger Haydon, Maurice Holland, Jr., Chris Howard, Allen Kaufman, Dan Kryder, George Lodge, Bill Mayer, Eileen McDonagh, Mike McGeary, David Mindell, Richard Nelson, Larry Owens, Andrew Polsky, Harvey Sapolsky, Mike Scherer, Bruce Seely, Phil Smith, Roe Smith, Jessica Wang, Charlie Weiner, Gregg Zachary, and two anonymous referees at Princeton University Press. I received feedback on the work from participants at meetings of the American Association for the Advancement of Science, American Political Science Association, Boston-Area Workshop on American Political Development,

Hagley Museum and Library, Kennedy School of Government Center for Business and Government, Kennedy School of Government Politics Research Group, Kennedy School of Government Faculty Research Seminar, Northeastern Political Science Association, and Society for the History of Technology.

I have been blessed with financial support from the MIT Political Science Department, the Center for Science and International Affairs at the Kennedy School of Government, the MIT Industrial Performance Center, and the Herbert Hoover Presidential Library. Since 1994 the Kennedy School of Government has provided a paycheck and a slush fund, for which I am most grateful. I owe a debt of gratitude to hardworking archivists around the country (at the locations listed in the bibliography) for their unfailing assistance and courtesy. Maryann Barakso and Dana Weinberg assisted in the research.

Gene Skolnikoff has been my guardian angel, and I cannot repay him for watching out for me. In an early comment on my work, he remarked that it was either "brilliant" or a "house of cards." I leave it to the perspicacious reader to decide which of these—or something entirely different—applies to the final product.

Abbreviations

AAA	Agricultural Adjustment Act (1933)
AAF	Army Air Forces
AAR	Association of American Railroads
ACC	American Construction Council
AEA	Atomic Energy Act (1946)
AEC	Atomic Energy Commission
AF of L	American Federation of Labor
AIP	American Institute of Physics
APC	Alien Property Custodian
ARA	American Railway Association
ARD	American Research and Development Corporation
ARDC	Air Research and Development Command, U.S. Air Force
ARPA	Advanced Research Projects Agency
ATP	Advanced Technology Program, National Institute of Standards and Technology
BEW	Board of Economic Warfare
BNA	Bureau of National Affairs
BOB	Bureau of the Budget
BRAB	Building Research Advisory Board, National Research Council
CCC	Civilian Conservation Corps
CEA	Council of Economic Advisors
CED	Committee for Economic Development
CIO	Congress of Industrial Organizations
CITP	Civilian Industrial Technology Program, proposed
CIW	Carnegie Institution of Washington
CMR	Committee on Medical Research, Office of Scientific Research and Development
CND	Council of National Defense
CPD	Committee on the Present Danger
CRADA	Cooperative Research and Development Agreement
CTI	Cotton Textile Institute
DARPA	Defense Advanced Research Projects Agency
DEIR	Division of Engineering and Industrial Research, National Research Council
DLC	Democratic Leadership Council
DOD	Department of Defense
DPC	Defense Plant Corporation
EHFA	Electric Home and Farm Authority

ERTA	Emergency Railroad Transportation Act (1933)
FAES	Federated American Engineering Societies
FDRL	Franklin Delano Roosevelt Library
FDR-PP	*Public Papers and Addresses of Franklin D. Roosevelt*
FHA	Federal Housing Administration
FLSA	Fair Labor Standards Act (1938)
FNMA	Federal National Mortgage Association
FRC	Federal Radio Commission
FTC	Federal Trade Commission
HBS	Harvard Business School
HHFA	Housing and Home Finance Administration
HHPL	Herbert Hoover Presidential Library
HOLC	Homeowners' Loan Corporation
HSTL	Harry S. Truman Library
IBAA	Investment Bankers Association of America
ICBM	Intercontinental Ballistic Missile
ICC	Interstate Commerce Commission
IMF	International Monetary Fund
JCAE	Joint Committee on Atomic Energy, U.S. Congress
JCS	Joint Chiefs of Staff
MIT	Massachusetts Institute of Technology
MITI	Ministry of International Trade and Industry (Japan)
NACA	National Advisory Committee for Aeronautics
NAM	National Association of Manufacturers
NAS	National Academy of Sciences
NASA	National Aeronautics and Space Administration
NBS	National Bureau of Standards
NDAC	National Defense Advisory Council
NDRC	National Defense Research Committee
NHA	National Housing Agency
NIH	National Institutes of Health
NIRA	National Industrial Recovery Act (1933)
NIST	National Institute of Standards and Technology
NLRA	National Labor Relations Act (1935)
NPPC	National Patent Planning Commission
NRA	National Recovery Administration
NRC	National Research Council
NRE	National Research Endowment, proposed
NRF	National Research Foundation, proposed
NRPB	National Resources Planning Board
NSB	National Science Board
NSC	National Security Council
NSF	National Science Foundation

NSRB	National Security Resources Board
NTIS	National Technical Information Service
ODM	Office of Defense Mobilization
OMB	Office of Management and Budget
ONR	Office of Naval Research
OPA	Office of Price Administration
OPM	Office of Production Management
OPRD	Office of Production Research and Development, War Production Board
OSD	Office of the Secretary of Defense
OSRD	Office of Scientific Research and Development
OTD	Office of Technical Development, War Production Board (proposed)
OTM	Office of Technological Mobilization (proposed)
OTS	Office of Technical Services, Department of Commerce
OTSS	Office of Technical and Scientific Services, Department of Commerce
OWMR	Office of War Mobilization and Reconversion
PSRB	President's Scientific Research Board
PWA	Public Works Administration
PWPP	*Postwar Plan and Program* (1943)
RCA	Radio Corporation of America
RDB	Research and Development Board, Department of Defense
RFC	Reconstruction Finance Corporation
SAB	Science Advisory Board
SAC	Strategic Air Command, U.S. Air Force
SBA	Small Business Administration
SBIC	Small Business Investment Company
SDI	Strategic Defense Initiative
SDPA	Small Defense Plants Administration
SEF	*Science, the Endless Frontier* (1945)
SSC	Superconducting Supercollider
SST	Supersonic Transport
SWPC	Smaller War Plants Corporation
TMC	Technology Mobilization Corporation (proposed)
TNEC	Temporary National Economic Committee
TTNP	*Technological Trends and National Policy* (1937)
TVA	Tennessee Valley Authority
UAW	United Auto Workers
UCWOC	United Construction Workers' Organizing Committee
UMT	Universal Military Training
UN	United Nations
USAF	U.S. Air Force

USDA	U.S. Department of Agriculture
USHA	U.S. Housing Authority
VEHA	Veterans' Emergency Housing Act (1946)
VEHP	Veterans' Emergency Housing Program
WIB	War Industries Board
WPA	Works Progress Administration
WPB	War Production Board
WRB	War Resources Board

FORGED CONSENSUS

The Malleability of American Liberalism and the Making of Public Policy

DAVID CUSHMAN COYLE, "engineer, eccentric, economist" (to quote *Time*), a purveyor of policy ideas who often had his finger on the pulse of New Deal thought, posed the following question in 1938: "What would a democratic, high-technology system be if we could attain it?"[1] The question demanded not only an understanding of what technology was and where it came from, but a vision of the political economy as well. The New Dealers struggled to answer Coyle's question and to realize that answer in practice. In so doing, they encountered opponents who thought differently about science, technology, politics, and economics and therefore supplied alternative answers. The struggle among these camps, in the crucible of depression, war, and cold war, revolutionized federal science and technology policy.

None of the combatants could legitimately claim full credit for the revolution. What has appeared to many observers in retrospect as a coherent "postwar consensus"[2] about federal science and technology policy masked numerous compromises, false starts, and out-and-out contradictions. Though revolutionary, postwar policy is best understood as a "hybrid" of competing visions, rather than the complete realization of any single one. Some aspects of the policy were forged out of a give-and-take among two or three schools of thought and were accepted across a wide political spectrum not as ideal but as the best that could be gotten under the circumstances. Other aspects of the policy rested on narrower bases. These have often been overlooked; the "postwar consensus" is in this regard a forgery of later observers. The hybrid has its roots in the nature of the federal policy process. No answer to Coyle's question could muster sufficient political backing to sweep through all the policy venues of the fragmented American state.

This book explores the genesis and germination of the hybrid. It traces the efforts of a series of key figures, policy entrepreneurs who extracted from their grand visions of the role of the state in a modern industrial economy concrete legislative and administrative proposals for revamping the governance of tech-

---

[1] Jordan A. Schwarz, *The New Dealers: Power Politics in the Age of Roosevelt* (New York: Knopf, 1993), 183 (citing *Time*, October 24, 1938); David Cushman Coyle, *The American Way* (New York: Harper and Bros., 1938), 28.

[2] Bruce L. R. Smith, *American Science Policy Since World War II* (Washington: Brookings, 1990), 36.

nological innovation in the United States. To make policy, they articulated their
ideas, acquired allies, searched for hospitable venues, struggled with one another, and, ultimately, explained what they had done, with more or less candor.

Secretary of Commerce Herbert Hoover, nicknamed (without cynicism) "the
great engineer," broke with American tradition and Jazz Age conservatism by
endorsing a federal role in the development of industrial technology. He saw
lasting value in the improvisations of World War I and consequently pressed for
cooperation within industry and between industry and government for the sake
of more rapid technological innovation in the 1920s. In the decade after
Hoover's downfall in the wake of the Crash of 1929, men like MIT President
Karl Compton and Assistant Attorney General Thurman Arnold came to the
fore, sharing the goal of solving the unemployment problem by creating new
industries based on new technologies, but advancing contending policies to
achieve it. Compton elaborated Hoover's vision, advocating a modestly as-
sertive state that would bolster private cooperation; Arnold called for an
aggressively active state that would "break the bottlenecks" that impeded
innovation.

As unemployment diminished and war loomed with the turn of a new decade,
another group of policy entrepreneurs, notably Vannevar Bush, President Roosevelt's science advisor, and Vice-President Henry Wallace, took the places of
Compton and Arnold on the Washington battlefield. Adapting ideas inherited
from the 1930s about the appropriate roles of the public and private sectors in
the governance of technological innovation, they jousted with one another and
with the military brass to meet the new challenge. At the end of the war, both
the economic and national security challenges remained on the minds of the
policy elite. Several factions committed to apparently incommensurable visions
of the state deadlocked over science and technology policy in the late 1940s,
an impasse that was broken only by the Korean War. With this war my narrative ends. The "postwar consensus" emerged, lubricated by defense dollars, in
a world of political and economic thought impoverished by McCarthyism.

Each step of the way, the actual policy diverged from the policy entrepreneurs' visions of what the American state ought to do about science and technology. What the state could and ultimately did do reflected not only the appeal
of these visions and the entrepreneurship of their proponents, but also the structure of policy-making institutions and the larger alignment of political, economic, and military forces. Science and technology policy was not made by a
few specialists working in isolation. There were intimate linkages between this
apparently narrow policy area and the grand politics and issues of the nation
between 1921 and 1953. Most importantly, the ideas that structured debates
over science and technology policy derived from ideological principles of
broad significance in national politics, creating connections that had serious
consequences for policy outcomes.

The decisions recounted here have profoundly shaped the nation's capacities for economic development and for war-making. The presence of a massive Department of Defense (DOD) research and development (R&D) program and the absence of a comparable civilian industrial R&D program (to name two important features of postwar science and technology policy) influenced not only the aggregate wealth and power of the United States, but also the distribution of wealth and power among its sectors, classes, and regions. Huntsville, Alabama, where the Confederacy meets the Space Age, epitomizes the consequences. Without DOD, modern Huntsville with its aerospace complex is unthinkable. In the big picture of twentieth-century American political and economic development, federal science and technology policy deserves an important place.

This history also bears on the contemporary policy debate. Many of the ideas advanced decades ago—and the conflicts among them—are still evident today, and the processes by which these ideas are converted into policy have changed less than one might think. While care must be taken in the use of historical analogies and prudence is required in assessing the durability of historical legacies, the story holds insights that are still useful. Perhaps by reconstructing and reinterpreting the past, we can help make a better future. That, in any case, is one subtext of this book.

THE "POSTWAR CONSENSUS": CRACKS
IN THE CONVENTIONAL WISDOM

Most studies of postwar science and technology policy rest on a few broad empirical observations. These observations, in turn, have been explained mainly by applying two general theories. Neither the stylized facts nor the explanatory traditions hold up under scrutiny. The conventional wisdom is not so much wrong as it is incomplete. It attempts to explain too narrow a slice of the federal government's activities and it does so by excluding important influences on them. One consequence is that the guidance that scholars provide to policy-makers is flawed.

The empirical basis of the conventional wisdom can be summed up in two policy principles: financial support for basic research and commercial "spinoff" from mission-oriented R&D. The primary federal role in science and technology since World War II has been that of a funder of R&D. Government support has been made available to academic researchers, because private support for science was too modest, and to public and private laboratories furthering broad federal missions, such as military security and space exploration. Sometimes technologies developed for government missions (or in university labs) serendipitously found commercial uses, but such "spinoffs," policy-makers agreed, were natural byproducts of government activity in a capitalist economy; no special policies were needed to facilitate the transfer of technology from public to private uses. Although government R&D spending was substantial, the heart of the U.S. national innovation system since World War II has been private investment in R&D in pursuit of profit. Both large and small firms have played important roles in this system.

This thumbnail sketch has several salient features. The government is committed to accelerating the pace of technological innovation. Its approach to doing so appears to be rational; the decision rules are clear. The division of labor between the public and private sector is well-demarcated and stable over time; private R&D spending takes precedence, with the public sector only filling in where markets fail (even if those market failures require enormous resources, as in the provision of national defense). And the system can be understood and policy assessed almost entirely in terms of R&D spending, aggregated at a high level of abstraction.

These stylized facts have motivated scholars to develop two strands of explanation for science and technology policy. The first draws on transaction cost economics. This approach contends that the policy and the institutions it has fostered are highly efficient for developing new scientific and technological knowledge and putting that knowledge to practical use. Corporate research labs, for example, provide concepts and devices tailored to the needs of firms more cheaply and with less uncertainty than labs run by trade associations or government agencies would. Fundamental scientific findings, by contrast, are rarely useful enough to any single firm to justify in-house support of basic research, but sufficiently valuable to the national economy to stimulate public spending on academic science. Transaction cost analysts postulate two mechanisms by which the test of efficiency may be applied. Public and private policy-makers may calculate the costs of alternative arrangements rationally and choose the most efficient ones. Or, such policies and institutions may emerge as the unintended result of an evolutionary selection process in a competitive market economy in which the inefficient are weeded out.[3]

The second explanatory style takes as a given that U.S. policy-makers and the public prefer markets over state action. Policy initiatives that support the market's hegemony in this political culture stand a chance of success; more collectivist initiatives inevitably fail unless they can draw on a compelling noneconomic rationale. Recurring efforts by officials in the White House and the Commerce Department over the past fifty years to inject the state more forcefully into civilian industrial R&D, for instance, have been doomed, the argument goes, by the overwhelming power of what Louis Hartz labeled "the liberal tradition in America." The American state's capacities to govern

---

[3] Christopher Freeman and Carlota Perez, "Structural Crises of Adjustment, Business Cycles, and Investment Behavior," in Giovanni Dosi et al., eds., *Technical Change and Economic Theory* (London: Pinter, 1988), 38–66; Herbert Kitschelt, "Industrial Governance Structures, Innovation Strategies, and the Case of Japan: Sectoral or Cross-National Comparative Analysis?" *International Organization* 45 (1991): 453–94.

technological innovation are stunted by comparison to other nations that do not hold these preferences so strongly.[4]

Transaction cost economics and (to use another phrase of Hartz) "liberal society analysis" both make important contributions to our understanding. Market forces and market ideology have deeply shaped institutional development and science and technology policy-making. But they do not tell the whole story, and their omissions and weaknesses matter.

One ground for questioning is empirical. The conventional wisdom takes for granted that science and technology policy has been stable in essential respects, particularly in ceding room to the free market. If one looks beyond the postwar period, however, significant variations jump out. In the nineteenth century, for instance, state governments and federal bureaus for agriculture, forestry, and mining, in partnership with private entrepreneurs, played extremely important roles in putting the natural resources of the hinterlands at the service of the new manufacturing industries. Even within the past fifty years, the empirical account that is the basis of the conventional wisdom overlooks vital activities of the federal government that influence scientific research and technological development, like the provision of intellectual property rights and the enforcement of antitrust laws.

The longer and broader view of the facts challenges transaction cost economics. This approach presumes a gradual evolution of policies and institutions under steady pressure for greater efficiency. The bureau system, however, emerged rapidly out of the crisis precipitated by the Civil War; so too did military R&D spending in World War II. "Efficiency" under such exceptional circumstances presumably means something different than it does in normal times, yet the basic patterns remained in place when peace was restored. The liberal society analysis has obvious difficulties accounting for a more expansive role for the American state. The political culture should have prohibited such activism.

The conventional wisdom also warrants a theoretical critique. Both approaches present a "postwar consensus" that is inevitable; plausible alternative policies are highly constrained on theoretical grounds. Transaction cost economics assumes that (1) there is a single best set of policies and institutions for the governance of technological innovation at any given moment, (2) this set of policies and institutions will be generated as an alternative by society, and (3) this alternative will be selected because of its efficiency advantages. Each of these assumptions is questionable. With regard to the first, differences in economic sectors and public missions may mean that any institutional framework will have widely varying results; what is most efficient in one area of science and technology may not be in another. Second, assuming that there is a set of

[4] Louis Hartz, *The Liberal Tradition in America* (1955; reprint, San Diego: Harcourt, Brace, Jovanovich, 1991); Harvey Averch, *A Strategic Analysis of Science and Technology Policy* (Baltimore: Johns Hopkins University Press, 1985); Smith (above, n. 2).

institutions that is most efficient on transaction cost grounds, the social system may not generate it as a possibility; large firms, for example, might stifle small competitors that would be able to develop a technology better. Third, even if one grants that the meaning of efficiency does not change (a condition to which I objected above), factors other than efficiency may influence the survival of institutions; economic competition may not be as severe a constraint, particularly on state institutions, as the transaction cost literature suggests.

The liberal society analysis is equally rigid. It assumes that what counts as a market and what counts as a failure are easily and consensually defined in the policy-making process. Again, part of the problem is that analysts' empirical compass has been too narrow; by concentrating on the development of academic science, in which market failure is not a deeply contested label, this tradition has tended to overlook conflicts over the development of industrial technologies that entail more subtle interpretations of the basic terms of liberalism. This view also takes as fixed the institutions and interests that defend the particular interpretation of liberalism represented by the "postwar consensus." Yet both institutional authority and interests are malleable. The power of business, for example, has waxed and waned throughout U.S. history, and its opposition to state activism, including policies like federal funding of R&D for civilian industry, has by no means been written in stone. Business leaders' understanding of what is best for business depends on their beliefs and knowledge, which change with experience.

The conventional wisdom provides sobering advice to policy-makers considering new initiatives. It suggests that the range of possible science and technology policies in the U.S. experience is quite limited. Most attempts to change the path of institutional development will fail miserably, rejected because they introduce inefficiencies or by an unchanging liberal tradition. The conventional wisdom holds up for admiration a rational and easily described set of rules; indeed, these are embodied in a founding text, Vannevar Bush's 1945 report, *Science, The Endless Frontier.* This mythology obscures a more complex reality, a path of development that is more twisted and in which politics plays a more significant part than the conventional wisdom allows. To come to grips with this reality, I have tried a new approach, based on two general principles that follow directly from my critique. First, I cast a bigger net for empirical evidence. Second, I theorize science and technology policy-making as a political process.

A NEW APPROACH: THE EMPIRICAL BASIS

The first principle led to several choices. For one thing, rather than seeking the sources of the "postwar consensus" only in the postwar period, I have trolled backward into the interwar period, into waters relatively uncharted in the historiography. Even though the decisions of the late 1940s and early 1950s are widely acknowledged to have marked the most significant watershed in the history of U.S. science and technology policy, few scholars have looked carefully at their precedents.

In addition, I have considered a wide range of policy initiatives, including not only those that led to the establishment of enduring organizations, like the National Science Foundation, which have been thoroughly analyzed in the existing scholarship, but also those that did not leave as much of an institutional trace, like the effort to create a research program for the National Housing Agency, which have been overlooked. These unsuccessful initiatives represent potential alternative paths of development that the conventional wisdom rules out on principle, but which appeared to be viable enough at the time that significant coalitions formed to advance them. R&D funding is an important area of contestation, but not the only one; policy-makers fought over economic regulations, planning capabilities, and other issues as well. Although jarring to the modern ear, proposals that aimed at slowing the pace of technological innovation must be included to grasp the full picture.

A corollary to these decisions is my effort to pay attention to a broad array of policy arenas and actors. All three branches of the federal government participated in the policy-making process, and the outcome cannot be understood by concentrating solely on any one. Public officials, elected and appointed, played leading roles, but they were joined by private citizens motivated by economic gain, professional commitment, and intellectual curiosity. Moreover, these actors often made connections between science and technology policy and other policy areas. If science and technology policy was sometimes considered in isolation, as a matter of interest only to a tiny elite, it was at least as often considered to be an integral element of a larger political-economic project aiming to harness (or eliminate) an array of state powers for the common good.

All of these considerations suggest a sprawling story, and I will plead guilty on this count to a degree. American politics is so messy and confusing that no realistic policy history can be without inconsistencies and loose ends. However, adherence to my second principle has disciplined the study and, I hope, allowed me to avoid excessive confusion. A theory—a term I use loosely—of the science and technology policy-making process provided guidance in the research and construction of the narrative.

A NEW APPROACH: THE THEORETICAL ARGUMENT

My theory of science and technology policy-making has three components. It begins with the core of the conventional wisdom, the liberal tradition. As I noted above, free markets and belief in them have had a major effect on the governance of technological innovation in the United States. However, as the economy has grown more complex, the liberal tradition has been adapted to legitimate a wide range of government activities; my claim is that it sets only a loose boundary within which a wide range of science and technology policies is permissible. The second part of my argument is that competition among advocates of different versions of liberalism propels much of the federal science and technology policy process. Competing conceptions of the role of government are advanced by policy entrepreneurs and attract diverse coalitions that include public and private actors of many sorts. This competition can and often does proceed in many different policy-making venues in which the criteria for winning vary. As a result, my argument concludes, the competition among liberalisms is not a winner-take-all event; the outcome is inevitably a hybrid.

Liberalism, as Dorothy Ross has put it, imposes "distinct limits to American political discourse" by presuming a consensus about such values as private property, rationality, progress, and individual rights. These limits are particularly evident in the debate over policies that affect the economy. The market is considered to be the most desirable form of economic organization, because it is believed to both facilitate individual development and expand the wealth of the nation. Private property must be respected for the market to work, and it also provides a bulwark against the overexpansion of state power. The term "liberal" in this study usually denotes a preference for markets and private property in economic governance, although I occasionally use the term in the more expansive sense that Ross uses it and in its more colloquial sense, referring to the left wing of the American political spectrum. As the reader will see, however, even American "conservatism" is a species of liberalism.[5]

Although recent research has uncovered compelling evidence of republican and authoritarian alternatives to liberalism in U.S. history, in economic affairs, at least, a liberal consensus emerged in the nation by the turn of the twentieth century at the latest. Politicians and policy-makers who called for supplanting markets as a matter of economic principle (rather than as a means to expand other markets or to achieve other noneconomic liberal ends) have been marginal in the past hundred years. Both major political parties have consistently averred their faith in private property and markets. Even the debate over the governance of the labor market, the market that most critics of liberalism would argue is least free and least fair and that has in fact been noticeably altered by the state in this century, has been marked by a liberal consensus. Christopher Tomlins has shown how the last remnants of republican ideology were squeezed out of the labor movement in the 1900s and 1910s. Social democracy (much less socialism), which in the European democracies provided an alternative belief system for labor's political activists, never achieved the same status here, despite some brief moments of glory.[6]

---

[5] Dorothy Ross, *s.v.* "Liberalism," in *Encyclopedia of American Political History;* J. David Greenstone, *The Lincoln Persuasion: Remaking American Liberalism* (Princeton: Princeton University Press, 1992), 42–46.

[6] Joyce Appleby, *Liberalism and Republicanism in the Historical Imagination* (Cambridge:

Yet the liberal consensus has not led to unity about policy. Political battles erupted not only over which liberal ideals ought to govern in instances when they conflicted, but also over how established principles ought to be interpreted in the light of new social facts. The liberal preference for free markets and private property, for instance, offered few clues for reconstructing the global economy after the shattering impact of World War II. After fighting among themselves and with their British allies, U.S. policy-makers ultimately concluded that a liberal international trade regime had to be "embedded," as John Gerard Ruggie has put it, in a web of international governing institutions.[7] While markets have long depended on states to enforce contracts, twentieth-century political and economic conditions provided strong incentives for liberals to develop new ideas about how markets could be constituted and maintained through government action.

Science and technology pose particular challenges for liberal economic governance. The private sector, as transaction cost economics suggests, has engaged in extensive institutional experimentation, seeking advantages that will yield profits through the development of technologies that lower costs or provide new products. This century has seen the development of large corporate R&D laboratories, the venture capital industry, high-technology start-up firms, strategic technology alliances, and other novel organizational forms aimed at winning markets. Organizational creativity has often been supplemented by corporate political and legal activism; the "visible hand" of managerial capitalism is accompanied, as Leonard Reich notes, by the "iron fist" of corporate power. Reich, for instance, shows how General Electric used public relations and patent law as well as investments in R&D to dominate the early electric lamp market.[8] Policies that were designed to create and expand markets, like patent laws, can be twisted to subvert them.

While liberals have worried about private threats to existing markets for new and improved products, they have also been concerned that potential markets be brought to fruition. Academic research, for instance, may lead to products that would not be developed in the private sector because firms have too short a time horizon or too narrow a technological vision. Many liberals point to this market failure to justify government funding of university science. More subtle forms of market failure abound; these provide more difficult challenges to the liberal tradition. Firms in an atomized industry, for example, may be unable to invest enough in R&D individually to realize a new technology that would dramatically expand their markets. In such a case, liberal policy-makers might

Harvard University Press, 1992); Christopher L. Tomlins, *The State and the Unions: Labor Relations, Law and the Organized Labor Movement in America, 1880–1960* (New York: Cambridge University Press, 1985), 74–95; Nelson Lichtenstein, *The Most Dangerous Man in Detroit: Walter Reuther and the Fate of American Labor* (New York: Basic, 1995).

[7] John Gerard Ruggie, "International Regimes, Transactions, and Change: Embedded Liberalism in the Postwar Economic Order," *International Organization* 36 (1982): 379–416.

[8] Leonard S. Reich, "Lighting the Path to Profit: GE's Control of the Electric Lamp Industry, 1892–1941," *Business History Review* 66 (1992): 305–34.

encourage them to cooperate, force them to merge, invest public funds on their behalf, or let them drift. The liberal tradition provides no definitive guidance among such choices, all of which can be justified in liberal terms. Nor does it determine the extent to which the state ought to pursue such markets in the face of uncertainty about their potential, particularly at the expense of existing markets.

These problems of creating and maintaining satisfactory markets for processes and products utilizing new scientific and technological ideas are further complicated by the existence of a large nonprofit sector in the United States. University graduate departments, charitable foundations, and independent research institutes emerged to support and perform R&D around the turn of the twentieth century and have been major players in science and technology ever since. To some extent, this sector provides policy-makers with an easy solution to the conundrums posed above; foundations have stepped in to address market failures in academic research, for example. Yet, although voluntary cooperation for the public good is esteemed in liberal thought, the extent to which the government ought to rely on such efforts to solve market failures is not clear in the abstract.

The distinction between public and private activity, which in classical liberal theory is firm and clear, is thus blurry and convoluted in twentieth-century science and technology. Property rights regimes for new ideas, for instance, are plain at the margins: academic publications are public goods, freely used; product blueprints are tightly held. But in between these margins is a vast gray zone of "generic technological knowledge" (a term borrowed from Richard Nelson) of uncertain status, providing fodder for intellectual property litigation and being used by academic, government, and industrial researchers alike. It is a commonplace to point out the obsolescence of the "linear model" of innovation, in which the public good of academic science is unproblematically converted into profitable technology by private enterprise. New products emerge from complex exchanges of ideas and information among scientists, engineers, workers, and managers in universities, businesses, government agencies, and nonprofit institutions. Exactly what is public and what is private about technology—and what ought to be—remains poorly understood and hotly disputed.[9]

The liberal tradition therefore provides little more than a loose boundary for science and technology policy-making. A wide variety of government actions in this sphere may be compatible with the expansion of existing and potential markets. But the same tradition does provide a strong incentive to policy-makers to ensure the advance of science and technology. Progress is a central lib-

[9] Richard R. Nelson, "What Is Public and What Is Private About Technology?" Consortium on Competition and Cooperation, working paper 90–9, Center for Research in Management, University of California, Berkeley, 1990; Stephen J. Kline, "Innovation Is Not a Linear Process," *Research Management* 28 (July/August, 1985): 36–45.

eral value. Science represents intellectual progress, while new technologies form the basis for material progress. It is not surprising that U.S. science and technology policy-makers have developed many permutations of liberal governance in search of one that works well enough. Competing visions of the liberal state provide the basis for coalitions that contest the direction of policy development.[10]

These visions are advanced by "policy entrepreneurs,"[11] who draw from them specific proposals and assemble supporters both inside and outside government. These supporters may have obvious material or bureaucratic interests in the proposed policies, but often policy entrepreneurs help to shape or even create interests during the policy-making process. The malleability of interests and the opportunity for policy change is not the same at all times. Widely perceived crises are the most opportune moments to make change. Yet the distinction between crisis and stability is not hard and fast; there is almost always room for some creative policy entrepreneurship.

Policy entrepreneurs are rarely practical politicians. Politicians must be able to trim their sails when the winds change; they can rarely afford to be devoted to a rigid ideal of what the government ought to do. More commonly, the intellectual work involved in reinterpreting the liberal tradition to respond to new circumstances is performed initially by thinkers outside of government, such as academics and journalists. The broad visions of the state that these efforts lead to then spawn a swarm of specific policy proposals, linked by a shared conception of liberalism. Often the intellectuals themselves are moved to become policy entrepreneurs, serving as advisors or taking jobs in the capital. Some, like Herbert Hoover and Henry Wallace, even become politicians, although such figures tend to remain somewhat aloof from the hurly-burly, posturing, and compromising of everyday politics.

The policy entrepreneur's challenge is to secure sufficient support in venues that have the authority to make the changes that he or she envisions. This is an exercise in persuasion. Those who hold power must be convinced that the problems they face are caused by new circumstances to which old ideals must be adapted. The "causal story"[12] advanced by a policy entrepreneur provides the basis for creating new state capacities (or dismantling old ones) that will solve social problems. In science and technology policy entrepreneurship, causal stories describe the process of technological innovation (especially the place of market forces in that process), the prospect that a change in the pace or direc-

---

[10] Gary Gerstle, "The Protean Quality of American Liberalism," *American Historical Review* 99 (1994): 1043–73; Greenstone (above, n. 5), 35–65; Richard J. Ellis, "Radical Lockeanism in American Political Culture," *Western Political Quarterly* 45 (1992): 825–49.

[11] I use the term "policy entrepreneurs" in much the same way as John W. Kingdon does in *Agendas, Alternatives, and Public Policies,* 2d ed. (New York: HarperCollins, 1995), 122.

[12] This concept is taken from Deborah A. Stone, "Causal Stories and the Formation of Policy Agendas," *Political Science Quarterly* 104 (1989): 281–300.

tion of technological innovation will address a social problem, and the prediction that new policies will bring about this change. Typically, two or more causal stories, linked to two or more visions of the state, offer distinct options to political actors.

An example may be helpful. Karl Compton, then president of MIT, proposed to expand funding for university-based scientific research between 1933 and 1935. Compton argued that new technologies would help reduce unemployment, the central problem of those years. Universities, if well-supported, could be a major source of such innovations, and firms could use the ideas developed on campus to create new industries that would put people back to work. He therefore appealed to President Roosevelt and lobbied the public with a campaign built around the notion that "science makes jobs"; federal funding could make jobs by making science. Compton's view was contested hotly by those committed to the causal story that technological innovation caused unemployment by raising productivity without providing new opportunities for reemployment. Government support for scientific research would merely exacerbate the problem in their view. They pressed the president for measures that would regulate the pace of technological change in order to allow reemployment to proceed more smoothly.

The president is only one possible target for entrepreneurial persuasion. The federal system of separated powers and relatively open access provides many more. Members of Congress, agency heads, and judges as well as those who might have influence on them, such as corporate executives, labor union leaders, and interest group representatives, are potential recruits to the cause. Few of these possible participants in a coalition for policy change will be intimately familiar with the institutional organization of science and technology or the way that innovations are translated into jobs and profits (or military capabilities). They may have obvious vested interests that will be helped or hindered by the entrepreneur's proposal; agency heads, for instance, are loath to turn down expanded resources and authority. More commonly, however, interests in generating scientific knowledge and technological innovations are ambiguous. Effective entrepreneurs are able to use the causal stories and associated visions of the state to resolve this ambiguity, redefining interests that had earlier been conceived differently.

To continue the example, Compton's proposal that the federal government should fund scientific research was received skeptically by many of his colleagues in academe. Far from snuffling for a taste at the federal trough, they feared that such support would be the thin end of a wedge that would ultimately lead to civil servants dictating the research agenda. Compton shared this skepticism to a degree, and in seeking to allay such fears, he emphasized that technical experts should control the distribution of funding. His vision of the liberal state was hemmed in by sober expertise. Compton expended a great deal of energy in the early 1930s to persuade university presidents and academic scientists to rethink their interests, and he won many over.

The ambiguity of interests is particularly notable not only in areas in which what is at stake is rather remote from most people's lives, such as science and technology policy, but also in periods when public problems appear to be especially acute and baffling. When old remedies have been tried, the willingness to revise beliefs grows. Periods of economic depression and war mobilization, on which this study concentrates, therefore provide the most compelling instances of the dynamic that I describe here. Yet other historical moments have fostered science and technology policy entrepreneurship as well. Often crisis rhetoric is adopted as a tool of persuasion, as in the response to Sputnik in 1957. Perceptions, rather than objective indicators, determine the degree to which policy change is a serious possibility.

Policy entrepreneurship, then, is always present, but it is both more common and more likely to succeed in periods of crisis. Policy entrepreneurs typically face opponents who seek to build their own coalitions behind alternative conceptions of the liberal state. They also face choices. The American state is a complicated thing, and it is this fact that dilutes the triumph of even the most successful policy entrepreneur.

One of the most difficult choices facing a policy entrepreneur is the venue in which to pursue his program. The American state offers many options, not all equally promising to competing entrepreneurs. Its various policy venues differ in their responsiveness to particular ideas and political resources. Ironically, competitors may succeed on the same issue in different venues; science and technology policy is thus guided by more than one brand of liberalism when one looks across the branches and agencies of the federal government. Public policy is a patchwork. Yet the political process also creates pressure to rationalize the discrepancies and contradictions, to paper them over with a mythical consensus. By selective attention and by glossing over unwelcome details, politicians (and, more lamentably, scholars) portray a policy bred from a pure strain of liberalism, rather than a motley hybrid.

The Constitution alone virtually dictates this outcome. It provides for the separation of powers, giving Congress, the executive, and the courts influence over federal policy. Variation in the rules that govern these venues, such as those that set the timing of election or appointment, makes a coincidence of views across them unlikely. In addition, each venue requires a different coalition for victory; the president's say-so, for example, is not necessarily won with the same set of supporters that leads to a congressional majority. Moreover, the boundaries of each venue's jurisdiction are fuzzy. As Stephen Skowronek has argued, struggles over substantive policy and institutional authority are frequently intertwined.[13] Institutional authority changes with circumstances, too; presidential power, to take a conspicuous example, is greater in war than in peace. To this constitutional variety, each branch with its own winning coalition and potential authority, Congress has, over the past century or so, added regulatory commis-

[13] Stephen Skowronek, *Building a New American State* (New York: Cambridge University Press, 1982).

sions and agencies that have some independence from the executive, legislature, and judiciary and their own criteria for decision-making.

Policy entrepreneurs are thus venturing into an extremely convoluted landscape. In surveying the strategic options generated by this system of separated institutions sharing power, they see strengths and weaknesses in each. Congress typically has the broadest power but requires the most adept coalition-building. The courts and regulatory commissions usually have a more limited reach but make decisions on narrower grounds. The executive branch tends to fall somewhere in between on both scores, although it is occasionally possible for the president to make decisions with sweeping consequences on the basis of his own idiosyncratic opinions.

Policy entrepreneurs embark on their journey with an estimate of their resources and prospects, but little certain knowledge. Much depends on their persuasive skills and tactical virtuousity and those of their opponents. However, they cannot always control the timing of and context for their efforts, and these may powerfully affect the outcome. Presidents, for instance, may be diverted by crises or choose to trade off one policy area to achieve more important objectives in another. Policy entrepreneurship is often a matter of trial and error, of venue-shopping writ large.

The inconsistencies, even incoherence, in the development of the American state that result from this open, fragmented, and flexible system of policy-making have been widely noted. The process is said to be "roundabout"; the results, "uneasy," even "hapless."[14] In economic policy, for instance, the independent Federal Reserve Board regulates interest rates, the Congress and president together determine the fiscal surplus or deficit, and an array of federal and state agencies command, regulate, or supervise economic sectors (including defense, health care, transportation, energy, and finance) that constitute a quarter or more of the nongovernment share of the national economy. Postwar science and technology policy had a similar character. Court rulings on intellectual property in the 1940s and 1950s, for instance, derived from an expansive vision of the liberal state, even as congressional appropriations for civilian industrial R&D reflected a barely updated version of classical liberalism.

Yet, the patchwork character of policy regularly fades from view. When presidents and parties project their programs, for example, they naturally suppress activities that do not fit in. One level down, agency heads similarly portray clear missions, well-defined tasks, and a steady hand. Critics of those in power, ironically, have an incentive to picture the state as a monolith as well, so that their alternative is starkly presented against that backdrop. One job of political scientists is to revise these descriptions, to reveal the inconsistencies. Much recent work in American political development, such as that of Theda Skocpol and Stephen Skowronek, has tackled this chore with gusto. Science and technology

---

[14] James A. Morone, *The Democratic Wish* (New York: Basic, 1990); Barry Karl, *The Uneasy State: The United States from 1915 to 1945* (Chicago: University of Chicago Press, 1983); Skowronek 1982 (above, n. 13).

policy studies, however, have been little touched by this endeavor, tending to depict the American state's role in the governance of technological innovation as a pure breed descended from a visionary Vannevar Bush in 1945. When one digs into the roots of the "postwar consensus," one finds that its provenance is far more complex and, with that knowledge, one can see more clearly the resulting hybrid.[15]

FIVE VISIONS OF THE LIBERAL STATE AND THE GOVERNANCE OF TECHNOLOGICAL INNOVATION, 1921–1953

What are these roots? The central claim of this book is that post-World War II federal science and technology policy was a hybrid of five competing conceptions of the state advanced by policy entrepreneurs between 1921 and 1953. These policy entrepreneurs intended to preserve and expand free markets, while responding effectively to changes in circumstances that they perceived as threats to the nation's economic health and military security. The five visions of the state emerged sequentially in this period, and the influence of each ebbed and flowed over time and across policy-making venues. All left legacies to the postwar period.

Conservatism

One conception of the state, "conservatism," held that the state should limit its role in the economy, as much as possible, to the enforcement of property rights. Conservatives blamed the government for prolonging the Depression by disrupting business confidence with unpredictable and excessive taxes and regulation and by propping up wages through relief and support for unionization. They proposed that such policies be repealed. This view extended naturally to the governance of technological innovation; the state should stay out of it.

Conservatives viewed the military challenge as separable from the economic one. They recognized a need for the state to provide for defense, including military technological innovation, but believed that this sphere of activity could and should be isolated from the domestic economy. During the 1930s conservatives tended to lean toward isolationism as a way to minimize the threat that military policy posed to normal economic governance; when that position lost its viability, they sought to build institutional firewalls between military and civilian activity.

Conservatism held sway in the 1920s, advanced by Treasury Secretary Andrew Mellon, among others, in reaction to the perceived excesses of the Wilson period. The Depression was a devastating blow. Even Frank Jewett, the

---

[15] Theda Skocpol, *Protecting Soldiers and Mothers: The Political Origins of Social Policy in the United States* (Cambridge: Harvard University Press, 1993); Skowronek (above, n. 13).

president of Bell Telephone Laboratories, who was the most eminent conservative science and technology policy entrepreneur of the 1930s and 1940s, relaxed his stance in the face of 25 percent unemployment. The "Roosevelt recession" of 1937–38, however, revitalized conservatism. Jewett, who ascended to the presidency of the National Academy of Sciences in 1938, found a substantial audience, particularly in the House of Representatives, for his view that federal meddling with patent laws and research funding would slow the pace of scientific and technological progress and distort it according to the whims of government bureaucrats. He argued that AT&T (of which Bell Labs was the R&D arm) and similar firms had provided their customers with rapid improvements in performance and price under the established rules and that there was no reason to change them. Government intervention could lead nowhere but to unjustifiable curbs on liberty, especially in universities.

Jewett endorsed the institutional innovations that mobilized U.S. technological resources after 1940 and served as a key science and technology policymaker during World War II. Nonetheless, he saw the war as a unique circumstance, fraught with danger for the peace to follow, when a return to normalcy was in order. Jewett reasserted his conservative principles in the immediate postwar period, supporting congressional conservatives who watered down and killed off measures that would have expanded federal powers to intervene in science and technology for the purpose of stimulating economic growth. Senator Robert A. Taft of Ohio was the leader of the conservative coalition in Congress between World War II and the Korean War. Taft engaged military as well as civilian issues. When he found that he could not head off the maintenance of a large military establishment, he sought to bound its influence. Taft's efforts contributed to the adoption of a military strategy that was highly dependent on rapid technological innovation carried out in secretive institutions. When the Korean War burst the budget constraints that Taft had helped to impose, this strategy was fully implemented.

These consequences for the organization of military technological innovation constitute the most tangible, if indirect, legacy of the conservatives. Perhaps more important, however, was their obstruction, mainly in Congress, of entrepreneurial efforts motivated by other conceptions of the state. Despite the Depression, the conservative vision of the state proved so compelling that it reemerged as a vibrant pole of political debate.

Associationalism

Chief among the contenders that conservatism squeezed out from the right side of the ideological spectrum after the war was "associationalism."[16] The asso-

---

[16] Ellis W. Hawley, "Herbert Hoover, the Commerce Secretariat, and the Vision of an 'Asso-

ciationalists believed that markets failed on occasion because private economic decision-makers were ill-informed. If corporate executives understood the big picture, their decisions would incorporate enough concern for the public interest for it to be protected. The associationalists proposed the creation of institutions that would extract or develop this information and ensure that it was transmitted to the proper men. The state's role was to catalyze and support the development of these institutions, but preferably not to own them.

Science and technology were considered important targets for state action by associationalists like the engineer-cum-statesman Herbert Hoover. Unmitigated economic competition, they thought, inhibited innovation by inspiring fear that the risks taken would not be rewarded. Competition also contributed to the atomization of industry, which hindered long-term, large-scale investments in modern research and development. Associationalists proposed that the state see to it that the latest research findings and information about best practices be disseminated, so that industry would be continually rationalized toward ever-higher efficiency, shutting obsolete plants. Industrywide research facilities, run by industrial trade associations or, failing that, by government service agencies, would provide such knowledge efficiently. They would foster close relationships among research executives and among bench-level scientists and engineers across the industry to set R&D priorities, harmonize expectations, and diffuse knowledge. Such collective efforts were said to make the market work better by enhancing the decision-making of firms and providing consumers with better products.

Associationalism had its origin in the World War I mobilization. The chief virtues of associationalism in wartime were the same as in peacetime: the efficient production of new knowledge by pooling resources and preventing duplication, and the broad diffusion of knowledge throughout industry. Patriotism gave an added prod to firms less inclined to cooperate otherwise, particularly technological leaders that preferred to keep their advantages to themselves. Associationalists debated the extent to which the state ought to use its power to require cooperation in war and the extent to which the war analogy and any coercion it might justify should be employed during economic hard times.

Against the grain of the conservative administrations in which he served, Secretary of Commerce Hoover experimented with associational policies between 1921 and 1928, drawing heavily on experiences, colleagues, and public goodwill built up during World War I. Commerce's Bureau of Standards worked particularly to organize "sick" industries to develop new technological capabilities. Other bureaus in Hoover's department attempted to tear down barriers inhibiting the growth of high-technology industries, and the secretary himself chaired a private effort to get American industry to cooperate in the sup-

---

ciative State,' 1921–1928," *Journal of American History* 61 (1974): 116–40. Hawley and others who have drawn on his work also apply the terms *neocorporatist* and *technocorporatist* to the "associative" state.

port of academic science. As president, however, Hoover was paralyzed by the economic crisis and did little more to advance the associative vision.

Ironically, the administration of Hoover's nemesis, Franklin D. Roosevelt, attempted to solve the economic crisis with associative policies between 1933 and 1935. The National Recovery Administration (NRA) and, in science and technology policy, the Science Advisory Board (SAB) that Karl Compton and others attempted to attach to the NRA, were the vehicles for these experiments. As a general economic policy, the NRA was a disaster that discredited associationalism, particularly among conservatives who had found it a more attractive alternative than some of the more radical measures circulating in New Deal Washington. Yet in certain industries, such as railroads, durable NRA-like regulatory bodies were established that lasted for several decades. Far from realizing Compton's hopes, however, these organizations tended to retard the rate of technological change so as to preserve the established industrial order.

Even though the NRA experience discouraged associationalist entrepreneurs in the late 1930s, their vision of the state resurfaced in a modified form to guide the war mobilization of national scientific and technological capabilities in the 1940s. Vannevar Bush, who served as Roosevelt's science advisor as well as the director of the Office of Scientific Research and Development, effected this resurrection in synthetic rubber and other critical industrial sectors. While many of these experiments were abandoned after the war, they left traces in military procurement policy and elsewhere in the postwar system.

Reform Liberalism

The failure of the NRA in 1935 created an opening to advance a vision of the state that challenged existing economic institutions more than associationalism did. Political entrepreneurs wed to "reform liberalism" stepped into this vacuum, calling for the creation of new institutions and policies that could stop the abuses of private power that, they argued, unbalanced the free market.[17] Reform liberals in the executive branch, like Henry Wallace (who served as Secretary of Agriculture, Vice-President, and Secretary of Commerce) and Thurman Arnold (Assistant Attorney General for Antitrust), believed that financiers and large corporations wielded bargaining power so disproportionate as to disrupt the natural course of progress. The administrative state they envisioned would shoulder the burden of re-establishing markets through regulation, by providing aid to the less powerful in civil society, and even by becoming an economic actor itself.

[17] Alan Brinkley, "The New Deal Order and the Idea of the State," in Steve Fraser and Gary Gerstle, eds., *The Rise and Fall of the New Deal Order* (Princeton: Princeton University Press, 1989), 87–94; Alan Brinkley, *The End of Reform: New Deal Liberalism in Recession and War* (New York: Knopf, 1995), 1–14.

Technological innovation, in the view of reform liberals, was as subject to greed and myopia as any other aspect of economic life. Sometimes new technologies were used to shed labor and raise capital's share of income, leading to technological unemployment. Elsewhere in the economy, new technologies were suppressed by powerful interests, so that their own investments would not become obsolete. What the reform liberals wanted to do in these circumstances was to call forth the new technologies and assure that their fruits were distributed in a manner that led to economic expansion. To do this, the state would require the expertise to assess the direction of future technological advances and a supple set of capacities to resolve the specific failures of the market in each sector. In one industry the state might need to develop and commercialize technology itself; in another it might need to break a bottleneck that held back private competition that would spur innovation.

The Tennessee Valley Authority (TVA) was the reform liberals' flagship agency early in the New Deal, bucking the associative tide. Although the president was increasingly inclined to countenance state activism as the decade passed, conservative opposition in Congress in the late 1930s stymied reform liberal legislative initiatives in such areas as patents and the development of mass-produced housing. The courts proved to be a more promising venue for Arnold's pursuit of patent reform, although the final victories were delayed until after the war. These decisions ultimately proved to be the reform liberals' most significant contribution to postwar science and technology policy, shaping corporate technology strategies over several decades.

The reform liberals did not anticipate war. When it came, however, Arnold, Wallace, and their allies endeavored to coopt the bloated wartime state to pursue domestic as well as military ends. The war appeared to them to be an opportunity to prove the viability of reform liberal experiments that peacetime politics had precluded. But this assessment was wrong. In the hands of the military services and the business-dominated civilian defense bureaucracy, state capacities that the reform liberals had longed to put in place during the 1930s were turned to ends that reinforced the imbalances of the market, rather than busting open encrusted patterns of control. The "two-front" war, from the reform liberal perspective, was lost badly at home. The decline of reform liberalism carried right through the war's immediate aftermath, and its fate was sealed by the emergence of anticommunist conservatives, who painted Wallace and others as fellow travelers. Reform liberalism was largely displaced at the liberal end of the political spectrum by "Keynesianism" in the postwar years.

Keynesianism

The causal story of the Great Depression associated with the name of John Maynard Keynes (though he was neither its sole originator nor much responsible for its elaboration in the United States) did not place the blame as squarely on vested interests as reform liberalism did.[18] Instead, it took the Depression to be an almost mechanical malfunction. The problem, as Keynes showed in 1936, was a lack of effective demand that left the economy trapped at a low-level equilibrium. Neither consumer spending nor business investment was capable of snapping the economy out of this funk; the government had to do so, through deficit spending. In the ideal Keynesian state, the main job of government economic managers would be to calibrate the budget deficit or surplus to nudge aggregate economic indicators onto the right track. Fiscal policy, later supplemented by monetary policy (known together as macroeconomic policy), were the tools by which the state could ensure that the free market worked properly, without supplanting it any more than was necessary.

Science and technology played an ambiguous part in Keynesian thought. Keynesians agreed that they were essential ingredients of long-run economic growth but disagreed among themselves over the market's capacity to supply them sufficiently. For those in the policy elite who became known in the postwar period as "commercial Keynesians," such as the liberal businessmen of the Committee for Economic Development (CED), technological innovation was a natural outcome of private investment, which could be regulated by macroeconomic policy. Macroeconomic policy would establish the optimal level of investment, which would in turn remedy any shortage of new technologies (with some modest exceptions) as a byproduct. To another group of Keynesians, the "social Keynesians," market failures in the provision of science and technology for economic purposes appeared far more widespread. Without necessarily imputing that powerful corporations deliberately held back technological progress, as the reform liberals did, social Keynesians like the Harvard economist Alvin Hansen argued that the state should rectify these market failures as a component of the spending programs that were intrinsic to fiscal policy. These differences mirrored larger divides among the Keynesians which emerged as their views achieved wider acceptance in the 1940s.

The Keynesian idea that the state's main role ought to be to provide liquidity to an otherwise well-functioning market was prefigured in the early 1930s, particularly in housing and labor policy. By expanding the market, it was hoped that housing finance reform, for instance, would lead to the development of mass production technology for residential construction. The more distinctive concept of deficit spending as an element of macroeconomic management emerged in the wake of the 1937–38 recession, as the lessons of Keynes's *General Theory* were blended with indigenous American ideas. As articulated by Hansen, who served as an advisor to the National Resources Planning Board and the Federal Reserve Board, the vision of the Keynesian state was a sophis-

---

[18] Brinkley 1989 (above, n. 17); Ira Katznelson and Bruce Pietrykowski, "Rebuilding the American State: Evidence from the 1940s," *Studies in American Political Development* 5 (1991): 301–39. These authors use the term *fiscalism* for this conception of the state. *Keynesianism* is less precise, but more accessible, as discussed in Chapters 4 and 6.

	Conservative	Associative	Reform Liberal	Keynesian	National Security
1921					
2					
933					
37					

Strong   Moderate   Weak   Dormant

... the State in Science and Technology Policy: A Rough Illus-
... uence

... s of the state; their support dwindled as policy-makers and
... ainst the strictures of wartime governance. Even the back-
... curity state vision, Chapter 6 relates, lost power as con-
... e late 1940s. The Korean War, and the overarching Cold
... it was a part, blunted this surge, and prompted an un-
... etween conservatives, Keynesians, and national security
... 950s. This entente is the subject of Chapter 7.
... ns and principles of science and technology policy that
... 3 are familiar and have lasted through the Cold War and

ticated complement to reform liberalism, providing a rationale for spending on the aggressive scientific research and technological development policies, like those of the TVA, that the reform liberal economic program demanded.

World War II, however, detached Keynesianism from reform liberalism. Too much demand, rather than depressed consumption and investment, was the central threat in wartime. Instead of spending to promote the development of new industries, Keynesians recommended raising taxes to offset the stimulus of the war effort. Their apparent success at this task helped Keynesianism win new adherents after the war. In the conditions of postwar "exhilaration," however, in which additional government spending was not obviously indicated, the Keynesians divided. Hansen reiterated his prewar prescriptions in anticipation of a downturn that never came, the CED advocated limited funding of academic science and tax cuts to encourage private venture capital investment, and the Truman White House sought a politically viable mix of these variants in an era of resurgent conservatism.

The stalemate of the late 1940s was broken by the Korean War. Massive military spending required by the Cold War, including R&D spending, came to be seen by Keynesians as indirectly beneficial to the economy, raising the aggregate level of scientific and technological activity. As a source of new industries and cultivator of human resources, the military took the place in the scheme that Hansen had hoped to reserve for civilian science and technology policy. In addition to rationalizing military spending, Keynesianism's influence on the postwar period extended to the use of aggregate indicators, such as national R&D spending, as the central tools for assessing science and technology policy.

The National Security State

Military spending's most avid advocates were partisans of the "national security state."[19] These entrepreneurs argued that the most dangerous threats to the American way emanated from outside the United States, rather than from internal opposition or some organic defect in American capitalism. This was a novel situation in American history, brought on by technological changes that gave foreign states, such as Nazi Germany and Soviet Russia, the power to reach the eyes and ears of U.S. citizens and the potential to take direct military action against the United States. Only by privileging national security above all other purposes of the state, its advocates argued, could these threats to liberty and the free market be averted. The consequences of national security thinking for science and technology policy were clear; the United States must develop the military technologies that would guarantee security by any means necessary. If a foreign state took a substantial lead, it would be tempted to impose its will here.

[19] Daniel Yergin, *Shattered Peace: The Origins of the Cold War and the National Security State* (Boston: Houghton-Mifflin, 1977), 5–6.

World War II mobilizers inherited a very modest complex of institutions for military technological innovation that had just scraped along between the wars. This poor foundation and the urgency of military needs provided a convincing justification that much technological development during the war should be delegated to those in civil society who already possessed the appropriate organizational and human resources and hence could move most quickly: notably elite universities and large high-technology firms. This consideration, along with the reform liberal proclivity to divert resources away from strictly defined national security ends, fostered a wartime synthesis of the national security state and the associative state under the eye of Vannevar Bush. Bush's organizational creativity in utilizing nongovernment contractors and his technological enthusiasm diffused into the military services, particularly the air force, which made heavy investments in R&D as the war proceeded and hoped to maintain them afterward.

These aspirations were mostly frustrated in the immediate postwar period, from 1945 to 1950. Across the political spectrum, the expansion of the national security state was perceived as a potential threat to liberty as well as a drain on prosperity, whether by interrupting the free market, as Senator Taft thought, or by squeezing the state's domestic capacity to improve the market, as Secretary Wallace thought. With budget caps firmly in place, vicious civil wars broke out inside the Pentagon, between the military services and within them, over the extent to which these limited resources should be devoted to R&D and the acquisition of new technologies. As the foreign policy challenges of the early Cold War mounted, congressional conservatives acquiesced in increased military spending, but on the condition that the new resources be channeled to technological enthusiasts like air force General Curtis LeMay, who appeared to them less likely to impose on domestic liberty than the universal military training and overseas ground commitments preferred by Secretary of State George C. Marshall, the former army chief of staff. The air force and the navy also took virtual control of the new Atomic Energy Commission, dashing the hopes of a few remaining reform liberals, who had hoped to open a second front in the Cold War by using atomic power to subvert the market power of private electric utilities at home.

The Korean War shattered the barriers to the growth of the national security state. As the military budget quadrupled, there was enough money for everything. For Keynesians like Leon Keyserling, chairman of the Council of Economic Advisors under President Truman, military spending, once necessary, became virtuous; from an economic perspective, it was just another means of carrying out an expansionary fiscal policy. As the war dragged on, however, conservatives regained their bearings and, as in the late 1940s, pressed for smaller budgets to be spent on technologically intensive military forces. In this, too, Keynesians found virtue; their concern was that aggregate national R&D spending be raised. That military R&D spending was the majority of the ag-

gregate was of little concern; they reasoned th
itable commercial products. And, indeed, th
mental government program were impressi
computer, and electronics industries owe m

THE POSTWAR HYBRI

The claims made in the previous section
Rather than treat the five brands of liber
them in competition with one another.
tivities of contending science and t
growth and decline of the coalitions t
the plot line. This chronological str
of alternative outcomes to the post
gies to the present; the science an
structured by competing liberalis
guided policy entrepreneurship f

Chart 1 is a rough illustratio
sociationalism, reform liberalis
in science and technology pol
episodes that I trace are not fi
three, or four coalitions. No
throughout the entire period
leys.

Chapter 2 concentrates
vative assumptions were
challenges occurred at t
the first Roosevelt admi
of the Depression. Ass
spite a modest challen
of the NRA crippled
revived conservatism
strates that these vi
"Roosevelt recessi
some saw as a wa
as well.

This three-wa
World War II, a
ingly, dominate
triotic unity, h
the state conti
1930s. The e

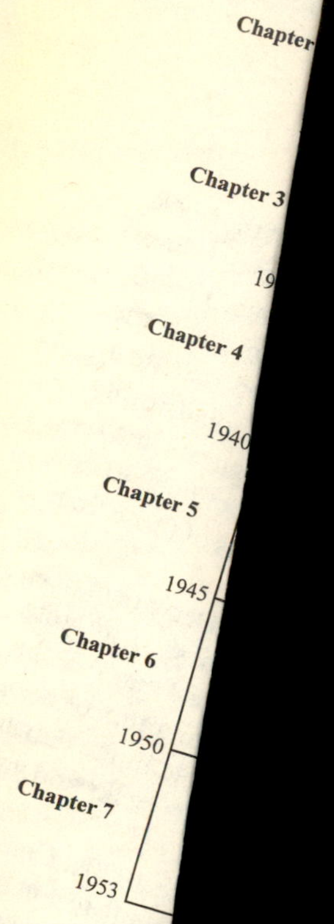

Chart 1. Visions of
tration of Their Infl

reform liberal vision
the public recoiled ag
ers of the national se
servatism surged in th
War buildup of which
comfortable embrace b
advocates in the early
Many of the institutio
were established by 195

beyond. The National Science Foundation, the national laboratories, the concept of spinoff, the analytical use of aggregate R&D spending statistics, and more were in place. Although some of these may seem to represent the triumph of a single vision of the state, most have roots in more than one. The technological capacities of the military services and the Atomic Energy Commission, for instance, may seem to be the pure product of the national security state ideal, yet my research shows that they owed debts to associationalism, Keynesianism, and conservatism as well.

This work also shines a spotlight on features of federal science and technology policy that fall outside the scope of the "postwar consensus" on basic research and spinoff. The new relationship between antitrust and patent law in the postwar period, for instance, to which many large corporations felt obliged to respond, derived from a reform liberal initiative of the late 1930s that was blocked by congressional conservatives and shunted into the courts. Hidden legacies of decades past, like this one, may constitute important resources for freeing contemporary science and technology policy from the blinders imposed by the conventional wisdom.

The roads that were not taken between 1921 and 1953 and the reasons why they were not taken may serve a similar purpose. The evidence I have gathered shows that serious science and technology policy initiatives that garnered substantial support were pursued at many points during these decades, but most of them failed to win approval. These failures were caused by many things, ranging from entrepreneurial miscalculation to unexpected war. But some patterns can be discerned. The most pronounced seem to be due to affinities between particular visions of the state and policy-making venues; Congress tended to be a conservative bulwark in this period, for example, while the president was more congenial to associationalist and reform liberal policy entrepreneurs.

More generally, the notion that the "postwar consensus" is a hybrid of several visions of the state ought to dissuade analysts from positing radical counterfactuals about what might have happened and, by extension, harboring excessive expectations about what could happen. The plausible alternative trajectories of development in the past, in my view, are also hybrids that, compared to the actual outcome, display a little more of one vision here or a little less of another there. I find it implausible, for instance, that federally funded civilian R&D programs on either an associationalist or reform liberal model would have served as a substantial counterweight to military R&D programs in the early Cold War had circumstances been only slightly different, as some have implied.[20] The revolution in science and technology policy wrought in the period of my study is not a single big bang, but rather was composed of many little revolutions.

---

[20] Stuart W. Leslie, *The Cold War and American Science: The Military-Academic Complex at MIT and Stanford* (New York: Columbia University Press, 1993).

The end of the Cold War combined with the continuing transformation of the nation's economic structure have raised some hopes that a new revolution may be in the offing. My tale is cautionary on this score. At the same time, however, it does offer some intriguing insights. Several liberalisms seem to characterize the science and technology policy debate of the 1980s and 1990s, and they recall those of the earlier period. The conservatism of the House Republicans of the 104th Congress, for instance, nearly equaled that of the Republican majority in the 80th Congress of 1947–48; President Bill Clinton's plans for public/private partnerships in technological development echo those of Hooverian associationalism. One might find that the relationship between these contemporary conceptions of the liberal state and the institutions of the federal government mirror those affinities that I touched on above as well.

Because these visions of the state are durable and economic and military circumstances are constantly changing, the policy process continually inspires policy entrepreneurs. The perceived failure of the Bush administration to adapt to the post-Cold War era prompted the Clinton administration's change of course. Congressional Republicans, in turn, were determined to obliterate the president's new ventures. Should these policies fail to alter the sense of economic insecurity that pervades the public mind, another round of intense conflict among policy entrepreneurs will surely follow.

While the process generates entrepreneurs, the hybrid quality of the twentieth-century American state typically provides them with exemplars and institutional bases on which to erect new programs. The legacies of old rounds of competition serve as platforms for new ones. Hoover's Bureau of Standards, working quietly in harmony with industry in the shadow of the Cold War military technology complex, for instance, became a major focus of congressional Democrats' and ultimately of President Clinton's technology policy in the 1980s and 1990s. It received a new name (the National Institute of Standards and Technology, or NIST), a strengthened mission, and an infusion of funds. Conservative attacks on NIST as a source of unneeded subsidy echo those of Republicans in the 1930s and 1950s.

These legacies and analogies, which provide fertile material for thinking about contemporary science and technology policy-making, will become clearer, I hope, as the reader proceeds, and I return to them in my concluding chapter. To pursue the parallel between the Clinton and Hoover approaches just one more step at this point, I offer the words of President Hoover's Research Committee on Recent Social Trends regarding the possibilities for revising the relationship between government and business in the United States:

> Observers of social change may look here for new types of politico-economic organization, new constellations of government, industry, and technology, forms now only dimly discerned; the quasi-governmental corporation, the government owned corporation, the mixed corporation, the semi- and demi-autonomous industrial groupings in varying relations to the state. . . . The hybrid nature of some

of these creations may be the despair of those theorists, both radical and conservative, who see the world only in terms of an unquestioning acceptance of one or the other of two exclusive dogmas, but these innovations will be welcomed by those who are less concerned about phobias than with the prompt and practical adjustment of actual affairs to the brutal realities of changing social and economic conditions.[21]

Hoover is the protagonist of the next chapter.

[21] President's Research Committee on Recent Social Trends, *Recent Social Trends in the United States,* vol. 1 (New York: McGraw-Hill, 1933), lxii.

The Republican Ascendancy and the Crash

ASSOCIATIVE UNDERCURRENTS
IN A CONSERVATIVE ERA, 1921–1932

THE INDUSTRIALIZATION of the United States was rapid. A nation that was little more than a vast wilderness pockmarked by scattered human habitation appeared to some of its founders to be nearly ungovernable in scale; the federal experience before the Civil War confirmed the prescience of this pessimistic minority. A half century after that war, the frontier was already a distant memory, the wilderness filled in. Telegraphs and railroads and then telephones and highways connected Americans, who had abandoned the land for the cities, where many worked in occupations undreamed of by their forbears. New technologies transformed the nation and nearly everything in it.

The federal government's role in this transformation was obscure. Army-trained engineers and federal/state cooperative agricultural experiment stations, for instance, visibly contributed to the nation's emerging scientific and technological capacities, but to say that these influences constituted a policy would be an exaggeration. The dominant force was corporate capitalism. World War I, however, revealed new possibilities for governance, at least to some of those who organized the U.S. effort. Herbert Hoover, who served as Secretary of Commerce throughout the Harding and Coolidge administrations, seized on the wartime experience and mobilized the men and organizations that were its legacy to advance a vision of the U.S. political economy in which cooperation within industry, facilitated by government, would accelerate the pace of scientific research and technological development. Hoover faced formidable opposition, particularly from his cabinet counterpart, Secretary of the Treasury Andrew Mellon, in his effort to make the young Commerce Department the center of such an associative state.

The conflict between conservatives and associationalists in the 1920s was played out in the White House and the Capitol, but most crucially in the court of business opinion. Hoover needed legal authority and funding to enable the Bureau of Standards and other Commerce units to do their part, but what he most needed was for firms to choose to work with these agencies and with one another. Mellon preached the gospel that small government was beautiful and pressed for tax cuts that would put more money in private hands to invest in science and technology, if they so chose; whether firms worked together was of little concern. The private initiatives that Secretary Mellon extolled suffused public consciousness, epitomized in the veneration of the General Electric Research Laboratory as the "House of Magic." As that laboratory's director, Willis Whitney, put it: "Research is religion and good business combined, and the organization that supports it, the giant corporation, is doing a public service."[1]

Secretary Hoover, too, admired the corporate research laboratories and world-class research universities built by the free market and the charitable foundations that sprang from its fortunes. He focused his energy on the stagnant "sick" industries and dynamic new industries. In both of these areas, he perceived opportunities for the federal government to catalyze new institutions and economic relations that would accelerate technological innovation. Hoover's programs hovered at the margins and rarely achieved the economic impact that he promised. Nonetheless, like the telephone on his desk, they helped to give him a "technological aura" (in the words of historian Barry Karl), which did not hurt at all when he ran for and won elective office for the first time in 1928.[2]

President Hoover, faced with a bewildering and demoralizing crisis, backed away from the associative vision of the state. Preoccupied, reasonably enough, with short-term issues, his administration did little to construct new modes of governance that cultivated long-term economic growth through the creation of new industries and the modernization of old ones. The president himself ultimately came to defend this paralysis, defining himself as a doctrinaire conservative against opponents who proposed changes that went far beyond what he found acceptable. In doing so, he contributed to the popular portrait of distance, rigidity, and ill-humor that his name still evokes, two-thirds of a century after Black Thursday, rather than the administrative innovator of great energy and intellect that his contemporaries both admired and despised.

THE AMERICAN TRADITION
IN SCIENCE AND TECHNOLOGY POLICY

The appropriate role of the U.S. government in science and technology has been debated since the nation's founding. Federal agencies were most active during the nation's first 150 years in collaborations with state governments to develop and promote new technologies in agriculture and other natural resource industries. To the nation's rise to global leadership in manufacturing in the late nineteenth century and the simultaneous emergence of a "distinctive American [technological] problem solving network," however, Washington made only in-

---

[1] George Wise, *Willis R. Whitney, General Electric, and the Origins of U.S. Industrial Research* (New York: Columbia University Press, 1985), 207–49.

[2] Barry D. Karl, *The Uneasy State: The U.S. from 1915 to 1945* (Chicago: University of Chicago Press, 1983), 80.

direct contributions.[3] Although sometimes significant, these actions mapped out only a small fraction of the policy terrain that other national governments were exploring and that the United States would explore itself as the twentieth century advanced.

The founders were deeply interested in science and technology and deeply divided about their governance. Benjamin Franklin was one of the great scientific minds of his age; Thomas Jefferson, a notorious enthusiast and tinkerer. A patent clause, giving Congress the power "to promote the Progress of Science and useful Arts," found its way into the Constitution. Yet the more important precedent set by the Constitutional Convention was its refusal to establish a national university. Such an institution fell under the rubric of "internal improvements," trespassing the limits set on federal power by defenders of the prerogatives of state governments. For the nation's first eighty-odd years, internal improvements, encompassing roads and canals as well as research and inventions, remained largely out-of-bounds for the central government. The failure of Samuel Morse to persuade Congress to take ownership of and promotional responsibility for the telegraph in the 1840s is but a minor footnote in this great constitutional struggle.[4]

That this struggle was waged mainly along sectional lines can best be seen by the effect of the Civil War on it. The antebellum antipathy to internal improvements was relegated to the dustbin of history after the Union victory as the federal government embarked on a massive program of industrial promotion. The tariffs, the concessions, and the rest of this program contributed to an explosion of technological dynamism. Railroads and steel were revolutionized; the electrical power and chemical industries, created. However, even as the old borders of the federal sphere were overrun, new ones were drawn. Unlike Imperial Germany or Meiji Japan, nations whose paths of industrialization paralleled that of the United States, the U.S. government did not target new technologies or construct institutions specifically designed to advance them. Government-run industrial research institutes and nationalized enterprises ran contrary to the American tradition.[5]

To European observers, the striking feature of American manufacturing technology in the second half of the nineteenth century was its use of interchangeable mechanical parts, which could be made by machine tools operated by unskilled laborers rather than skilled workers. This "American system" diffused

[3] Richard R. Nelson and Gavin Wright, "The Rise and Fall of American Technological Leadership: The Postwar Era in Historical Perspective," *Journal of Economic Literature* 30 (1992): 1937.

[4] A. Hunter Dupree, *Science in the Federal Government* (1957; reprint, paperback ed., Baltimore: Johns Hopkins University Press, 1987), 3–6, 48–49.

[5] Otto Keck, "The National System for Technological Innovation in Germany," in Richard R. Nelson, ed., *National Innovation Systems* (New York: Oxford University Press, 1993), 116–29; Hiroyuki Odagiri and Akira Goto, "The Japanese System of Innovation: Past, Present, and Future," in ibid., 79–81.

ticated complement to reform liberalism, providing a rationale for spending on the aggressive scientific research and technological development policies, like those of the TVA, that the reform liberal economic program demanded.

World War II, however, detached Keynesianism from reform liberalism. Too much demand, rather than depressed consumption and investment, was the central threat in wartime. Instead of spending to promote the development of new industries, Keynesians recommended raising taxes to offset the stimulus of the war effort. Their apparent success at this task helped Keynesianism win new adherents after the war. In the conditions of postwar "exhilaration," however, in which additional government spending was not obviously indicated, the Keynesians divided. Hansen reiterated his prewar prescriptions in anticipation of a downturn that never came, the CED advocated limited funding of academic science and tax cuts to encourage private venture capital investment, and the Truman White House sought a politically viable mix of these variants in an era of resurgent conservatism.

The stalemate of the late 1940s was broken by the Korean War. Massive military spending required by the Cold War, including R&D spending, came to be seen by Keynesians as indirectly beneficial to the economy, raising the aggregate level of scientific and technological activity. As a source of new industries and cultivator of human resources, the military took the place in the scheme that Hansen had hoped to reserve for civilian science and technology policy. In addition to rationalizing military spending, Keynesianism's influence on the postwar period extended to the use of aggregate indicators, such as national R&D spending, as the central tools for assessing science and technology policy.

The National Security State

Military spending's most avid advocates were partisans of the "national security state."[19] These entrepreneurs argued that the most dangerous threats to the American way emanated from outside the United States, rather than from internal opposition or some organic defect in American capitalism. This was a novel situation in American history, brought on by technological changes that gave foreign states, such as Nazi Germany and Soviet Russia, the power to reach the eyes and ears of U.S. citizens and the potential to take direct military action against the United States. Only by privileging national security above all other purposes of the state, its advocates argued, could these threats to liberty and the free market be averted. The consequences of national security thinking for science and technology policy were clear; the United States must develop the military technologies that would guarantee security by any means necessary. If a foreign state took a substantial lead, it would be tempted to impose its will here.

---

[19] Daniel Yergin, *Shattered Peace: The Origins of the Cold War and the National Security State* (Boston: Houghton-Mifflin, 1977), 5–6.

World War II mobilizers inherited a very modest complex of institutions for military technological innovation that had just scraped along between the wars. This poor foundation and the urgency of military needs provided a convincing justification that much technological development during the war should be delegated to those in civil society who already possessed the appropriate organizational and human resources and hence could move most quickly: notably elite universities and large high-technology firms. This consideration, along with the reform liberal proclivity to divert resources away from strictly defined national security ends, fostered a wartime synthesis of the national security state and the associative state under the eye of Vannevar Bush. Bush's organizational creativity in utilizing nongovernment contractors and his technological enthusiasm diffused into the military services, particularly the air force, which made heavy investments in R&D as the war proceeded and hoped to maintain them afterward.

These aspirations were mostly frustrated in the immediate postwar period, from 1945 to 1950. Across the political spectrum, the expansion of the national security state was perceived as a potential threat to liberty as well as a drain on prosperity, whether by interrupting the free market, as Senator Taft thought, or by squeezing the state's domestic capacity to improve the market, as Secretary Wallace thought. With budget caps firmly in place, vicious civil wars broke out inside the Pentagon, between the military services and within them, over the extent to which these limited resources should be devoted to R&D and the acquisition of new technologies. As the foreign policy challenges of the early Cold War mounted, congressional conservatives acquiesced in increased military spending, but on the condition that the new resources be channeled to technological enthusiasts like air force General Curtis LeMay, who appeared to them less likely to impose on domestic liberty than the universal military training and overseas ground commitments preferred by Secretary of State George C. Marshall, the former army chief of staff. The air force and the navy also took virtual control of the new Atomic Energy Commission, dashing the hopes of a few remaining reform liberals, who had hoped to open a second front in the Cold War by using atomic power to subvert the market power of private electric utilities at home.

The Korean War shattered the barriers to the growth of the national security state. As the military budget quadrupled, there was enough money for everything. For Keynesians like Leon Keyserling, chairman of the Council of Economic Advisors under President Truman, military spending, once necessary, became virtuous; from an economic perspective, it was just another means of carrying out an expansionary fiscal policy. As the war dragged on, however, conservatives regained their bearings and, as in the late 1940s, pressed for smaller budgets to be spent on technologically intensive military forces. In this, too, Keynesians found virtue; their concern was that aggregate national R&D spending be raised. That military R&D spending was the majority of the aggregate was of little concern; they reasoned that it would "spill over" into profitable commercial products. And, indeed, the economic fruits of this monumental government program were impressive. The contemporary aerospace, computer, and electronics industries owe much to it.

THE POSTWAR HYBRID AND ITS FUTURE

The claims made in the previous section are substantiated in the rest of the book. Rather than treat the five brands of liberalism separately, as I have above, I show them in competition with one another, in various groupings, over time. The activities of contending science and technology policy entrepreneurs and the growth and decline of the coalitions they mobilized behind their proposals form the plot line. This chronological structure allows one to assess the plausibility of alternative outcomes to the postwar hybrid. Furthermore, it suggests analogies to the present; the science and technology policy process continues to be structured by competing liberalisms that are the lineal descendants of those that guided policy entrepreneurship fifty or more years ago.

Chart 1 is a rough illustration of the relative influence of conservatism, associationalism, reform liberalism, Keynesianism, and the national security state in science and technology policy between 1921 and 1953. As one can see, the episodes that I trace are not five-way brawls but involve a shifting mix of two, three, or four coalitions. No single vision plays a significant role in the debate throughout the entire period, much less dominates it. Each has its peaks and valleys.

Chapter 2 concentrates on the Republican ascendancy of the 1920s. Conservative assumptions were questioned in this period by associationalists, but these challenges occurred at the margins of governance. As I discuss in Chapter 3, the first Roosevelt administration jettisoned conservative doctrine in the depths of the Depression. Associationalism flourished during this administration, despite a modest challenge from the new ideas of the reform liberals. The fiasco of the NRA crippled the associationalists and polarized the debate between a revived conservatism and an emboldened reform liberalism. Chapter 4 demonstrates that these views were voiced particularly clearly during and after the "Roosevelt recession" of 1937, although Keynesianism, which offered what some saw as a way to bridge the two poles, emerged as a factor in this period as well.

This three-way conflict was not fully resolved before the mobilization for World War II, as I show in Chapter 5. National security demands, not surprisingly, dominated the policy debate during the war. Beneath the surface of patriotic unity, however, serious conflicts over the domestic aims and structure of the state continued. These conflicts carried forward many of the fights of the 1930s. The end of the war brought the demise of both the associationalist and

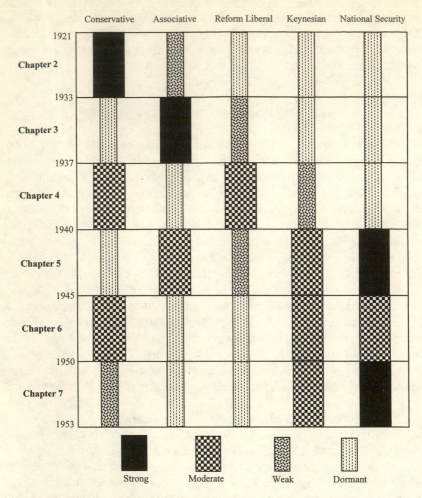

Chart 1. Visions of the State in Science and Technology Policy: A Rough Illustration of Their Influence

reform liberal visions of the state; their support dwindled as policy-makers and the public recoiled against the strictures of wartime governance. Even the backers of the national security state vision, Chapter 6 relates, lost power as conservatism surged in the late 1940s. The Korean War, and the overarching Cold War buildup of which it was a part, blunted this surge, and prompted an uncomfortable embrace between conservatives, Keynesians, and national security advocates in the early 1950s. This entente is the subject of Chapter 7.

Many of the institutions and principles of science and technology policy that were established by 1953 are familiar and have lasted through the Cold War and beyond. The National Science Foundation, the national laboratories, the concept of spinoff, the analytical use of aggregate R&D spending statistics, and more were in place. Although some of these may seem to represent the triumph of a single vision of the state, most have roots in more than one. The technological capacities of the military services and the Atomic Energy Commission, for instance, may seem to be the pure product of the national security state ideal, yet my research shows that they owed debts to associationalism, Keynesianism, and conservatism as well.

This work also shines a spotlight on features of federal science and technology policy that fall outside the scope of the "postwar consensus" on basic research and spinoff. The new relationship between antitrust and patent law in the postwar period, for instance, to which many large corporations felt obliged to respond, derived from a reform liberal initiative of the late 1930s that was blocked by congressional conservatives and shunted into the courts. Hidden legacies of decades past, like this one, may constitute important resources for freeing contemporary science and technology policy from the blinders imposed by the conventional wisdom.

The roads that were not taken between 1921 and 1953 and the reasons why they were not taken may serve a similar purpose. The evidence I have gathered shows that serious science and technology policy initiatives that garnered substantial support were pursued at many points during these decades, but most of them failed to win approval. These failures were caused by many things, ranging from entrepreneurial miscalculation to unexpected war. But some patterns can be discerned. The most pronounced seem to be due to affinities between particular visions of the state and policy-making venues; Congress tended to be a conservative bulwark in this period, for example, while the president was more congenial to associationalist and reform liberal policy entrepreneurs.

More generally, the notion that the "postwar consensus" is a hybrid of several visions of the state ought to dissuade analysts from positing radical counterfactuals about what might have happened and, by extension, harboring excessive expectations about what could happen. The plausible alternative trajectories of development in the past, in my view, are also hybrids that, compared to the actual outcome, display a little more of one vision here or a little less of another there. I find it implausible, for instance, that federally funded civilian R&D programs on either an associationalist or reform liberal model would have served as a substantial counterweight to military R&D programs in the early Cold War had circumstances been only slightly different, as some have implied.[20] The revolution in science and technology policy wrought in the period of my study is not a single big bang, but rather was composed of many little revolutions.

[20] Stuart W. Leslie, *The Cold War and American Science: The Military-Academic Complex at MIT and Stanford* (New York: Columbia University Press, 1993).

The end of the Cold War combined with the continuing transformation of the nation's economic structure have raised some hopes that a new revolution may be in the offing. My tale is cautionary on this score. At the same time, however, it does offer some intriguing insights. Several liberalisms seem to characterize the science and technology policy debate of the 1980s and 1990s, and they recall those of the earlier period. The conservatism of the House Republicans of the 104th Congress, for instance, nearly equaled that of the Republican majority in the 80th Congress of 1947–48; President Bill Clinton's plans for public/private partnerships in technological development echo those of Hooverian associationalism. One might find that the relationship between these contemporary conceptions of the liberal state and the institutions of the federal government mirror those affinities that I touched on above as well.

Because these visions of the state are durable and economic and military circumstances are constantly changing, the policy process continually inspires policy entrepreneurs. The perceived failure of the Bush administration to adapt to the post-Cold War era prompted the Clinton administration's change of course. Congressional Republicans, in turn, were determined to obliterate the president's new ventures. Should these policies fail to alter the sense of economic insecurity that pervades the public mind, another round of intense conflict among policy entrepreneurs will surely follow.

While the process generates entrepreneurs, the hybrid quality of the twentieth-century American state typically provides them with exemplars and institutional bases on which to erect new programs. The legacies of old rounds of competition serve as platforms for new ones. Hoover's Bureau of Standards, working quietly in harmony with industry in the shadow of the Cold War military technology complex, for instance, became a major focus of congressional Democrats' and ultimately of President Clinton's technology policy in the 1980s and 1990s. It received a new name (the National Institute of Standards and Technology, or NIST), a strengthened mission, and an infusion of funds. Conservative attacks on NIST as a source of unneeded subsidy echo those of Republicans in the 1930s and 1950s.

These legacies and analogies, which provide fertile material for thinking about contemporary science and technology policy-making, will become clearer, I hope, as the reader proceeds, and I return to them in my concluding chapter. To pursue the parallel between the Clinton and Hoover approaches just one more step at this point, I offer the words of President Hoover's Research Committee on Recent Social Trends regarding the possibilities for revising the relationship between government and business in the United States:

> Observers of social change may look here for new types of politico-economic organization, new constellations of government, industry, and technology, forms now only dimly discerned; the quasi-governmental corporation, the government owned corporation, the mixed corporation, the semi- and demi-autonomous industrial groupings in varying relations to the state. . . . The hybrid nature of some

of these creations may be the despair of those theorists, both radical and conservative, who see the world only in terms of an unquestioning acceptance of one or the other of two exclusive dogmas, but these innovations will be welcomed by those who are less concerned about phobias than with the prompt and practical adjustment of actual affairs to the brutal realities of changing social and economic conditions.[21]

Hoover is the protagonist of the next chapter.

[21] President's Research Committee on Recent Social Trends, *Recent Social Trends in the United States,* vol. 1 (New York: McGraw-Hill, 1933), lxii.

The Republican Ascendancy and the Crash

ASSOCIATIVE UNDERCURRENTS
IN A CONSERVATIVE ERA, 1921–1932

THE INDUSTRIALIZATION of the United States was rapid. A nation that was little more than a vast wilderness pockmarked by scattered human habitation appeared to some of its founders to be nearly ungovernable in scale; the federal experience before the Civil War confirmed the prescience of this pessimistic minority. A half century after that war, the frontier was already a distant memory, the wilderness filled in. Telegraphs and railroads and then telephones and highways connected Americans, who had abandoned the land for the cities, where many worked in occupations undreamed of by their forbears. New technologies transformed the nation and nearly everything in it.

The federal government's role in this transformation was obscure. Army-trained engineers and federal/state cooperative agricultural experiment stations, for instance, visibly contributed to the nation's emerging scientific and technological capacities, but to say that these influences constituted a policy would be an exaggeration. The dominant force was corporate capitalism. World War I, however, revealed new possibilities for governance, at least to some of those who organized the U.S. effort. Herbert Hoover, who served as Secretary of Commerce throughout the Harding and Coolidge administrations, seized on the wartime experience and mobilized the men and organizations that were its legacy to advance a vision of the U.S. political economy in which cooperation within industry, facilitated by government, would accelerate the pace of scientific research and technological development. Hoover faced formidable opposition, particularly from his cabinet counterpart, Secretary of the Treasury Andrew Mellon, in his effort to make the young Commerce Department the center of such an associative state.

The conflict between conservatives and associationalists in the 1920s was played out in the White House and the Capitol, but most crucially in the court of business opinion. Hoover needed legal authority and funding to enable the Bureau of Standards and other Commerce units to do their part, but what he most needed was for firms to choose to work with these agencies and with one another. Mellon preached the gospel that small government was beautiful and pressed for tax cuts that would put more money in private hands to invest in science and technology, if they so chose; whether firms worked together was of little concern. The private initiatives that Secretary Mellon extolled suffused public consciousness, epitomized in the veneration of the General Electric Research Laboratory as the "House of Magic." As that laboratory's director, Willis Whitney, put it: "Research is religion and good business combined, and the organization that supports it, the giant corporation, is doing a public service."[1]

Secretary Hoover, too, admired the corporate research laboratories and world-class research universities built by the free market and the charitable foundations that sprang from its fortunes. He focused his energy on the stagnant "sick" industries and dynamic new industries. In both of these areas, he perceived opportunities for the federal government to catalyze new institutions and economic relations that would accelerate technological innovation. Hoover's programs hovered at the margins and rarely achieved the economic impact that he promised. Nonetheless, like the telephone on his desk, they helped to give him a "technological aura" (in the words of historian Barry Karl), which did not hurt at all when he ran for and won elective office for the first time in 1928.[2]

President Hoover, faced with a bewildering and demoralizing crisis, backed away from the associative vision of the state. Preoccupied, reasonably enough, with short-term issues, his administration did little to construct new modes of governance that cultivated long-term economic growth through the creation of new industries and the modernization of old ones. The president himself ultimately came to defend this paralysis, defining himself as a doctrinaire conservative against opponents who proposed changes that went far beyond what he found acceptable. In doing so, he contributed to the popular portrait of distance, rigidity, and ill-humor that his name still evokes, two-thirds of a century after Black Thursday, rather than the administrative innovator of great energy and intellect that his contemporaries both admired and despised.

THE AMERICAN TRADITION
IN SCIENCE AND TECHNOLOGY POLICY

The appropriate role of the U.S. government in science and technology has been debated since the nation's founding. Federal agencies were most active during the nation's first 150 years in collaborations with state governments to develop and promote new technologies in agriculture and other natural resource industries. To the nation's rise to global leadership in manufacturing in the late nineteenth century and the simultaneous emergence of a "distinctive American [technological] problem solving network," however, Washington made only in-

---

[1] George Wise, *Willis R. Whitney, General Electric, and the Origins of U.S. Industrial Research* (New York: Columbia University Press, 1985), 207–49.

[2] Barry D. Karl, *The Uneasy State: The U.S. from 1915 to 1945* (Chicago: University of Chicago Press, 1983), 80.

direct contributions.[3] Although sometimes significant, these actions mapped out only a small fraction of the policy terrain that other national governments were exploring and that the United States would explore itself as the twentieth century advanced.

The founders were deeply interested in science and technology and deeply divided about their governance. Benjamin Franklin was one of the great scientific minds of his age; Thomas Jefferson, a notorious enthusiast and tinkerer. A patent clause, giving Congress the power "to promote the Progress of Science and useful Arts," found its way into the Constitution. Yet the more important precedent set by the Constitutional Convention was its refusal to establish a national university. Such an institution fell under the rubric of "internal improvements," trespassing the limits set on federal power by defenders of the prerogatives of state governments. For the nation's first eighty-odd years, internal improvements, encompassing roads and canals as well as research and inventions, remained largely out-of-bounds for the central government. The failure of Samuel Morse to persuade Congress to take ownership of and promotional responsibility for the telegraph in the 1840s is but a minor footnote in this great constitutional struggle.[4]

That this struggle was waged mainly along sectional lines can best be seen by the effect of the Civil War on it. The antebellum antipathy to internal improvements was relegated to the dustbin of history after the Union victory as the federal government embarked on a massive program of industrial promotion. The tariffs, the concessions, and the rest of this program contributed to an explosion of technological dynamism. Railroads and steel were revolutionized; the electrical power and chemical industries, created. However, even as the old borders of the federal sphere were overrun, new ones were drawn. Unlike Imperial Germany or Meiji Japan, nations whose paths of industrialization paralleled that of the United States, the U.S. government did not target new technologies or construct institutions specifically designed to advance them. Government-run industrial research institutes and nationalized enterprises ran contrary to the American tradition.[5]

To European observers, the striking feature of American manufacturing technology in the second half of the nineteenth century was its use of interchangeable mechanical parts, which could be made by machine tools operated by unskilled laborers rather than skilled workers. This "American system" diffused

---

[3] Richard R. Nelson and Gavin Wright, "The Rise and Fall of American Technological Leadership: The Postwar Era in Historical Perspective," *Journal of Economic Literature* 30 (1992): 1937.

[4] A. Hunter Dupree, *Science in the Federal Government* (1957; reprint, paperback ed., Baltimore: Johns Hopkins University Press, 1987), 3–6, 48–49.

[5] Otto Keck, "The National System for Technological Innovation in Germany," in Richard R. Nelson, ed., *National Innovation Systems* (New York: Oxford University Press, 1993), 116–29; Hiroyuki Odagiri and Akira Goto, "The Japanese System of Innovation: Past, Present, and Future," in ibid., 79–81.

rapidly through the economy, making possible the production of complex new goods such as sewing machines and bicycles. National policy-makers deserve some credit for this wave of innovation and the economic growth it spurred, because many of the people who carried the know-how between industries got their training in federal armories. Yet, although the armories' demands for interchangeability stimulated the invention of the American system, their influence on the economy through "spinning off" new technologies was unintended. It was just a happy side effect of military ideology. Like tariffs, the armories contributed indirectly to the advance of industrial technology.[6]

The federal government played a much more direct role in the resource extraction industries, the base on which the material- and energy-intensive American system of manufacturing rested. In mining, forestry, and agriculture, the government provided key public goods, beyond mere access to land and conventional property rights, that catalyzed the development of new technologies needed to satisfy the manufacturers' enormous appetite for inputs. The Geological Survey and the Forest Service, for example, created knowledge about materials processing as well as surveying the actual terrain. The U.S. Department of Agriculture (USDA) became the premier scientific organization of the federal government, and its scientific research bureaus became powerful models for advocates of a more active federal science and technology policy. New land grant colleges, made possible by federal/state cooperation, fostered research, education, and technical support for agriculture, mining, forestry, and the processing of raw materials. The colleges and bureaus formed regional triangles with firms that put the resource-rich hinterlands at the service of the new manufacturing industries.[7]

The Morrill Act of 1862, which established the USDA and the land grant college system, set these developments in train. Only secession made it possible for congressional majorities to be found for these internal improvements, which helped to firm up the Republican Party's "tariff-homestead axis," as Richard F. Bensel puts it, linking North and West. By the 1880s the bureaus had spawned loyal cadres of civil servants and built strong constituencies in Congress and the public. Their scope and authority steadily expanded before World War I. Moreover, state governments emulated and went beyond federal policy, creating "engineering experiment stations" to parallel those for agriculture. Forty

[6] David Hounshell, *From the American System to Mass Production, 1800–1932: The Development of Manufacturing Technology in the U.S.* (Baltimore: Johns Hopkins University Press, 1984); Merritt Roe Smith, "Army Ordnance and the 'American System' of Manufacturing, 1815–1861," in Smith, ed., *Military Enterprise and Technological Change* (Cambridge: MIT Press, 1985), 39–86.

[7] Paul A. David and Gavin Wright, "Resource Abundance and American Economic Leadership," pub. no. 267, Center for Economic Policy Research, Stanford University, 1991; Dupree (above, n. 4), 149–83, 195–214, 232–55; Louis Ferleger and William Lazonick, "The Managerial Revolution and the Developmental State: The Case of U.S. Agriculture," paper presented at the Business History Conference, Boston, March 19–21, 1993.

such stations were ultimately set up, often working with local manufacturing firms as well as resource extraction industries and state agencies.[8]

Although the Morrill Act authorized a federal role in the advancement of the "mechanical" as well as the "agricultural" arts, the U.S. government, unlike the states, did not take up this mandate. Federal/state cooperation was not extended from agricultural experiment stations to engineering experiment stations. Decades of effort were required just to found a Bureau of Standards in 1901, years after comparable organizations had been established abroad, and another decade and more passed before it was on a firm footing; Congress had deleted the offensive word *National* from the name in the meantime.[9] A "conservative consensus," bearing a family resemblance to the "postwar consensus" of my title, held sway between the Civil War and World War I. Neither the Wilson administration's progressive initiatives nor World War I displaced this "consensus," which provided the backdrop for Herbert Hoover's policy entrepreneurship.

THE U.S. NATIONAL INNOVATION SYSTEM IN THE 1920S: THE DYNAMIC PRIVATE SECTOR AND THE "CONSERVATIVE CONSENSUS"

To Americans of the 1920s, the world seemed to rush by faster and faster. Cars transformed daily life and drove the economy. By 1925 a new Ford rolled off the assembly line every ten seconds. Four years later, there was one car for every five people in the United States. Cars were only the most visible sign of new industrial technologies that pervaded the country. New technologies were even implicated in the era's scandals, when German patent rights expropriated during World War I were sold off by cronies of the U.S. Attorney General in exchange for kickbacks in 1923.[10] The pace of change was breathtaking for those on top of the wave, and even more so for those whom it buried. Whether enthused or enraged, most citizens rightly attributed the appearance of new technologies to the large corporations that had come to dominate the economy toward the end of the previous century. These firms set the technological pace and developed new organizational means to push it. University science was not far behind, finding the wherewithal during this decade to move to new heights in

[8] Richard F. Bensel, *Yankee Leviathan: The Origins of Central State Authority in America, 1859–1877* (New York: Cambridge University Press, 1990), 69–73, 82; Dupree (above, n. 4), 149–83; Bruce Seely, "Research, Engineering, and Science in American Engineering Colleges," *Technology and Culture* 34 (1993): 346–58; Nathan Rosenberg and Richard R. Nelson, "American Universities and Technical Advance in Industry," *Research Policy* 23 (1993): 324–26.

[9] Dupree (above, n. 4), 271–77; Rexmond C. Cochrane, *Measures for Progress* (Washington, D.C.: U.S. Department of Commerce, 1966), 38–47.

[10] William E. Leuchtenburg, *The Perils of Prosperity, 1914–1932,* 2d ed. (Chicago: University of Chicago Press, 1993), 178–202, 94.

basic research as well as make significant contributions to industry. The mainstream of the policy elite, led by Treasury Secretary Andrew Mellon, contented itself with cheering on these dynamic institutions. The conservatives largely ignored those few who doubted either the value of technological innovation or the adequacy of the federal role in its governance, reveling in the prosperity and adulation of the automobile age.

The emergence of very large firms between the Civil War and World War I was a precondition for the extraordinary expansion of private investment in R&D in the 1920s. To stabilize the new industrial order they had brought into being, the managers of these firms sought ways to systematize improvements in production and to secure a steady stream of new products. The earliest of these efforts led to the establishment of materials testing units and consulting relationships with academic and independent private experts in the steel and railroad industries in the 1870s. Managers in the new science-based industries of the "second industrial revolution" of the 1890s found such arrangements inadequate. They saw many promising opportunities to generate profitable new products, and they feared being surprised by competitors. In the first decade of the twentieth century, electrical and chemical engineering firms like General Electric, AT&T, and Dupont integrated backward into knowledge creation, establishing central research laboratories.[11]

This organizational innovation diffused widely after World War I, as the National Research Council's (NRC) periodic survey of industrial laboratories indicates. The number of firms that said they had a lab grew from 526 in 1921 to 1,000 in 1927 to 1,620 at the end of 1930. The director of the NRC's Division of Engineering and Industrial Research (DEIR), Maurice Holland, estimated total industrial research spending to be $200 million in 1927, twice that of government. The largest private research organization, Bell Telephone Laboratories, had a budget of about $20 million per year by the end of the decade.[12]

The contrast between Thomas Edison and Willis Whitney of General Electric illustrates the integration of R&D into the corporate enterprise between 1900 and 1930. After being forced out of the electricity business in the 1880s, Edison sought to commercialize a series of product ideas that emerged from his "invention factory," such as the phonograph, motion pictures, and the dictating machine. Despite his technical brilliance, Edison's companies were continually

---

[11] Alfred D. Chandler, *Scale and Scope: The Dynamics of Industrial Capitalism* (Cambridge: Harvard University Press, Belknap Press, 1990), 1–46; Leonard Reich, *The Making of American Industrial Research* (New York: Cambridge University Press, 1985).

[12] *Bulletin of the National Research Council,* nos. 16 (December 1921), 60 (July 1927), and 81 (January 1931); Maurice Holland, "On the Frontier of Industry," *American Bankers Association Journal,* (June 1927) 870–72; Maurice Holland and William Spraragen, "The Railroad and Research," January 16, 1933, Dugald C. Jackson papers, MIT Archives (hereafter "Jackson papers"), Box 5. Early R&D statistics fluctuate substantially and should be viewed as merely indicative. They should not be interpreted as comparable with more recent figures, which are based on more systematic definitions and gathered with better survey instruments.

outflanked by competitors that meshed marketing and legal considerations more effectively with product design and manufacturing. Whitney's GE was masterful at this balancing act. GE Labs monitored the firm's competitors and potential competitors; it received feedback from the sales, marketing, and manufacturing departments as well as input from outside specialists. Whitney created a lab culture that put the firm's mission ahead of technical virtuosity. GE's technological capabilities, backed by patents, helped it to build extraordinary market share, with over 90 percent in its lead product, electric lamps.[13]

The increasing technical sophistication of American corporations was mirrored in the nation's universities, though there is no simple cause-and-effect relation between industry and academe. Leading academic scientists, mired in the "genteel poverty" (as Robert Kohler puts it) of the nineteenth century, sought the means to realize their expansive view of the university's role in society and to explore an expensive research agenda. Telescopes and tropical diseases bore little obvious relation to the agricultural and mechanical arts that federal and state governments were inclined to support, and a persistent hunt for private patronage therefore ensued. In the first two decades of the twentieth century, academic fund-raising desires outstripped traditional sources of support, such as tuition, state appropriations, alumni contributions, and local fortunes. Although scientific research became a major activity of leading universities in these years, far beyond its place in the previous century, academic ambition still exceeded academic ability to pay.[14]

Many universities turned to business to fill the financial void. The disciplines of chemical and electrical engineering, in particular, were closely linked to industry. However, corporate interest in funding academic research was far from enthusiastic unless universities ceded substantial control of the agenda and the findings, sacrifices that many academics found too great. MIT, for instance, made a major effort in the 1920s to provide research services to industry but was unable to find a market. At the same time, its perceived abandonment of any semblance of the ideal of pure science sparked discontent in the school's faculty and governing board.[15]

Fortunately for a few aspiring institutions, large private foundations emerged

[13] Andre Millard, *Edison and the Business of Invention* (Baltimore: Johns Hopkins University Press, 1990); Wise (above, n. 1), 130–66, 207–49, 250–81; Leonard S. Reich, "Lighting the Path to Profit: GE's Control of the Electric Lamp Industry, 1892–1941," *Business History Review* 66 (1992): 321, 327, 331.

[14] Robert E. Kohler, *Partners in Science: Foundations and Natural Scientists, 1900–1945* (Chicago: University of Chicago Press, 1991), 7; Roger L. Geiger, *To Advance Knowledge: The Growth of American Research Universities, 1900–1940* (New York: Oxford University Press, 1986), 77–93.

[15] Rosenberg and Nelson (above, n. 8), 327–32; John W. Servos, "The Industrial Relations of Science: Chemical Engineering at MIT, 1900–1939," *Isis* 71 (1980): 531–49; Spencer Weart, "The Physics Business in America, 1919–1940: A Statistical Reconnaissance," in Nathan Reingold, ed., *The Sciences in the American Context: New Perspectives* (Washington: Smithsonian Institution Press, 1979), 301–5. David Noble, *America by Design* (New York: Knopf, 1977), overdraws the case for corporate dominance.

as patrons in these years. In the first flush of noblesse oblige at the turn of the century, fortune holders personally bequeathed huge sums to new independent research institutes, bypassing the universities. The Carnegie Institution of Washington's $10 million stake in 1902, for instance, equaled Harvard's endowment. This approach, however, created the twin dangers of duplication and competition with existing academic activities, and the new institutes inevitably cannibalized established reservoirs of academic expertise. As foundation management professionalized, it was inexorably drawn to support scientific research at universities.[16]

Foundation funding of academic science grew a hundredfold by the mid-1920s. But this game was only for the elite; a few foundations gave and a few universities received. As Wickliffe Rose, who became "central banker to the institutional world of western science" during the decade, said, the goal was to "make the peaks higher." By 1930 MIT had seen the light; at the urging of high-technology industrialists on its board, it remodeled itself to meet conditions laid down by the Rockefeller interests, who had rejected its earlier applications for funds.[17]

In most accounts of these developments in industry and academe in the 1920s, the federal government is absent. This view accurately reflects the dominant rhetoric of the period. Presidents Harding and Coolidge invested much effort in tearing down remnants of war mobilization agencies and fledgling activist policies put in place by prewar progressives. In doing so, officials in these administrations believed themselves to be aiding the development of science and technology by freeing private institutions from governmental burdens and intrusions. No policy was more important in this regard than taxation, and no figure more important than Andrew Mellon, who served an unprecedented and still unmatched three presidents as Secretary of the Treasury. Historian Michael Parrish captures the man's vision: "Low tax rates, low interest rates, sound money, a balanced federal budget, and a minimum of government regulation—these were Mellon's definition of good government." Mellon had made millions in technologically dynamic industries like oil and aluminum as well as in banking, but his conservatism reflected principle as well as interest. Reversing Wilson's progressive tax policies, and especially cutting the top tax brackets, Mellon believed, would unleash new investment, including investment in new industries and new products, that would expand industry and employment and sustain prosperity.[18]

[16] Geiger (above, n. 14), 59–67; Daniel J. Kevles, "Foundations, Universities, and Trends in Support for the Physical and Biological Sciences, 1900–1992," *Daedalus* 121 (1992): 195.

[17] Robert E. Kohler, "Science, Foundations, and American Universities in the 1920s," *Osiris*, second series, 3 (1987): 135–64; Kevles 1992 (above, n. 16), 203; Christophe LeCuyer, "The Making of a Science-Based Technological University: Karl Compton, James Killian, and the Reform of MIT, 1930–1957," *Historical Studies in the Physical and Biological Sciences* 23 (1992): 158–80.

[18] Michael E. Parrish, *Anxious Decades: America in Prosperity and Depression, 1920–1941* (New York: W. W. Norton, 1992), 16; John D. Hicks, *Republican Ascendancy, 1921–1933* (New

The conservative vision of the federal government in the 1920s did not entirely preclude direct support for science; business commentators on government policy did not automatically rule it out. But any such positive functions, however modest, required taxation for their support; given the high rates left behind by the war, there was simply no contest between these priorities. By 1928 Mellon had essentially succeeded in restoring the prewar status quo in tax policy, and the administration took credit for the economic successes under this regime. Along with wartime taxes, the military establishment, including its modest initiatives in military technological innovation (discussed in Chapter 5), was rolled back after the war. The rollback did not extend as far as the USDA, land grant colleges, and similar legacies of the Civil War era. But they hardly thrived, either. A. Hunter Dupree's account of the period states blandly that "activity and expenditures increased during the decade without essentially changing the government's research establishments."[19]

The absence of bold spending programs, however, should not lead to the inference that the federal government played no role in U.S. science and technology in the 1920s. As David Mowery has shown, the strengthening of patent protection, enforced by the federal judiciary, encouraged firms to invest in their own research laboratories and to aggressively gather up the work of independent inventors, confident that they would reap the rewards. While these policies favored large firms with deep pockets and sharp lawyers, they also forced many smaller firms to make investments in R&D and patent protection to defend themselves, as leaders of science, industry, and government continuously exhorted them to do. Intellectual property law was abetted by antitrust policy. Early interpretations of the Sherman Act had encouraged firms like GE to buy out, rather than collude with, competitors whose technology threatened, improved upon, or complemented their own. The relaxation of antitrust policy after World War I enhanced the incentive to snap up external inventions and small competitors to maintain control of key technologies. By taking advantage of these rules, some corporations were able to create exceptionally deep positions of technological control, positions that served as intimidating barriers to new entrants and gave them the assurance that only they would be able to appropriate the benefits of long-term R&D projects.[20]

York: Harper & Bros., 1960), 53–54; Andrew W. Mellon, *Taxation: The People's Business* (New York: MacMillan, 1924).

[19] James W. Prothro, *The Dollar Decade: Business Ideas in the 1920s* (Baton Rouge: Louisiana State University Press, 1954), 116; Hicks (above, n. 18), 107; Leuchtenburg (above, n. 10), 98; Dupree (above, n. 4), 302–25, 331–36, quote from 334; David K. van Keuren, "Science, Progressivism, and Military Preparedness: The Case of the Naval Research Laboratory, 1915–1923," *Technology and Culture* 33 (1992): 710–32.

[20] David C. Mowery, "Firm Structure, Government Policy, and the Organization of Industrial Research, 1900–1950," *Business History Review* 58 (1984): 504–31; Dale S. Cole, "Applying Scientific Knowledge to the Small Plant," *Industrial Management* 73 (March 1927): 155–60; David C. Mowery, "The Relationship between Intrafirm and Contractual Forms of Industrial Re-

These indirect effects do not entirely exhaust the influence of federal policy. Although Secretary Mellon overshadowed Presidents Harding and Coolidge, there were other Secretaries, not to mention Senators, Representatives, and many others who were not always willing to go with the main current in Washington. Mellon was forced to return to Congress several times, for instance, before he got his tax bill through. Beyond damming the conservatives when they could, advocates of alternative visions of the state occasionally found eddies in which they could go against the flow; the "conservative consensus," like the later "postwar consensus," was less monolithic in practice than in rhetoric. The strongest countercurrent swirled around the man whom Parrish labels "Harding's most controversial cabinet selection," Secretary of Commerce Herbert Hoover.[21]

HERBERT HOOVER AND THE ASSOCIATIVE STATE

Herbert Hoover was a lucky as well as a talented man. World War I crushed almost everyone who came into contact with it, from the front lines to the highest levels of government. But not Hoover. For him the war was more bracing than harrowing, a chance to grow rather than be ground down. It proved to be his defining political experience, molding the ideology that animated his postwar activities and yielding the popularity that propelled him briefly into presidential contention in 1920. Hoover's associationalism idealized the administrative experience of the war. Imbued with moral authority and technical competence, the associative state would facilitate private action toward the general good. Efficiency and productivity were prominent among the values to be advanced, and science and technology were essential instruments for advancing them. Although the Hoover-for-president boomlet fizzled, the office of Secretary of Commerce proved to be a surprisingly powerful platform for policy entrepreneurship. Hoover was Secretary of Commerce and undersecretary of all other departments, Washington wags said.[22] Secretary Hoover was an abnormality in the age of normalcy. He had a positive, though still limited, conception of government that contrasted with the negative conception held by Secretary Mellon. Even though they shared much common ground, including an antipathy toward those who wanted government to slow the pace of technological change, the two secretaries had fundamentally different instincts. Consequently, the associative and conservative factions fought some important battles, as Hoover sought to extend his department's reach throughout the entire economy.

---

search in American Manufacturing, 1900–1940," *Explorations in Economic History* 20 (1983): 366–69.

[21] Parrish (above, n. 18), 19.

[22] Ellis W. Hawley, "Herbert Hoover, the Commerce Secretariat, and the Vision of an 'Associative State,' 1921–1928," *Journal of American History* 61 (1974): 121.

1914 found Hoover in London, a rich man entering middle age and yearning to get something more out of life, to make a mark in public service. Early in the war, with little hesitation, Hoover dropped his business activities for good to organize relief efforts, first for American tourists caught in the maelstrom, then for the nation of Belgium, and ultimately for the entire continent after the war. He also undertook a range of tasks at home, most importantly as U.S. Food Administrator. From these posts, he built a web of connections in the political, business, and academic communities, winning admiration across party lines.[23]

The basic lesson that Hoover took away from the war and the chaos that followed it was that government could and indeed must take an active role in articulating national goals and coordinating private and public action toward achieving them. A complex technological society simply could not solve all its problems spontaneously. Yet Hoover retained a deep skepticism of politics and government; they were prone to ignorant demagogues and rigid bureaucratic placeholders. In place of legislation, which he noted is "always clumsy," he preferred "self-governance" by committees that bridged the public and private sectors, bringing together representatives of key organizations, advised by experts.[24]

Although it was drawn from war, Hoover considered this lesson to be directly applicable to economic policy, the crucial challenge of peacetime. American capitalism was not fundamentally flawed, Hoover believed, but was plagued on occasion by ill-informed individual decisions that could be remedied by learning and cooperation. Business executives who reacted to bad news by cutting prices and production, thereby driving the economy in its downward phase, for instance, would come to recognize that the business cycle was an artifact of irrational herd behavior. Given a basic scientific understanding of the economy and mechanisms for sharing their knowledge of current activity, they would understand that it was in their self-interest to maintain a steady hand in the face of adversity. Public and private interest thus merged through self-governance. As historian Guy Alchon has put it, Hoover took "a microeconomic approach to macroeconomic coordination."[25]

Trade associations were to be the primary instruments for achieving self-governance. Being private and voluntary, they were flexible and could draw easily on outside expertise. The state could play a useful role by helping to organize such associations and by providing technical support to them. Perhaps the most important function of these associations was the provision of authoritative statistics to allow firms to harmonize production, avoiding booms and busts. This

---

[23] Joan Hoff Wilson, *Herbert Hoover: Forgotten Progressive* (Boston: Little-Brown, 1975), 31–78.

[24] Hoover, speech, May 7, 1924, Herbert Hoover papers, Herbert Hoover Presidential Library (hereafter "Hoover papers") "Bible" (speech file), item 378.

[25] Guy Alchon, *The Invisible Hand of Planning: Capitalism, Social Science and the State in the 1920s* (Princeton: Princeton University Press, 1985), 4.

job was especially crucial in atomized industries made up of small firms. The market could be perfected through associative mechanisms, "giving the small unit the same advantages which are already possessed by big business."[26]

Associative ideals also had important implications for science and technology policy, and no one was more conscious of this than Secretary Hoover. Before becoming the Great Humanitarian during World War I, Hoover was merely a successful mining engineer. After the war, he became the Great Engineer, or, as the progressive engineer Morris Cooke labeled him, "the engineering method personified." Hoover believed firmly in the benevolence of science and technology, almost as a law of nature. He was widely seen as a symbol of progress, and he capitalized on this image politically. Science was essential for solving social and economic problems and helping citizens to live more satisfying lives.[27]

Self-governance therefore aimed not only at economic stability, but at growth and modernization as well. High domestic wages and tariffs on low wage foreign competition, both of which Hoover endorsed as proper objects of trade association activity, were intended to spur investments in research and capital equipment. He sought common ground with labor unions as well as trade associations on principles that would eliminate barriers to innovation and encourage productivity growth. "Efficiency" and "elimination of waste" were to be promoted through discoveries in "scientific management" that these discussions would reveal.[28]

In addition to providing financial and organizational incentives to firms, Hoover believed that trade associations and the federal government had direct responsibilities to stimulate scientific research and technological development. "Discovery and invention," he declared, "are now no longer the function of the garret genius. They are the result of deliberate organized exploration by our men of pure Science." The function of government needed to be enlarged to recognize this fact and to ensure that the expansion of knowledge kept pace with social needs. Hoover's Department of Commerce, the secretary hoped, would catalyze this expansion.[29]

[26] "Hoover Disavows Policy Favoring Business Combines in Big Units," *Journal of Commerce,* June 5, 1925, Hoover papers, "Bible" (speech file), item 493; William J. Barber, *From New Era to New Deal: Herbert Hoover, the Economists and American Economic Policy, 1921–1933* (New York: Cambridge University Press, 1985), 8–13.

[27] Edwin T. Layton, Jr., *The Revolt of the Engineers: Social Responsibility and the American Engineering Profession* (Cleveland: Press of Case Western Reserve University, 1971), 179; Vernon Kellogg, "Herbert Hoover and Science," *Science* 73, February 20, 1931, 197–99; Barry D. Karl, "Presidential Planning and Social Science Research: Mr. Hoover's Experts," *Perspectives in American History* 3 (1969): 361–62.

[28] "Questions for Secretary's Conference," May 18, 1923, Hoover papers, Commerce series, Box 129, "Commerce Department, Conference—Secretary's 1921–1923"; Hoover, Address to US Chamber of Commerce, May 12, 1926, Hoover papers, "Bible" (speech file), item 579, HHPL; Barber (above, n. 26), 27–40; Layton (above, n. 27), 179–200.

[29] "On to Greater Discovery!" *Industrial and Engineering Chemistry,* September 1923, Hoover papers, "Bible" (speech file), item 31A.

World War I bequeathed Secretary Hoover an organizational as well as an ideological legacy. He drew particularly on the experience and personnel of the War Industries Board (WIB), the industrial mobilization agency that had been headed by his rival, Bernard Baruch. The WIB served as a buffer between the peremptory and uninformed demands of Congress and the armed services on the one hand, and industrialists tempted by profiteering on the other. By organizing industry and infusing it with both patriotic sentiment and economic information, the WIB tried to harmonize public and private purposes, avoiding both government domination that might be carried over into peacetime and price-gouging that would disrupt the war effort. Many of the Progressive scientists and engineers who had helped to formulate the WIB's approach and "dollar-a-year" men on loan from business who had tried to put it into practice migrated to Hoover's Commerce Department. Arch Shaw, chief of the WIB's Conservation Division, for instance, became one of the secretary's key economic advisors.[30]

Yet the WIB was far from a smoothly operating machine that merely implemented the associative ideology. It emerged out of chaos in March 1918, survived only to the war's end in November of that year, and in any case deviated substantially in practice from voluntarism. Baruch was not afraid to use force when he thought it necessary to achieve national ends, and he had the power to do so. Hoover did not attend to this aspect of the WIB experience, which was obscured by postwar propaganda. The problem of coercion would haunt his efforts to realize the associative vision.

The Department of Commerce was little more than a hodgepodge of disconnected bureaus when Hoover was confirmed as secretary. He invested a great deal of energy and political capital in molding it into a broad and coherent organization that could promote the associative vision. Commerce absorbed the Patent Office and the Bureau of Mines during Hoover's tenure, took on new responsibilities in radio and aeronautics, reached out to help a number of industries organize themselves into associations, and dabbled in a host of lesser aspects of policy and governmental organization. He even built the department a grand home on Constitution Avenue, a "temple of Commerce" that still bears his name.[31]

To get the power and the funds to construct this bureaucratic empire, Secretary Hoover grappled with Secretary Mellon, who controlled the budget and had better access to the White House, especially under President Coolidge. Mellon's supporters viewed Hoover with suspicion, accusing him on occasion, as the *Commercial and Financial Chronicle* wrote in August 1922, of "gradual

---

[30] Robert D. Cuff, *The War Industries Board: Business-Government Relations during World War I* (Baltimore: Johns Hopkins University Press, 1973); Jordan A. Schwarz, *The Speculator: Bernard Baruch in Washington, 1917–1965* (Chapel Hill: UNC Press, 1981), 79–88, 219–27; Schwarz, *The New Dealers: Power Politics in the Age of Roosevelt* (New York: Knopf, 1993), 32–34.

[31] Hawley 1974 (above n. 22), 139; Wilson (above n. 23), 83–86.

and insidious nationalization." In response Hoover testified to the efficiency with which his department spent its appropriations, doing more with each dollar. He repeatedly averred his commitment to the preeminence of business in American society and to competition as the main mechanism for economic governance. Yet there was more and more for his organization to do in pursuing what economic historian William J. Barber describes as "a degree of governmental intervention without peacetime precedent in U.S. history."[32]

The differences between conservatives and associationalists, which are detailed in subsequent sections of this chapter, should not be exaggerated. Hoover believed that the nation's economic organization was fundamentally sound and that his efforts would perfect it, not overhaul it. He supported Mellon's tax policy, including the view that reduced taxation would stimulate private technological innovation, even though he sought a larger fraction of the federal revenues that remained for Commerce Department programs. Mellon, for his part, endorsed cooperation within industry, albeit without the governmental involvement that Hoover advocated; the Mellon Institute in Pittsburgh, which he co-founded in 1913, aimed to facilitate industrial cooperation privately.

The administration put forward a united face against members of Congress and others who questioned the advance of science and technology and the increasing scale of corporate organization, which both Hoover and Mellon celebrated. These doubts were expressed popularly in a variety of ways, from the intellectual alienation of Charles Beard to the religious fundamentalism of the Scopes trial, although they were usually drowned out by adulation of new technology in the popular press. Doubts about science and technology occasionally manifested themselves in political efforts of some potency. The 1924 presidential election, for example, in which "Battle Bob" LaFollette ran an independent campaign centered on the issues of antitrust enforcement and utility nationalization, prompted the administration to join ranks. Hoover took to the stump arguing that under LaFollette's program "invention will decline. . . . So far as I am aware, no single vital invention has ever come out of Government-owned utilities." In 1928 Senator Clarence C. Dill's bill providing for the forfeiture of patents by firms convicted under the Sherman Act, targeted at "trusts" in high-technology industries like radio and electrical power, passed the Senate. Senator George Norriss's bill to restart the mothballed Muscle Shoals complex as a government-run yardstick to motivate inefficient private utilities passed both houses of Congress and arrived on the President's desk, where it was vetoed. Usually, however, these gadflies could be ignored; their vision did not coalesce until the next decade. The rather narrow differences between Mellon's conservatives and Hoover's associationalists, fought out mainly in the private

[32] "Questions for Secretary's Conference," August 26, 1922, Hoover papers, Commerce series, Box 129, "Commerce Department, Conference—Secretary's 1921–1923"; speech to Commerce Department employees, March 9, 1925, Hoover papers, "Bible" (speech file), item 452; Barber (above, n. 26), 41.

sector, rather than the large gap between both of these groups and the skeptics, defined the scope of serious science and technology policy debate in the 1920s.[33]

THE BUREAU OF STANDARDS: SCIENCE AND TECHNOLOGY POLICY FOR "SICK" INDUSTRIES

In keeping with his general confidence in the U.S. economy and his limited resources, Hoover's science and technology policy worked at the margins. General Electric and General Motors were faring well, but the so-called "sick" industries needed a federal push to govern themselves more productively and efficiently. The sick industries tended to be old and composed of small units that did not benefit from economies of scale. No matter how low their taxes were, Hoover contended, they lacked the incentive to invest in new technology, instead competing on price by sweating labor and cutting wages. Associationalism provided firms in these industries with a way to overcome the collective action problem that inhibited such investment. Trade association research programs, supported jointly by the membership, could develop and diffuse improved practices and equipment. Consumers, workers, managers, and shareholders would all share in the benefits.

Commerce's Bureau of Standards was the main locus for this effort. Hoover gave the bureau his close personal attention and sought to augment its authority and budget. The bureau's program took as its blueprint *Waste in Industry,* a postwar study by the Federated American Engineering Societies (FAES), of which Hoover was president, that grew out of the work of the WIB Conservation Division. *Waste in Industry* examined six sick industries and discovered massive waste, due in large part to management's inability to use the latest technology effectively. It proposed an array of initiatives to address these deficiencies, including programs for simplification, standardization, and scientific research, which the bureau took up. The bureau targeted particular efforts along these lines toward two of the industries examined by the FAES, textiles and home-building.[34]

---

[33] Carroll W. Pursell, Jr., "'A Savage Struck by Lightning': The Idea of a Research Moratorium, 1927–1937," *Lex et Scientia* 10 (1974):146–58; Leuchtenburg (above, n. 10), 120–40; Herbert Hoover, "Government Ownership," radio address, September 29, 1924, Hoover papers, "Bible" (speech file), item 400, HHPL; U.S. Senate, Committee on Patents, *Forfeiture of Patent Rights on Conviction under Laws Prohibiting Monopoly,* 70th C., 1st s., 1928.

[34] Committee on Elimination of Waste in Industry of the FAES, *Waste in Industry* (Washington: FAES, 1921); "Simplified Practice: What It Is and What It Offers," U.S. Department of Commerce pamphlet, 1924, available in Littauer Library, Harvard University, 1; *Fourteenth Annual Report of the Secretary of Commerce* (Washington: Commerce Department, 1926); William R. Tanner, "Secretary Hoover's War on Waste, 1921–1928," in Carl E. Krog and Tanner, eds., *Herbert Hoover and the Republican Era* (Lanham, MD: University Press of America, 1984), 1–6.

The Bureau of the Budget, established in Mellon's Treasury Department in 1921 to centralize fiscal management and enforce the spending cuts imposed by the Harding administration, opposed Secretary Hoover's ambitions. In fiscal 1924, for instance, the budget director, H. M. Lord, imposed an overall ceiling on the Department of Commerce of $19.6 million, rejecting Hoover's $25.2 million proposal, which included a 28 percent increase for the Bureau of Standards. The following year, Hoover appealed Lord's strictures to the president: "Such an allotment of funds to this Department renders it impossible to conduct the work of the Department in an efficient manner or to meet the service absolutely demanded by industry, commerce, agriculture, and the public." Hoover called for an additional $10 million for the Departments of Interior, Agriculture, Labor, and Commerce, declaring cuts in "reproductive services" to be false economies. "[R]eal economy," he concluded "lies in building up our national assets. . . ." Coolidge relented only a little, providing an increment of $750,000 for Commerce, far less than the $1.8 million that Hoover had specified as the minimum acceptable. Although it did not fully satisfy Hoover, the bureau's expansion was steady during his secretaryship. Between fiscal years 1921 and 1929, the bureau's regular funds nearly doubled, from $1.27 million to $2.31 million. Budget growth continued into Hoover's presidency, peaking at $2.75 million and over 1,000 staff in fiscal 1932. New capital facilities, like a hydrological laboratory, were provided for as well. While no match for Bell Labs' $20 million annual budget, the bureau was a source of pride to Hoover, and its fans made much of it as "the largest physical laboratory of its kind in the world."[35]

Simplification and standardization, in the associative vision, were supposed to bring the benefits of Ford-style mass production to the sick industries. Fewer product lines meant longer runs; greater interchangeability meant that suppliers competed on quality and efficiency, rather than by locking customers into their products. With Hoover at the controls, the Bureau of Standards launched a publicity crusade in 1922 to spread "productivity consciousness" and convert competition-minded businessmen to cooperation under government auspices. The bureau's new Division of Simplified Practice spearheaded the drive to convince executives to commit their firms to a seven-step process of simplification. Its centerpiece was a conference run by a trade association to develop a consensus on the revision of practices; the association then bore the responsibility for disseminating the results. The division quickly reported success in the paving brick industry, which reduced 66 varieties of brick to 5; from fiscal 1924

[35] "Commerce Department, Appropriations, FY 1924" and "FY 1925," Hoover papers, Commerce series, Boxes 125 and 126; Hoover to President, November 5, 1923, Hoover papers, Commerce series, Box 606, "Treasury Department, Bureau of the Budget, HM Lord, 1922"; table attached to 1934 budget estimates, Hoover papers, Presidential series, Cabinet Offices, Box 14, "Department of Commerce—Standards"; Herbert Hoover, *Memoirs,* vol. 2 (New York: McMillan, 1952), 73; Cochrane (above, n. 9), 242.

on, some 15–20 industries were reported to have been simplified in this manner each year. At the end of Hoover's secretaryship, the division claimed credit for the adoption of its recommendations in 95 industries and estimated the benefits to the nation's $18 billion manufacturing sector at $600 million. Standardization contrasted with simplification by requiring research as well as industrial cooperation. On this front the Bureau of Standards worked closely with national engineering societies as well as with trade associations, ultimately issuing a 400-page "Standards Yearbook" to compile its efforts. In some cases it attempted to use the leverage of government procurement to promote standardization, developing specifications for purchase by all federal agencies.[36]

Hoover was adamant that simplification and standardization were voluntary processes. The Department of Commerce, he said in 1922,

> has no authority beyond friendly interest in this matter. . . . These things can be accomplished enduringly only by cooperation between the producer, the distributor and consumer with the help of the government to bring them together. There is no question of governmental interference in business. Such help as we can offer in experience and experts and in getting interested groups—of producers and consumers both—together is given only upon the expressed wish of the trades themselves.

But not everyone perceived it this way. The *Manufacturers' Record,* for instance, encapsulated one complaint in its headline "Standardization by Bureaucratic Methods Destructive of Initiative." Trade associations and engineering groups often perceived the bureau to be heavy-handed. Particularly in fragmented industries, the bureau was often unable to secure voluntary compliance with its recommendations. Firms threatened by simplification and standardization simply flouted associative blandishments, despite the fanfare that surrounded these programs. Such resistance gravely diminished the effectiveness of the effort. Apart from a few examples, some as trivial as the hotel china industry, simplification and standardization did not dramatically improve the health of the sick industries.[37]

"Waste," as understood by Hoover, encompassed the inability of firms to de-

[36] "Wilhelm, Donald, 1919–1922 April," Hoover papers, Commerce series, Box 147; *Tenth Annual Report of the Secretary of Commerce* (Washington: Department of Commerce, 1923), 138–40; *Twelfth Annual Report of the Secretary of Commerce* (Washington: Department of Commerce, 1925), 19; R. M. Hudson to Hoover, July 15, 1927, Hoover papers, Commerce series, Box 145, "Simplified Commercial Practice"; *Sixteenth Annual Report of the Secretary of Commerce* (Washington: Department of Commerce, 1929), xxxiv; Tanner (above, n. 34), 16; Cochrane (above, n. 9), 254–62.

[37] Memo to *World's Work,* December 1922, Hoover papers, Commerce series, Box 145, "Commerce Department, Simplified Commercial Practices"; *Manufacturers' Record,* June 12, 1924, HHPL, reprint file; Layton (above, n. 27), 207–10; Peri Arnold, "Ambivalent Leviathan: Herbert Hoover and the Positive State," in J. David Greenstone, ed., *Public Values and Private Power in American Politics* (Chicago: University of Chicago Press, 1982), 120–22.

velop new technological opportunities through research as well as the failure to exploit existing opportunities through simplification and standardization. Associationalists thought the government should provide expertise and a forum for the development of industrywide priorities and programs. The secretary's *Report* for 1924 put it this way: "It is well recognized that the brunt of the cost of industrial research should be borne by industry; nevertheless, there are many important problems of a fundamental nature common to industry which can best be handled by active participation of a public research institution. . . ."[38]

The Bureau of Standards used its research associates program, which entailed the stationing of scientists paid by private sources at bureau facilities, as one mechanism to fill this gap. Each associate worked on an agenda designed by a joint committee of government personnel and experts from his industry. Research findings were required to be published and disseminated throughout the industry; they could not be patented. Like the simplification and standardization programs, the research associates were expected to be most useful for industries characterized by small firms. The Portland Cement Association, for instance, put up to eight research associates at the bureau during the 1920s to work on topics like the behavior of cement in large structures.[39]

Although it nominally dated from the end of World War I, the research associates program did not really take off until 1924. At the program's peak in 1929, the bureau hosted 98 associates from 48 industries at a cost of about $200,000 to the bureau and an estimated $500,000 to outside sponsors. Another 900 industrial researchers participated in program planning. Although this in-kind private contribution added substantially to the bureau's budget, its national impact must be viewed in the context of approximately $200 million in private industrial research spending annually. The research associate scheme took a prominent place in contemporary assessments of the research scene not because of its size or scientific output, but because it symbolized the ideal of voluntary, cooperative progress.[40]

Hoover claimed that voluntary cooperation would pay off handsomely for the textile industry. Although still among the nation's largest employers, this industry had been on a downhill path for decades. Plagued by foreign competi-

[38] *Eleventh Annual Report of the Secretary of Commerce* (Washington: GPO, 1924), 154.

[39] U.S. House of Representatives, Committee on Appropriations, *Appropriations, Department of Commerce, 1929,* 70th C., 1st s., 1928, 95–96; George K. Burgess, "Bureau of Standards Cooperation in Industrial Research," in Malcolm Ross, ed., *Profitable Practice in Industrial Research* (New York: Harper and Brothers, 1932), 153–72; Duff B. Abrams, "The Contributions of Scientific Research to the Development of the Portland Cement Industry in the United States," pub. no. 1886, American Academy of Political and Social Sciences, May 1925; Edward J. Mehrens, "Concrete: Yesterday, Today, Tomorrow," American Concrete Institute pamphlet, February 1935, available in Widener Library, Harvard University.

[40] House Appropriations 1928 (above, n. 39), 95–96; *Seventeenth Annual Report of the Secretary of Commerce* (Washington: GPO, 1929), 163; Ross (above, n. 39); Edward R. Weidlein and William A. Hamor, *Science in Action* (New York: McGraw-Hill, 1931).

tion and regional division, it was the archetype of atomization and sweatshop practices that the associationalists abhorred. The "new competition" from synthetic fabrics was piled on top of these difficulties in the 1920s. Small textile manufacturers were suddenly put at the mercy of big chemical firms that had large research programs that they could not hope to match. The "new cooperation," an observer sympathetic to Hoover's efforts put it, was "the only sane course of action."[41]

In the first half of the decade, Hoover pressured the textile industry to develop a system for gathering and distributing price and production statistics, skirting the strictures laid down by the Supreme Court to prevent such a system from evolving into a price-fixing scheme. Producers evinced little interest until the onset of a major downturn in the industry in 1925. Only after the failure of traditional free-market responses, like expanding production to make up for revenue lost due to falling prices, did a substantial enough fraction of the industry, especially in the South, join together to form a trade association, the Cotton Textile Institute (CTI), that was to implement the "new cooperation." Hoover turned down an offer to step down from Commerce to become "czar" of CTI, which opened its doors in October 1926. Along with programs on industrial statistics and cost accounting, the CTI created a New Uses Division. Inspired by Hoover, the founders of CTI, Louis Galambos states, "hoped to start an R&D program comparable to those employed in oligopolistic industries" such as paper and chemicals with which textiles now competed. They were to be disappointed. Although the New Uses Division sponsored a research associate at the Bureau of Standards, most of its efforts went into advertising and publicity stunts, like inducing Mrs. Hoover to wear the right dress for National Cotton Week.[42]

Hoover conceded that the industry had only itself to blame for failing to make more effective use of the Bureau of Standards, but he moved nonetheless to provide more direct support for textile R&D. His staff developed a $450,000 research program in late 1926, the general outlines of which (although not the budget) were transmitted to Congress. This effort led to an initial appropriation of $50,000, shared between the Commerce and Agriculture Departments, for research on new uses of cotton, including such possibilities as tire treads, wallboards, and tiles. To put this program on a firmer footing, Hoover, after much tugging and hauling with the Treasury Department, was able to secure in 1930

[41] Franklin D. Jones, *Trade Association Activities and the Law* (New York: McGraw-Hill, 1922), 105; U.S. Department of Commerce, *Trade Association Activities* (Washington: GPO, 1923), 176–77.

[42] Louis Galambos, *Competition and Cooperation: The Emergence of a National Trade Association* (Baltimore: Johns Hopkins University Press, 1966), 89–107, 121–22 (quote from 107); Hoover to Stuart Cramer, August 3, 1926, Hoover papers, Commerce series, Box 598, "Textiles"; Hoover, address to National Association of Cotton Manufacturers, April 7, 1925, Hoover papers, "Bible" (speech file), item 466.

a bill devoting to it the proceeds of a $1.8 million fund garnered from the sale of German dye patents seized during World War I. The editor of *Textile World* hailed the Textile Foundation established under this act as the fulfillment of Hoover's prediction that the industry would have to cooperate on behalf of research.[43]

By then Hoover had already received the magazine's endorsement for the presidency: "Under his guidance, the Department of Commerce has achieved a position of service and effectiveness, which in our opinion, has never been surpassed by any department of any Government in modern history." The leadership of CTI joined in and maintained its support for President Hoover even in the grimmest days of the Depression. Yet these voices never fully represented the industry as a whole. CTI was unable to restore order in the textile market in 1927–28, and even with enhanced authority, could do next to nothing after the market collapsed in 1929. Recalcitrant manufacturers continued to expand production and cut wages in order to stay above water, rather than to respond to the public interest as the associationalists conceived it by calibrating their output to that of the market as a whole. And, despite the effort that Hoover put into textile research, even the Textile Foundation was little more than a public relations showpiece, a bit of symbolic cooperation in a dog-eat-dog business.[44]

Another sick industry to which Hoover devoted much attention was housing. As in textiles, in which disgust with sweating labor reinforced the drive to enhance competitiveness, associationalism in housing found moral sentiments and economic imperatives to be in harmony. Good homes made it possible to inculcate the Hooverian creed of "American individualism" on which the nation's future rested; only if families were strong would personal initiative be balanced by social responsibility without the deadening hand of the state. Hoover viewed home-building as an economic "balance wheel" as well as a socially valuable institution; he was vitally aware of its volatility. Not surprisingly, he used the Commerce Department to promote voluntary cooperation in planning and research to introduce mass production methods that he hoped would stabilize output.[45]

[43] Hoover, address, April 7, 1925 (above, n. 42); Edward Pickard to Hoover, December 14, 1926, and W. W. Carman to George Akerson, August 26, 1927, Hoover papers, Commerce Series, Box 170, "Cotton—Legislation, 1926–1927"; Herbert A. Ehrman, "Cotton in the Rubber Tire and Tube Industry," August 15, 1929, Hoover papers, Presidential Series, Cabinet Offices, Box 13, "Commerce—BFDC—Promotion of Domestic Production"; "Textile Foundation Bill," June 10, 1930, *Public Papers of the Presidents—Herbert Hoover, 1930* (Washington: GPO, 1976), 222; Douglas G. Wolf, "Herbert Hoover's Prediction of Organized Research in Textiles About To Be Fulfilled," *Textile World,* August 9, 1930, HHPL, reprint file, 24–26.

[44] Galambos (above, n. 42), 113–69; "Twelve Words," *Textile World,* August 6, 1927, HHPL, reprint file; George A. Sloan to president, September 20, 1932, Hoover papers, PSF, Box 303.

[45] Wilson (above, n. 23), 55–58; Hoover, "Statement to Planning Committee of the Conference on Home Building and Home Ownership, September 24, 1930," in W. S. Meyers, ed., *State Papers of Herbert Hoover* (New York: Doubleday, 1934), 372–74; Hawley 1974 (above, n. 22), 133–34.

The secretary worked energetically to fortify construction trade associations. By exchanging information about current activities and future plans, firms belonging to associations were supposed to avoid speculative overbuilding. Among other benefits, the smoothing of the cycle would create confidence that would induce investments in new technologies. In 1922 a Hoover-organized conference led to the establishment of the American Construction Council (ACC), which was to serve as the overarching federation of construction trade associations. Hoover even induced the Democratic vice-presidential nominee of 1920, Franklin D. Roosevelt, to run it. Hoover organized the lumber industry, too, into the Central Committee on Lumber Standards and the National Committee on Wood Utilization, largely to encourage the more efficient use of lumber in housing. He was also instrumental in the Better Homes movement, designed to demonstrate to consumers and builders alike that homes could be well-built, attractive, modern, and affordable.[46]

These mechanisms for private cooperation were supported by a new Division of Housing in the Bureau of Standards. Following up on the FAES finding that the home-building industry wasted $3 billion per year, the division set a goal in 1921 of cutting construction costs by 10 to 20 percent. It organized committees that included local officials and industry representatives to develop model building codes and zoning regulations. With the assistance of the USDA's Forest Products Laboratory, it embarked on a vigorous program of simplification and standardization, for example, with respect to the dimensions of lumber. Codes and standards both held out the promise of more assembly-line production of housing components. The bureau's research associate program, moreover, was dominated by building materials trade associations, like those for tile and terra cotta. Hoover was also active in the areas of housing labor and finance, both of which he viewed as having significant roles to play in modernizing the industry.[47]

Hoover must have been heartened by entrepreneurs like Foster Gunnison who struggled to make a go of mass-produced housing in the 1920s. Yet, de-

[46] Charles W. Wood, "Greatest of American Industries Adopts Plan," *The World,* June 18, 1922, HHPL, General Accession 598, Box 1, "Clippings 1922"; Arnold (above, n. 37), 121–23; Ellis Hawley, "Three Facets of Hooverian Associationalism: Lumber, Aviation, and Movies," in Thomas K. McCraw, ed., *Regulation in Perspective* (Cambridge: Harvard University Press, 1981), 101–8; Janet Anne Hutchinson, "American Housing, Gender, and the Better Homes Movement, 1922–1935" (Ph.D. diss., University of Delaware, 1989).

[47] "Three Billion Dollar Loss in Building Waste," *New York Evening Post,* July 22, 1921, HHPL, General Accession 598, Box 1, "Clippings, 1921"; Housing Division memo, undated, 1921, Hoover papers, Commerce series, Box 63, "Building and Housing 1921"; "Hoover Presents New Building Code," *New York Times,* January 22, 1923, General Accession 598, Box 1, "Clippings January–April 1923"; John M. Gries, "Elimination of Waste in Building Industry," undated, James S. Taylor papers, HHPL (hereafter "Taylor papers"), Box 3, "Commerce Department"; *Fourteenth Annual Report of the Secretary of Commerce* (above, n. 34), 184–85. On Hoover and housing finance and labor, see Chapter 4 of this book.

spite grand claims of achievement—that, for instance, the lumber industry was "Exhibit A of government by cooperation"—the limitations of the associational vision were plainly apparent. Housing led the great boom, peaking in 1925 at 937,000 units worth about $4.5 billion (nearly 5 percent of national income). By the time Hoover ascended to the presidency, housing was an ominous leading indicator of the impending Crash. In 1929 only 509,000 units worth about $3.5 billion (less than 3 percent of national income) were built. The housing cycle had grown more, not less, erratic.[48]

Hoover's housing technology policy encountered substantial local resistance. In many communities, close ties between distributors, contractors, local officials, and labor unions inhibited innovation. Indeed, collusion among these groups subverted markets in ways that disturbed him. Such collusion was nearly legitimated by Supreme Court decisions beginning in 1925, decisions that Hoover did much to bring about, but from which he later recoiled. Yet Hoover's conception of the associative state did not encompass using federal power to break the "building blockade," a point on which he clashed with Roosevelt, who left the ACC after only brief service.[49]

THE DEPARTMENT OF COMMERCE AND THE MANAGEMENT OF HIGH TECHNOLOGY

The sick industries' importance lay in their enormous employment and the danger that their instability would infect the entire economy. At the other end of the spectrum were brand-new industries of little present consequence but enormous growth potential. Beyond these lay unknown future industries that only scientific research would reveal. Associationalists saw a role for the federal government in creating the institutions, whether public, private, or mixed, that would ensure the full development of these possibilities. The new industries' difficulties were more varied than those of the sick industries, in which a consistent remedy of organizational and technological rejuvenation was applied, and Hoover and his aides struggled to adapt their associative ideals to each. Aviation, for example, was plagued by extremely high development costs. As in a sick industry, associationalist policy for aviation aimed at lowering the risk of investment by promoting standardization and stabilizing the market. Radio, by contrast, did not suffer from a lack of innovation, but a profusion. Radio equipment manufacturing and broadcasting needed to be managed so that helter-

---

[48] Hounshell (above, n. 6), 310; Hawley 1981 (above, n. 46), 108; Nathaniel S. Keith, *Politics and the Housing Crisis Since 1930* (New York: Universe Books, 1973), 17; *Verbatim Record of the Proceedings of the Temporary National Economic Committee* (Washington: Bureau of National Affairs, 1940), vol. 1, nos. 1–3, 7, 68.

[49] Ellis W. Hawley, "Herbert Hoover and the Sherman Act, 1921–1933: An Early Phase of a Continuing Issue," *Iowa Law Review* 74 (1989): 1067–1103.

skelter entrepreneurial efforts did not cancel one another out and alienate the public. The producers of academic science, the third "industry" dealt with here, were already organized, but they lacked a market. Secretary Hoover undertook to induce support from the industrial users of their research findings.

The airplane had its first flight in Kitty Hawk, North Carolina, but U.S. aircraft builders were quickly surpassed by Europeans. World War I led to an extraordinary boom that closed the gap, but it was followed by an equally extraordinary bust. From a peak rate of 21,000 planes per year when the Armistice was signed, production fell to just 263 in 1922. This economic instability, unlikely to be solved by a revival of military demand and compounded by public concern about safety, intimidated potential investors. Hoover characteristically tried to solve the problem by organizing a trade association, the Aeronautical Chamber of Commerce, to stabilize and promote the business. The chamber's goals, including the establishment of federal regulatory authority and subsidies (via airmail contracts), went well beyond what Hoover normally considered to be appropriate, but he made exceptions for them in the light of aviation's peculiar problems and profound promise. The chamber and the department also pursued more conventional associationalist projects through joint committees, such as standardization and safety codes.[50]

The R&D to support these efforts to put aviation on a stable mass-production basis drew on remnants of the war mobilization. The National Advisory Committee for Aeronautics (NACA), an independent agency established in 1915, conformed well to the associationalist vision, conducting aerodynamic research under the direction of industrial-government-academic committees. The NACA had managed to broker a cross-licensing agreement for aviation patents, along the lines of that in the auto industry, with the goal of sharing technology throughout the industry, although disputes over design rights left it far from the harmonious technical community that the associationalists dreamed of. The Bureau of Standards, too, conducted research for use throughout the aviation industry, particularly on engines. Hoover also aided academic aeronautical researchers, not from the federal purse but by inducing the Guggenheim family (which like Hoover had made its fortune in mining) to establish a $2.5 million fund for their support. The work done by these bodies produced results that advanced aircraft technology significantly. The NACA's wind tunnel, in particular, was an invaluable facility for common use in design and development.[51]

After a lengthy and frustrating battle in Congress, Hoover secured the creation of an Aeronautics Branch in 1926, formalizing the Commerce Depart-

---

[50] David D. Lee, "Herbert Hoover and the Development of Commercial Aviation, 1921–1926," in Krog and Tanner, eds. (above, n. 34), 36–65.

[51] Alex Roland, *Model Research: The National Advisory Committee for Aeronautics, 1915–1958* (Washington: NASA, 1985), 51–123; Lee (above, n. 50), 52; Rosenberg and Nelson (above, n. 8), 329–30.

ment's cooperative work to promote and regulate civil aviation. By the late 1920s, aided greatly by the demand stimulus of airmail as well as stunts like Lindbergh's flight, the industry was booming again. It did not, however, approximate the mass production model held up by Hoover. Supporters of independent inventors, whom key members of Congress viewed as "the true source of innovation," feared that the associationalist system would debase the market into an "aircraft trust." Using their leverage on military and naval affairs committees, they prevented military authorities, who represented a crucial slice of the market, from participating in Hoover's system. Mass production in aviation would have to wait until the next war.[52]

The radio craze of the 1920s was unforeseen by manufacturers or policymakers. The technology of radio appeared to be stalled at the end of World War I by a patent deadlock, in which General Electric, AT&T, and United Fruit each controlled components whose joining would create a promising product. Goaded by the navy, which wanted the technology for intercontinental communication to remain in American hands, these firms formed the Radio Corporation of America (RCA) to pool their patents, jointly develop technology, and divide the market. RCA was expected to provide products for point-to-point communication, until Westinghouse forced its way into the pool in 1920 with the ingenious KDKA, the nation's first radio broadcasting station.

Broadcasting created an enormous mass market for radio equipment; by 1928 there were some 10 million receivers. Early radio receiver technology was so simple that start-up firms simply infringed RCA's patents with impunity. Stations proliferated as well, some 500 vying for listeners within a year after KDKA's first broadcast informed Pittsburgh of the election results. Interference quickly became intolerable. In contrast to aviation, innovation in radio technology was cheap and rapid. For the Secretary of Commerce, the challenge was to ensure the market did not choke itself off; the industry came to the same conclusion by mid-decade and joined forces with Hoover to secure government regulation. Congressional critics of the "Radio Trust" denied Hoover an outright victory, vesting authority in an independent Federal Radio Commission (FRC) rather than Commerce in 1927, but in practice the FRC came under Commerce's wing.[53]

The radio patent pool, however leaky, was faintly troubling to the associationalists. Such a pool seemed, on the one hand, to be a voluntary cooperative device to avoid protracted litigation and secure joint access to a shared reservoir of knowledge, "a democratization of ownership [and] . . . a clearinghouse

[52] Hawley 1981 (above, n. 46), 112–14; Jacob A. Vander Meulen, *The Politics of Aircraft* (Lawrence: University of Kansas Press, 1991), 41–82 and quote from 5.

[53] Hugh G. J. Aitken, *The Continuous Wave: Technology and American Radio, 1900–1932* (Princeton: Princeton University Press, 1986); Cochrane (above, n. 9), 286; Philip T. Rosen, *The Modern Stentors: Radio Broadcasting and the Federal Government, 1920–1934* (Westport, CT: Greenwood Press, 1980).

for the advancement of inventions" in the words of an enthusiast. The pool could fuel industrial competition through rapid technological progress. On the other hand, the pool's members could choose to use their combined legal power to stifle diffusion and prevent nonmembers from advancing the art further. If patents were absolute property, then patent-holders could do what they liked with them, including sit on them.[54]

The Supreme Court provided confused guidance on the issue. In a landmark case in 1931, the Court held that a pool of patents for refining gasoline organized by Standard Oil of Indiana was legal. Justice Brandeis remarked in his opinion that in some cases cooperation could facilitate competition, just as Hoover believed. Some commentators interpreted the ruling to provide carte blanche for the creation of patent pools, but more careful readers noted that Brandeis reserved the power to declare pools that gained too much control over a market to be in violation of the antitrust law. The Justice Department was already moving in this direction in 1930, forcing RCA (which did not really object) to offer its patents to all comers for a reasonable royalty and to do away with the pool's restraints on competition among the partners in RCA. This "open patent pool" in radio seemed to be a useful model for preventing abuses, yet it required the employment of the coercive power of law, superseding the voluntary cooperation that Hoover esteemed.[55]

While the radio and aviation industries avidly sought government oversight and assistance, academic scientists were more mistrustful of federal power. This sentiment was evident in the organization of the National Research Council (NRC), which was formed in 1917 to expand the scientific resources on which the war effort could draw. George Ellery Hale, an astronomer who was the NRC's moving force, conceived of it as a private organization carrying out public functions. He hoped that the NRC's expert committees would have the power to allocate war research funds, although military officers typically thought otherwise. After the war, a brief legislative effort to secure peacetime federal support for academic research, to be doled out by the NRC, foundered in the face of opposition from engineering experiment stations and land grant colleges. Yet the financial shortfall in science was soon, and more congenially, filled by grants from Rockefeller and Carnegie foundations. The NRC meta-

[54] Benjamin S. Kirsh, *Trade Associations in Law and Business* (New York: Central Book Co., 1938), 273–74; Laurence I. Wood, *Patents and Antitrust Law* (New York: Commerce Clearing House, 1942), 96–117, 128–37.

[55] *Standard Oil Co. (Indiana) v. U.S.* (283 US 163), April 13, 1931; "Is the Patent Monopoly Waning?" *Journal of the Patent Office Society* 13 (1931): 363–67; Samuel R. Wachtell, "Restraints of Trade and Patent Pools," pamphlet reprint from *New York Law Journal,* April 15–22, 1933, available in Harvard Law School Library; "Radio Patent and Copyright Questions," *Journal of the Patent Office Society* 12 (1930): 327–30; "The RCA Consent Decree," *George Washington Law Review* 1 (1933): 513–16.

morphosed into a sort of "trade association for science," promoting coopera-tion, defining research agendas, and administering foundation-funded graduate fellowships.[56]

Secretary Hoover saw the NRC's significance to lie not only in the pursuit of truth, but in industrial development as well. "Pure research," he often said, "is the raw material of applied science." Hoover enthusiastically agreed to Hale's request in late 1925 to lead an effort to broaden the NRC's funding base by seek-ing support from business for a National Research Endowment (NRE). In an-nouncing the drive, which set a goal of $20 million, he argued that international economic competition required U.S. business to support U.S. universities, its primary source for trained personnel and new ideas. The NRE's backers then embarked on an elaborate educational campaign, "a little mass psychology," Hoover called it, to convince leaders of the petroleum, electrical, railroad, tex-tile, and steel industries, among others, of this business necessity.[57]

The usual conservative objections to Hoover's policy entrepreneurship did not apply to the NRE, since it sought no public money or authority. Secretary Mellon even lent his name to the cause, although nothing more. Yet few indus-trialists agreed with Arthur D. Little that supporting the fund represented "en-lightened self-interest." At first the NRE met with concerns about the tax con-sequences of industrial gifts, but a more fundamental objection soon appeared: many firms that considered giving to the NRE could not see how they would reap its benefits. Hale and Hoover labored to make the connection between aca-demic research and industrial profits plain to managers like Baltimore & Ohio Railroad president Daniel Willard, but public and private interest too obviously diverged. As Lance Davis and Daniel Kevles have shown, what little fund-rais-ing success the NRE had was with monopolists, who had a much higher prob-ability of extracting benefits from their gifts than did firms in competitive in-dustries. Even in these cases, the evidence suggests that contributions were typically made out of personal loyalty, rather than genuine conviction. The ef-fort dragged on into the Hoover administration until the Depression finally put an end to it. Not until the federal government required it, by means of an ap-propriation from general tax revenues to the National Science Foundation in

[56] Daniel J. Kevles, *The Physicists* (New York: Knopf, 1977), 117–54; Kevles, "Federal Legis-lation for Engineering Experiment Stations: The Episode of World War I," *Technology and Culture* 12 (1971): 182–89; Kohler 1987 (above, n. 17), 140.

[57] Herbert Hoover, "The Nation and Science," *Science* 65, January 14, 1927, 26; Herbert Hoover, "The Vital Need for Greater Financial Support of Pure Science Research," *Circular and Reprint Series of the National Research Council,* no. 65, December 1925; "Declaration of the Trustees of the National Research Endowment," January 1926, and Hoover to Frank Jewett, Feb-ruary 27, 1926 (incl. quote), Hoover papers, Commerce series, Box 425, "National Academy of Sciences—National Research Endowment." The National Research Endowment was known at times as the National Research Fund; for simplicity's sake, I use only the former term.

1950, would industry contribute much money to the abstract cause of university research.[58]

TRIUMPH, CRISIS, PARALYSIS: THE HOOVER ADMINISTRATION

Despite abject failures, like the NRE, and disappointments glossed over, like the textile and housing technology programs, Secretary Hoover could reasonably claim that the energy and idealism that he brought to the Commerce Department had had a hand in the scientific and technological dynamism of the 1920s. The department's policies had facilitated the diffusion of mass production, supported productivity growth, and nurtured new industries. The secretary had consolidated an organizational base in his department and had begun to wear down conservative resistance in the administration and Congress. The presumed beneficiaries of Hoover's efforts in the private sector, however, were harder to persuade. Only when threatened with crisis, as in the collapse of textiles and the chaos of radio broadcasting, did a large enough spectrum of firms in an industry seem to perceive their interest in his efforts as clearly as he did.

Secretary Hoover's ascent to higher office in 1928, succeeding Calvin Coolidge, a stalwart conservative if ever there was one, should not be read as the triumph of his vision of the state. Old Guard Republicans had a stronger claim on him as chief executive than as cabinet officer, and his responsibilities in the new role were more varied and taxing. As president, Hoover would have had to be less of a policy entrepreneur and more of an arbiter of interests, even had catastrophe not struck. At most he stood for a gradual transition in governance philosophy, "the old order's candidate for ushering in the new order painlessly," in Barry Karl's words.[59] Ironically, in light of his experience in the Commerce Department, Hoover did not move to reorganize industry along associational lines when the crisis that defined his presidency set in. He took the nation's economic problems to be short-term and financial, rather than secular and structural, and he was vexed as always by the conundrum of coercion. In the second half of his term, the president was forced to play defense, as a newly Democratic Congress, animated by fears of technological unemployment, attacked the basic value of progress itself.

In his first run for elective office, Hoover did not make the case for a change of course. He ran on the administration's record, and his mandate was to main-

---

[58] Arthur D. Little, "The Contribution of Science to Manufacturing," *Annals of the American Academy of Political and Social Sciences* 119 (1925): 9; Willard to Hoover, June 10, 1926, Hoover to Robert A. Millikan, July 2, 1926, Holland to Hoover, August 5, 1926, all in Hoover papers, Commerce series, Box 426, "National Academy of Sciences—National Research Endowment—Railroads and Pure Science"; Lance E. Davis and Daniel J. Kevles, "The National Research Fund: A Case Study in the Industrial Support of Academic Science," *Minerva* 12 (1974): 207–20.

[59] Karl 1969 (above, n. 27), 408.

tain prosperity, to keep up the good work. In fact, he relied largely on his reputation to carry him through the campaign, making only seven speeches and avoiding direct debate. In these pronouncements, Hoover identified research and invention as factors that contributed to the economic health of the nation and took credit for their expansion in the 1920s. While he occasionally mentioned that cooperation offered opportunities to further accelerate technological innovation, he gave no indication of planning dramatic new departures in this direction. Nor did the first year of the Hoover administration suggest this— the president's priorities lay elsewhere.[60]

Hoover viewed with alarm the rampant speculation that doubled the value of the Dow-Jones index of industrial stocks in the first eight months of 1929. He feared that when the plungers were brought to earth, as they inevitably would be, they would bring productive investors down with them. After the Crash, which modest anticipatory measures had failed to forestall, Hoover quickly took to the hustings, exhorting state and local governments, business, and trade associations to boost spending to counter the liquidation. He sought to rebuild consumer and investor confidence, calling for "systematic, voluntary measures of cooperation." The president ignored Secretary Mellon's advice to stand back and let the market do its job. On the other hand, he had neither the inclination nor the resources, given the federal budget's relatively small size, to boost federal spending to a level that might have made a difference.[61]

It soon became clear that Hoover had exaggerated his claim that the response to his call for cooperation had been "remarkable and satisfactory." Worse, the depression began to undermine the institutional foundations that Hoover saw as essential for long-term economic growth. Firms slashed their internal R&D budgets, up to 60 percent in the case of General Electric, the "house of magic" that had astounded Americans a few short years earlier. The NRC's Division of Engineering and Industrial Research (DEIR) estimated that about 10,000 out of 25,000 industrial research workers had lost their jobs by 1933. Such cuts severely affected trade association research programs, since most firms placed them even lower on their priority lists than in-house R&D. The Bureau of Standards research associates program, for instance, fell from its peak of 98 scientists in 1929 to half that in 1933, while the NRC approached bankruptcy.[62]

[60] Wilson (above, n. 23), 122–37; Herbert Hoover, *The New Day: Campaign Speeches of Herbert Hoover, 1928* (Stanford: Stanford University Press, 1928), 33–34, 105–7, 151, 183, 202.

[61] Barber (above, n. 26), 71–74, 78–84; Herbert Stein, *The Fiscal Revolution in America* (Chicago: University of Chicago Press, 1969), 12–24; Fred Israel, ed., *State of the Union Messages of the Presidents,* vol. 3 (New York: Chelsea House, 1966), 2752.

[62] Israel, ed. (above, n. 61), 2754; "Industrial Research Laboratories of the U.S.," *Bulletin of the National Research Council,* no. 91, August 1933; "Report of the Chairman to the Executive Board for the Period July, 1933—April, 1934," April 25, 1934, Jackson papers, Box 5, Folder 341, p. 19; "Trade Associations Hit Hard as Depression Breeds Ill Will," *Business Week,* April 29, 1931, 7–8; *Twenty-first Annual Report of the Secretary of Commerce* (Washington: GPO, 1933), 45; corre-

The president's fear that the disease had spread to the economy's vital organs was being realized. Yet, he made few moves to defend the scientists, engineers, and inventors whom he had called "our most priceless national possessions." The 1931 White House conference on home building and home ownership, for instance, included in its goals the establishment of a "science of housing" and devoted a long chapter in its report to housing technology. The research organization it proposed was wholly private, however, and stood no chance of securing funding in the grim conditions of the Depression housing market. Rather than seeking to use the state to accelerate technological innovation as part of the solution to the Depression, the president continued to use exhortation, blamed foreigners, and fell back on the old tool of budget economies.[63]

President Hoover's unwillingness to push for the relaxation of antitrust laws exemplifies his paralysis. By 1930 business organizations, particularly in the sick industries, had raced ahead of the president to take associationalism to its next logical step. If cooperation was the key to stability and growth, and a few opportunists could scuttle voluntary cooperation, why not give trade associations the power to force the misfits to go along? The most well-known of many plans for mandated cooperation was advanced in September 1931, by Gerard Swope, the president of General Electric. In order to remove the "psychology of fear" that was prolonging the Depression, Swope proposed that all firms be required to join trade associations. The associations would manage prices and production, under government supervision, while ensuring that workers received an array of welfare benefits, including unemployment insurance and pensions. The Swope Plan called for trade associations to mandate simplification and standardization as well as any other activities that would support industrial growth and development, presumably including R&D.[64]

But the president consistently rejected industrial self-governance of the Swope stripe (with an exception made for natural resource industries, in which

spondence of Jackson, William Spraragen, and Maurice Holland, 1932, in Jackson papers, Box 4, Folders 316–17.

[63] Herbert Hoover, "Address on the Fiftieth Anniversary of Thomas Edison's Invention of the Incandescent Electric Lamp," October 21, 1929, *Public Papers of the President, Herbert Hoover, 1929* (Washington: GPO, 1976), 337–41, quote from 339; John M. Gries and James Ford, eds., *Housing Objectives and Programs* (Washington: National Capitol Press, 1932), xx and 27–100; Hoover to William Chadbourne, May 18, 1931, Hoover papers, Presidential series, Box 73, "Better Homes"; Ellis W. Hawley, "'Industrial Policy' in the 1920s and 1930s," in Claude Barfield and William Schambra, eds., *The Politics of Industrial Policy* (Washington: American Enterprise Institute Press, 1986), 74; Karl 1983 (above, n. 2), 81–99.

[64] "Plan for Stabilization of Industry by the President of the General Electric Company," *Monthly Labor Review,* November 1931, 45–53; "Trade Association Is Keystone of Swope Stabilization Plan," *Business Week,* September 23, 1931, 12; "Friendly Critics of Swope Plan Want to See It Given Fair Trial," *Business Week,* September 30, 1931, 15; Hawley 1989 (above, n. 49), 1085–1101; Robert F. Himmelberg, *The Origins of the National Recovery Administration: Business, Government and the Trade Association Issue, 1921–1933* (New York: Fordham University Press, 1976), 88–165.

conservation could be invoked as a justification). Indeed, he sanctioned more aggressive antitrust enforcement by the Justice Department, as demonstrated by the RCA consent decree. Coercion and price-fixing made the Swope Plan a step toward the European monopoly system, rather than the realization of enlightened American individualism. If firms were unable to perceive their long-term interests, to learn the scientific basis for management, or to trust one another, Hoover could see no justification for the federal government to act on their behalf.

While Hoover attempted to rein in those who took associationalism too far, he also faced opponents who thought that his policies had caused or exacerbated the Depression. When the Democrats took control of Congress in 1930, they vigorously pursued an alternative agenda. Although Congress was enthusiastic about some spending measures, like the Reconstruction Finance Corporation (RFC), which was forced on the administration, federal R&D budgets were slashed across the board. Total federal R&D spending fell from $43 million in fiscal 1932 to $25 million in fiscal 1934. The USDA, the Department of the Interior, and the NACA all suffered major cuts, and Commerce Department research took the worst blows of all. From its "banner year" in 1931, the Bureau of Standards lost a third of its staff and budget. Industrial research at the bureau was cut by an estimated 70 percent.[65]

Given the president's previous job, the attack on the Commerce Department budget is not surprising. A number of lines were pursued. Journalist Frederick J. Schlink accused the bureau of selling out the public interest to conduct research for industry. The bureau's "shower of grace" economic theory, he argued, presumed that bureau research would eventually redound to consumers' benefit, but the government provided no mechanism to guarantee that it did. Arthur D. Little, on the other hand, saw the bureau's work with industry crimping his own consulting business as the market shrank. Little threatened to take his complaints to the House Appropriations Committee. Stuart Chase, who worked with Schlink at times, voiced the most profound challenge, claiming that mechanization caused unemployment, making it "one of the chief plagues of mankind." Many working people sympathized with this argument. Although the American Federation of Labor (AF of L) never retracted its 1919 endorsement of federal research for its contribution to productivity growth and social welfare, the union expressed deep concern about technological unemployment,

[65] George W. Gray, "Science Shares in National Planning," *New York Times Magazine,* January 21, 1934, 7; Roland (above, n. 51), 124–54; Carroll W. Pursell, Jr., "The Administration of Science in the Department of Agriculture, 1933–1940," *Agricultural History* 42 (1968): 232–33; "Curtailment of Activities in Connection with Scientific Research," 73rd C., 1st s., 1933, S. docs. 77, 102, and 105 (all with same title and date); U.S. House of Representatives, Committee on Appropriations, *Department of Commerce Appropriation Bill, 1934* (Washington: GPO, 1933), 4, 15, 167; Science Advisory Board, *Report, July 31, 1933—September 1, 1934* (Washington: National Research Council, 1934), 62–63.

estimating in 1932 that 55 percent of laid-off workers would not recover their jobs. Even the president harbored some doubts. His Committee on Recent Economic Changes had reported its worries about this issue well before the Crash, and the problem weighed on his mind. Yet he was as paralyzed on this issue as on others, promising the AF of L only that the issue would be thoroughly studied.[66]

Congressional appropriators clearly got these messages. While congressional records do not reveal the motivations of the members, there can be little doubt that many viewed programs of the type developed by the Bureau of Standards in the 1920s to be counterproductive for the economy and a threat to both business and labor. The notion that the state was doing more harm than good in this respect was one that recurred in the next administration.

CONCLUSION: THE ASSOCIATIVE STATE AT A TURNING POINT

The "conservative consensus" of the 1920s made it possible for corporations and universities to establish vital institutional foundations on which the "postwar consensus" would build. Major U.S. firms and many minor ones, too, embarked on a spending spree in research, development, and technology acquisition, confident that they would recoup these investments with a handsome gain. Industrial research employment quadrupled in the 1920s. The Depression-era cutbacks that so troubled DEIR proved to be just a hiccup; corporate research not only made up the lost ground, but doubled its employment yet again before 1940. The nation's research universities, too, were transformed in the 1920s, rising to world leadership in many fields, thanks to a great extent to private foundation patronage. In physics, for instance, even before the wave of prominent European emigrés arrived in the 1930s, the prestige of U.S. journals had far surpassed that of their counterparts abroad. Like the corporate research labs, academe weathered some tough times in the Depression and rebounded rapidly. The production of Ph.D.'s lagged behind industrial research employment only slightly, growing more than fivefold between 1920 and 1940.[67]

[66] Stuart Chase and F. J. Schlink, "A Few Billions for Consumers," *The New Republic,* December 30, 1925, 153–55; Schlink, "Government Bureaus for Private Profit," *Nation,* November 11, 1931, 508–11; Cochrane (above n. 9), 303–9; Stuart Chase, *Men and Machines* (New York: Macmillan, 1929), 205; "Directing Technical Progress," *American Federationist* 39 (1932): 1099; Committee on Recent Economic Changes, *Recent Economic Changes in the United States* (New York: McGraw-Hill, 1929), 876–79; Hoover to Roy A. Young, May 24, 1930, Hoover papers, Presidential series, Box 73, "Better Homes"; Herbert Hoover, "Address to the American Federation of Labor," October 6, 1930, *Public Papers of the President, Herbert Hoover, 1930* (above, n. 43), 411–15.

[67] National Resources Planning Board, *Research—A National Resource,* vol. 2 (Washington: GPO, 1940), 37–38, 168, 174–76; David C. Mowery and Nathan Rosenberg, *Technology and the Pursuit of Economic Growth* (New York: Cambridge University Press, 1989), 61–66; Weart (above, n. 15), 298.

The achievements during the Republican ascendancy of GE and MIT, DuPont and Caltech, to name just a few, were impressive and enduring. But to see in the 1920s only a conservatism that enabled these institutions to pursue their independent aspirations is to miss the vision of cooperation in science and technology among firms and between industry, academe, and government which inspired the highest hopes of many leaders in science and business, with Secretary of Commerce Herbert Hoover at their head. Certainly, the "new cooperation" never inspired the depth of commitment that private institution-building did, and Hoover, as historian Ellis Hawley has shown, was unable to fashion a "department of economic development and management" with an "economic general staff."[68] Hoover's Bureau of Standards, with other government agencies, like the NACA, and the trade association research programs that they helped to establish, did make contributions at the margins to the gadgets that made the twenties roar. More importantly, the bureau became permanent home in the federal government for the associative ideal, a Hooverian legacy that Congress was able to draw on when it periodically devised new programs for government-industry-academic technology partnerships over the next six decades.

The most direct legacy of associative science and technology policy-making in the 1920s was its impact on the New Deal, a legacy that ex-President Hoover bitterly renounced. By the time he sought reelection, Hoover found himself in an impossible bind. Politically, he had become the representative of conservatism, seen as the loyal son of the old regime even though he had initially been the black sheep of the family. He had little choice but to defend the legacy of the 1920s, for to do otherwise would alienate core Republican supporters. Temperamentally he was an activist, but he much preferred acting in accordance with a prepared plan. He was uncomfortable improvising when his plans did not elicit the expected responses and when reacting to the initiatives of foes. He seemed unable either to modify his own vision of government in light of the new circumstances or to turn in a new direction.[69] Hoover's immobility, magnified by the truly terrible economy of 1932, opened the door wide to his successor. His administrative innovations and his breaches of tradition were forgotten. Ironically and unacknowledged, Franklin D. Roosevelt built on Hoover's ideological foundations. Taking a page from the Swope plan and infusing it with the fears of technological unemployment, the new president rather haphazardly ushered in a brief spell of coercive associationalism.

[68] Hawley 1974 (above, n. 22), 121, 138.

[69] For this characterization, I draw on Stephen Skowronek, *The Politics Presidents Make: Leadership from John Adams to George Bush* (Cambridge: Harvard University Press, 1993), 279–85, and Michael Rogin's discussion of this book at the 1994 Annual Meeting of the American Political Science Association in New York City.

Trial and Error

SCIENCE, TECHNOLOGY, AND ECONOMIC POLICY IN THE FIRST

ROOSEVELT ADMINISTRATION, 1933–1936

FRANKLIN D. ROOSEVELT gained the presidency by providing his fellow citizens with a clear idea of where he would take them: to better times. All that remained unclear was how he would get them there. The federal government's involvement in the nation's economic life would certainly grow, but the president's advisors and congressional supporters differed among themselves over its precise role. Unlike Herbert Hoover, FDR was a professional politician; he came to office to solve problems, with less concern than Hoover about the specific ways in which the state and the market ought to interact. "Dr. New Deal" prescribed "bold, persistent experimentation," spurring policy entrepreneurship along more than one untrodden path.[1]

The metaphors that Roosevelt employed were not accidental. Although science and technology were deeply implicated in the economic crisis, they were also widely understood to be keys to its solution, as the Technocrat boomlet of 1932 illustrates. One set of early New Deal policy entrepreneurs tried to bring the gravity-free ideas of the Technocrats down to earth, envisioning a science of government that would channel social action so that the benefits of new technologies were more widely shared. These reform liberals hoped to design, as Secretary of Agriculture Henry Wallace put it, an administrative state that would be "as precise and powerful as an automobile engine."[2] They scored a stunning though limited legislative victory in the establishment of the Tennessee Valley Authority (TVA), a regional economic development agency with a mandate to invest in science and technology for the public interest. Delegated substantial flexibility in this regard, TVA board member David Lilienthal began to put reform liberal ideals to a practical test.

Yet the early New Deal's main economic policies were influenced less by Lilienthal and his comrades than by the heirs to Hooverian associationalism. This faction believed that the state could best help reignite the stalled machin-

---

[1] "The Country Needs, the Country Demands Bold, Persistent Experimentation," address, May 22, 1932, in Samuel Rosenman, ed., *Public Papers and Addresses of Franklin D. Roosevelt,* (New York: Random House, 1938) (hereafter "*FDR—PP*"), vol. 1, 639.

[2] Henry A. Wallace, "The Social Advantages and Disadvantages of the Engineering-Scientific Approach to Civilization," *Science* 79, January 5, 1934, 4.

ery of production and distribution by delegating to industry powerful means for "self-government." Most firms could and would learn to cooperate for the common good, in the view of policy entrepreneurs like MIT President Karl Compton, and the chiselers who refused to see the identity between self- and public interest would be forced by law to go along. The associationalist experiment was performed primarily by the National Recovery Administration (NRA), to which Congress passed the problem of the Depression in 1933. Although reform liberals had supported the NRA's establishment, they were quickly outflanked in its implementation, as their opponents in the private sector seized control of the crucial policy venues in the NRA, the industrial code authorities

The NRA experiment was brief. Within months it was boiling over, and it was little more than an unidentifiable mess when the Supreme Court shut it down after less than two years. Compton, like many who had hoped that enlightened self-government under federal auspices would speed the development and widely diffuse the benefits of new technology, was bitterly disappointed by the experience. Government, and much of industry, too, associationalists perceived, rejected the equation of self- and public interest. Perhaps worse, the self-governors sometimes found that the identity of interest lay in protection from, rather than acceleration of, technological change. The railroad industry, to which Compton's Science Advisory Board devoted substantial effort, exemplifies this disappointment. As the New Deal metamorphosed in the mid-1930s, the associationalists parted company with it, pursuing cooperation privately and opposing the rickety state they left behind.

TECHNOCRACY, TECHNOLOGY, AND THE ECONOMY IN THE 1932 PRESIDENTIAL CAMPAIGN

Technocracy is one of those crackpot movements in American politics that reveals far more about the pathologies of the public psyche than it informs the practical tasks of policy-making. Its appearance during the election season of the Depression's deepest trough riveted elite attention on issues of massive popular concern that the major presidential campaigns had avoided or fudged. The absurd proposals of the Technocrats made no contribution to the resolution of these issues, but they did pave the way for the somewhat more carefully contrived initiatives of the election's victors.

It is doubtful that Herbert Hoover could have done anything to win reelection in 1932. In any case, he spent much of the summer and fall cloistered in the White House, brooding. When he finally ventured out in October, the incumbent adopted the negative tactic of painting his opponent as un-American and posing the election as a choice between two philosophies, his own traditional individualism and the challenger's dangerous statism. With respect to science and technology, Hoover admitted that they might pose new problems, but he contended that voluntary cooperative measures could cope with these minor difficulties as well as ensure that new scientific frontiers would be explored. For the majority of voters in that autumn of despair, it was no contest. Hoover's posture as a conservative ideologue freed Roosevelt to experiment as he wished.[3]

Roosevelt's campaign revealed no clear agenda; what little he did say with regard to science and technology was ambivalent and ambiguous. He implied, on the one hand, that the era of rapid expansion and innovation was over, that the challenge of the day was to manage existing resources more equitably. On the other hand, he conveyed a sense of optimism and the conventional Progressive faith in efficiency and improvement. Running not to lose and keeping his policy options open, Roosevelt allowed voters a generous measure of interpretation, encompassing contradictions.[4]

Roosevelt's tenor reflected the popular mood. The perceived connection between the labor-displacing effects of mechanization and the mass unemployment of the Depression provoked a grassroots Luddism rarely seen in U.S. history. Harry Truman, recently elected County Judge in Independence, Missouri, for instance, oversaw hand labor on roads that would have been constructed with power machinery just a few years earlier. This hostility, however, was mixed with desire for the good life that technology made possible. The AF of L's *American Federationist* agonized that science was becoming "the enemy of the wage-earner. But science is inherently the ally of humanity." The scientific celebrities of the 1920s lost little of their luster. When Thomas Edison died in October 1931, fulsome praise with nary a hint of criticism was the order of the day.[5]

The brief life of the Technocracy movement from August 1932 to January 1933 encapsulated the popular confusion. Rising from utter obscurity to be the nation's "new mouthwash," as Will Rogers put it, the Technocrats claimed that technological unemployment would rise to apocalyptic levels unless the price system was replaced with a system based on energy values and run by experts. By taking full advantage of science and technology, said Howard Scott, the supreme Techocrat, such a system would allow everyone in the nation a living standard equivalent to $20,000 per year, with a four-hour workday four days a week, and retirement at age 45. What his "scientific techniques of decision ar-

---

[3] Arthur M. Schlesinger, Jr., *The Crisis of the Old Order, 1919–1933* (Boston: Houghton-Mifflin, 1957), 430–35; "Text of Herbert Hoover's Madison Square Garden Speech," *New York Times,* November 1, 1932, 12.

[4] Daniel R. Fusfeld, *The Economic Thought of Franklin D. Roosevelt and the Origins of the New Deal,* 2d ed. (New York: AMS Press, 1970), 219–20; "Invention in the New Deal," *Journal of the Patent Office Society* 16 (1934): 251; Schlesinger 1957 (above, n. 3), 420–26; "New Conditions Impose New Requirements," address, September 23, 1932, *FDR–PP,* vol. 1, 742–56.

[5] William E. Leuchtenburg, *The Perils of Prosperity,* 2d ed. (Chicago: University of Chicago Press, 1993), 257; David McCullough, *Truman* (New York: Simon and Schuster, 1992), 196–97; "A Principle of Balance," *American Federationist* 38 (1931): 1056–1057; "Inventor and the World," *The New Republic,* November 4, 1931, 312–13.

rivation" lacked in specificity, Scott compensated for in the public relations appeal of pseudo-technical mumbo jumbo. "Responsible sections of the business community," worried National Industrial Conference Board President Virgil Jordan, were making the "pole vault" of logic that the Technocrats required with surprising ease. Over ten thousand people turned out for a Technocrat rally at the Hollywood Bowl in early 1933.[6]

Technocrat demagoguery provoked a strong backlash from the corporate and scientific establishment. Men like MIT's Compton, GE's Gerard Swope, and GM's Alfred P. Sloan lambasted the movement's nightmarish prediction of 20 million technologically unemployed and sought to reclaim for themselves the dream of better living through chemistry. Such attacks quickly revealed that Scott was a phony. Yet the man was not the movement. Technocracy's appeal was in part, as *The New Republic*'s George Soule noted, its promise of a rational, planned solution to a crisis that was reaching epic proportions. While the Technocrats' plans were ridiculous, the new president and the new Congress would offer more plausible ones.[7]

SCIENCE, TECHNOLOGY, AND "PLANNING"

The New Deal routed conservatism from the capital. The banking panic during the lame-duck period gave Roosevelt a mandate that went beyond his electoral triumph. He seized it, squelching the panic and constructing a sprawling program of emergency state action in agriculture, banking, foreign affairs, and industry that touched almost every aspect of the economy. The felt need for action was acute: "We were faced with a condition and not a theory," said the president two-thirds of the way through his famous Hundred Days.[8] But "New Deal" was little more than a label. Although the mood of government activism was widely shared, competing policy entrepreneurs offered different causal stories on which that activism would be premised as well as contending visions of the state to which it would lead.

One fault line was whether technology caused unemployment. Compton, Swope, and many of their fellow associationalists did not think so, preferring

---

[6] H. E. Howe, "The New Mouthwash," *Industrial and Engineering Chemistry,* February 1933, 123–24; J. George Frederick, "What Are Technocracy's Assertions?" in Frederick, ed., *For and Against Technocracy* (New York: Business Bourse, 1933), 10–13; Howard Scott, *Introduction to Technocracy* (New York: John Day, 1933), 47; Virgil Jordan, "Technocracy—Tempest on a Slide Rule," *Scribner's,* February 1933, 65–69. The most complete description of the movement is William E. Akin, *Technocracy and the American Dream* (Berkeley: University of California Press, 1977).

[7] "Leaders Put Faith in Machine Age to End Depression," *New York Times,* January 9, 1933, 1; George Soule, "A Critique of Technocracy's Five Main Points," in Frederick, ed. (above, n. 6), 95–108.

[8] "Second Fireside Chat," May 7, 1933, *FDR—PP,* vol. 2, 160.

to blame chiselers, as I discuss below. Reform liberals, such as Roosevelt brain-truster Rexford Tugwell, refused to render such a sweeping verdict. They were by no means opposed to science, as their critics sometimes claimed; indeed, if anything, they made too much a fetish of "the machine" and worshiped progress. However, they did see an important place for the state in adapting society to new technology, thereby avoiding ills like technological unemployment. By developing new administrative capacities, the government could slow the pace of displacement, aid workers affected by it, and accelerate the development of new technologies to create jobs to absorb them. The reform liberals disagreed among themselves about which of these three elements ought to have the highest priority. But Congress and the president never gave Tugwell's ideas for regulating the impact of technology on labor an institutional test bed of the sort they gave Lilienthal and those more focused on job creation in the TVA.

The reform liberal proposals that gave most credence to the critics, tapped the deepest popular root, and were most summarily dismissed in policy circles called for a research moratorium and a tax on labor-displacing machines. From the cigar maker's point of view, the threat of technological unemployment was overwhelming; jobs for skilled hand-rollers had practically disappeared. Father Charles Coughlin, the notorious radio priest, gave voice to this anguish: "Save our factories! Protect our machinery! Let inventors discover new ways and means to lift the burden of labor from the backs of men! But for God's sake save our American laborer and farmer who depend upon each other and upon whom ultimately depend the owners of machinery and the Constitution of this nation." Voices like Father Coughlin's merged with those of the Technocrats and older strains of populism at the margin, linking machines, debt, Rothschilds, and other evil elites in nefarious conspiracies. Such rumblings in the heartland echoed but distantly in the capital. Representative William Connery, chairman of the House Labor Committee, offered a bill that would tax new machines to discourage layoffs, but it was a symbolic gesture, going nowhere but the hometown newspaper.[9]

In Washington, where Connery resided far from the obsolete shoemakers of his Massachusetts district, direct resistance to technological innovation was taken to be foolish and futile. The real challenge, to the capital's sophisticates, was shortening the "lag" between the appearance of new technologies and the "adaptation" of social institutions to them, to use the terms of the sociologist William F. Ogburn. It was technological lag or "maladaptation" that slowed the reabsorption of displaced workers, causing technological unemployment. In a

[9] Carroll W. Pursell, Jr., "'A Savage Struck by Lightning': The Idea of a Research Moratorium, 1927–1937," *Lex et Scientia* 10 (1974): 146–58; Mary Anderson, "When Machines Make Cigars," *American Federationist* 39 (1932): 1375–81; Charles E. Coughlin, *Eight Lectures on Labor, Capital, and Justice* (Royal Oak, MI: Radio League of the Little Flower, 1934), 11; "Bill Planned to Tax Machine Production," *New York Times,* September 24, 1933, IV:6; Glenn Harrison Speece, *After Roosevelt* (New York: Alliance Press, 1936), 182–86, 223–40.

booklet prepared for the youth workers of the Civilian Conservation Corps (CCC), Ogburn made clear his rejection of the machine tax: "People who do not want to change are called conservatives. They want to bring back the Good Old Days. But we know that sort of thing is foolish. We can't bring back the Good Old Days, no matter how much the old men want them. For the machine is forever changing things. Some of the conservative old men try to pass laws to stop change. One might as well brush back the tides with a broom . . . It is Youth to whom we must look—not old men. They must learn to adjust themselves to the Machine." The state had to take the lead in this process, because capitalists had neither the incentive nor the expertise to help society adapt. Capitalism was "awkward, slow, and frequently unjust," Tugwell stated. Expert civil servants could redress these failures, alleviating the conflict between capital and labor as a result and allowing everyone to reap the full fruits of scientific progress.[10]

The reform liberals offered a panoply of rules and taxes aimed at reducing technological unemployment which were more forward-looking than the research moratorium and machine tax. They argued for mandatory dismissal compensation, for instance, to discourage layoffs and give laid-off workers the means to retrain themselves. Stronger unions could also aid retraining, it was said, as well as avert violent machine-wrecking by the untutored rank and file. Employment exchanges could aid those who had developed new skills to find the work that they needed. But the idea that towered above all of these was the regulation of wages and working hours.[11]

Technological unemployment was not the only motivation for legislation to set minimum wages and maximum hours of work. A complementary causal story attributed unemployment to a shortage of purchasing power, in part because capitalists were keeping too much of the surplus created by mechanization for themselves. Shorter hours would spread the work among more citizens; putting a floor under wages would ensure that they had more money to spend. Drawing on works advancing these themes, such as Arthur Dahlberg's *Jobs, Machines, and Capitalism,* Senator Hugo Black took the lead in the spring of 1933, presenting a bill mandating a thirty-hour week. Appearing before Representative Connery, Black's co-sponsor in the House, W. A. Calvin of the Boilermakers' Union, stated this aspect of the case for the bill: "The benefits accrued . . . by reason of inventions and labor-saving devices should not be confined to a special group, a minority. . . . If this measure becomes law you will be making a tremendous stride toward the equalization of the benefits of mechanized industry." The passage of the Black bill by the Senate in early April prompted the administration into action.[12]

[10] William F. Ogburn, "You and Machines," pamphlet published by the American Council on Education, 1934, available in Widener Library, Harvard University; Rexford Guy Tugwell, *The Industrial Discipline and the Governmental Arts* (New York: Columbia University Press, 1933), 179.

[11] Paul Douglas, "Technological Unemployment," *American Federationist* 37 (1930): 923–50.

[12] Arthur Dahlberg, *Jobs, Machines, and Capitalism* (New York: MacMillan, 1932), 27–30;

The president endorsed the ideas behind the Black bill but found its mandate to be rigid and heavy-handed. He preferred to provide some flexibility and ambiguity, both to permit more competent administration and to allow himself to broaden the coalition behind the legislation. After a complex series of negotiations, the administration advanced the National Industrial Recovery Act (NIRA), which bowed to concern about technological unemployment and to practically every other theory of the Depression in a hodgepodge welter of statutory objectives. The NIRA delegated authority to industrial trade associations operating under the supervision of a National Recovery Administration (NRA) which were supposed to write and enforce codes of fair business practice, specifically including permissible hours of work and minimum wages.[13]

In practice, the statute was so vague that its meaning had to be fought out during its implementation; the president had succeeded in shifting the central arena for policy-making from the legislative branch to the executive branch. The critical issue in this fight (to which I return later in this chapter) was whether industry would govern itself, as the associationalists who joined the grand NIRA coalition expected, or whether government supervision would have real teeth, as the reform liberals hoped. A *Newsweek* headline in October 1934 summed it up: "'Enforcement,' Says Board; 'Self-Rule,' Cries Industry." Wages and hours, "the essence of the plan," as the president stated, were the main bones of contention. As the labor conflict took center stage under the NRA in the massive strike wave of 1934, social justice and the distribution of income almost entirely displaced technological unemployment in justifications for the reform liberal program. This conflict led to such landmark legislation as the National Labor Relations Act of 1935 (NLRA) and the Fair Labor Standards Act of 1938 (FLSA), subjects too large to address adequately here. Yet concern about technological unemployment continued to flicker; a contemporary observer noted, for instance, that the FLSA was "designed in part as a compulsory 'share the work' program."[14]

Although reform liberals in the early New Deal emphasized adapting the labor market to new technology, they did not leave the task of developing new industries to absorb laid-off workers entirely to the private sector. The TVA, centered on the World War I surplus chemical plants at Muscle Shoals, Ala-

---

Arthur M. Schlesinger, Jr., *The Coming of the New Deal* (Cambridge: Riverside Press, 1958), 90–92; U.S. House of Representatives, Committee on Labor, *Six Hour Day—Five Day Week,* 72d C., 2d s., 1933, 119.

[13] Robert Himmelberg, *The Origins of the National Recovery Administration* (New York: Fordham University Press, 1976), 181–218.

[14] "Third Fireside Chat," *FDR—PP,* vol. 2, 302; "'Enforcement,' Says Board; 'Self-Rule,' Cries Industry," *Newsweek,* October 27, 1934, 32; Paul H. Douglas and Joseph Hackman, "The Fair Labor Standards Act of 1938 I," *Political Science Quarterly* 53 (1938): 491. In the large literature on the NRA, see especially Ellis W. Hawley, *The New Deal and the Problem of Monopoly* (Princeton: Princeton University Press, 1966) and Donald Brand, *Corporatism and the Rule of Law* (Ithaca: Cornell University Press, 1988).

bama, and the huge dam built to power them, was their great hope in this respect. To the long-running debate on public power and Muscle Shoals, the new administration contributed a grand conception of a comprehensive regional planning corporation "clothed with the power of government but possessed of the flexibility and initiative of a private enterprise." Flood control and electricity provided by dams, modernized farming practices, and industrial development, beginning with fertilizer production at Muscle Shoals, would all be integrated in one giant package that would transform the region's impoverished, semifeudal economy.[15]

TVA had to have state-of-the-art technology if it was to meet its statutory responsibility to serve as a "yardstick" for power production to keep the private utilities honest. For the fertilizer plants, the challenge posed by the TVA bill's sponsors was even greater: "the operation of experimental plants on a larger scale than has ever before been undertaken in the history of the world, for the purpose of discovering new methods of production of fertilizers with the objective of cheapening the cost of fertilizers, not only to farmers in the Tennessee Valley, but everywhere in the nation." Congress therefore gave the TVA the power to compel licensing of patents for electrical machinery and fertilizer production and the authority to maintain and operate its own laboratories.[16]

David Lilienthal, the hard-charging former Public Utility Commissioner of Wisconsin, translated the congressional mandate into concrete (literally) actions of the TVA. Lilienthal was convinced, by temperament and experience, that bureaucrats in business, especially in the power companies, constantly threw up barriers to progress that the state constantly had to break down. One such effort aimed at installing the revolutionary new van de Graaf electricity transmission system in the Tennessee Valley, a move that Lilienthal hoped would lengthen the "yardstick" against which TVA's private competitors were measured. Although a deal with MIT to develop this system was negotiated, it foundered on ideological conflict, as the historian Larry Owens has shown. MIT's report noted, "We felt that a contract along the lines demanded by the Tennessee Valley Authority would place in the hands of the government a powerful tool for combating private public-utility interests throughout the country and we refused to become party to such practice." TVA had slightly more success developing low-budget electrical appliances for the home and equipment for the farm that it hoped would increase electricity sales as well as make life more enjoyable for its hardscrabble constituency. It designed such items as har-

---

[15] "Muscle Shoals Development," message from the president, 73d C., 1st s., 1933, H. Doc. 15; Thomas K. McCraw, *TVA and the Power Fight, 1933–1939* (Philadelphia: J. B. Lippincott, 1971), 26–36.

[16] "Muscle Shoals and Tennessee Valley Development," 73d C., 1st s., 1933, S. Rept. 23, 2; "Muscle Shoals," 73d C., 1st s., 1933, H. Rept. 48, 9; U.S. House of Representatives, Committee on Military Affairs, *Muscle Shoals,* 73d C., 1st s., 1933, 68; F. M. Scherer et al., *Patents and the Corporation,* 2d ed. (Boston: Patents and the Corporation, 1959), 73.

vesters, hay driers, and storage freezers and provided incentives for manufacturers to do the same.[17]

TVA's most impressive technological innovations were made in fertilizer production, under the leadership of board member Harcourt Morgan. The fertilizer companies, which were denounced by the American Farm Bureau Federation at the House hearings on TVA as "antiquated as an oxcart," rightly feared TVA. The industry was notorious for adulterating its product, and the South was the region that used fertilizer most heavily. Working with local scientists and engineers, the USDA, and the Research Corporation, TVA designed and constructed a phosphate plant at Muscle Shoals. By 1936 it had shipped 25,000 tons of fertilizer. TVA experts made important strides in process technology and in the product itself, developing super-concentrates to reduce the costs of shipping and use; the agency held seven patents related to the manufacturing of phosphate fertilizers. TVA also placed emphasis on diffusing techniques for proper use of its products, establishing demonstration farms as (in Lilienthal's words) "a living channel of communication between the layman and the technician, a needed stimulus to science, invention, and industry."[18]

When he took a tour of the Tennessee Valley in 1936, Stuart Chase, the journalist and social commentator whose intellectual journey drew a bright line from the Technocrats to the TVA, could scarcely contain his enthusiasm for what the New Deal had wrought there. The TVA epitomized the "middle road" of democratic planning, similar to that of Sweden. It represented progress, not Washington paper-pushing: "The patents are held by the government, and the development will be non-profit government business—unless the Liberty League lawyers contrive to get hold of it and lock it up in their economy of judicial scarcity. Dams, yes. But perhaps here is something more important."[19] Despite Chase's propagandizing, TVA was an isolated regional experiment. The

[17] David E. Lilienthal, "Business and Government in the Tennessee Valley," *Annals of the American Academy of Political and Social Sciences* 172 (1934): 45–49; Larry Owens, "MIT and the Federal 'Angel': Academic R&D and Federal-Private Cooperation Before World War II," *Isis* 81 (1990): 211; Gregory B. Field, "'Electricity for All': The Electric Home and Farm Authority and the Politics of Mass Consumption, 1932–1935," *Business History Review* 64 (1990): 32–60; Clarence L. Hodge, *The Tennessee Valley Authority: A National Experiment in Regionalism,* reissue (New York: Russell and Russell, 1968), 105–8; TVA, *TVA—1933–1937* (Washington: GPO, 1937), 64–66.

[18] House Military Affairs Committee (above, n. 16), 83, 253–85; TVA, "Soil . . . People, and Fertilizer Technology," pamphlet, 1949, available in Widener Library, Harvard University; *Annual Report of the Tennessee Valley Authority for Fiscal Year 1934,* 74th C., 1st s., 1935, H. doc. 82, 3–4, 37–40; TVA, 1937 (above, n. 17), 39–53; TVA, "Fertilizer Science and the American Farmer," pamphlet, 1958, available in Littauer Library, Harvard University; David E. Lilienthal, *TVA: Democracy on the March* (New York: Harper and Bros., 1944), 83.

[19] Stuart Chase, "The New Deal's Greatest Asset" (four parts), *Nation,* June 3, 1936, 702–5; June 10, 1936, 738–741; June 17, 1936, 775–77; June 24, 1936, 804–5; quote from 741.

linkages between governmental administrative capacities, purchasing power, and technological innovation that it seemed to demonstrate were not replicated elsewhere in the country. Indeed, the central thrust of early New Deal economic policy owed little to the reform liberals' vision of the state. Ironically, this early failure would prove handy, allowing them in the second term to move into the vacuum left by the pathetic results of the great associationalist experiments begun in 1933.

COOPERATION FOR PROGRESS AND PROTECTION: THE ASSOCIATIVE IMPULSE IN THE EARLY NEW DEAL

As the failed van de Graaf deal suggests, the corporate and scientific establishment, for whom self-government was the mantra, viewed the TVA with dismay. They feared a more autonomous state, particularly one vested with technological capabilities. Yet many in their ranks recognized that the Depression required changes in American capitalism. "If only they could achieve the necessary organization, thought many hard pressed businessmen," the historian Ellis Hawley states, "and if only some means were provided to force the chiselers into line, then prices might be fixed at profitable levels to all, and production, employment, and wages might be maintained at satisfactory levels." The heirs to Hoover's vision believed that the Great Engineer had had the right idea but had overestimated the capability of business to put aside short-term interests for long-term ones. The state had to provide the means for industrial self-government to overcome the recalcitrant minority.[20]

In research and development the new, improved associationalism promised an end to free riding and the security to invest funds without fear of crank inventors and nuisance patents. By taking prices and wages out of competition, the policy would make firms compete on the basis of service and quality, to which technological innovation could make major contributions. As Joseph Schumpeter later rationalized it, restrictions on trade practices like those envisioned by the associationalists were "incidents, often unavoidable incidents, of a long-run process of expansion which they protect rather than impede." The New Deal associationalists hoped that the institutional innovations made by the Hoover Commerce Department in the governance of science and technology would be improved and expanded. The sociologist S. C. Gilfillan of the University of Chicago, for instance, proposed mandatory membership in trade associations that could levy fees to support research programs. These associations would also manage patents pooled by all their members. Gilfillan claimed his ideas "would substitute intelligent trade and national planning for haphazard development of inventions, prevent duplication of effort, pour as much funds

[20] Hawley (above, n. 14), 40.

as seem fit into each research deemed hopeful and desirable . . . [and suppress wasteful spending on patent litigation]."[21]

Most associationalist rhetoric reflected the deep faith averred by General Electric research director Willis R. Whitney: "If industrial research were done by more and better people, we should have less unemployment and perhaps none. This is perfectly obvious."[22] Yet, although denunciations of "the machine" were rare, the associationalists, like the reform liberals, were divided in the enthusiasm with which they pursued technological solutions to the Depression. For every Whitney, there was a southern cotton textile mill owner who wanted the associative state to protect him from more sophisticated northern competitors. The fear of technological disinvestment among such people mirrored the fear of technological unemployment within labor. Hence, associationalists who shared a vision of the state differed over whether that state ought to accelerate or restrict technological innovation. As the policy debate played out in the industry-level venues set up under the NIRA and other early New Deal policies, such as the Emergency Railroad Transportation Act, these camps clashed repeatedly. The protectionists were both more aggressive in their efforts and more powerful in the "sick" industries in which these policies had the most effect. The associative vision of the state was ultimately tarred by the affiliation.

Like their reform liberal partners in the grand coalition, associationalists who backed the NIRA fell prey to wishful thinking. They pinned their hopes on those sections of the act that relaxed the antitrust laws and authorized the so-called "constitutions" of self-government, the industrial trade practice codes. As the economist Edward S. Mason cynically put it in 1934, the possibility of state-sanctioned cooperation through codes was "the bait calculated to make wage increases more palatable." Yet, in the crisis atmosphere of 1933, the smell was simply too enticing. Some 546 codes bloomed, covering "an almost unbelievably wide range and variety of trade practices."[23]

The mechanics of code writing were unclear in the statute and chaotic in practice. Self-organized industry was supposed to take the lead, but their efforts were to be overseen by the NRA in Washington, including its Consumer, Labor, and Industrial Advisory Boards, which were authorized to represent these constituencies at all code hearings. To this array of institutionalized interests, the enterprising Karl Compton, along with Johns Hopkins president Isaiah Bow-

---

[21] Joseph A. Schumpeter, *Capitalism, Socialism, and Democracy* (New York: Harper [Colophon ed.], 1975), 87–88; "Patents and the 'New Deal'," *Journal of the Patent Office Society* 16 (1934): 92; S. C. Gilfillan, "A New System for Encouraging Invention," *Journal of the Patent Office Society* 17 (1935): 970.

[22] W. R. Whitney, "Accomplishments and Future of the Physical Sciences," *Science* 84, September 4, 1936, 213.

[23] Edward S. Mason, "Controlling Industry," in *The Economics of the Recovery Program* (New York: Whittlesey House, 1934), 39; Leverett S. Lyon et al., *The National Recovery Administration: An Analysis and Appraisal,* 2d ed. (New York: Da Capo Press, 1972), 29, 563.

man, the new president of the National Research Council (NRC), hoped to add a Science Advisory Board (SAB) to serve as a comparable voice on behalf of technological innovation in the codes. They sensibly proposed that the SAB focus on older industries, like textiles and steel, that were likely to be tempted to use the NRA for protection from new technologies. On this score Compton and Bowman were frustrated. While they ultimately succeeded in establishing an entity called the SAB, chaired by Compton, on July 31, 1933, it had no voice in the NRA but rather helped government officials like Agriculture Secretary Wallace solve administrative problems that involved science. Compton was added instead to the Industrial Advisory Board, which was chaired by his patron Gerard Swope. He continued, however, to nurture hopes that the SAB would play a more significant role in economic and industrial policy.[24]

In addition to attempting to gain a seat at the table in code negotiations, the progressive associationalists also sought to lead by example, through the writing of model codes. The earliest model codes emanated from the Hoover Commerce Department's Bureau of Foreign and Domestic Commerce in 1932 and called for cooperation in product and process research as well as in simplification and standardization. In 1933 Maurice Holland of the NRC Division of Engineering and Industrial Research (DEIR) drafted a paragraph on industrial research for inclusion in the model code being prepared by the NRA and made extensive efforts to interest trade association executives in the subject. Like Compton, Holland was rebuffed by industry executives on the one hand and reform liberals in the government on the other; both model and actual NRA codes typically ignored research or even authorized controls on modernization.[25]

The failure of model codes is not surprising, given the diverse impact of the Depression on U.S. industries. High technology industries, in which most research was done, suffered far less than industries that were sick already in the 1920s. On occasion the newer industries used associationalist rhetoric to supply ideological sanction in the early 1930s for their established practices for managing technological innovation, such as the patent pool. The pool for RCA's radio patents, for instance, was said to be intended to avoid "economic waste

[24] Robert Kargon and Elizabeth Hodes, "Karl Compton, Isaiah Bowman, and the Politics of Science in the Great Depression," *Isis* 76 (1985): 308–10; Carroll W. Pursell, Jr., "The Anatomy of a Failure: The Science Advisory Board, 1933–1935," *Proceedings of the American Philosophical Society* 109 (1965): 342–43; Albert L. Barrows, Assistant Secretary, NRC, to R. A. Millikan, July 15, 1933 (with attachment, "Preliminary Science Approach to the Industrial Recovery Program" by Maurice Holland), in Millikan papers, California Institute of Technology Archives, File 7.15. I retrieved the Barrows letter thanks to a citation by Kargon and Hodes.

[25] NRA Division of Review, "The So-Called Model Code: Its Development and Modification," 1936, Hagley Library, Imprints Collection; "Report of the Chairman to the Executive Board for the Period July, 1933–April, 1934," April 25, 1934, Dugald C. Jackson papers, MIT (hereafter "Jackson papers"), Box 5, Folder 341, 19; Maurice Holland, "Summary of Analysis . . . with Recommendations for Future Development," October 5, 1934, National Academy of Sciences Archives (hereafter "NAS Archives"), NRC, Engineering and Industrial Research Division, "Analysis. . . ."

and business disorganization," although this was little more than a post hoc rationalization. The boom in autos and aviation, which continued through the hard times, was attributed in part to patent pools established in the 1910s and revised in the 1920s.[26]

In the codes themselves, however, the high technology industries stuck to the bare minimum required by law, wage and hour regulations, and disputed these bitterly. The chemical industry even used its vaunted technological capacity as a symbolic weapon in this conflict. Article IX of its code stated that the industry's "main product and purpose" was "the extension of chemical knowledge in the public interest" and that its "peculiar relation . . . to national defense, national health, national industry, and national agriculture must be constantly borne in mind." These grandiose phrases sanctified the efforts of the DuPonts and others to evade the collective bargaining provisions that the NRA was forcing on many industries; they had no practical significance and were inserted in negotiations with the administration in order to avoid the appearance of setting a precedent for sectors that could not claim such noble aims.[27]

However appealing it might be in the abstract, the new improved associationalism in high technology industries required that firms share their most vital assets. But there was no interest in sharing, nor could such an interest be created no matter how many times associationalists tried to persuade high-technology executives. Even the patent pools hailed by reformers excepted the most important inventions, those likely to lead to significant competitive advantages. In any case, whatever ideological defense technological dynamism provided to high technology executives soon wore thin as they came under attack in Congress (as "merchants of death" and worse) and, even more seriously, from unions on the shop floor.

In the sick industries, the associative impulse had more real consequences for the governance of technological innovation, but they tended to be protectionist, the opposite of what Compton and Holland had hoped for. Railroading, for instance, was among the sickest of industries. The nation's second largest industry after agriculture at the outset of the Depression, it had been in decline for decades as new modes of transportation captured passenger and freight traffic. The Depression cut the industry's already-falling revenues in half between 1929 and 1933; employment dropped by 40 percent. Some 42,000 miles of

---

[26] "The RCA Consent Decree," *George Washington Law Review* 1 (1933): 513–16; Samuel R. Wachtell, "Restraints of Trade and Patent Pools," pamphlet reprinted from *New York Law Journal,* April 15, 1933, available in Harvard Law School Library; W. Ellison Chalmers, "The Automobile Industry," in George B. Galloway, ed., *Industrial Planning under Codes* (New York: Harper and Bros., 1935), 314–16; George Bittlingmayer, "Property Rights, Progress, and the Aircraft Patents Agreement," *Journal of Law and Economics* 31 (1988): 230–35.

[27] "Code for Chemical Manufacturing Industry Approved," *Industrial and Engineering Chemistry,* news edition, February 20, 1934, 57–59; correspondence of Alfred E. Sloan and Lammot Dupont, November 1933, and Lammot DuPont, draft letter, March 2, 1934, both in Lammot DuPont papers, Box 15, Hagley Museum and Library.

track, or one-sixth of the national total, was held by bankrupt firms. In 1932 the Reconstruction Finance Corporation (RFC) poured $337 million into the railroads without stemming the red ink. The evident futility of the RFC's attempt to prop up the industry with low-cost loans prompted conflict between associationalist and reform liberal camps over railroad policy as the new administration took shape. Like the NIRA, which was also passed on June 16, 1933, the Emergency Railroad Transportation Act (ERTA) was an uneasy compromise, providing for voluntary reorganization under the auspices of industry committees, to be guided by a Federal Coordinator of Transportation whose coercive power was uncertain. In this milieu Compton's SAB sought to accelerate the pace of technological innovation in the railroad industry.[28]

This effort built on a similar initiative by Holland's DEIR in 1932, which had run into a stone wall. Frustrated by the intransigence of the railroad executives, Dugald Jackson, the patriarch of the MIT Electrical Engineering Department, who chaired the division, joined forces with Compton to approach the new coordinator, Joseph Eastman. On October 11, 1933, Compton and Eastman announced the formation of the Committee on National Railway Research Organization to consider the establishment of a laboratory that would conduct fundamental research for the benefit of the entire railroad industry at an initial cost of $500,000 per year. The committee's members included several research directors from major corporations outside the railroad industry. Its chair was held by Bell Labs' Frank Jewett, who had been persuaded by the crisis in the railroad industry and by the analogy between the railroad network and the communications network that his firm managed alone, to temporarily set aside his conservative leanings. Powerful railroad executives, led by General W. W. Atterbury of the Pennsylvania Railroad, also accepted places on the committee.[29]

Jewett and the other nonrailroad men worked hard to reassure the rest of the members that they sympathized with the industry's dire predicament and meant to be constructive. After the first meeting, Jewett was upbeat, confiding to Jackson that General Atterbury (whom he took to be the bellwether of the railroad members) was "favorable to some form of cooperative solution." By early 1934 the committee had reached a consensus that the railroads needed "an improved mutual organization for stimulating, directing, and planning the utilization of the results of the research." The committee's report, which was made public in

---

[28] Hawley (above, n. 14), 227–31; Earl Latham, *The Politics of Railroad Coordination* (Cambridge: Harvard University Press, 1959); James S. Olson, *Herbert Hoover and the Reconstruction Finance Corporation, 1931–1933* (Ames: Iowa State University Press, 1977), 97–98.

[29] William Spraragen to Jackson, November 12, 1932 (Folder 334); Jackson to Eastman, July 20, 1933 (Folder 335); Compton to Holland, September 7, 1933 (Folder 336); Holland, "A Plan for Centralized and Coordinated Railroad Research Organization," September 20, 1933 (Folder 337); Holland, "Steps in Establishing a Central Scientific Laboratory for Railroad Transportation Industry," September 23, 1933 (Folder 336); press release, October 11, 1933 (Folder 338), all in Jackson papers, Box 5.

October 1934, called for the new laboratory to be supported by "equitable annual levy" on the industry's firms.[30]

Coordinator Eastman received the report with open arms: "I . . . look forward to the speedy establishment of a centralized railroad research department." Jackson and Jewett immediately began prospecting for a director. Yet nobody got the job, because the railroads did not create it. The American Association of Railroads (AAR), which was the closest equivalent to an NRA code authority in the industry, simply shelved the report, leaving Eastman's office to fret in April 1935 that the proposed Department of Planning and Research "seems to be in a state of suspended animation." Rather than seek technological solutions, the industry preferred to displace the Federal Coordinator altogether, a goal it accomplished in 1936. Its idea of damage control was to use the powers granted by the state to trade associations to protect itself from change as much as possible, rather than to mount the best competitive counterattack. The AAR did not establish a technical research department until 1943, and then only in response to antitrust proceedings alleging that it was impeding the adoption of new technology.[31]

The railroads at least nominally considered the prospect of investing more in technological innovation. Many other "sick" industries blatantly established capacity, production, and machine hour controls with the intention of preventing such investments. The textile industry, for instance, organized quickly to impose such controls through NRA codes. Fred Feiker, a Hoover associate who edited *Mill and Factory,* called for the textile codes to be administered with an eye toward reducing costs, eliminating wastes, and developing "our mechanical ingenuity and our management ability," but this was beyond the NRA's capacity. To do so, it would have had to distinguish between the mere "stretchout" of labor, which was to be banned, and true innovation, which was to be welcomed. Instead, when the Johnson and Johnson Company tried to "press the case for efficiency as opposed to stabilization" in early 1934, the historian Louis Galambos shows, it was rejected by General Hugh Johnson, the NRA's highest official. The textile codes had the dual effect of impeding sweatshop exploitation in more backward mills and preventing the most modern mills from working to capacity.[32]

---

[30] Minutes, notes, and statements from committee meeting, December 18, 1933 (Folder 339); Jewett to Jackson, December 29, 1933 (Folder 339); notes and minutes of subcommittee meeting, March 9, 1934 (Folder 340); Jewett to committee, June 22, 1934 (Folder 342); all in Jackson papers, Box 5. The final report is reprinted in Science Advisory Board *Report, 1934–35* (Washington: National Research Council, 1935), 459–77.

[31] Eastman to Compton, October 15, 1934; Jewett to Jackson, October 17, 1934; Jackson to Jewett, October 24, 1934 (Folder 344), all in Jackson papers, Box 5; Latham (above, n. 28), 164–94; Lockwood to Jackson, April 11, 1935, Jackson papers, Box 5, Folder 346; U.S. Senate Committee on Military Affairs, *Technological Mobilization,* 77th C., 2d s., 1943, 305–6; "Rail Worrying," *Business Week,* November 13, 1943, 81.

[32] Frederick M. Feiker, "Blessed by the President," *Mill and Factory,* August 1933, 22; Louis

The iron and steel industry, suffering from a "cataclysmic" decline in sales, also found this sort of self-government appealing. Its code contained production and capacity controls that the trade journal *Iron Age* hoped would help lead to "brain competition," rather than brutal price-cutting; these same provisions might plausibly have constrained innovation, particularly in smaller firms that had no voice in the code authority but were nonetheless subject to the code. In practice, however, the provisions were never utilized because of the enormous overcapacity in the industry during the NRA years. Still, critics complained that the NRA had realized the industry's aim of protection from the introduction of new steel-making technology.[33]

About 15 to 20 percent of the codes ultimately contained provisions, like those in textiles and steel, that regulated the pace at which plants were modernized. As the most authoritative contemporary assessment of the NRA, carried out by the Brookings Institution, put it, "By admitting capacity control provisions into codes, the NRA in effect certified it to be in the public interest that the present amount and ownership of productive equipment be frozen in its existing pattern. . . ." Even if the practical effect was actually modest, the perception that "the NRA codes were full of restrictions on the introduction of new equipment" (in the words of the economist Sumner Slichter) was disillusioning for associationalists who had hoped they would promote progress rather than protection and unnerving for the capital goods industries that hoped to sell that new equipment.[34]

The cataclysmic experience of steel was magnified in the backbone of the capital goods sector, machine tools, which experienced a decline in sales of 87 percent between 1929 and 1933. Unemployment, it was clear, was concentrated in this sector. In the wish list that was the NIRA, manufacturers of capital goods had sought solace in Title II, which authorized over $3.3 billion in public works spending. The investment banker Alexander Sachs helped inspire these sections of the legislation and had hoped to implement them in conjunction with General Johnson's NRA; instead, the president gave control of these funds to Secretary of the Interior Harold Ickes, whose tightfistedness and fear of corruption

Galambos, *Competition and Cooperation: The Emergence of a National Trade Association* (Baltimore: Johns Hopkins University Press, 1966), 252; Charles Frederick Roos, *NRA Economic Planning* (Bloomington, IN: Principia Press, 1937), 360–70; "Research and the New Deal," *New York Times,* October 23, 1933, 14.

[33] "Iron and Steel Industry Code of Fair Competition as Amended May 30, 1934," pamphlet, Hagley Library, Imprints Collection; Meredith B. Givens, "Iron and Steel Industry," in Galloway (above, n. 26), 146; "A Law That We Cannot Repeal," *Iron Age,* June 1, 1933; Federal Trade Commission, *Report to the President with Respect to the Basing-Point System in the Iron and Steel Industry* (Washington: GPO, 1935), 26–28.

[34] Lyon et al. (above, n. 23), 647; Arthur R. Burns, *The Decline of Competition: A Study of the Evolution of American Industry* (New York: McGraw-Hill, 1936), 465–71, 508–12; Sumner Slichter, *Union Policies and Industrial Management* (Washington: Brookings Institution, 1941), 205.

was legendary. Ickes had no intention of seeing the government directly pick up the slack in capital goods, and Sachs soon departed the administration.[35]

Karl Compton encountered a similar roadblock in his effort to wedge university science into the definition of public works. Just as the NRA put muscle into previously voluntary trade associations, Compton's program to "Put Science to Work" went a step beyond Hoover's plan for a National Research Endowment (NRE). Although the federal government would provide funds for academic R&D projects, it was to vest authority for their administration and oversight in the academics themselves. Compton's plans for scientific self-government were twice referred by the president to Ickes and twice rejected as outside the scope of the authority of the NRA. "Evidently," the *New York Times* noted, "the term 'public works' is narrowly construed."[36]

These abortive efforts to expand the idea of public works presaged things to come. Both capital goods and science would eventually receive direct federal subsidies, mainly from the Department of Defense, but not until after the Second World War. The entrepreneurs behind these efforts also began advocating a new policy, tax breaks for research spending, toward which modest steps were taken before the war, although countervailing provisions in the tax code greatly diluted the effects. Such subsidies, both direct and indirect, did not require the sort of industrial reorganization envisioned by either the reform liberals or the associationalists.[37]

THE FALLOUT OF THE ASSOCIATIVE EXPERIMENT

By the time that the NRA was killed by the Supreme Court in 1935, the results of associative experimentation in science and technology policy were in. By and large they were negative. Across the ideological spectrum, commentators agreed that the "meaning of the NRA" was a futile "showdown with progress." While most Americans answered the president's question, "Are you better off

[35] Fred Colvin, "The Machine Tool Industry," in Galloway (above, n. 26), 301–10; NRA Code Hearings, no. 277, *Machine and Allied Products* (Washington: Recordak Corp, 1934), reel 48, 7–23; Jordan A. Schwarz, *The New Dealers: Power Politics in the Age of Roosevelt* (New York: Knopf, 1993), 96–102; Alexander Sachs, "NRA Policies and the Problem of Economic Planning," in *America's Recovery Program* (New York: Oxford University Press, 1934), 107–92.

[36] Science Advisory Board *Report, 1933–34* (Washington: National Research Council, 1934), 267–83; Karl T. Compton, "Put Science To Work!" *Technology Review* 37 (1935): 133–35, 152–58; "Science and Public Works," *New York Times,* July 17, 1933, 12; Kargon and Hodes (above, n. 24), 314–15; Daniel J. Kevles, *The Physicists* (New York: Knopf, 1977), 254–58, 265–66; Joel Genuth, "Groping Towards Science Policy in the United States in the 1930s," *Minerva* 25 (1987): 238–68.

[37] "Report of the Capital Goods Expenditures Committee of the Business Advisory Council," November 22, 1935, Pierre S. DuPont papers, Entry 1173–3, Hagley Museum and Library; Machinery and Allied Products Institute, "Capital Goods Industries and Postwar Taxation," pamphlet, 1945, Hagley Library Imprints Collection; Bernard Wolfman, "Federal Tax Policy and the Support of Science," *University of Pennsylvania Law Review* 114 (1965): 171–86.

than you were last year?" in the affirmative, the NRA had little to do with it. Indeed, the short tenure of the agency and its dubious effectiveness in enforcing any of its regulations suggest that the critics overstated the degree to which technological change actually slowed down. R&D spending, both in corporations and universities, recovered after 1933 with little change in the institutional arrangements by which science and technology were governed. If anything, the NRA mainly seems to have had the unintended consequence of spurring innovation by raising labor costs and the power of unions. Although this effect was not as pronounced as that of the Agricultural Adjustment Act (AAA), the beneficiaries of which bought tractors that sent sharecroppers packing across the South, it helped set in motion a positive feedback between wages, innovation, and productivity that would be institutionalized after World War II.[38]

In some economic sectors, however, the associationalists managed to remake industrial governance, transforming emergency measures into permanent specialized regulatory authorities, particularly in the natural resource and transportation industries. The railroad industry, for instance, freed itself from the coordinator in 1936, with the support of its unions. Trainmen who had ridden the rails their entire lives feared technological unemployment as deeply as the executives feared technological disinvestment. Cemented by dismissal compensation and other palliatives to ease these fears, the labor/management condominium of decline sheltered for the next several decades under the benign neglect of the Interstate Commerce Commission (ICC). By controlling competition and by setting rates on the basis of historical performance, the ICC provided neither the incentive nor the funds to invest in new technologies.[39]

Regulation did not necessarily have to induce technological stagnation. The electric utility industry, for instance, was given ample incentive by regulators (typically at the state level) to invest in advanced equipment; indeed, such investments were often the only way that they could make more money. Although

[38] Garet Garrett, "Machine Crisis," *Saturday Evening Post,* November 12, 1938, 12–13, 61–68, quote from 61; Bernhard Stern, "Restraints Upon the Utilization of Inventions," *Annals of the American Academy of Political and Social Sciences* (November 1938): 13–32; Harry Jerome, *Mechanization in Industry,* National Bureau of Economic Research pub. no. 27 (1934), 18–22; "First Fireside Chat of 1934," June 28, 1934, *PP-FDR,* vol. 3, 314; A. Hunter Dupree, *Science in the Federal Government,* 2d ed. (Baltimore: Johns Hopkins University Press, 1987), 346; National Industrial Conference Board, meeting minutes for October 26, 1933, National Industrial Conference Board papers, Box 6, Hagley Museum and Library; E. E. Lincoln to Willis Harrington, February 20, 1934, Willis F. Harrington papers, Box 19, Hagley Museum and Library; Bruce J. Schulman, *From Cotton Belt to Sunbelt: Federal Policy, Economic Development, and the Transformation of the South, 1938–1990* (New York: Oxford University Press, 1991).

[39] "Make Technical Progress Social Progress," *American Federationist* 43 (1936): 682–83; *Verbatim Record of the Proceedings of the Temporary National Economic Committee* (Washington: Bureau of National Affairs, 1940), vol. 13, no. 11, 395–99, 407–15; Latham (above, n. 28), 222–25, 259–65; Aaron J. Gellman, "Surface Freight Transportation," in William M. Capron, ed., *Technological Change in Regulated Industries* (Washington: Brookings Institution, 1970), 169–78.

the utilities did little R&D themselves, their purchasing power, the steady growth of the market until the 1970s, and the engineering esprit of some particularly aggressive utilities, which served as "lead users," motivated competing electrical equipment manufacturers to offer a steady stream of bigger and better products, which many utilities quickly adopted. The TVA was among these "lead users," although it is doubtful that its efforts served as a "yardstick" for private utilities in the way that its advocates had originally hoped. The federal role in developing new electric power generation technology was largely confined to the new and special postwar field of nuclear power. The impact of regulatory authorities on science and technology in sectors such as railroads and electric power, although hardly trivial, has been virtually invisible to observers of the "postwar consensus" in science and technology policy.[40]

The real impacts of associationalist entrepreneurship on science and technology, however, may well have been less significant than the perceptions that the NRA and its ilk were opposed to progress. The grand coalition that had passed the NIRA and ERTA dissolved in an orgy of finger-pointing well before *Schechter* (the decision which declared the NIRA unconstitutional). The president and the extraordinary 74th Congress of 1935–36, it soon became clear, cast the blame for the chaos on the associative vision of the state; most associationalists, finding the state being used by the reform liberals in ways that they could never countenance, moved into outright opposition. Only a few lamented, with Federal Trade Commissioner Nelson Burr Gaskill, that the "NRA almost discovered the true public interest in this matter of regulation of competition and then turned back." More commonly, they retreated to conservative rhetoric, assailing the emerging administrative state as antithetical to the "enterprise system." Such a state would soon be compelled by its very nature to dominate every aspect of a market society, including science and technology, which formed, as the Conference Board's Virgil Jordan put it in 1935, "the essence of the enterprise system."[41]

One manifestation of this apocalyptic turn in the associative interpretation of political trends was the joint scientific research committee of the American Institute of Physics (AIP) and the National Association of Manufacturers (NAM). A descendant of Karl Compton's "Put Science to Work" campaign of 1934–35, the joint committee's most visible activity was the sponsorship of major speeches to the NAM's annual Congress of American Industry. In this context in December 1937, Compton assailed the notion of government-funded re-

---

[40] Richard F. Hirsh, *Technology and Transformation in the American Electric Utility Industry* (New York: Cambridge University Press, 1989), 36–81; Bruce A. Smith, *Technological Innovation in Electric Power Generation, 1950–1970* (East Lansing: Michigan State University Public Utility Papers, 1977).

[41] Meeting minutes, National Industrial Conference Board, January 23, 1936, 37–38, and May 16, 1935, 29, National Industrial Conference Board papers, Boxes 7–8, Hagley Museum and Library.

search for its inefficiency and susceptibility to "political domination." Lammot Dupont, whose family bankrolled the viciously anti-Roosevelt American Liberty League, echoed Compton's complaints about "oppressive" government policies from the same platform, claiming that federal labor, regulatory, and tax policies inhibited new product development.[42]

Yet the associative impulse in science and technology policy was far from dead. Associationalists continued to admire, for instance, the salutary effect of the German cartel system on research, even though they often despised the system as a whole. German firms pooled technical resources while their American competitors had to go it alone. Leading associationalists admitted, however, that Hoover had been right about the dangers of state building; they therefore returned to their old chief's voluntarist agenda in the late 1930s. The opening of the Mellon Institute's new building in 1937 provided an occasion for these sentiments to surface. The "Parthenon of granite and limestone" would be, in the view of the *New York Times,* the "salvation" of small manufacturers who could band together to match the research resources of large firms. Edward Weidlein, the institute's director, emphasized the importance of constructive cooperation for industrial success, supplanting destructive price competition. The Institute's flagship program, the Industrial Fellowship System, served 142 fellows on the newly expanded campus, about half again as many as the Bureau of Standards' research associates program had involved at its peak in 1930.[43]

The industrialists with whom Compton and Weidlein associated in these endeavors were reviled by reform liberals, who by the second term claimed exclusive rights to the label "New Dealers." During the same week in 1937 that the new Mellon Institute building opened, for instance, the Justice Department opened a new antitrust suit against Alcoa, the prize property of patron Andrew Mellon (who was "known to rank as Economic Royalist No. 1 with the present Administration"). Similarly, the chairman of Compton's AIP-NAM committee, M. H. Eisenhart of Bausch and Lomb, came under attack in 1940 for dominating the military optics business by abusing the patent laws in collusion with German manufacturers.[44] The antitrust offensive marked a new stage in the de-

[42] "Proposal for Science-Industry Relationship . . . ," April 13, 1937, NAS Archives, Institutions-Associations-Individuals, "National Association of Manufacturers, 1937"; Karl T. Compton, "Symposium on Science and Industry," *Review of Scientific Instruments,* January 1938, 6–9; Lammot Dupont, "Industry's Outlook," reprinted in *Congressional Record,* 75th C., 2d s., 359–60. Compton's other activities, notably his support of the Randolph bill, suggest that he had not entirely given up on securing federal funding for academic research.

[43] National Research Council, "Research Consciousness Among Leading Industrial Nations" (1937), reprinted in Harold Vagtborg, *Research in American Industrial Development* (New York: Pergamon, 1976); William L. Laurence, "Scientists Open Mellon Institute," *New York Times,* May 7, 1937, 15; William L. Laurence, "Mellon Institute," *New York Times,* May 7, 1937, 24; E. R. Weidlein, "Broad Trends in Chemical Research, *Industrial and Engineering Chemistry,* January 10, 1938, 10–11; W. A. Hamor, "Research at the Mellon Institute, *Science* 87, April 29, 1938, 360–63.

[44] "Politico-Aluminum," *Business Week,* May 1, 1937, 13–14; Thurman Arnold to Robert Jack-

velopment of the reform liberal agenda for the governance of technological innovation. As the power of the "New Dealers" reached its apogee in the administration in the late 1930s, they relied less on the TVA-style development of new technologies that Stuart Chase so admired and more on the regulatory shaping of business behavior. The central figure in this effort was Thurman Arnold, a voluble, dapper intellectual who was named Assistant Attorney General for Antitrust in March 1938.

son, May 18, 1940, in Gene Gressley, ed., *Voltaire and the Cowboy: The Letters of Thurman Arnold* (Boulder: Colorado Associated University Press, 1977), 305–6.

Breaking Bottlenecks and Blockades

THE HEYDAY OF REFORM LIBERALISM, 1937–1940,

AND ITS POSTWAR CONSEQUENCES

FOR A PRESIDENCY premised on restoring the nation to prosperity, the collapse of its most important economic policy initiative might reasonably have signaled electoral danger. Yet the demise of the National Recovery Administration in 1935 was flanked by the extraordinary Democratic congressional victories of 1934 and Roosevelt's own landslide reelection in 1936. The economic recovery somehow overcame the drag placed on it by the NRA. Casting off the associative inclinations of its predecessor, the 74th Congress (1935–36) enacted legislation, like the National Labor Relations Act, that was so radical by American standards that it seemed to some to portend the realization of the reform liberal vision of the state. In the wake of the 1936 election, "anything seemed possible" to Roosevelt men like clothing industry unionist Sidney Hillman.[1]

Roosevelt's most avid partisans were to be bitterly disappointed. The president overinterpreted his mandate, bringing disaster on himself with his plans for reforming the Supreme Court and the executive branch. The sharp economic downturn that began in the fall of 1937 was even more disillusioning. The president's enemies, galvanized by the court fight, interpreted the "Roosevelt recession" as confirmation that the New Deal was smothering the vital sources of growth. While still mainly on the defensive, rejuvenated conservatives and erstwhile associationalists frustrated the administration's legislative program in the 75th and 76th Congresses and even began to dream of bringing back 1920s-style "normalcy."

In left-leaning circles of the administration, just the opposite interpretation took hold. Given the current configuration of economic power, the first-term strategy of raising wages and farm prices was bumping up against its limits. Reform liberals thought that the financial and corporate elite were withholding investment and sopping up purchasing power by raising prices, choking off job creation. It was the state's responsibility in this situation to assert the public interest in expanding markets, guided by expert advice. Thurman Arnold of the Justice Department applied this logic to large patent-holders, accusing them of suppressing and restricting the development and diffusion of inventions that

---

[1] Steve Fraser, *Labor Will Rule* (New York: Free Press, 1991), 375.

would lead to new industries; he employed antitrust law in order to burst open these "bottlenecks" to growth-enhancing technological innovation.

The emerging Keynesian interpretation of the recession complemented reform liberalism during the late 1930s. In this view economic difficulties were inevitable because the private sector had exhausted most of the technological avenues that could lead to growth. Government had to step into this "mature" economy, as Keynes's disciple Alvin Hansen of Harvard called it, not only by bolstering purchasing power and by regulating corporations, but also by engaging in deficit spending to finance its own investments. Hansen's and Arnold's ideas fused in the administration's plans for the economically vital housing industry. Its program of financial reform, federally funded public housing, housing technology research, and antitrust enforcement constituted an effort not just to stimulate building and sales, but to transform the industry's backward craft techniques into modern mass production.

The reform liberal-Keynesian coalition in the executive branch found it difficult to build congressional majorities behind their initiatives. Their greatest legislative successes came in the relatively restricted arena of the appropriations committee; on the floor, symbolic measures, like the establishment of the Temporary National Economic Committee, were much more likely to pass than were changes in substantive law, like patent reform. Unable to construct winning coalitions in Congress, reform liberal policy entrepreneurs sought the president's favor to make the most of authority already delegated to the executive. And, as the old guard retired from the bench, Arnold in particular sought to make science and technology policy through the courts, with some eventual success.

THURMAN ARNOLD AND THE PATENT BOTTLENECK: REFORM VISION AND LEGISLATIVE STALEMATE

Alan Brinkley has cogently shown how the reform liberal vision of the state came to the fore in the executive branch as fall turned to winter in 1937. Having rejected associationalism as a result of their experience with the NRA, the self-styled "New Dealers" took the recession as a wake-up call. Unless they acted to expand the state's economic governance capacities, they feared a future of permanent stagnation under the heavy hand of entrenched capital. The railroads, the power companies, the investment bankers, and the giant manufacturing firms had shown that they still could stifle purchasing power and that they would do so if it suited their self-interest, rather than, as the associationalists had vainly hoped, acting on behalf of the public interest.[2]

[2] Alan Brinkley, "The New Deal and the Idea of the State," in Steve Fraser and Gary Gerstle, eds., *The Rise and Fall of the New Deal Order* (Princeton: Princeton University Press, 1989), 87–89.

Reform liberals continued to express interest in mandatory dismissal compensation and other labor law reforms to combat technological unemployment, but the more pressing challenge they perceived was, as the president put it in his 1940 State of the Union message, "to face the task of finding jobs faster than inventions can take them away." For this aspect of their program the concepts of technological lag and adaptation, which had been prominent in the first term, provided little guidance. The lag theory led instead to a vision of government that was reactive at best, with little control over the pace and direction of technological innovation. *Technological Trends and National Policy* (*TTNP*), a National Resources Committee report chaired by W. F. Ogburn, the lag theory's progenitor, illustrates the point; it was a pastiche of views with no policy punchline. Although *TTNP* was published with great fanfare in July 1937, garnering no less than nine articles in the *New York Times* on the day after its release, its tepid call for each federal department to establish a branch to monitor changing technology and its social impact was ignored.[3]

Assistant Attorney General Thurman Arnold advocated a more vigorous program, in which the state would ensure that new industries based on new technologies emerged to employ those laid off as older industries were modernized. Arnold employed imaginative new tactics to mold his antitrust division into an effective tool for this purpose. He elaborated an economic and legal critique of contemporary patent practices to guide the work. He was unable, however, to push legislative patent reform through a Congress in which the conservative coalition had been energized by Roosevelt's blunders, and had to settle for symbolism rather than new legal authority.

Arnold was an expert on symbolism. Before his appointment in March 1938, the Yale law professor had characterized the Sherman Act as a "pure ritual" to appease the seething masses, an "escape valve" for reform energy. Yet Arnold demonstrated that he had a far more positive, even expansive, view of antitrust law. He saw the law not as a vehicle for a crusade against big business, but as an antirecession policy that could help to stimulate consumer demand and spread the benefits of mass production to everyone. He went out of his way to make sure his audience knew he did not think bigness in business was a "curse," as Louis Brandeis had argued. Rather, Arnold was concerned to prevent only those price controls that went beyond "efficient mass production" and "orderly marketing." As he entitled a chapter in his 1940 book, *The Bottlenecks of Business,* "The Test Is Efficiency and Service—Not Size."[4]

[3] David Lynch, *The Concentration of Economic Power* (New York: Columbia University Press, 1946), 307–10, 337, 352; "Text of President's Message," *New York Times,* January 4, 1940, 12; National Resources Committee, *Technological Trends and National Policy* (*TTNP*), (Washington: GPO, 1937), 26, viii; *New York Times,* July 18, 1937, I:1, 20, 21; IV:8; XI:6.

[4] Thurman W. Arnold, *The Folklore of Capitalism* (Garden City, NY: Blue Ribbon Books, 1937), 207, 216; Thurman W. Arnold, "What Is Monopoly?" *Vital Speeches* 4, July 1, 1938, 567–70; Thurman W. Arnold, *The Bottlenecks of Business* (New York: Reynal and Hitchcock, 1940), 116.

During Arnold's five-year tenure, his division instituted 215 investigations and 93 lawsuits, or almost as many as had been pursued in the first forty-eight years of the Sherman Act. Its budget quadrupled, to about $2 million, and its professional staff grew from about 35 to well over 200, adding economists for the first time. Arnold's tactical innovations included sophisticated public relations blitzes, industrywide investigations, criminal prosecutions, and drastically expanded settlement by consent decree. When the consumers whom he claimed to represent were silent (as they often were), Arnold was not above using what he knew to be antiquated small-town symbolism to win support from those who found the machine tax appealing. In fiscal 1942, for instance, Arnold won the division's largest budget ever, over the objections of the Bureau of the Budget, by making an end run on the Senate floor with the assistance of southern and western Senators.[5]

The heart of Arnold's effort, however, was opening, expanding, and modernizing markets. Technological innovation loomed so large in this regard that the first important systematic program that the antitrust division initiated after he took office, and in which he employed all of his new tactics, aimed at preventing the abuse of patents. For Arnold and his successor, Wendell Berge, unfreezing the status quo in production meant not only upsetting the establishment, but ensuring that the economic power that was released thereby was put to constructive use in the development of new products from which consumers could benefit. Corporate control of patents had long been a hobbyhorse of populist activists, but, impelled by the division's campaign, the issue rapidly achieved new prominence. "Interest in the American patent system," the Commerce Department reported in late 1938, "has been more widespread in the last 12 months than at any time in two generations." Even the president was induced to express concern, calling in a message on April 29, 1938, for amendment of the patent law.[6]

The patent reform effort was driven by the perception of a mismatch between economic reality and legal theory. The economic reality was that the private governance of technological innovation had been transformed since the nine-

[5] Gene Gressley, ed., *Voltaire and the Cowboy: The Letters of Thurman Arnold* (Boulder: Colorado Associated University Press, 1977), 47; Corwin Edwards, "Thurman Arnold and the Antitrust Laws," *Political Science Quarterly* 58 (1943): 340; Berge to William Ayers, April 4, 1944, Wendell Berge papers, Library of Congress (hereafter "Berge papers"), Box 28; Leo Tierney to Robert Jackson, February 23, 1938, Berge papers, Box 23; *Congressional Record,* 77th C., 1st s., May 19, 1941, 4186–4204; *Annual Report of the Attorney General for Fiscal Year 1938* (Washington: GPO, 1938), 59–60. Gressley supplies the best general introduction to Arnold; see also Alan Brinkley, "The Antimonopoly Ideal and the Liberal State: The Case of Thurman Arnold," *Journal of American History* 80 (1993): 557–79.

[6] *Annual Report of the Secretary of Commerce* (for fiscal year 1938), cited in *Verbatim Record of the Proceedings of the Temporary National Economic Committee* (Washington: BNA, 1940), (hereafter "TNEC Transcripts") vol. 1, Reference Data Section I, January 5, 1939, 12; U.S. President, "Strengthening and Enforcement of Antitrust Laws," 75th C., 3d s., 1938, S. doc. 173, 9.

teenth century. No longer the province of the fabled inventor in the garret, industrial research and development had systematized innovation and brought it under the aegis of the giant corporation. A Works Progress Administration (WPA) study published in 1940 found that half of all industrial research personnel were hired by forty-five companies and that the thirteen biggest research employers accounted for a third. "The whole [R&D] complex creates an economy quite different from the individualistic enterprise system of which textbooks still speak; it is becoming a planned economy—at least on the technical side," wrote reformer David Lynch. A few corporate executives, Lynch concluded, could exert disproportionate and malevolent control over the nation's development.[7]

Firms exercised this control, the critique continued, not merely by directing large-scale R&D spending, but by using the patent law to choke off alternative competing possibilities. The legal theory of the patent held that it was a temporary monopoly that induced individuals to invent useful things and disseminate know-how about them by publishing the patent claim. Large patent-holders, however, had devised ways to expand the scope and extend the length of this state-sanctioned monopoly. The government, the legal critic Mortimer Feuer argued, had passively accepted for too long the fiction that the patent was a limited property right when it was in fact "the greatest single monopolistic device."[8] The critics asserted a public responsibility to ensure technological dynamism (and its economic benefits) when private patent practices subverted it.

The most egregious practice of which big firms were accused was the suppression of their own useful inventions that they feared would cut into the profits yielded by their established products. Although the Supreme Court had sanctioned the right of a patent-holder *not* to make or permit use of a patented invention in 1908, representatives of business vehemently denied that they engaged in this practice. AT&T, for instance, which held about 9,500 patents in 1938, came under investigation for suppression by the House Patent Committee and the new Federal Communications Commission in the mid-1930s, prompting violent denunciations by Bell Telephone Laboratories president Frank Jewett.[9]

---

[7] George Perazich and Philip M. Field, *Industrial Research and Changing Technology* (Philadelphia: Works Progress Administration, 1940), v, 14, 17, 49–50; Lynch (above, n. 3), 108. Perazich and Field's figures were widely cited. David Mowery has argued more recently that the concentration was less than the WPA found; David C. Mowery, "The Relationship between Intrafirm and Contractual Forms of Industrial Research in American Manufacturing, 1900–1940," *Explorations in Economic History* 20 (1983): 370.

[8] Mortimer Feuer, "The Patent Monopoly and the Anti-Trust Laws," *Columbia Law Review* 38 (1938): 1145–46.

[9] Feuer (above, n. 8), 1147–51; Jewett to Senator Joseph O'Mahoney, January 24, 1939, RG144, Box 93, "Executive Committee—Resolutions"; Jewett to Charles E. Wilson, September 13, 1937, NAS Archives, SAB Series, Agencies and Departments, "National Resources Committee, Committee on Study of Problems in Field of Technology, 1936–1937."

A somewhat less offensive but far more widespread practice was the restrictive patent license. Patent-holders regularly restricted the geographical territory in which their licensees could sell products, limited the field of business in which a patented item could be used, dictated the pricing policies of licensees, and set production quotas related to the use of the patent. While the jurisprudence was more ambiguous in these cases than in suppression, the Supreme Court had gone so far in 1926 as to uphold license provisions that fixed the final sale price and method of sale of an unpatented item that had been made by using the licensed patent. General Electric, the beneficiary of this ruling, was a favorite target of patent reformers. It held a controlling patent position in the electric lighting field and, despite numerous legal challenges from competitors, used this power to retard the diffusion of fluorescent lighting in the 1920s and 1930s. GE generated half of its profits in the 1920s by selling incandescent lighting and still controlled 87 percent of the lighting market in 1939.[10]

Suppression and restrictive licensing, it was alleged, were supplemented by a wide range of practices that utilized the deep pockets and legal firepower that large firms could draw upon. Patent reformers put forward an array of remedies to these ills, from the provision of legal and financial assistance to small litigants to the imposition of penalties for filing intimidating lawsuits. Above all, they sought to give the federal government the power to compel patent licensing. With compulsory licensing (including the power to deny royalties), they argued, an agency or the courts would have the leverage to channel business practice toward lower prices, higher production, and faster innovation, expanding the economy and satisfying consumers. But despite public interest in the "patent question," Congress did next to nothing about it, continuing the long frustration of reform legislation in this policy area. The House Patent Committee, as Representative Charles Kramer (who soon became the committee's chair) contemptuously said in 1938, awoke from its "Rip van Winkle" sleep every ten years or so, came "out of the hills and got a shave and a haircut and then go [sic] back." A 1935 committee investigation into aviation, radio, and telephony ended in disarray. Even the far less critical and more modest proposals of a Science Advisory Board (SAB) committee chaired by MIT's Vannevar Bush in that same year left no legislative trace. Representative W. D. McFarlane's 1938 compulsory licensing bill, which *Business Week* intimated had been authored

[10] Feuer (above, n. 8); Walton Hamilton, *Patents and Free Enterprise,* TNEC monograph no. 31, 76th C., 3rd s., 1941, 80–82; Arthur A. Bright, Jr., and W. Rupert MacLaurin, "Economic Factors Influencing the Development and Introduction of the Fluorescent Lamp," *Journal of Political Economy* 51 (1943): 429–50; Leonard S. Reich, "Lighting the Path to Profit: GE's Control of the Electric Lamp Industry, 1892–1941," *Business History Review* 66 (1992): 305–34. Mark Clark has shown that suppression did occur, at least in AT&T; the Bell system suppressed the magnetic tape recorder in order to maintain customers' trust that they could discuss immoral topics on the phone without fear. Mark Clark, "Suppressing Innovation: Bell Laboratories and Magnetic Recording," *Technology and Culture* 34 (1993): 515–38.

by the Justice Department, shared the same fate, after a pathetic hearing in which witness after witness opposed the bill.[11]

The McFarlane fiasco prompted the administration to give up on the bill and focus on bringing the patent issue into the proceedings of the Temporary National Economic Committee (TNEC). The TNEC was a peculiar body, composed of three members from each house of Congress and the heads of six executive agencies, with a mandate to investigate the president's claim in the April 29 message that private power was "seriously impairing" prosperity in the United States. Its first hearings, in December 1938, took up the patent question, relying on materials turned up by Arnold's investigations. TNEC staff, on loan from the antitrust division, contrasted the beneficial patent system of the automobile industry with the abuses of the glass industry. The technological dynamism of autos was seen to have been sparked by Henry Ford's unwillingness to go along with a rigid patent pool organized by the Automobile Manufacturers' Association. In the glass container industry, however, the TNEC found an "AAA in milk bottles," according to its chairman, Senator Joseph O'Mahoney. Patent contracts controlled by the Hartford-Empire and Owens-Illinois companies guaranteed prices, restricted production, and stifled innovation.[12]

These hearings, pressing the reform liberal view that vigilant oversight and active intervention by the state were needed to ensure the adequate progress of industrial innovation, were immediately followed by hearings that advanced the SAB's view that the patent system was fundamentally sound and needed, at most, modest tinkering. The second set of TNEC hearings was organized by the Commerce Department and featured Commerce officials like Commissioner of Patents Conway Coe (who was said to be "hopping mad" at Arnold), prominent patent attorneys, and corporate research directors. The witnesses roundly denounced compulsory licensing as an infringement of property rights and a deterrent to innovation, endorsing Bush's statement that the patent system was "decidedly a democratic affair."[13]

---

[11] U.S. House of Representatives, Committee on Patents, *Compulsory Licensing of Patents,* 75th C., 3d s., 1938, 248; U.S. House of Representatives, Committee on Patents, *Pooling of Patents,* 74th C., 1st s., 1935; "Storm over Patent Pools," *Business Week,* October 26, 1935, 30–31; Compton to Daniel Roper (Secretary of Commerce), February 5, 1935, and press release, December 6, 1935, both in NAS Archives, Executive Board, Science Advisory Board, Committee on Relation of Patent System, "1934–1935;" *TNEC Transcripts,* vol. 1, 458–63; "Patent Reform," *Business Week,* March 5, 1938, 38–39.

[12] Representative W. D. McFarlane to Roosevelt, February 16, 1938, Franklin D. Roosevelt papers, FDRL (hereafter "Roosevelt papers"), OF 808, "1937–1939"; U.S. President (above, n. 6); *TNEC Transcripts,* vol. 1, 121–404; "Scene I: Edsel Ford and Knudsen," *Business Week,* December 3, 1939, 12–13; "Patent Probe Begins Mildly—But," *Business Week,* December 10, 1939, 14–15; "'Pay Dirt' in Glass Containers," *Business Week,* December 17, 1939, 14–15.

[13] *TNEC Transcripts,* vol. 1, 405–540, quote from 438; "What Changes in Patent System?" *Business Week,* January 28, 1939, 17–18.

TNEC's equivocations strengthened the conservative position of key Members of Congress and of disillusioned associationalists in the business and scientific establishment. A "Modern Pioneers" dinner, for example, mounted by the joint committee of the National Association of Manufacturers and the American Institute of Physics to celebrate the 150th anniversary of the patent law in 1940, was the venue for attacks on Thurman Arnold and "certain sinister, subversive groups." A patent, the dinner speakers agreed, recalling the old Republican rhetoric, was the homestead of the modern pioneer, from which no state should have the power to sunder him. House Patent Committee Chairman Kramer appointed an advisory committee controlled by opponents of legislative patent reform, which duly reported back do-nothing proposals. Despite the lobbying of Harry Hopkins, the new Secretary of Commerce, the House refused to pass anything besides technical modifications of Patent Office procedures. As the *New York Times* editorialized, these changes "hardly touch[ed] the larger issues raised by industrial research, invention, and business methods."[14]

The "magnificent failure" of the TNEC, as *Business Week* labeled it, came as no surprise to Arnold. The committee's unusual structure guaranteed that disagreements within and between the executive and legislative branches would be reproduced within it. As Arnold wrote, "Any proposed amendment [to the antitrust law] is caught between the extreme trust busters and the extreme appeasers, and nothing ever happens. This has been true for forty years and will continue to be true. Amendments will follow enforcement and not precede it." While the antitrust division supplemented its budget through the TNEC's appropriations and used TNEC hearings as a platform for publicity, Arnold discounted the toothless committee as a vehicle for substantive policy change. Instead, Arnold turned to case law, believing that a judiciary made over by Roosevelt appointments would be more sympathetic to the reform liberal critique of the patent system than Congress.[15]

SECOND BEST SUCCESS: THE ANTITRUST DIVISION
AND PATENT JURISPRUDENCE

"Will wonders never cease!" remarked Attorney General Homer Cummings to the president in conveying a favorable lower-court ruling in an antitrust case against Alcoa in late 1937. *Alcoa*'s progress through the courts epitomizes the

[14] "Twentieth Century Pioneers," *Business Week,* March 2, 1940, 20; *United States Patent Law Sesquicentennial Celebration, April 10, 1940* (Washington: GPO, 1940); "Report of the National Advisory Council to the Patents Committee of the House," *Congressional Record,* 76th C., 3d s., April 1, 1940, A2205-A2207; Hopkins to President of Senate, June 3, 1939, RG40, Office of the Secretary, General Correspondence, Box 567, File 83191/27; "Five Patent Bills," *New York Times,* August 11, 1939, 14.

[15] "TNEC—Magnificent Failure," *Business Week,* March 22, 1941, 22–31; Arnold to William Chenery, May 5, 1939, in Gressley, ed. (above, n. 5), 284.

slow triumph of Arnold and, after him, Berge. Filed with a flourish in the late 1930s, the case was set aside for national security purposes after Pearl Harbor. Reopened as the war came to a close, *Alcoa* provided the New Deal antitrust division's crowning moment in 1945, when Judge Learned Hand used the case to establish a more lenient standard for proving antitrust violations and oversaw the diffusion of the firm's formidable technological capabilities to its new competitors. The *Alcoa* precedent defined a hidden legacy of reform liberals in the postwar period, the legal shaping of corporate R&D decision-making.[16]

The influential monograph *Patents and Free Enterprise,* prepared for the TNEC by Walton Hamilton, Arnold's former colleague at Yale, best summarized the state of the law that stimulated optimism among patent reformers. Hamilton argued that two conflicting lines of patent law decisions were available to judges. One, developed by the conservative courts of the Republican era, conceived of patents merely as property and provided for full freedom of contract. This approach, Hamilton contended, had caused the patent system to stray "far from its constitutional purpose" of promoting "the progress of Science and useful Arts." The patent system under this doctrine "not only delays novelties and arrests the rate of advance, but it may . . . create a situation hostile to new ideas and throw a barrier across the development of a technology." The alternative approach asserted the constitutional purpose as a public interest that permitted the limitation of property rights. In these cases judges had taken the initiative to determine whether patent-holders had adequately promoted technological innovation, and judged them by this standard.[17]

Ethyl Gasoline, a 1938 decision that enjoined DuPont, General Motors, and Standard Oil of New Jersey from employing important restrictive licensing practices, followed this second line of opinions. Sensing an opportunity to build legal momentum, Arnold used the $155,000 that flowed to him from the TNEC to develop new cases that drew on *Ethyl.* Rather than filing them one at a time, Arnold chose to build up evidence in a whole group of cases, in order to create both a symbol and a stronger legal foundation for his policy. His first target was glassmaker Hartford-Empire, which had been cast as the villain at the TNEC hearings in December 1938. A series of highly publicized suits, Arnold hoped, would raise employment, lower prices, and result in more rapid technological advance by encouraging firms throughout the economy to change their standard operating procedures.[18]

[16] Attorney General Homer Cummings to Roosevelt, December 6, 1937, Roosevelt papers, PSF, Box 56, "Cummings, 1937"; Richard Caves, *American Industry: Structure, Conduct, Performance,* 5th ed. (Englewood Cliffs: Prentice-Hall, 1982), 94–111.

[17] Hamilton, (above, n. 10), 142, 60, 163.

[18] Cummings to Roosevelt, February 10, 1938, Roosevelt papers, OF 277, "1938"; "Pyrrhic Victory Over Ethyl," *Business Week,* June 10, 1939, 8; "Nine against Ethyl," *Business Week,* March 30, 1940, 17; TNEC, "Public Hearings on Patents," undated, RG144, Box 93, "Indirect Results of TNEC"; Luther A. Huston, "Trust Suit Names Glassware Group," *New York Times,* December 11, 1939, 17; "Patent Battles Begin," *Business Week,* December 16, 1939, 18–20.

Hartford-Empire, filed at the end of 1939, was followed by the institution of eleven more patent cases in the next fifteen months. Justice, for example, filed a complaint alleging that the Pullman Company had prevented the railroads from using "modern, lightweight, streamlined cars manufactured by competing companies." Arnold appealed to the House Appropriations Committee to expand his fiscal year 1941 budget (taking up the slack left by the end of the TNEC) so that he could accelerate the pace of the patent investigation. "1941," wrote *Business Week,* "will be known to antitrust students as the patent year." In August of that year, the first court-overseen settlement compelling a patent-holder to issue a license was reached.[19]

The year 1941, however, was to be more famous for other reasons, in antitrust policy as well as in American politics generally. The defense mobilization had begun to take over the economy in late 1940, and, in 1941, perhaps 10 percent of the GNP was devoted to direct federal military spending, up from about 3 percent in the previous year. From the beginning, military procurement was concentrated on the nation's largest and most technologically advanced firms, such as Standard Oil of New Jersey, DuPont, Alcoa, and General Electric, the same firms that figured prominently on the antitrust division's hit list. Conflict between the mobilization authorities and the Justice Department was inevitable, and in 1941 it became acute. Patents topped the bill in this fight. Arnold pressed the case for continued strict antitrust enforcement, even under conditions of military emergency, by alleging that monopoly power stifled production and innovation in the military as well as the civilian sector and thereby raised both government and consumer costs. The war, he argued, was between industries and economic systems, not just armies. Unless vigilant antitrust authorities prevented "economic sabotage," the defense effort would be for naught. Beyond making the mobilization more effective and cost-efficient, antitrust enforcement would help maintain the semblance of a market system under war conditions that tended to preempt markets. Arnold saw his effort to be a keystone of the "middle way" between controls and the free market economy, which was, after all, among the liberties for which the war was being fought.[20]

Arnold sought to seize the high ground on national security as early as 1939

[19] "Strategy of the Patent Battle," *Business Week,* March 29, 1941, 25; press release, Department of Justice, July 12, 1940, RG144, Box 92, "Department of Justice—General"; U.S. House of Representatives, Committee on Appropriations, *Department of Justice Appropriation Bill for 1941,* 76th C., 3d s., 1940, 309–11; *U.S. v. Kearney and Trecker,* August 22, 1941, cited in U.S. Senate, Judiciary Committee, Subcommittee on Patents, Trademarks, and Copyrights, *Compulsory Patent Licensing under Antitrust Judgments,* 86th C., 2d s., 1960, 55.

[20] Thurman Arnold, "Monopolies Have Hobbled Defense," *Reader's Digest,* July 1941, 51–55; Arnold, "Defense and Restraints of Trade," *The New Republic,* May 19, 1941, 687; Arnold, speech to Illinois Association of Real Estate Boards, September 20, 1940, RG144, Box 92, "Department of Justice—Thurman Arnold," 1–3; Arnold, "War Monopolies," *The New Republic,* October 14, 1940.

by investigating such industries as beryllium, magnesium, aluminum, tungsten carbide, synthetic rubber, and military optical goods. He was particularly keen to demonstrate that collusion between German and American firms damaged the nation's technological base. In some cases, antitrust investigators claimed, patent deals led American firms to forswear the development of technologies that the Germans ultimately put to military use. In others, American firms gave away "vital secrets," as Senate Patent Committee chairman Homer Bone put it, to induce German firms to reach cartel agreements. In the case of military optics, for example, Arnold argued that the German firm Zeiss used the "patent weapon" to extract excessive profits from the navy in the sale of rangefinders for cruisers. The American supplier, Bausch and Lomb (whose president chaired the NAM-AIP committee on scientific research founded by Karl Compton), had agreed to Zeiss's conditions to boost its own profits; because of market-splitting arrangements among American optical firms, there was no alternative source for the equipment. Threatened with public exposure of the case, Bausch and Lomb agreed in July 1940 to a consent degree providing for royalty-free licenses for war production and "reasonable" royalties thereafter. Similar settlements were reached in other cases.[21]

Although these investigations convinced some of Arnold's conservative opponents that patent rights ought to be abridged because national security was at stake, they provoked powerful new opposition from the military services and war mobilization agencies. In April 1941 Attorney General Robert Jackson was forced to grant what amounted to a blanket exemption from the antitrust laws for defense contractors. Once the United States actually entered the war, the infighting over antitrust policy escalated into what assistant budget director Wayne Coy called "one of the most bitter scraps I have seen in the Government for some time." Complaints from the service secretaries ("Mr. Hitler himself could hardly have chosen a surer way to embarrass our munitions production today," said Secretary of War Henry Stimson) forced FDR to call in his troubleshooter, Judge Samuel Rosenman, to resolve the dispute. Rosenman brokered a memorandum of understanding on March 20, 1942, that gave the mobilization authorities the power to go beyond the exemption and postpone antitrust suits filed before the war.[22]

---

[21] "Strategy of the Patent Battle," *Business Week,* March 29, 1941, 25–29; U.S. Senate, Committee on Patents, *Patents,* 77th C., 2d s., 1942, 3; Arnold to Jackson, May 18, 1940, in Gressley, ed. (above, n. 5), 305–6; Elliott H. Moyer to Wendell Berge, April 22, 1947, Berge papers, Box 43; "Folklore of Magnesium," *Time,* February 10, 1941, 64–66.

[22] Commissioner of Patents to Secretary of Commerce, February 4, 1941, RG40, Office of the Secretary, Box 565, File 83191/5; "Patents and Defense," *New York Times,* August 10, 1940, 12; Robert Jackson to John L. O'Brian, April 29, 1941, attached as Appendix C in Moyer to Berge, April 22, 1947; and Biddle to O'Brian, October 4, 1941, both in Berge Papers, Box 43; Arnold to Jackson, September 9, 1942, in Gressley, ed., (above, n. 5), 330–34; Coy to Grace Tully, March 5, 1942; Stimson to Roosevelt, March 4, 1942; Biddle to Rosenman, March 7, 1942; "Anti-Trust Procedure Memorandum," undated (probably March 20, 1942); Rosenman to Roosevelt, March 27,

Arnold's loss in this conflict led him to turn to Congress not for legislative action but for publicity. Working with committees chaired by Senators Harry Truman, Homer Bone, and Harley Kilgore, Arnold made the term *cartel* notorious through investigations of the metals, drugs, chemicals, and electrical equipment industries. Jersey Standard came in for particularly rough treatment for its handling of synthetic rubber patents and its dealings with the German trust I.G. Farben. Although they did little to alter military contracting practices, these charges contributed to public support for harsh measures taken against German firms, notably the seizure of all enemy patents by the Alien Property Custodian (APC) in April 1942, which made the federal government the nation's largest patent-holder. An APC study published after the war found that 75 percent of the patent contracts it took over contained some restrictive licensing provisions.[23]

Although its most celebrated cases were postponed because of military opposition, the antitrust division persisted in litigating cases that were judged by the mobilization authorities not to disrupt essential war production. In *Morton Salt* (1942), *Univis* (1942), *Masonite* (1942), and *Mercoid* (1944), Justice Department lawyers convinced the Supreme Court to chip away at patentees' supposed right of free contract. Supplementing *Ethyl,* these decisions established that patent-holders could not force licensees to set prices under most circumstances nor could they force licensees to purchase unpatented products as a condition of their use of the patented product. Led by the solid bloc of Roosevelt-appointed Justices William Douglas, Frank Murphy, and Hugo Black, Court majorities began to accept that, in Douglas's words: "It is the public interest which is dominant in the patent system. . . . The patent is a privilege."[24]

The price of what critics called "Thurman Arnoldism" was Arnold's being kicked upstairs, to a judgeship on the Circuit Court of Appeals for the District of Columbia in January 1943. Wendell Berge, however, proved to be a worthy successor at the helm of the antitrust division, perhaps more effective under the circumstances for being less flamboyant than Arnold. In November 1943, with the support of Vice-President Henry Wallace, Attorney General Francis Biddle, and Senator Kilgore, Berge began reopening postponed cases. His most dan-

1942; all in Rosenman papers, FDRL, "Anti-Trust"; Rosenman to Roosevelt, March 14, 1942, OF 277, FDRL, "1939–1943." The memorandum of understanding is reprinted in *Annual Report of the Attorney General for Fiscal Year, 1942,* mimeo in Littauer Library, Harvard University, 9–10.

[23] Moyer to Berge, April 22, 1947, Berge papers, Box 43; Fritz Machlup, "The Nature of the International Cartel Problem," in Corwin Edwards et al., *A Cartel Policy for the United Nations* (New York: Columbia University Press, 1945), 1, 11; Senate Patent Committee (above, n. 21); U.S. Senate, Committee on Military Affairs, *Scientific and Technological Mobilization,* 78th C., 1st and 2d s., 1943–44.

[24] Bureau of National Affairs (BNA), *Patents and the Antitrust Law: Analyses from BNA's Antitrust Trade Regulation Report* (Washington: BNA, 1966), 6, 22; Frank P. Huddle, "Patent Reform," *Editorial Research Reports,* May 25, 1945, 393–94; Arthur M. Smith, "Recent Developments in Patent Law," *Michigan Law Review* 44 (1946): 917–22.

gerous move was the investigation of General Electric, whose president, Charles E. Wilson, was running the War Production Board and vigorously opposed Berge. In August 1944 the president decided that the investigation should move forward; the smell of victory in the war, the looming election, the need to placate supporters of the recently dumped Wallace, and the long-run national security argument against international cartels combined to sway Roosevelt's choice.[25]

The antitrust offensive culminated in a series of important patent decisions in the late 1940s. *Alcoa* (1945), the overarching precedent that shifted the basis of all antitrust judgments from intent to actual market share, was closely linked to the disposition of the government's huge holdings of aluminum plants built and operated by Alcoa during the war. After negotiations in which the Attorney General, the courts, and antitrust activists in the Senate were deeply involved, Alcoa agreed to part with some of these plants and to license its key patents without a royalty. *Hartford-Empire* (1945) and *National Lead* (1947) established the principle of compulsory licensing as a remedy for antitrust violations. Although the Court did not sanction royalty-free compulsory licensing, this harsh remedy was nonetheless imposed by some judges relying on these precedents. Other cases prohibited exclusive patent pools that led to price and market restrictions. By and large, the broad interpretations of *General Electric* (1926) and *Standard Oil* (1931) that sanctioned restrictive licenses and patent pools were reversed by the end of the 1940s.[26]

The pursuit of the reform liberal vision in patent policy thus ended with a judicial bang and a congressional whimper. The bang was a dramatic change in the jurisprudence relating the antitrust and patent laws. The prominent attorney Gilbert Montague, in an adulatory letter to Wendell Berge, called it a revolution, one of the two great legal victories of the New Deal (the other being the regulatory precedent set by the National Labor Relations Board). Compulsory licensing became accepted as "one of the most common forms of relief in antitrust cases," according to a 1960 study by the Senate Judiciary Committee.

[25] Alfred Jones, memo, June 18, 1942, enclosed in Jones to Wallace, May 8, 1945, RG40, Office of the Secretary, General Correspondence, Box 567, File 83191/5, 4; Arnold to Roosevelt, January 16, 1943, Roosevelt papers, OF 51s; Berge to section heads, November 8, 1943, Berge papers, Box 27; Wallace diary entry for August 11, 1943, in John Morton Blum, ed., *The Price of Vision: The Diary of Henry A. Wallace, 1942–1946* (Boston: Houghton Mifflin, 1973), 234; Senate Military Affairs Committee (above, n. 23); Berge to Biddle, March 30, 1944, Berge papers, Box 28; "Wendell Berge: Anti-Trust Chief," *Tide,* April 1, 1944, in Berge papers, Box 43, "Wendell Berge."

[26] Harold Stein, "Disposal Of The Aluminum Plants," in Stein, ed., *Public Administration and Policy Development* (New York: Harcourt, Brace & World, 1952), 313–63; Margaret B. W. Graham and Bettye H. Pruitt, *R&D for Industry: A Century of Technical Innovation at Alcoa* (New York: Cambridge University Press, 1990), 239–71; BNA 1966 (above, n. 24), 5–9, 26–34; Simon N. Whitney, *Antitrust Policies: American Experience in Twenty Industries* (New York: Twentieth Century Fund, 1958), 400–401.

The committee counted 107 such judgments involving about 40,000 to 50,000 patents (out of a total of about 600,000) between 1941 and 1959. Among the technologies covered were semiconductors (AT&T), computers (IBM), and nylon (Dupont).[27]

More importantly, the revolution in patent and antitrust law seems to have had a wide impact on business practices without diminishing overall business investment in R&D. For example, a detailed history of Dupont has shown that, beyond complying with court judgments, the company changed its technology strategy to rely more heavily on its own R&D. The company's leaders recognized that the prewar practice of acquiring small competitors was less viable in the new, tougher antitrust environment. Similarly, U. S. business used restrictive patent pools, the *Antitrust and Trade Regulation Reporter* said in 1966, "relatively infrequently . . . or with great circumspection," and they no longer posed a serious enforcement problem. These new practices, then, created space to grow for innovative small companies that might have been snatched up by giants before the war, while at the same time they contributed to the growth of central corporate research laboratories. The weakening of patent protection for large firms in the postwar period may also have contributed to the relative decline in the importance of patents and the corresponding rise in reliance on tacit knowhow and other mechanisms for appropriating the gains from investments in technological innovation. The changes in patent policy brought about by the entrepreneurship of Arnold and Berge thus contributed to both the distinctive strengths and the distinctive weaknesses of the U.S. national innovation system in the postwar period, even though they fall outside the "postwar consensus."[28]

Obviously these changes occurred far too late to have an impact on the recession of 1937–38. As a short-term economic policy, the reach of antitrust enforcement was quite limited, as its enthusiasts reluctantly recognized. The fiscal jolt of expanded government spending was a much more powerful pick-me-up. Wartime federal budgets proved to be the ultimate stimulant, of course. Yet, before the war, Keynesian entrepreneurs were already building momentum, allying in those peaceful days with "Thurman Arnoldism."

ASSAULTING THE HOUSING TECHNOLOGY BLOCKADE: REFORM LIBERALISM MEETS KEYNESIANISM

"Keynesianism" is a term of convenience, rather than a precise designation; the "Keynesian" causal story, that economic downturns stemmed from a shortage of purchasing power, predates John Maynard Keynes's *General Theory*. The

[27] Montague to Berge, January 10, 1944, Berge papers, Box 27; Senate Judiciary Committee (above, n. 19), 1, 5; David C. Mowery and Nathan Rosenberg, "The U.S. National Innovation System, in Richard R. Nelson, ed., *National Innovation Systems* (New York: Oxford University Press, 1993), 39–40.

[28] F. M. Scherer, "Antitrust, Efficiency, and Progress," *New York University Law Review* 62

National Industrial Recovery Act of 1933, as we have seen, was intended (by some of its supporters at least) to raise wages for precisely this reason. Keynes's work codified this analysis, amplified its intellectual appeal immensely, and identified new policy instruments. Keynes divided aggregate demand (as he termed purchasing power) into consumption, investment, and government spending, and he attributed the lion's share of the blame for the depression to a lack of investment. Low expectations of future sales, a preference for liquidity, risk aversion, and "animal spirits," among other factors, caused the shortfall in this component of aggregate demand. It was the state's responsibility to compensate for it.[29]

Keynes did not investigate deeply the microeconomic mechanisms by which compensatory government action to boost demand would be converted into economic growth. As Joseph Schumpeter put it (with characteristic hyperbole) in his memorial to Keynes: "All the phenomena incident to the creation and change in apparatus [of production in Keynes's model], that is to say, the phenomena that dominate the capitalist process, are thus excluded from consideration." Many Americans who took up the Keynesian cause, however, took more interest in these mechanisms than the master did; some identified technological innovation as a vital link between deficit spending and economic growth. Alvin Hansen, for example, a Harvard economist who trained the first wave of American Keynesians, argued in his presidential address to the American Economic Association in 1938 that two of the three ultimate sources of economic growth, population growth and territorial expansion, had been exhausted, leaving the third, technological innovation, to bear the burden, much as Schumpeter, his Harvard colleague, thought. Parting company with Schumpeter, however, and taking his cue from Keynes, Hansen viewed private enterprise as incapable of creating the innovations that would fuel new growth industries. Instead, entrenched monopoly power was restricting new product innovation while advancing labor and capital-saving process innovation. Keynesian compensatory spending had therefore to serve the role of creating new investment opportunities, particularly technological opportunities, as well as expanding consumer

(1987): 998–1019; Richard Levin, "The Semiconductor Industry," in Richard R. Nelson, ed., *Government and Technical Progress* (New York: Pergamon, 1982), 75–79; David Hounshell and John K. Smith, *Science and Corporate Strategy: DuPont R&D, 1902–1980* (New York: Cambridge University Press, 1990), 246–49; BNA 1966 (above, n. 24), 29; Mowery and Rosenberg (above, n. 27), 50–52; Margaret Graham, "Industrial Research in the Age of Big Science," *Research on Technological Innovation, Management, and Policy* 2 (1985): 47–79.

[29] Bradford Lee, "The Miscarriage of Necessity and Invention: Proto-Keynesianism and Democratic States in the 1930s," in Peter A. Hall, ed., *The Political Power of Economic Ideas: Keynesianism Across Nations* (Princeton: Princeton University Press, 1989), 129–70; J. M. Keynes, *The General Theory of Employment, Interest, and Money,* Harvest/HBJ edition (San Diego: Harcourt, Brace, and Jovanovich, 1964); J. M. Keynes, "Some Consequences of a Declining Population," in Donald Moggridge, ed., *The Collected Writings of John Maynard Keynes,* vol. 14 (London: MacMillan, 1973), 124–33.

demand. In addition to becoming a welfare state, Hansen claimed, "the government is becoming an investment banker." Hansen's view that, absent aggressive state action, the "mature" economy was destined for "secular stagnation" resonated with his students, many of whom departed Cambridge, Mass., for Washington, D.C., upon completing their degrees.[30]

Hansen and his followers identified a number of opportunities for federal investments, including the electrical technologies being developed by government agencies like the Tennessee Valley Authority, the Electric Home and Farm Authority, and the Rural Electrification Administration. But they held out particular hope for housing. They believed (with Schumpeter and Ogburn, among others) that the prefabricated house was likely to be one of the most socially and economically significant inventions of the coming decades. According to Peter J. Stone and R. Harold Denton, whom the TNEC commissioned to review housing policy, "The construction industry affords the largest single unexploited outlet for investment funds—outlets which are so necessary to maintain a proper balance in our economic system." Without even taking into consideration its value as social reform, there could be no more important way in which the ideal Keynesian state could spend the taxpayers'—and borrowed—money than on housing investment.[31]

The 1937–38 recession catapulted the Keynesian analysis to the attention of the highest policy-makers. Changes in taxing and spending, claimed Keynesians like Marriner Eccles of the Federal Reserve and White House advisor Lauchlin Currie, had precipitated the downturn, and an aggressive spending and lending program was required to end it. Although "splending" foundered in Congress, the administration was nonetheless able to take a number of stimulative fiscal and monetary steps, including pushing down mortgage interest rates and creating a secondary mortgage market. These measures capped a series of policy innovations, dating back to the Hoover administration, that greatly expanded federal control of housing finance costs. Yet the housing market rebounded far more weakly in the late 1930s than did the economy as a whole. In 1937 only 300,000 units of housing were built; in 1938, only 350,000; and in 1939, only 450,000—still less than half the peak year of 1925. Less than a million people were employed in the entire construction industry, compared to an average of nearly 2 million in the 1920s. The failure of housing policy

[30] Joseph A. Schumpeter, "John Maynard Keynes, 1883–1946," *American Economic Review* 36 (1946): 512; Alvin H. Hansen, "Economic Progress and Declining Population Growth," *American Economic Review* 29 (1939): 1–15. Hansen, *Full Recovery or Stagnation?* (New York: Norton, 1938), 318; Richard V. Gilbert et al., *An Economic Program for American Democracy* (New York: Vanguard, 1938).

[31] Joseph A. Schumpeter, *Capitalism, Socialism, and Democracy* (1942; rpt. New York: Harper Colophon edition, 1975), 68; *TTNP,* (above, n. 3), viii; Peter J. Stone and R. Harold Denton, *Toward More Housing,* TNEC monograph no. 8, 76th C., 3d s., 1940, xv.

was graphically depicted by the first Census of Housing, made in 1940: 49 percent of the national housing stock was structurally substandard or lacked a private bath.[32]

The failure of private investment in housing to respond to financial reform and interest rate cuts prompted vigorous policy entrepreneurship aimed not merely at injecting liquidity into this vital sector, but at bringing about a mass production revolution in residential construction. The business was dominated by archaic, handwork practices and held together by men whose crudeness was matched only by their venality. These practices kept costs high, meaning, according to one report, that there were "no new dwellings at all for families in the lower third income group, and very few for families in the middle third." Without mass production, there could be no mass market. Yet the industry's technological backwardness was protected by market-sharing and price-fixing agreements among firms and unions as well as by simple coercion, and these protections were buttressed by custom and often enshrined in law. Local building codes, for instance, required the use of techniques and materials that perpetuated established arrangements.[33]

The way to burst the housing "blockade," argued Miles Colean of the Federal Housing Administration (FHA), the most articulate and authoritative commentator on this issue, was for the federal government to attack all of the barriers simultaneously. In addition to more expansive federal housing finance policies, Colean called for public procurement of housing on a large scale to serve as a testbed for mass production. Local authorities would have to be overseen so that federal funds for public housing were not simply siphoned off by inefficient small-time builders. Colean also advocated a massive expansion of federal housing R&D, to provide the science and technology on which mass production would be based. And he endorsed aggressive antitrust enforcement in the construction industry, too. The monopolies of materials manufacturers, collusion among distributors, and featherbedding of contractors and unions all deserved to be challenged by the Justice Department's crusaders. By taking these steps, in Colean's view, the state would provide the powerful central force that the housing industry lacked. The history of U.S. housing showed that mar-

[32] Herbert Stein, *The Fiscal Revolution in America,* rev. ed. (Washington: American Enterprise Institute, 1990), 115–23; Jordan A. Schwarz, *The New Dealers: Power Politics in the Age of Roosevelt* (New York: Knopf, 1993), 85–86; Fraser (above, n. 1), 409–10; Nathaniel S. Keith, *Politics and the Housing Crisis since 1930* (New York: Universe Books, 1973), 17–29; National Resources Planning Board, *Housing: The Continuing Problem* (Washington: NRPB, June 1940), 32; Robert Lasch, *Breaking the Building Blockade* (Chicago: University of Chicago Press, 1946), 284; *TNEC Transcripts,* vol. 4, 346–48.

[33] Charles E. Noyes, "Restraints of Trade in the Building Industry," *Editorial Research Reports,* April 23, 1940, 311–28; NRPB (above, n. 32), 8–22; *TNEC Transcripts,* vol. 4, 457–98; Corwin Edwards, "The New Antitrust Procedures as Illustrated in the Construction Industry," *Public Policy* 2 (1941): 325–26; "The Month in Building," *Architectural Forum* (October 1939) 50.

ket forces alone would not produce a Henry Ford who would be able to appropriate benefits for himself *and* serve a mass public by seeing the house as a system that could be designed and assembled with the average family in mind. In
the absence of strong policies, the individual buyer would continue to be at the
mercy of predatory manufacturers, distributors, builders, and unions against
which he could exercise little bargaining power. Colean hoped that operative
(large-scale) builders and prefabricated housing manufacturers would eventually capitalize on the investment opportunities that the federal program would
create and make it obsolete. But, until that day, the public interest demanded
that large-scale procurement, extensive research, and vigorous antitrust enforcement supplement housing finance reform.[34]

Entrepreneurship on behalf of each of these aspects of Colean's vision accelerated in the wake of the recession of 1937–38. Senator Robert F. Wagner
led the fight in Congress for the expansion of public housing under the aegis of
the newly formed United States Housing Authority (USHA). Robert Davison
of the John B. Pierce Foundation pressed for administration support of a federal housing R&D program loosely modeled on the National Advisory Committee for Aeronautics (NACA). Thurman Arnold made residential construction
enforcement the antitrust division's biggest and most expensive program, engaging, at its high-water mark in 1940, more than half of the division's staff.[35]

PUBLIC HOUSING FOR MASS PRODUCTION

The story of public housing in the 1930s and 1940s is a rich and complex one,
bound up with the issues of race, social reform, and federalism which constitute a central dynamic of twentieth-century American politics. This section
sketches only a few of the main events in that story, concentrating on major efforts to use public housing specifically to accelerate technological innovation.
These efforts failed in part because their proponents underestimated the difficulty of economically mass-producing attractive homes and in part because
their opponents effectively defended a conservative conception of the state
against what they called socialism. Even the passage of the landmark Housing
Act of 1949, perhaps the Fair Deal's greatest legislative monument, appeared
to an enthusiast as a "hollow victory"; its public housing provisions were never
fully implemented, nor did the public housing that was built fulfill the inflated
hopes of the act's authors.[36]

[34] "The Trouble with Building Is . . . ," *Fortune,* June 1938, 46–50, 92–103; Miles L. Colean,
The Role of the Housebuilding Industry (Washington: National Resources Planning Board, July,
1942); Colean, *American Housing: Problems and Prospects* (1944; reprint New York: Twentieth
Century Fund, 1949).

[35] Edwards 1943 (above, n. 5), 347.

[36] Richard O. Davies, *Housing Reform during the Truman Administration* (Columbia: University of Missouri Press, 1966), 136.

As early as the Hoover administration, the federal government adopted modest measures to finance low-income housing. In President Roosevelt's first term, too, steps were taken in this direction; Secretary of Interior Harold Ickes's cautious administration, however, limited construction to only 22,000 houses over the four years. Senator Wagner found this pace unacceptable for both social and economic reasons. The Wagner-Steagall Housing Act of 1937, which established the USHA, pushed Ickes aside and permitted Wagner to install his partisans in key positions. Even though the act was watered down by opponents like Senator Harry Byrd and its program was never fully funded, the USHA managed to finance the building of 56,000 units in 1939 and 73,000 in 1940. The USHA's primary mode of operation was the provision of loans to local housing authorities. Its early years were spent largely in the "missionary" work of setting up authorities under state and local law and getting them going with any projects that they had on the drawing board. Despite Wagner's long-term hopes for mass production, the government's capacity for public housing built like traditional housing needed to be established before any futuristic schemes that might test local attitudes—particularly those of the AF of L's craft unions—could be attempted.[37]

World War II created conditions more conducive to technological innovation in public housing and boosted federal authority to carry it out. The mobilization drained materials and labor from the residential construction industry at the same time that it created tremendous demand for housing near newly built defense plants and military bases. In 1940 the president established the Office of the Defense Housing Coordinator, superseding USHA, and Congress passed the Lanham Act, authorizing the building of 700,000 units to house defense workers. Congress expressed its unease with public housing and marked off the war as an exceptional circumstance by requiring that Lanham Act housing be temporary and forbidding its conversion to peacetime use. These constraints accelerated the development of "demountable" (movable) prefabricated housing. Walter Reuther, president of the United Auto Workers (UAW), sought to seize this opportunity for the benefit of UAW workers, who had experience assembling complex products. His plan for factory-produced housing, like his more famous plan for mass production of airplanes, was given short shrift by the Office of Production Management (OPM), the main war mobilization agency, in 1941. Even after Pearl Harbor, old-style "bricks and mortar" thinking dominated defense housing construction. Local coercion and cumbersome rules, drafted (according to Reuther's CIO) under the influence of the AF of L, inhibited bold experimentation. The craft unions, for their part, fired back that

---

[37] Keith (above, n. 32), 19–39; Roger Biles, "Nathan Straus and the Failure of U.S. Public Housing, 1937–1942," *Historian* 52 (1990): 33–46; Robert F. Wagner, "The Ideal Industrial State," *New York Times Magazine*, May 9, 1937, 9–10, 21–23; James T. Patterson, *Congressional Conservatism and the New Deal: The Growth of the Conservative Coalition in Congress, 1933–1939* (Lexington: University of Kentucky Press, 1967), 155, 318–22.

prefab housing was shoddy and that the government had no place in foisting it on the public. While the federal government never made a full-scale commitment to housing innovation during the war, its modest experiments and the pressure of labor and materials shortages combined to demonstrate to Reuther that his vision of mass-produced housing was technologically feasible.[38]

Postwar demand for housing, pumped up by the GI bill, surpassed even wartime demand. Reuther, anticipating the postwar crunch as early as 1943, modified his earlier proposals, advocating the mass production of houses in converted aircraft plants. *Fortune*'s April 1946 special issue on housing reflected the popularity of these ideas. The editors noted "openings for spectacular increase in the amount of housing value the dollar can buy" and mooned at length over Buckminster Fuller's prototype house. Fuller's house was built with surplus war materials and tools and could be delivered, he claimed, for 50 cents per pound or about $3700. "[W]hen you go into the house it feels as if, for the first time in your life, you had walked into the twentieth century," *Fortune*'s correspondent exclaimed. Although *Fortune* naturally looked to the expansion of demand to force private builders to adopt new technologies, the Veterans' Emergency Housing Act (VEHA) of 1946 had already given the federal government a stake in prefabricated housing.[39]

The VEHA, as its name suggests, was intended as a short-term crisis measure. It was the brainchild of Housing Expediter Wilson Wyatt, the former mayor of Louisville, whom President Truman had brought in to give his efforts on veterans' housing some pizzazz. Wyatt believed that traditional construction techniques were inadequate to solve the crisis, and he proposed that the federal government force prefab housing into the market by guaranteeing the purchase of a large number of prefab houses, providing loans to housing manufacturers, and directing surplus plants and machinery to them. "[W]e are talking about houses on mass-production principles," he told the Senate Banking Committee, "developed and built in the factory, that would not look or be in any wise different than a conventional house except that the cost should be lower." Such an industry would not develop without the state certifying to manufacturers that there was a market and to buyers that the product was sound. Wyatt set a goal of 850,000 prefab homes by the end of 1947.[40]

[38] Davies (above, n. 36), 11; Biles (above, n. 37), 42–44; Nelson Lichtenstein, *The Most Dangerous Main in Detroit: Walter Reuther and the Fate of American Labor* (New York: Basic, 1995), 154–74; "Reuther Housing Plan," *Architectural Forum* (March 1941); 172–78; and replies, *Architectural Forum* (May 1941), 58–64; "The Battle of the 'Prefabs,'" *Business Week,* August 15, 1942, 37–44; National Housing Agency, *Second Annual Report* (Washington: GPO, 1943), 42–44; Bureau of Labor Statistics, *New Housing and Its Materials, 1940–1956,* bull. no. 1231, August 1958.

[39] John Morton Blum, *V Was for Victory: Politics and American Culture during World War II* (New York: Harcourt, Brace, and Jovanovich, 1976), 102–5; Frank Cormier and William J. Eaton, *Reuther* (Englewood Cliffs: Prentice-Hall, 1970), 215–17; "The Promise of Shortage," *Fortune,* April 1946, 102; "Fuller's House," *Fortune,* April 1946, 167.

[40] "Mr. Wyatt's Shortage," *Fortune,* April 1946, 105–9, 252; U.S. Senate, Committee on Banking and Currency, *Veterans' Emergency Housing Act of 1946,* 79th C., 2d s., 1946, 82.

Wyatt's detractors, like Senator Robert A. Taft of Ohio, found this goal preposterous. The government, Taft said, would need a "crystal ball" to know whether this technology was ready for market. Wyatt's Veterans' Emergency Housing Program (VEHP) was a fiasco that proved the skeptics right. Wyatt failed to anticipate the difficulties inevitable when new technologies are scaled up. He also refused to take into account the differences between prefab prefab and conventional homes, which he instead wished away, though they mattered greatly to homebuyers. Furthermore, the program's administration was "amateurish," according to the Prefabricated Home Manufacturers' Institute; by mid-1948, ten of the fifteen firms that received loans through it had gone bankrupt. Only 37,000 prefab houses were built in 1946 and 1947, a far cry from Wyatt's goal.[41]

The VEHP proved to be an entertaining and educational diversion from the long-running debate over peacetime housing policy, which was stalled between 1945 and 1949 over the issue of public housing. Senator Taft, despite his colleagues' complaints that he was becoming a socialist, endorsed public housing from 1942 on, so long as it was locally controlled and carefully fenced in so that it did not compete with private housing. Taft's support swung enough votes that the Senate would reliably pass bills that included public housing provisions. In 1946 and 1948 the upper chamber did so, only to find that the House Banking Committee led by Representative Jesse Wolcott killed them. Backed by a shrill banking and real estate lobby that feared any public housing as the thin end of the wedge of a government takeover, Wolcott was not shy about the "basic question of socialism versus Americanism. . . ." President Truman, who made a housing bill one of his highest priorities, ultimately had a laugh on Wolcott. The president's lambasting of the "do-nothing Congress" for its failure to deal with housing was a keystone in his stunning electoral comeback in 1948. Propelled by the Democratic victory, a comprehensive housing bill finally passed the House in 1949, although not without a fistfight between 83-year-old Representative Adolph Sabath and 69-year-old Representative E. E. Cox on the House floor. Cox's denunciation of the measure as "'a socialistic scheme' designed to create 'a vast omnivorous bureaucracy'" typified the opposition. The 1949 Housing Act authorized 135,000 public housing units to be constructed each year for six years.[42]

Yet Representative Wolcott had the last laugh. Congress never appropriated enough funding to meet the Housing Act's goals; in the first fifteen years after its passage, construction averaged less than 25,000 units of public housing per year. This level of public procurement in a market of more than a million units was simply too small to catalyze massive changes in housing technology. More

[41] *Congressional Record,* 79th C., 2d s., April 8, 1946, 3326–29, 3350–51; National Housing Agency, *Fifth Annual Report* (Washington: GPO, 1946), 18–19, 31–35, 42; Davies (above, n. 36), 50–58; U.S. House of Representatives, Committee on Banking and Currency, *General Housing,* 80th C., 2d s. (Washington: GPO, 1948), 116; Senator Ralph Flanders, *The High Cost of Housing,* report for the Joint Housing Committee, 80th C., 2d s., 1948, 146.

[42] Davies (above, n. 36), 33–34, 110; Keith, (above, n. 32), 86.

importantly, public housing proponents seemed to have lost their enthusiasm for bold technological experimentation, perhaps learning from the failures of the VEHP. Simply siting and building any form of public housing was difficult enough without fighting the craft unions and challenging citizens' expectations of what housing in their town ought to look like. Geographical variation and substantial local control over public housing would have made it difficult for even half of the 25,000 units per year to roll off a single assembly line in any case. Finally, the means-testing and stigmatization of public housing in the United States probably would have doomed the diffusion of even the most successful mass-produced units. As the experiments of the 1960s would show, middle-class homebuyers did not want to live like their less-fortunate fellow citizens. Buckminster Fuller's fifty-cents-a-pound house was to be little more than a flight of practical fancy.

HOUSING R&D

Large-scale public procurement of housing was intended to provide a stable, savvy, forward-looking buyer for new designs, materials, and techniques. The New Dealers of the late 1930s also wanted to intervene on the supply side to force-feed housing's technological development. Federal technical guidance and R&D funding, preferably channeled into a central housing laboratory affiliated with a central housing agency, would inject the sophistication of science into the muddy traditionalism of the construction business. But, like their hopes for public housing, reform liberal and Keynesian hopes for housing R&D were dashed, despite the authorization of a major program in the 1949 Housing Act. The building industry turned against the idea after 1945, when its leaders came to the conclusion that they would be unable to control the direction of federally funded housing R&D, and they were able to abort the embryonic research program of the Housing and Home Finance Agency (HHFA) through the appropriations process in the early 1950s.

The Bureau of Standards was the center of federal efforts in the 1920s and early 1930s to simplify and standardize home construction. The bureau's building and housing division was decimated during Roosevelt's first term and only modestly revived in the late 1930s. The bureau's incremental approach to housing research, in which industrial and local interests had a strong say, frustrated housing technology policy entrepreneurs. In 1938 Robert Davison, director of housing research at the John B. Pierce Foundation, wrote the White House, complaining of the bureau's timidity. Unless it changed its *modus operandi,* the federal program would never produce a Model T house that ordinary families could afford. With the blessing of James Roosevelt, the president's secretary, Davison pressed his case the following year before the TNEC, recommending that a federal housing research agency modeled on the National Advisory Committee for Aeronautics (NACA) be established. Revolutionary rather than evolutionary steps were required. The call for an independent housing research laboratory was echoed by Mordecai Ezekiel (economic advisor to Secretary of Agriculture Henry Wallace), by Alvin Hansen, and by Senator Harley Kilgore, who introduced a bill to establish one.[43]

Davison's testimony impressed the TNEC, prompting it to add the expansion of technological research to its list of recommendations on housing. The TNEC's housing monograph enthused, "[T]he desirability of aid by the Federal government is not questioned." Miles Colean's view was harsher: "Present efforts in this direction are hopelessly inadequate." The Commerce Department, during Harry Hopkins's brief tenure as secretary in 1938–1940, hatched plans to do something about the problem, proposing a $3 million, three-year appropriation to get started in fiscal 1941. Commerce was vague about the operational details of the housing R&D program, particularly on the crucial question of the programmatic power of established industrial interests relative to governmental or academic technical experts and representatives of emerging industries. Davison's use of NACA as a model suggested high-technology associationalism, but it also raised the specter of NRA-style protectionism, should the new organization be dominated by the construction establishment. Senator Kilgore, on the other hand, analogized his proposal for housing research to the federal agricultural R&D system, in which the government set the direction and pace of innovation. Bad timing eliminated the need to iron out these details; the Budget Bureau persuaded President Roosevelt to table the Commerce plan in the name of defense spending.[44]

The war stalled this agenda entirely, with the exception of the modest housing R&D program of the War Production Board's Office of Production Research and Development (OPRD) in 1943–1944. The pressure of the war did create a logical administrative home for any major federal housing R&D program that might emerge, the National Housing Agency (NHA), established by executive order in February 1942. The NHA's first leader, John Blandford, who had spent the 1930s at the Tennessee Valley Authority, a hotbed of innovative housing experiments, carefully toed the administration line of "first things first," linking all wartime housing priorities to the war effort. By 1943, though, he began quietly moving toward a postwar housing policy. Blandford was firm

[43] Rexmond C. Cochrane, *Measures for Progress* (Washington, D.C.: U.S. Department of Commerce, 1966), 331; *TNEC Transcripts,* vol. 4, 380, 565–74; Davison to Roosevelt, May 5, 1938; Roosevelt to Lyman Briggs, May 23, 1938; Patterson to Roosevelt, June 11, 1938; James Rowe to Davison, July 7, 1938, all in Roosevelt papers, OF 3D; Ellis W. Hawley, *The New Deal and the Problem of Monopoly: A Study in Economic Ambivalence* (Princeton: Princeton University Press, 1966), 180; Alvin Hansen, *After the War—Full Employment* (Washington: National Resources Planning Board, January, 1942), 19; U.S. Senate, Committee on Banking and Currency, *General Housing Act of 1945,* 79th C., 1st s., 1946, 1178–83.

[44] *TNEC Transcripts,* vol. 4, 625; Stone and Denton (above, n. 31), xix, 146; Colean 1949 (above, n. 34), 23; Roosevelt to Averell Harriman, January 11, 1940, Roosevelt papers, OF 3D.

on the need to keep the federal housing program centralized, and he strongly supported public housing. He was also convinced that the federal government must take the lead in "stimulating full utilization of technical resources and supplementing them to the extent required." Blandford suggested that the NHA survey housing research, identify existing facilities that could carry out the work, and create additional facilities if the need for them was apparent. Senator Kilgore, who, with Senator Wagner, reintroduced his bill for a central housing research laboratory in 1944, wanted the government's role to be more aggressive; stealing a line from Vannevar Bush, he told the Senate Banking Committee the next year, "Science is truly an endless frontier—there is no limit to the values and savings that can be offered the housing consumer through a continuing program of housing research."[45]

Blandford's view on housing R&D accorded, not coincidentally, with Senator Taft's; Taft's support was essential for any housing bill to pass the Senate in the immediate postwar period. Breaking ranks with those who opposed any federal role in housing R&D, such as the AF of L, the lumber dealers, and U.S. Savings and Loan League, Taft took the NACA model seriously, picturing the NHA as a catalyst and coordinator of research across the residential construction industry, to which its own programs might contribute in a modest way. He categorically rejected the larger and more authoritative organization called for by Kilgore. Taft secured the ambivalent support of representatives of building materials makers, realtors, and home builders, while only the CIO adopted Kilgore's reform liberal vision. Reassured by Blandford, the Taft subcommittee endorsed "appropriate measures for coordinating the results of existing research and initiating original inquiries that will insure a sound basis for both public and private decisions," recommended appropriations of $12.5 million over five years, and gave the NHA administrator the authority to organize the research as he saw fit. After President Truman sent Blandford to China with General Marshall and appointed Wilson Wyatt as his replacement in early 1946, the discretion that Taft had sanctioned suddenly appeared much more threatening. Housing industry interests that had gone along with Taft on federal research in 1945 now denounced the research provisions of the housing bill as "unsound" and likely to lead to government competition with private industry. The bill died, with the debate unresolved.[46]

[45] Keith (above, n. 32), 40–50; National Housing Agency, "Housing Costs and Cost Reduction," December 1944, pamphlet available in Littauer Library, Harvard University, 38; Senate Banking Committee, 1946 (above, n. 43), 1181; U.S. Senate, Special Committee on Postwar Economic Policy and Planning, Subcommittee on Housing and Urban Redevelopment, *Post-War Economic Policy and Planning,* part 6, 79th C., 1st s., 1945, 1299–1301.

[46] Senate Postwar Planning Committee (above, n. 45), 1299–1301, 1653–55, 1680–81, 1989–90, 2002, 2018, 2044, 2079; "A Hundred Million Dollars for Housing Research," *Housing Progress,* Fall 1945, reprinted in Senate Banking Committee, 1946 (above, n. 43), 606–11; NHA, *Third Annual Report* (Washington: GPO, 1944), 56–57; U.S. Senate, Special Committee on Post-

While Congress wrangled, the NHA quietly did what it could to promote technological innovation in the housing field. It took credit for diffusing new techniques developed during the war, conducted reviews and tests related to prefabricated housing under the VEHP, and forged technical relationships with the established housing research units in other government departments and academic institutions. The NHA program was hamstrung, however, by its temporary authority, its lack of appropriations or authorization for R&D, and the plain fact that Congress had obviously not reached a conclusion on the matter.[47]

Housing R&D played an important role in the housing debate of the 80th Congress. The Congressional Joint Committee on Housing, which came to the center of that debate in 1947, adopted the view of Senator Ralph Flanders, who thought that a federal initiative to overcome antiquated craft methods of construction was among the most compelling reasons to pass a housing bill. The committee's majority report called for "an extensive program of technical research" and advocated giving HHFA (which had succeeded NHA) authority to "initiate and coordinate research," although it did not recommend specific new facilities. Senator Joseph McCarthy, who used the Joint Committee's hearings to hone his inquisitorial technique, dissented. McCarthy's minority report specified that the technical responsibilities of HHFA were to be restricted to standardization and code development. McCarthy's view resonated among House Republicans and manufacturers, builders, and realtors, who bitterly attacked the housing bill's research provisions as "bureaucratic control," "an entering wedge," and "dictatorship." Although the bill escaped Chairman Wolcott's committee, much to his surprise, the House Rules Committee bottled it up. After an extended conflict pitting the president and the Senate majority against the House leadership, Congress passed only what Truman called a "phony housing bill" authored by Senator McCarthy. The Housing Act of 1948 forced HHFA to shut down its small existing research program and limit its technical efforts as McCarthy had specified in his report.[48]

Truman used the housing issue effectively in the campaign of 1948, and the bill that was bottled up the year before squeaked through the House Rules Committee of the 81st Congress and thus passed into law as the Housing Act of 1949.

war Economic Policy and Planning, *Postwar Housing,* 79th C., 1st s., 1945, 16; Senate Banking Committee, 1946 (above, n. 43), 7, 440–43, 567, 597–99; Keith (above, n. 32), 63–64.

[47] NHA, *Fourth Annual Report* (Washington: GPO, 1945), 41–44; NHA, *Fifth Annual Report* (Washington: GPO, 1946), 31–35; HHFA, *Second Annual Report* (Washington: GPO, 1948), 50–55.

[48] HHFA 1948 (above, n. 47), 50, 73; Flanders (above, n. 41), part I; Joint Housing Committee, *Housing Study and Investigation: Final Majority Report,* 80th C., 2d s., 1948, H. Rept. 1564, 1, 15, 22; "The Controversy over a Long-Range Federal Housing Program," *Congressional Digest,* (June–July 1948): 165–92; S. Rept. 1019, 80th C., 2d s., 1948, 3–4; U.S. House of Representatives, Banking and Currency Committee, *General Housing,* 80th C., 2d s., 1948, 776–78, 882, 891, 944–46, 1035; U.S. Senate, Special Subcommittee on HR 9659, *Housing Act of 1948,* 80th C., 2d s., 1948. S. doc. 202.

The act did not specify the structure or size of HHFA's R&D program. The agency, taking Blandford's old suggestion, based its research budget proposal of $11 million on a survey of the industry. Its proposal was not aimed at a "single miracle solution" but at "progressive and cumulative results, large and small, that can be put to practical day-to-day use as they become available." Even this modest, realistic approach, hedged with references to consultation and cooperation with industry and to bolstering private enterprise, proved too much for the Budget Bureau and the House Appropriations Committee, which chopped the program to $2 million for fiscal 1950. In fiscal 1951, HHFA tried to bump its research budget up to $3.3 million, but instead it was cut to $1.8 million. The next year, the House used the opportunity of the Korean War to kill off this appropriation entirely. HHFA spent 1952 and 1953 closing out its research division. Its cumulative spending amounted to only $4.3 million over four years.[49]

In the meantime the opponents of HHFA R&D mounted a counterattack by establishing the Building Research Advisory Board (BRAB) of the National Research Council in 1949. BRAB provided a veneer of coordination to private housing R&D that appeased the sentiment to avoid the "do-nothing" label that Truman had pinned on the industry and its congressional supporters in 1948. BRAB secured an HHFA contract to survey industrial R&D and put an optimistic spin on what it found. When HHFA departed the research scene, BRAB, a mockery of the New Dealers' original vision for housing R&D, became the authoritative voice on the subject. Prewar housing technology policy entrepreneurs were utterly defeated. Their cherished central housing agency was stripped of its tiny technical capability, which had been established only after years of effort, punctuated by near misses. The reform liberal vision narrowed between the 1930s and 1950s, forsaking breakthroughs for incrementalism and centralization for the power to initiate just a bit of independent research. Instead, the nation got BRAB, a nongovernmental organization beholden to just those interests that critics argued were holding back housing innovation. Indeed, when the reform liberals got something of a second wind during the Kennedy Administration, BRAB and its congressional allies were there to gut the effort for federal housing R&D again. President Johnson's Great Society was only slightly more successful, yielding the short-lived Operation Breakthrough, a crash program run by NASA engineers as part of the War on Poverty, which was a miserable failure.[50]

[49] Davies (above, n. 36), 87–115; HHFA, *A Handbook of Information on Provisions of the Housing Act of 1949* (Washington: HHFA, 1950), 81; Shurman to Haeger, March 3, 1949, RG207, HHFA Subject File 701; HHFA, *Annual Report for 1950* (Washington: GPO, 1950), 18–22, 62–68; HHFA, *Annual Report for 1951* (Washington: GPO, 1951), 60–64; HHFA, *Annual Report for 1952* (Washington: GPO, 1952), 66–72; HHFA, *Annual Report for 1953* (Washington: GPO, 1953), 55–57; John H. Frantz to Lewis E. Williams, January 8, 1951, RG207, HHFA Subject File 121, Box 43; U.S. Senate, Committee on Appropriations, *Independent Offices Appropriations for 1952,* 82d C., 1st s., 1951, 616–25.

[50] Dorothy Nelkin, *The Politics of Housing Innovation* (Ithaca: Cornell University Press, 1971);

ANTITRUST ENFORCEMENT IN THE RESIDENTIAL
CONSTRUCTION INDUSTRY

The final element of the reform liberal thrust in residential construction was the most ballyhooed and flamed out the most rapidly. Acting on behalf of what he understood to be his consumer movement's fondest dream, home ownership, Thurman Arnold engaged the antitrust division's shock troops in a scorched-earth campaign. Arnold hoped to bring present prices down and to speed the introduction of newer, cheaper housing technologies by breaking the hold of monopolies of all sorts on this business. But in the end Arnold was the one who was burned. For legal and political reasons, and perhaps out of personal antipathy, Arnold's guns zeroed in on the building trade unions. When the Supreme Court handed Arnold his most bitter defeat by exempting labor unions from the antitrust laws in *United States v. Hutcheson* (1941), an opinion authored by Supreme Court Justice Felix Frankfurter, Arnold found he had alienated a powerful constituency just when he needed it most in his struggle with military industry. Aggressive antitrust enforcement not only did little to change the homebuilding industry, it disrupted Arnold's larger reform liberal project.

Arnold attributed housing's failure to recover after the Roosevelt recession to its high costs, which barred the middle and working classes from the market. "Unreasonable restraints of trade, nearly all of which are probable violations of the law, are," he told the TNEC, "the most conspicuous reasons for high construction costs." Unless free competition was established, Arnold warned, the technological progress that was required to bring costs down would never occur. He scored every aspect of the housing industry for monopolistic practices that perpetuated anachronistic techniques. Building material manufacturers used patent contracts and predatory practices to crush innovative competitors. Distributors colluded with manufacturers to inhibit access to new materials in exchange for regional monopolies. Contractors, trade unions, and local officials worked together to keep out new designs and methods. All along this tightly linked chain were barriers to the introduction and diffusion of new technologies that would serve the public interest.[51]

Arnold laid plans, therefore, to attack all the links at once. Manufacturers, distributors, contractors, and unions in several different regions of the country would be investigated. The division's efforts and the restrictive practices they attacked would be widely publicized to the press and in speeches. As in his other

---

Building Research Advisory Board, *A Survey of Housing Research* (Washington: HHFA, 1952); Winfield Best and Eugene Tilleux, "Results of a Survey of Housing Research," *Housing Research* (Winter 1951–52): 25–26; John M. Quigley, "Residential Construction," in Richard R. Nelson, ed., *Government and Technical Progress: A Cross Industry Analysis* (Washington: American Enterprise Institute, 1980), 393–400; Davis Dyer and David Sicilia, *Labors of a Modern Hercules: The Evolution of a Chemical Company* (Boston: Harvard Business School Press, 1990), 368–71.

[51] *TNEC Transcripts,* vol. 4, 458–60; "For Building, Anti-Trust Treatment," *Business Week,* July 15, 1939, 52.

investigations, Arnold hoped to change the behavior and thinking of the industry and to mobilize the public, not merely to slap the wrists of a few miscreants. Public relations were as much a part of the campaign as lawsuits. Corwin Edwards, a prominent economist who was brought into the Justice Department from the Federal Trade Commission to run the construction investigation, put it pithily: "The process is much broader than the proceedings." Only an industrywide attack could change the industry's psychology and thus get the "maximum economic effect," Wendell Berge wrote Arnold as the campaign unfolded. Otherwise, the division would simply reinforce the notion that "this is just another instance of sporadic antitrust enforcement which accomplishes very little economically."[52]

The Justice Department's residential construction investigation was announced publicly in May 1939, when, as *Architectural Forum* put it, Thurman Arnold promised to "strafe Building from top to bottom." By the end of the summer, he was laying people off from other investigations in order to hire new ones for housing. Within a few months this investigation came to center on building trade unions. The other targets did not disappear entirely. Arnold filed suits against the hardboard industry alleging patent abuses, against the lumber industry alleging price fixing, and against networks of contractors alleging collusion. Indeed, as of December 1939, only 30 out of 239 indictments returned by federal grand juries cited labor unions or union officials. But labor occupied the public eye and the attention of the antitrust division's staff. Perhaps this focus derived from Arnold's perception that the case against the construction trade unions was the weakest in the entire investigation and from his belief that he could not afford any losses. Perhaps Arnold wanted to demonstrate his bona fides to consolidate his support among key agrarian members of Congress. Perhaps he believed these unions to be the most significant of the barriers to innovation in construction and the most outrageous flouters of his authority, and he hoped to give more progressive competing unions a better opportunity.[53]

Although accused of wanting to destroy the labor movement like some of his predecessors in the job, the Assistant Attorney General for Antitrust had no intention of prosecuting union organizers or the closed shop. A more accurate charge was that Arnold desired a "benevolent dictatorship," to install himself as "the self-appointed guardian of what he calls 'technological progress,'" as one AF of L critic put it. Arnold argued that union "autocrats" stifled workers'

[52] Edwards 1941 (above, n. 33), 322–27; Berge to Arnold, May 31, 1939, Berge Papers, Box 24.

[53] "The Month in Building," *Architectural Forum* (June 1939): 2; Arnold to staff, August 1939, Berge papers, Box 24; John H. Crider, "Breaking a Bottleneck," *Survey Graphic* (February 1940): 74; "New Test for Patents," *Business Week,* March 16, 1940, 19–20; "The Month in Building," *Architectural Forum* (April 1941); 2–4; Thurman Arnold, speech to Illinois Association of Real Estate Boards, Chicago, September 20, 1940, RG 144, Box 92, "Department of Justice—Thurman Arnold," 11–13; Frank C. Waldrop, "Trust Busting against Labor," *Washington Herald,* November 10, 1939, in Berge Papers, Box 54; Arnold to Freda Kirchwey, December 14, 1939, in Gressley, ed. (above, n. 5), 298–99.

natural inclination to adopt new techniques. He aimed to unlock this creativity and raise the standard of living of the rank and file, whose support he always claimed, along the way. Arnold cited in particular the support of "progressive" unions for his cases against building trade unions. By this he meant the CIO, which in October 1939 announced an organizing drive headed by Alma Lewis, the brother of CIO founder John L. Lewis, in the AF of L-dominated construction industry. Echoing UAW leader Walter Reuther's plans for mass-produced housing, the United Construction Workers' Organizing Committee (UCWOC) declared that "20th century building methods are demanded. . . . Jurisdictional disputes, racketeering, restraints on production and the whole mass of craft unionism is outmoded." The CIO's drive for "modern factory production technics" in housing got a boost from Arnold, who regaled the TNEC with an account of violent clashes with the AF of L over the erection of prefabricated homes in Belleville, Illinois.[54]

The AF of L for its part disputed the antitrust division's capacity to distinguish between practices that prevented technological innovation, which Arnold wanted to ban, and those that assisted workers in making a transition when technological improvements displaced them, which Arnold claimed to support. What employers and the state saw as the forced hiring of unnecessary labor, for instance, might reasonably be understood by unions as a buffer against casual and cavalier layoffs. Arnold's approach would preempt craftsmen's judgments about which innovations constituted true advances and which were simply shoddy substitutions that compromised safety and yielded profits for builders without giving the consumer any value. The federation urged that the distinction between innovative and anti-innovative practices be made in bargaining with management, rather than by the Department of Justice. Skepticism of the reform liberal vision of the state underlay the AF of L's views. Just as builders feared mass-produced public housing as an entering wedge for socialism, the building trade unions feared Arnold's antitrust prosecution as the entering wedge for a full-fledged assault on labor. Today's "administrative aggression" was tomorrow's "dictatorship." Whatever the CIO's private representations to Arnold with respect to its construction industry organizing effort, its convention, too, assailed the use of antitrust prosecution against unions. [55]

[54] Joseph A. Padway, "Mr. Arnold Gets Stopped," *American Federationist* (March 1941): 12; Louis P. Goldberg, *American Federationist* (March 1940): 262–70; Thurman Arnold, "The Antitrust Laws and Labor," speech to American Labor Club, New York City, January 27, 1940, Berge Papers, Box 32; Noyes (above, n. 33), 323–24; "The Month in Building," *Architectural Forum* (September 1939): 4, (March 1940): 4, and (September 1940): 4; *Proceedings of the Fourth CIO Convention* (n.p., 1941): 115; *TNEC Transcripts,* vol. 14, 32–33.

[55] "Labor and the Anti-Trust Laws," *American Federationist* (June 1940): 622–29; *TNEC Transcripts,* vol. 13, 540; National Resources Planning Board, *Housing: The Continuing Problem* (Washington: GPO, 1940), 35; David Kaplan, "Men and Machines," *American Labor Legislation Review* 30 (1940): 90–95; "Anti-Trust," *American Federationist* (May 1940): 471–73; "Labor and the Anti-Trust Laws," *American Federationist* (June 1940): 622–29; "Blunderbuss," *Nation,*

The first indictments of labor unions and leaders were handed down in November 1939, by grand juries in Cleveland, Pittsburgh, Washington, D.C., New York City, and St. Louis, where "Boss Carpenter," William Hutcheson, one of the most powerful figures in the AF of L, was among those tagged. The antitrust prosecution of labor unions sparked what one correspondent called "the wildest internal riot yet seen in the New Deal." The Justice Department was embarrassed by the support its policy won in right-wing circles, but Arnold was able to parlay that support, along with that of rural Members of Congress won over by his food-processing campaign, to secure increased appropriations. He overcame Budget Bureau objections that were ostensibly based on the budget demands of the defense program but rumored to be the product of AF of L influence.[56]

The Justice Department took credit for securing immediate economic gains from prices lowered in 1939 and 1940 as a result of its intimidation of the "autocrats" and their collaborators, while its cases against them slowly wended their way through the courts. The AF of L refused to enter into negotiations with Arnold, setting its face against what Federation official Joseph Padway termed "ruthless, brutal, inconsistent, damaging, and destructive" Justice Department practices. In *Hutcheson,* the Supreme Court dealt Arnold a crushing blow. In Arnold's view the decision put consumers, honest employers, and progressive workers at the mercy of the established interests in housing, food, clothing, and other consumer and defense industries. The ruling would be used, he believed, to prevent the introduction of new technologies, especially those that used unskilled workers. At a hearing of the TNEC ten days after the case came down, Arnold vowed to fight on, including cases against unions that excluded efficient methods or prefabricated materials, and against the "make-work" system in general.[57]

Arnold did press two more cases against unions under the Sherman Act, in-

---

December 2, 1939, 596–97; *Proceedings of the Second Constitutional Convention of the CIO* (n.p., 1939).

[56] "Boss Carpenter," *Fortune* April, 1946, 118–25, 276–82; "The Month in Building," *Architectural Forum* (September 1939): 4, and (December 1939): 2; "Building Trust-Busters Eye 1940," *Business Week,* January 6, 1940, 15–16; Edwards 1941 (above, n. 33), 333; Frank C. Waldrop, "Trust Busting Against Labor," *Washington Herald,* November 10, 1939, Berge Papers, Box 54; "The Month in Building," *Architectural Forum* (February 1940): 2; Harold Smith, memo of conference with President, February 7, 1940, Harold D. Smith papers, FDRL, Box 3; U.S. House of Representatives, Committee on Appropriations, *Department of Justice Appropriation Bill for 1941,* 76th C., 3d s. (Washington: GPO, 1940); *Congressional Record,* 77th C., 1st s., Senate, May 19, 1941, 4186–4204.

[57] Edwards 1941 (above, n. 33), 335; clippings for March 3, 1940, Berge papers, Box 54; E. B. McNatt, "Recent Supreme Court Interpretations of Labor Law (1940–1941)," *Journal of Business* 14 (1941): 359–61; Arnold to Robert Jackson, February 21, 1941, in Gressley, ed. (above, n. 5), 312–15; Arnold to Reed Powell, February 21, 1941, in *ibid.,* 315–17; *TNEC Transcripts,* vol. 14, 53–60.

cluding one against the International Hod Carriers Union for attempting to prevent the introduction of ready-mixed concrete in Chicago, but the Court declined to review lower-court judgments against Arnold, citing *Hutcheson.* Legislation to overturn the decision never materialized either. Arnold was unable to win administration approval to reopen the issue during the war, leaving the antitrust division with only the tool of talk to convince unions to act "responsibly" and support technological innovation. The residential construction campaign was virtually abandoned in the wake of *Hutcheson.* Moreover, the fight that led to the decision robbed the antitrust division of potentially valuable support in the patent fights Arnold had picked with the military services, war mobilization agencies, and large defense contractors in 1940–1941 and in its later efforts to regain the momentum in 1944. Common cause was achieved in some conflicts over reconversion, but on more substantial issues, such as a permanent postwar economic policy, the rift was never fully repaired.[58]

POSTWAR HOUSING AND THE DIVERGENCE OF REFORM LIBERALISM AND KEYNESIANISM

The men who labeled themselves "New Dealers" in the late 1930s wore that label like a badge of courage in the face of congressional hostility. The "Roosevelt recession" of 1937–38 unified them; it forced them to revise their account of the recovery from the Depression for which they had claimed credit, to cast blame for the downturn, and to propose new measures. The causal story they developed was complex, concealing hidden fault lines among them. The channels of healthy economic development, including the development of technological innovations that would lead to new jobs and new industries, they agreed, were blocked because investment was lacking. Whether this shortfall was due to an intentional capital strike, as one extreme of the administration had it, or was an inevitable malfunction in a rusting economic machine, as others argued, made little difference. No matter where a New Dealer stood on this spectrum, he could support federal action to break bottlenecks, as called for by Thurman Arnold, and make new investments, as advocated by Alvin Hansen.

Reform liberals and Keynesians agreed in particular on the importance of an aggressive program to transform housing technology, as articulated by Miles Colean in response to the sluggish market of the late 1930s. As we have seen, almost every element of this program was defeated by conservative opposition or undermined by the mistakes and weaknesses of its advocates. Large-scale

---

[58] Thurman W. Arnold, *Fair Fights and Foul: A Dissenting Lawyer's Life* (New York: Harcourt, Brace and World, 1965), 116–17; Memorandum for the Solicitor General, December 3, 1942, Francis Biddle papers, FDRL, "Antitrust"; Wendell Berge, "Labor Must Share Responsibility," *St. Louis Post-Dispatch,* April 16, 1945, in Berge papers, Box 57; Brinkley 1993 (above, n. 5).

public housing on the assembly-line model performed dismally in its only real test; the Veterans' Emergency Housing Program of 1946 placed unrealistic demands on the prefab industry to mass-produce a house for which neither it nor the public was prepared. The more realistic public-housing goals of the National Housing Agency and its successors could not be pursued, due to tenacious congressional and industrial opposition, which pictured these agencies as bent on taking over the entire industry. Federal spending on housing R&D encountered similar obstacles. An early window of opportunity closed with the mobilization in 1940; by the end of the war, opponents of "socialism" tagged such spending as an element of the takeover conspiracy. Not even Senator Taft's support could overcome this opposition, especially when the Korean War again provided a plausible argument for cutting domestic spending. For both public housing and housing R&D, the 1949 Housing Act proved a false promise.

Antitrust enforcement, which completed the reform liberal approach to housing technology, beached itself, too, on the grounds of government takeover, put forward largely by the American Federation of Labor. The AF of L's fear that later Assistant Attorneys General for Antitrust would not be as understanding as Arnold prompted it to blast his campaign. Its success, in *Hutcheson,* crushed the Justice Department's hope that, by eliminating restraints of trade, it would open the door to a construction revolution. Ironically, the most concrete result of the three-pronged effort was the creation of an associationalist entity, the Building Research Advisory Board (BRAB) of the National Research Council. Yet, rather than fulfilling Hoover's dream of a force for industrywide progress, BRAB was aimed at blocking institutional change that would facilitate technological innovation in housing. BRAB was the voice of the old order.

Despite these failures, the immediate postwar period brought a major restructuring of the housing industry and housing technology. The emergence of large-scale "operative builders," who were just a glimmer in the eye of Colean in the 1930s, stimulated the introduction of new materials, standardized designs, prefabricated components, and power tools in the 1940s. The most crudely balkanized fiefdoms of the craft unions gave way as well. By 1949 more than 50 percent of all residential construction in the United States was done by specialist firms, with the largest 1 percent accounting for a third of the output. The leading firm, Levitt and Sons, which built its first Levittown in 1947, consciously modeled their approach on the auto industry. As historian Marc Weiss has shown, the technological tranformation was powered largely by federal housing finance programs put in place during President Roosevelt's first and second terms and by the GI Bill. The conviction of prewar reform liberals that private dictatorships would extort any new purchasing power supplied by the state proved wrong. By cutting interest rates, standardizing mortgage lending, and reducing the risks to lenders, the federal government helped to create a mass market that proved to be a Schumpeterian "gale of creative destruction" in homebuilding. Alvin Hansen's view that such consumption-oriented measures had to be supplemented by government investment in new technologies for economic growth to return, quickly lost favor among Keynesians.[59]

The doubts about reform liberalism among Keynesians, illustrated so vividly in the postwar history of housing policy, began before the war. Little legislation to boost public investment passed in the late 1930s, and yet the economy nonetheless renewed its recovery. Alternative policies that ignored investment and aimed instead to shift the aggregate consumption function upward, such as progressive taxation and social welfare spending, had the virtue of being somewhat more politically palatable while still providing the fiscal stimulus that Keynesians sought. If, from Hansen's perspective, stimulating consumption without stimulating investment was only half a policy to counter secular stagnation, it was better than no policy at all. Perhaps, too, expanded consumption might arouse the animal spirits of investors and make public investment superfluous.[60]

"Demand management" of this sort stranded Thurman Arnold. If the arteries of the economic organism could be unclogged merely by increasing the volume of consumption, then the invasive surgery of antitrust enforcement was no longer required. Although the antitrust division doggedly pursued cases against patent miscreants and "labor's hidden hold-up men" (as Arnold put it in *Reader's Digest*), it slowly sank into legalism, increasingly making prosecutorial choices by the odds of victory rather than the contribution to economic policy.[61] The judiciary, in any case, had definite limits as an agency to govern technological innovation. Except in rare cases, judges lacked the expertise and authority to take into account the technological prospects of industrial structures on which they ruled. Without new patent or antitrust legislation or public investment in new technologies, the division stood alone, making the most of its second-best strategy of case law development. This effort did wring significant changes from the legal system, such as compulsory patent licensing, but inevitably yielded diminishing returns.

The war mobilization briefly delayed the estrangement of the reform liberals from the Keynesians and, indeed, the fissioning of the Keynesians among

[59] Bureau of Labor Statistics, *Structure of the Residential Building Industry in 1949,* bull. 1170, November 1954; Marc A. Weiss, *The Rise of the Community Builders: The American Real Estate Industry and Urban Land Planning* (New York: Columbia University Press, 1987); Glenn H. Beyer, *Housing and Society* (New York: MacMillan, 1965), 204–11; Bureau of Labor Statistics, *New Housing and Its Methods, 1940–1956,* bull. 1231, August 1958.

[60] Alan Brinkley, *The End of Reform: New Deal Liberalism in Recession and War* (New York: Knopf, 1995), 136; William J. Barber, "Government as a Laboratory for Economic Learning in the Years of the Democratic Roosevelt," in Mary O. Furner and Barry Supple, eds., *The State and Economic Knowledge: The American and British Experiences* (New York: Cambridge University Press, 1990), 120–22.

[61] Thurman Arnold, "Labor's Hidden Hold-Up Men," *Reader's Digest,* June 1941, 136–40; Marc A. Eisner, *Antitrust and the Triumph of Economics* (Chapel Hill: University of North Carolina Press, 1991), 76–89.

themselves. National security was a potent weapon in the battle for both public investment and antitrust enforcement. While the new rationale did not instantaneously dissolve all obstacles, the New Dealers gained important allies in their guise as "all-outers" fighting the final battle against the "scarcity economics" that they still affiliated with the NRA, big business, and now fascism. At the same time, however, military officers and dollar-a-year men on loan from corporate America increasingly took control of the public investment agenda at the working level. Ultimately, these new players shoved "Thurman Arnoldism" aside. Keynesian theory, by contrast, was put to the test, not to stimulate consumption but to restrain it in order to make room for huge military spending programs. The war worked a transformation. When, at war's end, the challenge of unemployment once again rivaled the challenge of military mobilization for policy-making attention, divisions between reform liberals and Keynesians that had been cracks became chasms too large to bridge.

CHAPTER 5

Old Fights, New Accommodations

WARTIME EXPERIMENTS AND THE DEMISE
OF REFORM LIBERALISM, 1940–1945

THE ANTITRUST OFFENSIVE and the related reform liberal and Keynesian policy initiatives of the late New Deal, like the NRA and its associationialist kin of the New Deal's early phase, did not end the Depression. As measured by the real gross national product, the United States was poorer in 1939 than it had been in 1929.[1] Despite the coming of World War II, the unresolved struggle over anti-Depression policy never entirely disappeared. In crafting the mobilization and managing the war effort, processes that provided extraordinary opportunities to redefine the relationship between state and market, competing policy entrepreneurs carried the conflicts of the 1930s forward into the 1940s. Yet the setting had changed dramatically, and new players joined the game. The mobilization and war powerfully revived the vision of the national security state, dormant since World War I. In the name of defending free enterprise and democracy, military officers and defense officials challenged liberal norms in a huge swath of economic sectors. Neither conservatives, associationalists, reform liberals, nor Keynesians had given much thought to national security before 1939, and they struggled to accommodate this purpose for state action with that of economic prosperity. On the other hand, after decades of neglect, national security advocates lacked the resources to achieve their urgent goals. "Total war" forced all sides to come to new accommodations, which sometimes served as a means to win old fights at home as well as new ones abroad.

The U.S. military was particularly ill-prepared technologically. Military R&D was poorly funded in the interwar period, and many officers had little taste for newfangled weapons nor an understanding of how they ought to be developed. Once given some money and an appreciation for modernization (an appreciation instilled most effectively by an imminent threat from technologically superior forces), men like General Brehon Somervell of the Army Supply Forces and General Leslie Groves of the Army Corps of Engineers at their most brazen simply tried to force innovations out of the private firms and civilian scientists on whom they were unhappily dependent. The predilection of national

---

[1] Christina D. Romer, "What Ended the Great Depression?" *Journal of Economic History* 52 (1992): 761.

security advocates for centralization and hierarchy appears on the surface to make for a common cause with reform liberalism, and, indeed, reform liberals like Vice-President Henry Wallace sought to build this alliance. Wallace's vision of the state, however, encompassed purposes and activities that competed with national security, even during the crisis period. Rather than dilute their efforts in the cause of reform, the military men learned to mute their preference for hierarchy when they needed to secure scientific and technological resources.

The science and technology policy entrepreneurship of Vannevar Bush, who moved from MIT to Washington to become president of the Carnegie Institution in 1939, contributed enormously to both the increasing technological sophistication of the national security state-builders and their adoption of some associationalist approaches to the governance of innovation. Bush and his colleagues, drawing on academic and industrial centers of technical excellence that had far outpaced the services between the wars, designed and managed a potent set of organizations that contributed important new weapons and devices to the war effort. But, in spite of the rhetoric of "total war," Bush was careful to define and patrol a boundary between military and civilian science and technology. With the defense establishment behind him, he held in check the entrepreneurship of Wallace and other reformers who tried to use national security rhetoric to blur that boundary and establish a federal R&D presence in economic sectors that they thought would stimulate postwar growth.

Bush's success owed much to the president. The mobilization and war temporarily moved the main arena for policy-making back to the executive branch, as Congress delegated sweeping emergency authority. Ironically, New Dealers who had fought in the 1930s for just such a shift found that control of key administrative positions slipped from their grasp as national security gained significance. The nation's need for immediate, massive production required that the state secure the cooperation of those, like Bush, who could put the scientific brainpower and industrial might of research universities and corporations at its disposal. As the demands of foreign and military policy grew and the bureaucracy exploded in size, the White House delegated increasing authority to establishment appointees in the mobilization agencies. Bush's exceptional political skills and rapport with Roosevelt made his already-strong position that much stronger.

Much more suddenly than it came, the war ebbed, leaving behind a raft of wartime experiments. A resurgence of conservatism and the return of Congress to its central place in policy-making in the immediate postwar period destroyed the weakest of these experiments, the modest wartime programs that reform liberals had managed to push through. Henry Wallace's journey from a heartbeat away from the Presidency to the middle of nowhere personified their demise. The disappearance of reform liberalism cleared the way for Keynesianism to serve as the lodestone of the left in the postwar United States. Direct state participation in technological development for economic policy purposes was forsworn, and the institutions that might have effectively carried out a reform liberal science and technology policy were pruned down to nearly nothing. As the postwar international system took shape, conservatives also challenged the far more massive and much sturdier organizational innovations of the national security state and posed a new peacetime conundrum for the associationalists who had managed the growth of that state during World War II.

SLEEPING GIANT: MILITARY INNOVATION BETWEEN THE WARS

For many Europeans, the shattering experience of World War I made it clear that war, technological change, and political and economic development were, for better or worse, intimately linked. "Sombart," noted Lewis Mumford in 1934, "looks upon 1914 as a turning-point for capitalism itself." Yet, war and military technological innovation did not figure much in the ideas of the state and its relationship to the economy that animated political action in the interwar United States. When the threat of war and then war itself engulfed the nation, this ideological absence had to be filled quickly and, as a result, rather haphazardly. The fundamental reasons for the void, of course, were the lack of a perceived threat to the United States and the country's lack of interest in conquering territory held by a technically competent foe. This geopolitical foundation was cemented, though, by ideology.[2]

For conservatives, the military represented an enduring threat to local political control and individual liberty, which they took to be the wellsprings of invention, among other good things. This sentiment was among those that stimulated the antipathy of Presidents Harding and Coolidge to military spending and enhanced their support for the arms limitation treaties they negotiated. Most politically influential associationalists, too, hoped to minimize the role of the military in the state. Although Bernard Baruch kept alive the flame of that associative paragon, the War Industries Board, which he had chaired during World War I, Herbert Hoover spurned Baruch's advice, seeking, for instance, to wrest the aircraft industry from the clutches of the military while he was Secretary of Commerce. Reform liberals, too, were skeptical about technological innovation for war. They saw military research spending as a wasteful perversion of state power that diminished social welfare, "more distorted," said the British physicist J. D. Bernal (a favorite of reform liberal thinkers), "than . . . [the] worst industrial research."[3]

---

[2] Lewis Mumford, *Technics and Civilization* (1934; reprint with a new introduction, San Diego: Harvest/Harcourt, Brace, and Jovanovich, Paperback, 1963), 422; Richard J. Samuels, *Rich Nation, Strong Army: National Security and the Technological Transformation of Japan* (Ithaca: Cornell University Press, 1994), 4–9.

[3] William E. Leuchtenburg, *The Perils of Prosperity, 1914–1932,* 2d ed. (Chicago: University of Chicago Press, 1993), 106–19; Jordan A. Schwarz, "Baruch, the New Deal, and the Origins of

Not surprisingly, the dominant fact of the interwar U.S. military was its small budget, leading inevitably to a lack of investment in force modernization and even a paucity of new technological options should such modernization have been desired. Two decades after the armistice at Versailles, only a thin residue remained of the veneer of organization for war that had been laid on the U.S. national innovation system during World War I. The Army Ordnance Department, for example, conducted a major review in 1919 prompted by wartime deficiencies, but the department failed by 1939 to come close to achieving the goals that were set. Motorized artillery, the review's highest priority, made "scant headway," in the words of the department's official history. The antitank weapon fielded in the late 1930s was "obsolete before it was standardized." Only one model of experimental tank could be tested each year; hence, heavy tank design was "virtually abandoned."[4]

The navy, the object of Assistant Secretary Franklin D. Roosevelt's affection during World War I, when he butted heads with his Commander-in-Chief over a variety of high-technology schemes, fared slightly better. The Naval Research Laboratory (established in 1923) survived the interwar period, albeit only by making itself useful to other bureaus by conducting routine testing; its 1930 breakthrough in aircraft detection by radar failed to win the funding merited by the findings. Other naval agencies were able to support secret, sole-source contracts to develop high-technology items like rangekeepers and bombsights, skirting procurement regulations that required competitive bidding. But such arrangements were both peculiar and modest; the Navy Bureau of Ordnance spent only $427,000 to have Carl Norden, a resident alien of German descent, design the world's best bombsight. The navy, characteristically, refused to share the Norden bombsight with the army, even though naval aviators had little use for it in torpedo and dive bombing while the Army Air Corps was desperate to make high-altitude bombing more precise.[5]

Both the army and the navy invested in aviation, developing the autopilot and

the Military-Industrial Complex," in Robert Higgs, ed., *Arms, Politics, and the Economy: Historical and Contemporary Perspectives* (New York: Holmes and Meier, 1990), 1–21; Samuel P. Huntington, *The Soldier and the State: The Theory and Politics of Civil-Military Relations* (Cambridge: Belknap, 1957), 290; Ellis W. Hawley, "Three Facets of Hooverian Associationalism: Lumber, Aviation, and Movies, 1921–1930," in Thomas K. McCraw, ed., *Regulation in Perspective* (Cambridge: Harvard University Press, 1981), 95–124; J. D. Bernal, *The Social Function of Science* (London: George Routledge and Sons, 1939), 182.

[4] Constance M. Green, Harry C. Thomson, and Peter C. Roots, *The Ordnance Department: Planning Munitions for War* (Washington: Department of the Army, 1955), 178, 196.

[5] Otis L. Graham, Jr., and Meghan Robinson Wander, eds., *Franklin D. Roosevelt—His Life and Times: An Encyclopedic View* (Boston: G. K. Hall, 1985), 10; Daniel J. Kevles, *The Physicists* (New York: Knopf, 1977), 289–91; David K. van Keuren, "Science, Progressivism, and Military Preparedness: The Case of the Naval Research Laboratory, 1915–1923," *Technology and Culture* 33 (1992): 710–36; David A. Mindell, "'Datum for Its Own Annihilation': Feedback, Control, and Computing, 1916–1945" (Ph.D. diss., MIT, 1996); Stephen L. McFarland, *America's Pursuit of Precision Bombing, 1910–1945* (Washington: Smithsonian Institution Press, 1995).

the aircraft carrier, but military support in this field was so inconsistent between the wars that most U.S. aircraft firms sustained themselves, if at all, through foreign sales and sheer entrepreneurial enthusiasm. In the 1930s the Army Air Corps strove for organizational independence through its long-range bomber development program, which promised to free the airmen from merely supporting ships and troops. The appropriations for this endeavor, however, rose only slowly, even after the president's dramatic call following the Munich summit for 20,000 bombers to be built, and the procurement process was plagued by conflicts over design rights and private profits. Other aspects of military aviation, like fighter airplanes and logistics, suffered from neglect. In 1939 the U.S. candy industry was still larger than the aircraft industry. Military R&D spending barely broke $10 million as the decade closed and lagged far behind the comparable Agriculture Department budget.[6]

The military officers running technology development programs between the wars were often well-trained engineers, cognizant of the state of the art in civilian industry and abroad. Their bêtes noires included field officers who could not see beyond the end of a gun as well as a Congress and administration chary with cash. Some military bureaus, especially in the Army Air Corps and navy, drew on the technological capacities of private firms, but to a far lesser extent than they later would. The services continued to operate substantial arsenal facilities, like the Naval Aircraft Factory in Philadelphia and the Portsmouth Naval Shipyard, and their relationships with contractors were rocky and burdened by red tape. Most of the mechanisms set up during World War I to permit the military to draw on independent civilian scientists and engineers atrophied. The National Research Council (NRC) had been established in 1916 to permit the National Academy of Sciences (NAS) to reach beyond its relatively narrow membership to provide the armed services with advice on problems like submarine detection. Although the NRC continued to advise the government on a few issues in the interwar years, its most important function was the administration of private graduate fellowships. The National Advisory Committee for Aeronautics (NACA), created in 1915 to coordinate aviation-related research, was somewhat more dynamic. It was one of the few institutions within which experts from the two services, firms, and academia exchanged technical information. Yet NACA spent the 1930s fighting budget cuts and bureaucratic rivals that threatened its very existence.[7]

[6] Michael S. Sherry, *The Rise of American Air Power* (New Haven: Yale University Press, 1987), 22–75; McFarland (above, n. 5), 26–44; Mark S. Watson, *Chief of Staff: Prewar Plans and Preparations* (Washington: Department of the Army, 1950), 44–47; Jacob Vander Meulen, *The Politics of Aircraft* (Lawrence: University of Kansas Press, 1991), 55–79, 182–220; Walter Millis, *Arms and Men: A Study in American Military History* (New York: G. P. Putnam, 1956), 269–73; Gerald T. White, *Billions for Defense: Government Financing by the Defense Plant Corporation during World War II* (University, AL: University of Alabama Press, 1980), 1; National Resources Planning Board, *Research—A National Resource*, vol. 1 (Washington: GPO, 1938), 69–70.

[7] A. Hunter Dupree, *Science in the Federal Government,* 2d ed. (Baltimore: Johns Hopkins Uni-

The United States' military mediocrity in the 1920s and 1930s contrasted sharply with the sophistication of its civilian economy. American mass-production techniques and consumer goods were famous around the globe. American corporations steadily added R&D facilities and expanded R&D funding throughout the interwar period, with only a brief hiccup in the depths of the Depression. American universities, too, attained world eminence, a process aided but not caused by refugees from European fascism. When President Roosevelt turned decisively toward a defense buildup in the wake of Munich, the nation had a strong civilian technological base to draw on for military purposes but lacked the state capacity to do so effectively.

VANNEVAR BUSH AND THE STRUCTURING
OF WARTIME MILITARY INNOVATION

The president's wild targets for bomber-building, which rose to 50,000 during Nazi Germany's western offensive, hardly gave the military establishment a blank check to meet them. Many voters opposed such a program and even the general staff thought it badly unbalanced. Congress was therefore reluctant to provide the funds before the fall of France, and only Pearl Harbor precipitated full-scale delegation of mobilization authority to the executive. Beyond this, the military's technological backwardness, the urgency of its need, and the impressive capabilities of the nation's high-technology corporations and academic powerhouses virtually guaranteed that civilian scientific and technical institutions would be adapted to military needs during the mobilization and the war. In practice these pressures forced a de facto alliance with prewar associationalists and conservatives, like Vannevar Bush, MIT President Karl Compton, Harvard President James Conant, and Bell Telephone Laboratories President Frank Jewett. Bush, by virtue of the special relationship that he established with the president and his canny tactics with respect to Congress, had particular influence on the organization of military technological innovation and helped to cushion its impact on firms and universities. As the notorious clashes between General Groves and his scientists at Los Alamos demonstrated, the accommodation of military and civilian approaches was not always easy. But it was successful nonetheless in helping the Allies to victory, perhaps in part (as the historian Larry Owens has suggested) because its haphazard quality allowed for so much organizational experimentation. The consequences of the wartime effort for the postwar period were profound, none more so than the conversion of the military brass to gung-ho technological enthusiasm.

The foreign policy conflict that convulsed the United States after the German

versity Press, 1987), 302–43; Alex Roland, *Model Research: The National Advisory Committee for Aeronautics, 1915–1958* (Washington: NASA, 1985), 1–146.

invasion of Poland crosscut the ideological boundaries that divided Americans over economic issues. For all Bernard Baruch's interwar labors, business remained cool to mobilization, even, in many quarters, after the fall of France. Industrialists feared overbuilding, they feared that labor would gain the upper hand, they feared government bureaucracy, and they feared cutting into sales; 1941 was the second biggest year for cars in history. A *Fortune* survey of executives in October 1940 found that 60 percent had reservations about rearmament. Unionists were at odds, too. Walter Reuther of the United Auto Workers put management on the defensive by proposing that the auto industry build 500 planes a day in 1940, but many in the rank and file found John L. Lewis's skepticism of the buildup (if not his endorsement of Wendell Wilkie) more congenial. Congressional opponents of mobilization ultimately forced the president to sacrifice his domestic priorities to pay for military appropriations. The collapse of France secured only the barest of majorities to pass the selective service bill in the House of Representatives.[8]

The president's authority to suspend normalcy was thus granted haltingly and, even after Pearl Harbor, on an emergency basis only. Like a drunk who stashes the car keys before opening the bottle, Congress took steps to contain the war's effect on the state. The mobilization agencies that began to appear in Washington in 1939 and proliferated after 1940 were time-limited to the special circumstances that gave birth to them. The status quo ante of U.S. government was always, de jure at least, just a peace treaty or two away. In any case FDR sent mixed messages, covering himself politically. He established the War Resources Board (WRB), which counted Karl Compton among its members, in mid-1939, but dismissed it when New Dealers and isolationists complained at the end of that year. The end of the phony war the following spring prompted the creation of the National Defense Advisory Commission (NDAC) in the WRB's place. However, its chairman, William Knudsen of General Motors, was hardly the "all-outer" whom the interventionists expected; NDAC's authority was never clearly established. Similarly, the president left the cautious Jesse Jones in charge of the Reconstruction Finance Corporation and its new subsidiary, the Defense Plant Corporation (DPC); Jones's foot-dragging on

---

[8] Terrence J. Gough, "Soldiers, Businessmen, and U.S. Industrial Mobilization Planning between the World Wars," *War and Society* 9 (1991): 63–99; Gregory Hooks, *Forging the Military-Industrial Complex: World War II's Battle of the Potomac* (Urbana: University of Illinois Press, 1991), 130–31; Barton J. Bernstein, "The Automobile Industry and the Coming of the Second World War," *Southwestern Social Sciences Quarterly* 47 (1966): 22–33; David Brody, "The New Deal and World War II," in John Braeman, Robert H. Bremner, and Brody, eds., *The New Deal: The National Level* (Columbus: Ohio State University Press), 281–84; Hadley Cantril, *Public Opinion 1935–1946* (Westport, CT: Greenwood Press, 1978), 346; Nelson Lichtenstein, *Labor's War at Home: The CIO in World War II* (New York: Cambridge University Press, 1982), 26–43; Richard N. Chapman, *The Contours of Public Policy, 1939–1945* (New York: Garland, 1981), 69–85; Barry Karl, *The Uneasy State: The U.S. From 1915 to 1945* (Chicago: University of Chicago Press, 1983), 200.

plant financing was soon legendary and would come back to haunt him after Pearl Harbor. This ramshackle administrative apparatus may well have expressed Roosevelt's own qualms about building a national security state. He never centralized control of war production, preferring ad hoc governance that left him as the final arbiter.[9]

Nonetheless, for all his backing and filling, Roosevelt richly appreciated those who shared his enthusiasm for fighting the fascists. Among them was Vannevar Bush. In his two decades at MIT, Bush established a reputation as a brilliant inventor, an imaginative researcher who blended electrical engineering with mathematics and physics, and a savvy administrator in Compton's reform presidency. With his friends Compton, Conant, and Jewett, who joined him at the core of the wartime technical leadership, Bush was an early believer in military preparedness. Alerted by the influx of eminent emigrées and deeply concerned by Nazi repression, the group came to the conclusion in 1937 that the United States needed to take more radical steps to modernize its military forces. In 1938 they engineered the election of Jewett to the presidency of the National Academy of Sciences; he was the first industrial scientist to hold the post. After Bush moved to Washington (where he assumed the chairmanship of NACA as well as heading up the Carnegie Institution), they began to agitate more aggressively against the "Colonel Blimp" view—that research would never pay off fast enough to help win a war—that they thought characterized the military services. They worked quietly behind the scenes at first. Bush, for instance, wrote Herbert Hoover at Stanford in April 1939, informing him of the services' lack of interest in radar and requesting his assistance in building an elite consensus behind a more active antiaircraft research program.[10]

Despite his enthusiasm for technological preparedness, Bush, like most Americans, considered the mobilization and the war to be peculiar circumstances and the national security state to be (as Owens writes) "an intrusion to be limited, carefully controlled, and always feared." Although he partook of the entrepreneur's disdain for bankers and big business, Bush's political philosophy was much closer to that of the New Era than the New Deal. He called Hoover, not Roosevelt, "chief." Like Compton in the 1930s, Bush sought to

[9] Alan Brinkley, *The End of Reform: New Deal Liberalism in Recession and War* (New York: Knopf, 1995), 177–82; Luther Gulick, "The War Organization of the Federal Government," *American Political Science Review* 38 (1944): 1166–79; Civilian Production Administration (CPA), Bureau of Demobilization, *Industrial Mobilization for War, Volume I, Program and Administration* (Washington: GPO, 1947), 8–23; Robert Dallek, *Franklin D. Roosevelt and American Foreign Policy, 1932–1945* (New York: Oxford University Press, 1979), 199–232.

[10] Carroll Pursell, "Science Agencies in World War II: The OSRD and Its Challengers," in Nathan Reingold, ed., *The Sciences in the American Context: New Perspectives* (Washington: Smithsonian Institution Press, 1979), 360; James G. Hershberg, *James B. Conant: Harvard to Hiroshima and the Making of the Nuclear Age* (Stanford: Stanford University Press, 1993), 111–34; Bush to Hoover, April 10, 1939, Vannevar Bush papers, Library of Congress, Manuscripts Division (hereafter "Bush papers, LC") Box 51, File 1261.

make sure that, to the extent possible, nongovernmental experts like himself were in charge of allocating resources and setting agendas for federally financed R&D. In May 1940 Bush brought a proposal to the attention of the president's right-hand man, Harry Hopkins. Hopkins had already been pondering the problem of military innovation and recognized Bush's capacity to put the nation's most prestigious technical resources, especially those in the private sector, at the service of the national security state. As Bush put it in his memoirs, "He was a New Dealer and I was far from it. Yet something meshed, and we found we spoke the same language." On June 15 the president approved the establishment of the National Defense Research Committee (NDRC), chaired by Bush. The other members were Compton, Conant, Jewett, Richard Tolman of Cal Tech, and representatives of the army, the navy, and the Patent Office.[11]

Bush quickly constructed a "remarkable, symbiotic relationship" with Roosevelt in the summer of 1940. As Congress delegated emergency war authority to the president, he in turn delegated science and technology policy matters to Bush. By the end of 1940, a winning coalition in this policy area was one that could win Bush's approval. As chairman of NDRC and, later, director of the Office of Scientific Research and Development (OSRD), Bush channeled $450 million into R&D projects large and small. His close relationship with Hopkins and Roosevelt also won him a powerful advisory role, formalized in the executive order establishing OSRD in 1941. The president regularly called upon him to adjudicate science- and technology-related matters. Bush was granted extraordinary administrative latitude, and Congress steered clear of his ultra-secret domain. He could and did, on occasion, even go over the heads of the chiefs of the armed services and win. Yet pulling rank, whether or not it led to military results, as Bush's projects often did, still posed risks. Bush's success was therefore equally predicated on "tact," as he put it, "and a due recognition of the primary responsibility of the armed services on military matters."[12]

Although Bush's agencies were the most elite of those that conducted R&D during World War II, they were not the only branches of the national security state concerned with military innovation. The war spawned a sprawling array of science and technology agencies with an elaborate division of labor. Interestingly, many analysts believe that the United States contributed to the Allied

[11] Larry Owens, "The Counterproductive Management of Science in the Second World War: Vannevar Bush and the Office of Scientific Research and Development," *Business History Review* 68 (1994): 518; Vannevar Bush, *Pieces of the Action* (Cambridge: MIT Press, 1970), 35; Kevles 1977 (above, n. 5), 297; Nathan Reingold, "Vannevar Bush's New Deal for Research, or the Triumph of the Old Order," *Historical Studies in the Physical and Biological Sciences* 17 (1987): 299–344.

[12] Stanley Goldberg, "Inventing a Climate of Opinion: Vannevar Bush and the Decision to Build the Bomb," *Isis* 83 (1992): 431; James P. Baxter, III, *Scientists against Time* (Boston: Little, Brown, 1946), 452; Kevles 1977 (above, n. 5), 298–301; "War in the Laboratories," *Time,* May 26, 1941, 58–62; Bush to Hopkins, March 13, 1941, Bush papers, LC, Box 51, File 1269. This letter proposes a single high-level science advisor who had the qualities mentioned in the quote; although the proposal was not accepted formally, it captures Bush's self-image.

victory less by developing new technologies than by mass-producing military systems from prewar or borrowed designs. The creations of OSRD and its brethren, for instance, had little impact on the infantryman's war before 1944. The atomic bomb, too, barely made an appearance before the war ended, and its military effect has been the subject of hot debate. The "technological high command" (as *Fortune* figured Bush and company) also missed opportunities that other nations spotted. Jet engines, missiles, submarine schnorkels, and long-range torpedoes were among the new devices that, Bush argued in 1949, might have led to German victory under slightly different circumstances. Nonetheless, American military innovations played a significant, if not decisive, part in winning the war.[13]

OSRD's forte was technology that had no prewar counterpart, notably radar, electronics, and the atomic bomb. MIT's famed "Rad Lab" received the largest proportion of the agency's funds. Aided by British breakthroughs, this work rapidly paid off in the Battles of the Atlantic and Midway. Other large OSRD contracts supported the development of the proximity fuze at Johns Hopkins and rocketry at Caltech. Bush's group also funded a wide array of smaller contracts that helped to develop technologies as diverse as computers and penicillin. And, of course, OSRD incubated the Manhattan Project, before transferring it to the Army Corps of Engineers in order to hide its budget and scale it up. Bush did his best to maintain the autonomy of OSRD's academic contractors, even as he shattered precedents in this aspect of state/society relations. Generous and flexible terms were offered to the universities that were allowed to join up, existing facilities were used to the extent possible, and technical decision-making was decentralized. Like Bush, most scientists and engineers working on OSRD contracts remained on the payrolls of private institutions. The committees that managed OSRD divisions thus bore at least a family resemblance to the research committees of industrial associations envisaged by Hoover in the 1920s, able to see across organizational boundaries to identify new opportunities and to pool knowledge to realize them. The state, however, bore the costs and reaped the benefits.[14]

The new niche that OSRD occupied was bounded by the established jurisdictions of the military bureaus and the NACA. Freed from prewar penury, the Army Air Forces (AAF), so renamed in June 1941, aggressively pursued new technology in a fashion somewhat similar to OSRD, but on a much larger scale (so big, in fact, that the NACA was marginalized). Like OSRD, the AAF ne-

[13] "Technological High Command," *Fortune,* April 1942, 63–67; Harold G. Vatter, *The U.S. Economy in World War II* (New York: Columbia University Press, 1985), 146; Alan S. Milward, *War, Economy, and Society* (Berkeley: University of California Press, 1977), 186; Vannevar Bush, *Modern Arms and Free Men* (New York: Simon and Schuster, 1949), 27–112.

[14] Joel Genuth, "Microwave Radar, the Atomic Bomb, and the Background to U.S. Research Priorities in World War II," *Science, Technology, and Human Values* 13 (1988): 276–89; Mindell (above, n. 5); Baxter (above, n. 12); Owens (above, n. 11).

gotiated flexible contracts that could accommodate unexpected technological advances of uncertain cost. Technological networks involving contractors, academics, and military officers emerged as a result of these contracts, with the procurement officials at Dayton's Wright Field at their hubs. These networks were formalized in coordination committees that built sufficient trust so that designs and technical information could be freely shared. An industrywide production council ultimately emerged as a trade association of Hooverian dimensions and infiltrated the AAF's long-range planning process. The capabilities of U.S. military aircraft, particularly long-range bombers, were augmented substantially thanks to these associative institutions. Even in this high-technology sector, however, considerable reliance was placed on prewar designs. The workhorse of the AAF, the Boeing B-17, for example, was first built in 1937; mass production of such designs, with the aid of automobile companies once the United States declared war, was the most significant technological capability the nation gained as a result of the air force's wartime activities. Modifications were retrofitted into the mass-produced planes after they rolled off the line. American pilots could be confident that some of their planes' components (like the Norden bombsight and radar countermeasures) outperformed their enemies', but they were less sure that they could outmaneuver or outrun them in a fight. The United States lagged behind Germany (and Great Britain) badly in jet propulsion, although this innovation came into service only after the war had been decided.[15]

The navy's technical bureaus kept as tight a hold on their traditional terrain as they could, sometimes but not always updating their ways of doing business to acquire and incorporate new technology more effectively. The Navy Bureau of Ordnance's new R&D division, for instance, directed the development of the proximity fuze, a tiny electronic device implanted in the nose of a shell; this project was carried out by OSRD's Section T and involved at its peak over 300 companies constituting a quarter of the nation's electronics capacity. As in aircraft, the production challenges and the rapid pace of innovation in electronics led to "a new and flexible approach to industrial economics," as one postwar review put it, in which intellectual property was "thrown open" and coordinating committees emerged to manage development. Bush took some credit for opening the navy to new ideas, helping to precipitate the appointment of his old MIT colleague, Jerome Hunsaker, to the new post of Coordinator of Naval R&D in mid-1941. Still, as late as October 1943, Bush lamented the navy's

[15] Sherry 1987 (above, n. 6), 187–90; Allen Kaufman, "In the Procurement Officer We Trust: Constitutional Norms, Air Force Procurement and Industrial Organization, 1938–1947," paper presented at the Hagley Museum, October 1995, 37–49; Roland, (above, n. 7), 173–98; Jonathan Zeitlin, "Flexibility and Mass Production at War: Aircraft Manufacture in Britain, the U.S., and Germany, 1939–1945," *Technology and Culture* 36 (1995): 46–79; William S. Hill, Jr., "The Business Community and National Defense: Corporate Leaders and the Military, 1943–1950" (Ph.D. diss., Stanford University, 1979), 84–103.

stubborn refusal to work with OSRD and to provide more central direction to its more parochial technical bureaus, like the Bureau of Ships.[16]

The army happily turned over some longer-range projects to OSRD in 1940 in order to concentrate its resources on mass production, but at the same time it jealously defended its most precious turf, such as tank design, from civilian outsiders. But, the army, like the navy, came to rely much more on contractors during World War II than it had in the past, in R&D as well as production. By the end of the war, about 80 percent of its R&D funds were disbursed externally. The Ordnance Department, for instance, worked closely with Chrysler and other auto manufacturers on tanks and tank engines. During the course of the war, "America's Industry-Ordnance team" developed over one hundred vehicles for combat and support use; in heavy tanks, though, the United States still lagged behind its enemies and allies. Secretary of War Henry Stimson, to whom Bush dedicated his postwar book, played a large part in easing the army's traditional resistance to technological innovation, especially facilitating the passage of externally developed technology into army use. Stimson employed MIT's Edward Bowles as his liaison to OSRD and other sources of such technology.[17]

The Manhattan Project, finally, was an administrative anomaly. Nominally within the Army Corps of Engineers, it was actually an independent entity with the highest wartime priorities, overseen (to the extent that a man like General Groves can be said to be overseen) by a top-level interagency policy committee chaired by Bush. It spent over $2 billion, employing many of the nation's most eminent scientists through OSRD contracts and procuring enormous experimental production facilities from some of the nation's most technologically sophisticated firms. Despite the deep participation of academic and industrial contractors, the project's facilities were something of a throwback to the arsenal system, a highly secret, vertically integrated national enterprise.[18]

The Manhattan Project aside, the federal government spent over $2 billion during the war on R&D, more or less equally divided among each of the three military services and OSRD. In aggregate, this spending was also about evenly shared among outside contracts and government programs. The contracts were highly concentrated, with the top 68 contractors, by one estimate, receiving

[16] Michael A. Dennis, "A Change of State: The Political Cultures of Technical Practice at the MIT Instrumentation Laboratory and the Johns Hopkins University Applied Physics Laboratory, 1930–1945" (Ph.D. diss., Johns Hopkins University, 1991); Arthur A. Bright, Jr., and John Exter, "War, Radar, and the Radio Industry," *Harvard Business Review* (Winter 1947): 256, 265; Harvey Sapolsky, *Science and the Navy: The History of the Office of Naval Research* (Princeton: Princeton University Press, 1990), 14–20; Bush to Conant, October 19, 1943, RG227, Entry 2, Box 5.

[17] Baxter (above, n. 12), 31–36; Green et al. (above, n. 4), 275–93, 225; Kevles 1977 (above, n. 5), 308–15.

[18] Richard G. Hewlett and Oscar E. Anderson, Jr., *The New World, 1939/1946* (University Park, PA: Pennsylvania State University Press, 1962); Richard Rhodes, *The Making of the Atomic Bomb* (New York: Simon & Schuster, 1986).

two-thirds of the total spent. In some areas academic, corporate, and government experts worked harmoniously together to develop and implement research agendas; in others, one "estate" (as Don Price later called them) of science or another dominated. Certainly, the enterprise as a whole never fully realized the associative vision that underpinned Bush's entrepreneurship. The capstone coordinating body, the Joint New Weapons Committee of the Joint Chiefs of Staff, remained, in Bush's words, "feeble." Although Bush's organizational aspirations were not attained, his proselytizing on behalf of science and technology as an element of long-term military strategy paid off. After the war OSRD's work and its sponsorship of elite scientific institutions was taken up vigorously by the military agencies themselves. High-ranking officers emerged from the war haunted by the "Maginot line" complex, fearing that they would always be prepared only to fight the last war and not the next one. Technology, the first report of the Secretary of Defense in 1947 put it, was a "factor of extreme consequence" in national security. R&D and innovation would have a favored place in the postwar national security state.[19]

PEACE BY OTHER MEANS: ASSOCIATIONALISM
AND REFORM LIBERALISM

The lines of demarcation between OSRD and the military's technical bureaus were never perfectly clear. Although Bush deferred out of political expediency to some of the services' claims to turf, he often went on the offensive, pushing the boundaries of civilian influence. Another set of fuzzy boundaries that Bush established and largely adjudicated distinguished "weapons and instrumentalities of war" from civilian products and processes. The former, which officially defined OSRD's scope, received massive support from the federal government. The latter, by contrast, were supposed to be out of the reach of the national security state. OSRD occasionally breached Bush's own rules, moving downstream into production and field service and backward into materials R&D as the war progressed. These endeavors made Bush uncomfortable, though, because he feared that "total war" would obliterate the prewar order entirely. Such was, in fact, the objective of reform liberals, like Maury Maverick of the War Production Board (WPB), Senator Harley Kilgore, and Vice-President Henry Wallace, who conceived of a "two-front war" to expand the New Deal at home and export it as well; war was peace by other means. On this border of his do-

---

[19] Smaller War Plants Corporation, *Economic Concentration and World War II* (Washington: GPO, 1946), 51–54; Bush to Conant, October 19, 1943, RG227, Entry 2, Box 5; *Second Annual Report of the Secretary of Defense* (Washington: GPO, 1949), 48; *First Annual Report of the Secretary of Defense* (Washington: GPO, 1949), 15; Michael S. Sherry, *Preparing for the Next War: American Plans for Postwar Defense, 1941–1945* (New Haven: Yale University Press, 1977), 127–34.

main, Bush tended to play defense, quashing reform liberal policy entrepreneurship. On those occasions when bottlenecks in the production of civilian goods or raw materials threatened the war effort, as in the case of synthetic rubber, he and his allies preferred associationalist policies, with which they had prewar affiliations, over other interventions to spur technological innovation.[20]

For reform liberals the war seemed at first to be a golden opportunity to create technological capabilities for the federal government that peacetime Congresses had rejected. In a total war anything that stretched materials in short supply or raised productivity might be justified on the basis of national security. Peacetime industrial R&D had demonstrated convincingly that it could do both. "Since the problems of this war will be total problems," an advocate of this point of view stated just after Pearl Harbor, "then a total mobilization of the field of scientific research must be had."[21] That this R&D might create new postwar growth industries and break the grip of prewar monopolists was never far from the minds of such advocates. Federally funded civilian industrial R&D, they hoped, might not only help win the war abroad, but the peace at home, too.

This argument was raised as early as August 1940, by Secretary of the Interior Harold Ickes, who proposed to the president an Office of Scientific Liaison under Ickes's jurisdiction. The White House referred the issue to Bush, who rejected the proposal in March 1941. The national security rationale for industrial R&D became more compelling to Bush after Pearl Harbor. In January 1942 Bush recognized a gap in such areas as conservation and substitute materials that had not been evident to him the previous spring and that neither OSRD nor the services would fill. He suggested to William Batt, a high WPB executive, that "a vigorous group be set up in WPB" and, hinting at the appeal of associationalist structures to him, noted that "there is an interesting opportunity for producing a beneficial exchange of rights among the units of an industry which should be explored." At times Bush spoke of the WPB spending up to $40 million on R&D.[22]

The idea floated by Bush was not taken up by Batt but instead by several WPB officials with ties to prewar reform liberal hotbeds, led by Maury Maverick. Maverick's job was to represent the claims of state and local governments within WPB, but he by no means confined himself to this task. His formative political experience was a two-term stint in Congress in the 1930s, during which

---

[20] Irvin Stewart, *Organizing Scientific Research for War* (Boston: Little Brown, 1948), 16–17; Norman D. Markowitz, *The Rise and Fall of the People's Century: Henry A. Wallace and American Liberalism, 1941–1948* (New York: The Free Press, 1973), 39–40.

[21] Cletus Miller to Maverick, January 12, 1942, RG227, Entry 13, Box 30.

[22] Ickes to President, August 19, 1940, Roosevelt papers, OF 2240; Knudsen to Roosevelt, February 18, 1941, RG179, PDF 282, "Research 1940–1941"; Roosevelt to Smith, February 20, 1941, Roosevelt papers, OF 872; Bush to Hopkins, March 13, 1941, Bush papers, LC, Box 51, File 1269; Smith to Roosevelt, March 17, 1941, Roosevelt papers, OF 2240; Ickes to Roosevelt, April 11, 1941, OF 2240; Bush to Batt, January 30, 1942, RG179, PDF 016.802, "Materials Division OPM—Personnel"; C. K. Leith, "Cooperation of the Laboratories of the Country," Verbatim Transcript of Proceedings, April 29, 1942, RG179, PDF 282M.

he had been a leader of a small reform liberal bloc that mixed patriotic rhetoric with advocacy of government-led economic development, modeled on the Tennessee Valley Authority (TVA). Maverick charted out a WPB bureau devoted to research, with industry sections for metals, fuels, chemicals, plastics and rubber, and other goods. He sought support for this plan directly from Vice-President Wallace, Senator Harry Byrd, Budget Director Harold D. Smith, and others. But, he highlighted in a memo to the WPB hierarchy, "Dr. Vannevar Bush said . . . that the idea I presented was in effect right." And indeed the president turned to Bush for counsel. Bush (on April 8, 1942) endorsed the idea of a WPB R&D organization in the abstract, and, although he viewed Maverick's plan as "more elaborate than is necessary," he thought that "this subject of internal organization is Mr. Nelson's problem."[23]

Bush probably hoped that Donald Nelson, the former Sears executive who chaired the WPB, would find the views of Maverick's opponents within WPB, such as the University of Wisconsin geologist C. K. Leith, more sensible. Leith had been one of the most conservative members of Karl Compton's Science Advisory Board in 1935 and was now a consultant to the WPB's minerals branch. He pointed out that, as in World War I, the NRC had already appointed a number of committees comprising university and industry experts to consult with WPB industrial units on technological problems. This mechanism worked well, in Leith's view, and could easily be expanded to accommodate any new demands that might be placed on WPB. Rather than a central office, as Maverick proposed, a coordinating committee headed by Leith would administer WPB R&D. Leith implied that the WPB should do little more than precipitate ongoing conferences on industrywide problems, at a cost of about $500,000 for the remaining months (May and June) of fiscal 1942.[24]

If Bush had hoped that Nelson would lean toward Leith's associationalism, his hopes were quickly dashed. Nelson put Maverick in charge of the committee to present a report on the subject. Maverick held a set of full-dress hearings during May that made a show of impartiality but tended to serve as a platform for ad hominem attacks on Leith and the "Old Man's Club." Leith's allies in the business-dominated industry branches that controlled the daily administration of WPB were frozen out of the process. On a parallel track, Nelson sought advice on the issue from the WPB Planning Committee (chaired by the pioneer Keynesian economist Robert Nathan), a bastion of New Deal liberalism within the WPB that was in constant conflict with the industry branches.[25]

[23] Stuart L. Weiss, "Maury Maverick and the Liberal Bloc," *Journal of American History* 57 (1971): 880–95; Maverick to James Knowlson, March 13, 1942, RG179, PDF 282, "Research—1942"; Bush to Roosevelt, April 8, 1942, RG179, PDF 027.33, "WPB—Organization—Proposed Units and Committees, 1941–1942."

[24] Joel Genuth, "Groping Towards Science Policy in the United States in the 1930s," *Minerva* 25 (1987): 261–63; Leith to Batt, April 15, 1942, RG 179, WPB PDF 073.011.

[25] Miller to A. C. C. Hill, March 21, 1942, RG179, PDF 027.33, "WPB-Organization-Proposed Units and Committees, 1941–1942"; C. I. Gragg to Hill, April 20, 1942, RG179, PDF 282, "Research-1942"; "Index to Files," RG179, PDF 073.011; Robert D. Leigh to Thomas Blaisdell,

Not surprisingly, both Maverick's committee and the planning committee endorsed reform liberal positions. Maverick called for a WPB Office of Technical Development (OTD), funded at $80 to 100 million, to centralize control of the board's R&D. (OSRD's budget for FY43, by comparison, was $73 million; it also received $61.8 million in transfers from the services.) OTD would operate under policies "representative of broad interests rather than of the technical knowledge of the Divisions." Nathan's group gave its support to a War Research Development Corporation of approximately the same size, authorized not just to do R&D but to build pilot plants and production facilities. As Fred Searls (a planning committee member whom Bruce Catton, author of the postwar polemic *Warlords of Washington,* described as "a crusty gentleman of the Republican persuasion") noted, this corporation would put an end to "buck-passing" among firms reluctant to jeopardize profits to contribute to national security. While Nelson pondered his options during the summer of 1942, Maverick put together a draft program that earmarked $25 million for transportation projects, such as the development of an air cargo plane; $15 million for materials, including synthetic rubber; and $10 million for housing R&D. He won the support of Roosevelt confidant Sam Rosenman and the *New York Times.* Bush maintained his pose of neutrality, ignoring Maverick's lobbying, but behind the scenes he had already begun to derail the plan. He agreed with Leith's concern that, following "the Thurman Arnold thesis," Maverick had invaded forbidden territory, committing WPB to "building up postwar industries."[26]

The first sign that Maverick was in serious trouble came in early August, when his budget was rejected. Soon thereafter General George C. Marshall denied Nelson's request to transfer Colonel Royal B. Lord, former chief engineer of the Farm Security Agency and the present chief of operations of Henry Wallace's Board of Economic Warfare (BEW), to serve as director of OTD. At the end of August, the *New York Times* reversed its editorial position, citing "dis-

---

April 30, 1942, RG179, PDF 282, "Research-1942"; Leith to A. I. Henderson, May 15, 1942, RG 179, PDF 073.011; Reid, "Conversation with Maury Maverick on Thursday, May 28, 1942," June 1, 1942. Transcripts of the Maverick committee hearings can be found in RG179, PDF 073.011. Upon reading the transcripts, Jewett pronounced, "I'm disgusted." Jewett to Batt, June 8, 1942, RG179, PDF 073.011. Bush was directed by Maverick to read a selection of the transcript pertaining to him (in which Maverick declared him "a patriot" rather than "a sacred cow"); he declared himself "amused and somewhat refreshed. There is so much that is serious in this war effort and one has to be so completely objective in most contacts, that it is occasionally pleasant to relax and not be quite as serious." Bush to Maverick, June 6, 1942, RG179, PDF 027.33, "WPB-Organization-Proposed Units and Committees, 1941–1942."

[26] Maverick to Nelson, May 29, 1942, RG179, PDF 282M; Nathan to Nelson, May 16, 1942; Nelson to Smith, July 9, 1942 (noted—"not sent"); Rosenman to Sidney Weinberg, July 2, 1942; and Leith to Amory Houghton, July 21, 1942, all in RG179, PDF 282, "Research-1942"; Bruce Catton, *The Warlords of Washington* (New York: Harcourt, Brace, 1948), 132; "Testing New Inventions," *New York Times,* July 20, 1942, 12; Searls to Nathan, June 7, 1942, RG179, PDF 073.01; Maverick to Bush, May 29, 1942; and Bush to Nelson, June 3, 1942, both in RG179, PDF 073.011; Bush to Frederic Delano, July 22, 1942, RG227, Entry 13, Box 34.

quieting opinions from Washington." In the meantime Maverick had turned to his friend Senator Harley Kilgore, an avid New Dealer from West Virginia, for leverage. On August 17 Kilgore offered S. 2721, embroidering on the main features of both Maverick's and Nathan's proposals. Kilgore proposed to create an independent Office of Technological Mobilization (OTM) and a $200 million Technology Mobilization Corporation accountable directly to the president. These agencies were to have the power to oversee all federal R&D, to draft technical personnel and facilities, and to compel patent licensing. They would be independent not only of the WPB's dollar-a-year men, whose defeat of Maverick was imminent, but of the military as well.[27]

Although the Kilgore bill would ultimately metamorphose into the postwar National Science Foundation Act, its initial effect on the administration was nugatory. In early September, at the suggestion of Batt, Nelson turned to Webster Jones, president of the Carnegie Institute of Technology and a man with whom Bush was comfortable, to organize WPB's R&D. As Batt wrote Leith, Jones put together "a very representative committee," consisting of executives of large firms, military research directors, and academics from MIT and other universities with OSRD contracts. The Jones committee wrote what Bush informed Nelson on October 21 was a "sound and well-considered" report; he had, he said, therefore filled in the War Department's Robert Patterson and the White House on it. Kilgore was conciliatory, even though he continued to hold hearings, declaring that Jones's report and S. 2721 were consistent.[28]

On November 23, 1942, Nelson issued an administrative order establishing an Office of Production Research and Development (OPRD) within WPB. OPRD officially gained many of the powers that Maverick had sought for OTD, such as the power to "carry technical development through to the production line stage" and to oversee all WPB R&D contracts. However, following the Jones committee's recommendations, OPRD's autonomy was constrained by "close contact with the Industry Divisions." More importantly, Jones proposed a budget of only $5 million.[29] OPRD, unlike the proposed OTD, was not going to have the resources to establish WPB as a powerful influence on the development of new industrial technology.

[27] "Index to Files," RG179, PDF 073.011 for August 5 and August 7, 1942; Milo Perkins to Nelson, August 10, 1942, Marshall to Nelson, August 10, 1942, and Lord to Nelson, August 28, 1942, all in RG179, PDF 073.012; J. H. Thacher to L. Gulick, August 6, 1942, RG179, PDF 073.0111; "Research Agency," *Business Week,* August 8, 1942, 58; "Inventions and the War," *New York Times,* August 27, 1942; U.S. Senate, Commitee on Military Affairs, *Technological Mobilization,* 77th C., 2d s., 1943, 1–4.

[28] Daniel Kevles, "The National Science Foundation and the Debate over Postwar Research Policy, 1942–1945," *Isis* 68 (1977): 5–27; memo to files on October 15 conference, RG179, PDF 073.011; Jones to Nelson, September 12, 1942, RG179, PDF 073.012; Jones to Nelson, September 25, 1942, RG179, WPB PDF 073.01; Batt to Leith, September 25, 1942, RG179, WPB PDF 073.014; Bush to Nelson, October 21, 1942, RG179, WPB PDF 073.018.

[29] Thacher to Gulick, November 4, 1942, RG179, PDF 073.017; Donald Davis to Nelson, December 1, 1942, RG179, PDF 073.014.

OPRD modelled its image on OSRD and claimed to be its equal. In OPRD Director Harvey Davis's view, as he stated to the House Appropriations subcommittee, OSRD was responsible for "what" was to be produced and OPRD was responsible for "how" and "from what." OPRD did make important contributions to the mass production of goods like alcohol and penicillin and to industrial processes like welding and lamination. Its proposals to work on radical new ideas, such as solar heating for houses, and on behalf of civilian agencies like the USDA and the National Housing Agency, however, were stifled by skeptics within WPB, in the "technological high command," and in Congress. Grander OPRD plans to "lay the foundation for new industries in every state and territory" were mere wind.[30]

The constraints on OPRD were tightened steadily over the course of the war, and its time horizon was shortened. In 1944 and 1945, it was confined to little more than troubleshooting—establishing, for instance, a "production economy" branch to explore new methods of quality control and labor-saving. OPRD was not allowed even to spend its full appropriation. Its total wartime spending of $9 million was 2 percent that of OSRD's, negligible in a war effort of some $90 billion annually. The establishment figures into whose hands Bush steered OPRD limited not only its scope and size, but its mode of operation as well. Most OPRD projects were first vetted by the WPB's industry branches, committees of the NRC, or professional associations; they were then contracted out. The results of these contracts were disseminated to all interested firms in an industry. This decentralized, consensual mode, dominated by technical elites, has far more in common with the associative conception of the state that Bush favored than with the reform liberal vision of Maverick and Kilgore.[31]

The synthetic rubber R&D program provides a useful contrast to OPRD. Maverick's group met repeatedly with rubber and chemical industry experts to flesh out such a program during the summer of 1942, when the rubber crisis reached a head. Had the WPB been able to assert its control of this matter, some in the agency noted, it would greatly shore up its image and its capacity to resist the armed services and other rivals that seemed bent on diluting its central

[30] "Statement on the Functions of OPRD," June 1, 1943, RG179, PDF 073.006; "What Benefits Have Accrued or Will Accrue to the People of Our Country from the Research Work Sponsored by OPRD," June 4, 1945, RG179, PDF 282, "Research-1942"; Peter Neushul, "Science, Technology, and the Arsenal of Democracy" (Ph.D. diss., University of California, Santa Barbara, 1993); Harvey Davis to Donald Davis, March 8, 1944, and April 15, 1944, both in RG179, PDF 073.006; Philip N. Youtz, "Programs for Regional Development of Industry," July 4, 1944, pamphlet available in Littauer Library, Harvard University.

[31] Davis to Nelson, June 5, 1944, RG179, PDF 073.002; Donald Davis to Donald B. Keyes, July 18, 1944, RG179, PDF 073.006; Nelson to Murray, August 12, 1944, RG179, PDF 073.003; "Office of Production Research and Development Operating Summary for the Period Ending August 30, 1946," RG179, PDF 073.008; OPRD budget justification for FY45, February 1, 1944, RG179, PDF 073.003, 8.

authority.[32] Instead, Bush's forces ensured that the rubber program was taken out of WPB and that many of the program's associationalist features were strengthened.

The United States was the world's largest importer of rubber before the war, creating a vulnerability that Japan eventually exploited by capturing regions providing 97 percent of the U.S. rubber supply. This vulnerability was recognized, but not acted upon, before Pearl Harbor. Although Standard Oil of New Jersey held key patents for making synthetic rubber (by virtue of a deal with the German giant I. G. Farben), it was unable to come to an agreement that would allow the big four rubber firms to exploit them. Jesse Jones, whose RFC was assigned the problem by the president, was reluctant to try to force an agreement that seemed to promise only to saddle the nation with expensive white elephant plants. In the wake of Pearl Harbor and Japanese victories in rubber-rich Southeast Asia, Jones and Jersey faced intense public displeasure, and the firm acceded to RFC-brokered industrywide cross-licensing and technical information-sharing agreements in early 1942. The Antitrust division of the Department of Justice forced further concessions by Jersey under these agreements just before its domestic activities were suspended in March 1942.[33]

Although the industry seemed to come to a modus vivendi under these agreements, the war over rubber continued within the government. In July Maverick's attempt to establish WPB's authority and congressional passage of a poorly conceived bill goaded Bush into action. He helped instigate the creation of the Rubber Survey Committee, composed of chairman Bernard Baruch and Bush's close allies James Conant and Karl Compton. The Baruch committee, tasked to review the situation and make recommendations, took the heat off the president with its aura of impartiality. By the same token, he was obliged to follow the advice in its report of September 10, 1942. Dragging Baruch along, Conant and Compton divorced the administration of synthetic rubber from WPB and RFC and created an independent office for rubber production. The Baruch committee also advocated a central rubber industry R&D program, beyond technology-sharing, which was duly begun in October 1942, under the leadership of two chemists from Frank Jewett's Bell Labs. In 1943 the government took over the administration of the Jersey-Farben patents on the condition that it continue to fund rubber R&D to the tune of at least $5 million per year. A government-funded rubber laboratory was established in Akron, Ohio, in 1944.

[32] F. H. Hoge, Jr., to A. C. C. Hill, July 27, 1942; Hoge to Nathan, July 29, 1942; and Hoge to Hill, August 13, 1942, all in RG179, PDF 073.011.

[33] Vernon Herbert and Attilio Bisio, *Synthetic Rubber: A Project That Had to Succeed* (Westport, CT: Greenwood Press, 1985), 39–60; Peter J. T. Morris, *The American Synthetic Rubber Research Program* (Philadelphia: University of Pennsylvania Press, 1989), 9–10; William M. Tuttle, Jr., "The Birth of an Industry: The Synthetic Rubber 'Mess' in World War II," *Technology and Culture* 22 (1981): 38–43.

When Jewett's scientists left the program, their places were taken by rubber industry research executives. In fact, in the immediate postwar period, the big four rubber companies established a system in which their research directors rotated through the directorship of the government program.[34]

In important respects, the wartime synthetic rubber R&D program reflected the associationalist vision. Synthetic rubber was governed independently of other industries; it had its own "czar." Its projects were collaborative and industrywide; results were shared. A government laboratory serviced the program, but control of the research agenda rested with committees of private experts, drawn from the leading firms. The state had little independent expertise and relied on the private sector to develop the new technology efficiently. The "guidance and the bringing about of voluntary research exchange," of which Bush had written to the president's uncle, Frederic Delano of the National Resources Planning Board in July 1942, led in the case of synthetic rubber to a dynamic postwar growth industry. Keith Chapman estimates that government support accelerated the commercialization of synthetic rubber by between twelve and twenty years. Combined with Germany's defeat, the program aided U.S. firms in taking world leadership. However, industrywide cooperation could not be sustained in the absence of the grave national security crisis that followed Pearl Harbor; even the Cold War was not an incentive sufficient to overcome suspicions among firms of the sort that sank the NRA. By 1957 Firestone had taken over the Akron lab, and federal funding of civilian R&D in this industry ended.[35]

The combination of policies that characterized synthetic rubber—technological cooperation under the threat of coercion and the prod of government-funded and tax-advantaged investment in plant and equipment—was not unique to that industry (although elsewhere more technological development was done within firms and less in joint programs like the one described above). In other sectors of the chemical industry, for instance, John K. Smith has shown, these policies induced rapid technological advance and postwar competition. Similar results were achieved in metal industries. In aluminum, for example, Alcoa's production technology was diffused during the war, and the postwar disposition of government-owned plants to Alcoa's competitors substantially altered the industry's monopolistic structure. Typically, however, the postwar competitors were the same as the prewar oligopolists; technological change was not usually accompanied by changes in the industrial structure.[36]

[34] James B. Conant, *My Several Lives: Memoirs of a Social Inventor* (New York: Harper and Row, 1970), 307, 315, 326; Tuttle (above, n. 33), 53–63; Morris (above, n. 33), 12–17.

[35] Bush to Delano, July 22, 1942, RG227, Entry 13, Box 34; Keith Chapman, *The International Petrochemical Industry* (Cambridge: Blackwell, 1991), 66, 76–82; Morris (above, n. 33), 30, 18–22, 50–54. Robert A. Solo, *Synthetic Rubber: A Case Study in Technological Development Under Government Direction,* study no. 18 prepared for U.S. Senate, Committee on the Judiciary, 85th C., 2d s., 1959, dissents from Chapman's assessment.

[36] John K. Smith, Jr., "World War II and the Transformation of the American Chemical Indus-

DEMOBILIZATION, CONSERVATIVE RESURGENCE, AND THE DEATH THROES OF REFORM LIBERALISM

In sharp contrast to World War I's effect on Hoover and Baruch, the associative experiments of World War II evoked little enthusiasm from their participants (with the exception of university scientists), despite their sometimes impressive results. Unless an industry faced collapse as government procurement declined or was considered so vital to national security that coercion was applied, wartime cooperation rapidly dissipated. On the other hand, even though it was weak and tiny, OPRD symbolized for its founders the reform liberal ideal for governing technological innovation. There was a huge disparity in the budgets of OPRD and OSRD and an even bigger disparity in their power and prestige, but Maverick wanted the agency he had precipitated to become permanent while Bush wanted his disbanded. OPRD was one of several reform liberal science and technology policy experiments that, although marginal to the war effort, nonetheless set precedents for government policy with respect to important areas of peacetime economic activity, such as the diffusion of new technologies and the provision of technical expertise to small manufacturers. Drawing an analogy between the challenge of the war and what they saw as the crucial postwar challenge of full employment, a reform liberal coalition, led by the new Secretary of Commerce, Henry Wallace, gathered together the remains of these efforts and tried to breathe new life into them during the first two years after the war. This time the reform liberals were blocked by a newly resurgent conservatism, particularly, as before the war, in Congress.

Less than a month after the death of President Roosevelt, Henry Wallace commented to President Truman that "the greatest shortcoming of the New Deal was that it did not back scientific research the way it should have." Secretary Wallace's effort to complete this aspect of the New Deal took two forms. He undertook administrative actions to make permanent and expand the reform liberals' wartime experiments, and he also supported Senator J. William Fulbright's effort to pass authorizing legislation. Wallace's qualifications for science and technology policy entrepreneurship were extraordinary. He was a pioneer in both agricultural economics and corn genetics, before serving as Secretary of Agriculture and vice-president. Influenced by his historical connections to the agricultural research system, Wallace believed that intense private competition, facilitated by state promotion and regulation, would best bring about innovation, efficiency, and prosperity. As he put it in his postwar tract, *Sixty Million Jobs* (1945), the nation could best achieve full employment

---

try," in E. Mendelsohn, M. R. Smith, and P. Weingart, eds., *Science, Technology, and the Military* (Dordrecht: Kluwer, 1988), 307–22; Margaret B.W. Graham and Bettye H. Pruitt, *R&D for Industry: A Century of Technical Innovation at Alcoa* (New York: Cambridge University Press, 1990), 239–71; White (above, n. 6), 88–112; John M. Blair, *Economic Concentration: Structure, Behavior, and Public Policy* (New York: Harcourt Brace, 1972), 380–85.

through stronger government authority to encourage "competition in productivity rather than competition in free booting."[37]

One building block for Wallace was the Alien Property Custodian's (APC) portfolio of German patents. Concentrated in the areas of chemicals and pharmaceuticals, electrical equipment, and plastics, it included about 5 percent of all unexpired U.S. patents, making the APC the largest patent holder in the country. The APC endeavored to bring the technologies it controlled into the widest possible use by offering nonexclusive, royalty-free patent licenses whenever possible and by making special efforts to reach out to small firms. It even organized road shows to take technical knowledge to firms that did not have a Washington presence. Besides the APC and OPRD, other building blocks for Wallace included the Technical Advisory Service of the Smaller War Plants Corporation (SWPC), which assisted small firms with production problems; the National Inventors Council, which encouraged independent inventors; and the Publications Board, which handled reports on U.S. and enemy wartime technology that might be of use to U.S. industry in peacetime.[38]

These programs, in conjunction with such Commerce stalwarts as the Bureau of Standards and the Patent Office, were to provide assistance to small business in technological development, one of nine basic tasks in the full employment program that Wallace's staff developed in the first half of 1945. The new president put his stamp on the plan in August, approving the transfer of OPRD and SWPC (except for surplus property functions) to Commerce, agreeing to seek supplemental appropriations for fiscal 1946 and increased appropriations for fiscal 1947, and guaranteeing that Wallace would be represented on any cabinet committee dealing with science and technology policy. Small-business assistance was highlighted as point 15 of Truman's 21-point reconversion program announced on September 6, 1945, and Wallace was assigned to oversee the passage and implementation of legislation related to this point.[39]

[37] Wallace, diary for May 4, 1945, in John M. Blum, ed., *The Price of Vision: The Diary of Henry A. Wallace, 1942–1946* (Boston: Houghton-Mifflin, 1973), 442; Henry Wallace, *Sixty Million Jobs* (New York: Reynal and Hitchcock, Simon and Schuster, 1945), 94. My sketch here draws on Blum's introduction, "Portrait of a Diarist," 1–49.

[38] Office of Alien Property Custodian, *Annual Report for the Period March 11, 1942–June 30, 1943* (Washington: APC, 1943), 4–5, 58–63, 73–77; Office of Alien Property Custodian, *Annual Report for Fiscal Year 1944* (Washington: APC, 1944), iii–iv, 90–108; Office of Alien Property Custodian, *Annual Report for Fiscal Year 1945* (Washington: APC, 1945), 97–119; Office of Alien Property Custodian, *Annual Report for Fiscal Year 1946* (Washington: APC, 1946), 4, 95–107; Smaller War Plants Corporation, "Technical Advisory Service," March 1945, mimeo, available in Littauer Library, Harvard University; *Annual Report of the Secretary of Commerce for 1946* (Washington: GPO, 1946), 28–29; John Gimbel, *Science, Technology, and Reparations* (Stanford: Stanford University Press, 1990), 27–30.

[39] Program Committee, draft report, July 7, 1945, RG40, Office of the Secretary, Box 1083, File 104377, 35–43; Wallace diary for August 17, 1945, in Blum, ed. (above, n. 37), 475–76; *Public Papers of the President, 1945* (Washington: GPO, 1961), 296; Truman to Wallace, October 19, 1945, and February 18, 1946, both in RG40, Office of the Secretary, Box 921, File 101199.

To house the former war agencies, the secretary set up the Office of Technical and Scientific Services (OTSS). For fiscal 1947 the president's Budget Message called for OTSS to receive $4.55 million. $1.5 million of the OTSS budget was to be devoted to resurrecting the R&D function of OPRD. $1 million of this was to be disbursed directly by OTSS through research contracts with engineering schools and other nongovernmental organizations. The other half-million dollars was to be funneled through the Bureau of Standards to support research on behalf of groups of small manufacturers. On top of this, about a quarter-million dollars was intended to create a staff of engineers who would be "technical liaison officers" between firms, state research organizations, and Commerce. The renamed National Inventors Service was retained at its wartime size, $75,000. In the president's proposed budget, then, the domestic component of OTSS was to be roughly the same size ($1.8 million) as the external grants program of the National Institutes of Health (NIH) ($1.7 million). As I discuss below, Wallace also hoped to have another $3 million available for OTSS to use, mainly for research support, contingent on the passage of the Fulbright bill. [40]

The remaining $2.7 million of the OTSS budget was earmarked to support the collection, editing, publication, and dissemination of enemy technical information and the declassification of U.S. war documents. Commerce was strongly committed to a policy of broad use of these findings, a policy that echoed that of the APC (which had become a unit of the antitrust division of the Department of Justice), with which Commerce worked closely. OTSS was to be complemented by field offices that Wallace planned to establish. About $2.1 million of the field office budget was requested "to carry on in 1947 services to small business which it [the Department of Commerce] has never before provided. The experience of the Smaller War Plants [sic] in recent years has demonstrated the need for such services. . . ." Technical advice was the most prominent of the services that Wallace hoped to provide to small manufacturers.[41]

Congress funded the OTSS R&D program for fiscal 1947 without fanfare, heedless of the raging debate over the proposed National Science Foundation (discussed in Chapter 6, below). Project suggestions were collected from the land grant colleges and the APC in the fall of 1946, regulations were issued,

[40] "Budget Message of the President for Fiscal Year 1947," in *The Budget of the U.S. Government* (Washington: GPO, 1946), xxxii–xxxiv, 327–28, 125; U.S. House of Representatives, Committee on Appropriations, *Department of Commerce Appropriation Bill for 1947,* 79th C., 2d s., 1946, 80; Wallace to Senator Josiah Bailey, January 25, 1946, RG40, Office of the Secretary, Box 1083, File 104373. Regarding the NIH comparison, an additional $500,000 was to be spent on research grants by the National Cancer Institute, which was not yet a unit of NIH.

[41] House Appropriations Committee, 1946 (above, n. 40), 72, 85–90, 401; Wallace to Bailey, January 25, 1946, RG40, Office of the Secretary, Box 1083, File 104373; "Justification of Increases by Project in Request for 1947 Funds for Field Operations as Compared with Estimated Obligations for Similar Projects in 1946," RG40, General Records Relating to Appropriations, 1910–1951, Office of the Secretary, Box 183, File 88117, "1947," 2.

and $878,000 of the $1 million budgeted was actually spent. Ironically, the program as implemented seemed more appropriate to Herbert Hoover's Commerce Department than Henry Wallace's. "Research is done for industry," the program's director stated, "after it has been demonstrated that industry wants the research done and wants the government to do it." Wallace's vision for the field offices fared even worse. House Republicans, with tacit Democratic support, nearly wiped out this line item, opposing what they saw as a Wallace grab for government control of business. Although the Senate restored some of the funding, technical advice was among the field office functions eliminated because of the cuts. Commerce was left unable to live up to the analogy that Wallace often made between its technological services for small businesses and USDA's for farmers.[42]

The enormous backwash of war-generated information proved to be more a burden than a boon to Wallace's plans. The majority of the OTSS budget was spent processing the vast inventory of U.S. military R&D findings and organizing missions for an "intellectual reparations" program that ultimately brought dozens of German military and civilian experts, millions of pages of documents, and tons of equipment to the United States. The sheer bulk of these materials made a mockery of OTSS's intention to diffuse the findings equitably. OTSS staff suspected, for instance, that the reports they received from Germany failed to reflect the value of the information that was being gathered; the large firms whose representatives dominated the missions simply kept the useful nuggets to themselves. To the extent that this information included tacit knowledge that could improve industrial productivity, the bias in the collection program toward the collectors themselves was inevitable, since such knowledge was available only to observers on the spot. In the words of historian John Gimbel, "individuals and firms got private access to 'intellectual reparations' that were originally intended for dissemination to the general public."[43]

Fears of a "spending psychology," evident in the discussion of Commerce in fiscal 1947, dominated the following year's congressional budget debate. By this time the Republicans had won control of both chambers, and Henry Wallace had left the administration after challenging the president's foreign policy in September 1946. Since Wallace symbolized for conservative members the infiltration of the administration by radicals, his old department was a natural target for them. The House Appropriations Committee report charged that Commerce unnecessarily continued war activities into peacetime without proper

[42] Green to Stone, February 10, 1947, RG40, OTS Records, Box 56, "NAM"; *Annual Report of the Secretary of Commerce for 1947* (Washington: GPO, 1947), 21–26; U.S. House of Representatives, 79th C., 2d s., 1946, H. Rept. 1890, 27; *Congressional Record,* 79th C., 2d s., May 3, 1946, 4426–34; *Congressional Record,* 79th C., 2d s., June 21, 1946, 7296–7300.

[43] Gimbel (above, n. 38), 71; John W. Snyder, *Battle for Production,* report of the director of the Office of War Mobilization and Reconversion (Washington: GPO, 1946), 70–71; Secretary of Commerce, 1946 (above, n. 38), 17–22.

statutory authority, and it ridiculed the research program, remarking that "[p]rivate research, with a profit motive, has done rather well in the U.S. thus far." Other congressional committees found Communists in the department. By 1949 only $200,000 remained of Wallace's original budget, barely enough to clear declassified military research reports.[44]

The ease with which the appropriation of the postwar science and technology policy of the Commerce Department was struck out shows that the emergency war legislation under which it was authorized and transferred was a shaky foundation for its extension into peacetime. Secretary Wallace recognized that Commerce in this regard had only a broad interpretation of its basic mandate "to foster, promote, and develop foreign and domestic commerce" to rely on. By coincidence Wallace found the most promising answer to this problem in legislation proposed in 1945 by Senator J. William Fulbright, the first-term Democrat from Arkansas. But it too foundered on the shoals of congressional conservatism.[45]

The earliest versions of the Fulbright bill, offered in the summer of 1945, were clumsily drawn and unsophisticated. After consultations with Senator Kilgore (whose NSF bill was being debated at the same time) and Secretary Wallace, a substitute emerged that expressed well the reform liberal vision of the federal government's role in the governance of industrial innovation. It called for an Office of Technical Services (OTS) within the Department of Commerce to

- evaluate inventions for commercial potential, develop them in federal facilities, and offer them for private exploitation,
- initiate and sponsor technological R&D on industrial problems of general importance in departmental laboratories or by contract,
- provide research and testing services to individual firms for a fee when private facilities were not available,
- reward inventive federal employees,
- develop and operate a central information clearinghouse for the findings of engineering and technological R&D carried out in both the public and private sectors,
- operate an industrial extension service to diffuse new technology, and
- "study and analyze the impact of science and technology on the economy, to develop such policies, to recommend such legislation, and to take such legally au-

---

[44] U.S. House of Representatives, 79th C., 2nd s., 1946, H. Rept. 1890, 3; U.S. House of Representatives, Committee on Appropriations, *Department of Commerce Appropriation Bill for 1948,* 80th C., 1st s., 1947, 92–136; U.S. House of Representatives, 80th C., 1st s., 1947, H. Rept. 336, 23; *Congressional Record,* 80th C., 1st s., July 3, 1946, 8250; U.S. House of Representatives, Committee on Appropriations, *Department of Commerce Appropriation Bill for 1949,* 80th C., 2d s., 1948, 69; Robert K. Stewart, "The Office of Technical Services: A New Deal Idea in the Cold War," *Knowledge* 15 (1993): 59–63; Jessica Wang, "Science, Security, and the Cold War: The Case of E. U. Condon," *Isis* 83 (1992): 238–69.

[45] Wallace to Bailey, January 25, 1946, RG40, Office of the Secretary, Box 1083, File 104373, 3.

thorized steps with respect to science and technology as are designed to promote full production and employment, to raise the standard of living"

After three days of hearings and further modest revisions, the Senate Commerce
Committee recommended the bill on January 29, 1946. (The famous fall 1945
hearings held by Senators Kilgore and Magnuson on their competing NSF bills
nominally considered the Fulbright bill as well, but in practice consideration
was delayed while Fulbright conferred with Wallace.) The committee's report
stressed the goal of accelerating the pace at which new technologies were put
into manufacturing practice, particularly in the context of international economic competition. The report enclosed a Commerce Department estimate that
the bill would require about $3 million in additional spending in FY47;
$2.5 million would have been allocated for R&D support and the rest to field
services.[46]

The handling of the Fulbright bill on the Senate floor was marked by confusion. At least one Senator thought it had passed before it was even called up.
Wallace reported to the president on April 12 that "the votes are available to
pass both bills" (i.e., Kilgore's and Fulbright's), but Senator Robert A. Taft
blocked full consideration. While the "considerations of political strategy" to
which Wallace chalked up the opposition surely figured in the senator's objections, they were grounded in more fundamental ideological disagreements.
Taft's delaying tactics paid off brilliantly when the Republicans were victori-
ous in the fall of 1946. Fulbright, with a new Republican co-sponsor, introduced
a scaled-down version of his bill in the 80th Congress, but it received a poor
committee referral and died once again.[47]

The 81st Congress finally passed a bill in 1950 that authorized the Commerce
Department to serve as a clearinghouse for the unclassified reports of the Department of Defense, Atomic Energy Commission, and other agencies. The
Publications Board was thus the only wartime experiment to prove its viability
in the postwar political environment. The clearinghouse authorized in 1950 ultimately became the current National Technical Information Service (NTIS).
The concepts of government-funded civilian industrial R&D and extension services died in the cradle. In Maury Maverick's inimitable phraseology, "The

---

[46] U.S. Senate, Commerce Committee, *To Establish an Office of Technical Services in the Department of Commerce,* 79th C., 1st s., 1945; Wallace to Bailey, November 21, 1945, RG40, Office of the Secretary, Box 1083, File 104373; U.S. Senate, 79th C., 2d s., 1946, S. Rept. 908.

[47] Harold Young to Bernard Gladieux, February 25, 1946, RG40, Office of the Secretary, Box
1083, File 104373; *Congressional Record,* 79th C., 2nd s., March 1, 1946, 1818; Wallace memo of
telephone conversation with Fulbright, April 1, 1946, Reel 66, frame 232; and Wallace memo of
telephone conversation with Mead, April 2, 1946, Reel 66, frame 235, both in Wallace papers (microfilm, University of Iowa collection); Wallace to Truman, April 12, 1946, RG40, Office of the
Secretary, Box 921, File 101199; Wallace to Truman, May 10, 1946, RG40, Office of the Secretary, Box 1029, File 104240; U.S. Senate, Committee on Expenditures in Executive Departments,
Technical Information and Services Act, 80th C., 1st s., 1947.

bones of the Smaller War Plants Corporation were transferred to the Department of Commerce and since have not even been seen in a glass case, much less rattled."[48]

CONCLUSION: VACUUM ON THE LEFT

The NTIS ultimately developed into a useful device for the diffusion of government technical information, but it was a far cry from what Wallace and Maverick had hoped for. The postwar American state had little capacity to analyze the evolution of the national industrial structure, to identify potential paths of technological and industrial development that the private sector had ignored, and to act on such information by conducting or supporting industrial R&D, diffusing technical findings, and breaking down private barriers to the exploitation of this new public knowledge. The reform liberal vision was a political failure. The wartime enmity of the national security state was an important reason for this failure. Its partisans' opposition to the "two-front war" was inevitable; Maury Maverick versus George Marshall was no contest. A more sympathetic figure in Bush's position might have been of some help, although his authority would still have been contingent on achieving military results. It is difficult to imagine Wallace, much less Maverick, matching Bush in this regard. WPB's industry branches were another source of opposition. Big business could at most be maneuvered into provisional support of associationalist schemes for mobilizing civilian R&D during the war, as the synthetic rubber episode shows. Small business, which the reform liberals claimed as their constituency, saw them as more likely to add to burdensome wartime regulations than to provide a technological edge against larger competitors; the SWPC was unable to mimic the USDA's success in cultivating farmers a few decades earlier.

Indeed, in the immediate postwar period, small business fears of the state were whipped into an anticommunist frenzy of which Wallace was one victim. Wallace's political ineptitude, the painful presidential transition, and the unexpected economic boom were further strikes against his science and technology policy initiatives. Moreover, the end of the war reverted the legislative status quo to its prewar condition, forcing Wallace to take the offensive in Congress, rather than relying on administrative action. Even though many of the most extreme right-wing members had departed before V-J Day and the Republican leadership was willing to play ball on such issues as housing and education, the rhetoric of "free enterprise" still rang freely, not only in the Republican 80th

[48] Stewart (above, n. 44), 65–68; House of Representatives, Select Committee on Small Business, *Problems of Small Business Related to the National Emergency, part 3,* 82d C., 1st s., 1951, 2051.

Congress, but in the 79th Congress (1945–46) as well. Conservative policy entrepreneurs thus occupied whatever space might have been created for reform
liberal entrepreneurship by the inevitable postwar diminution of the national security state. Postwar advocates of the national security state fought to stem this
shrinkage in any case and, as we shall see, found enemies among both Taft Republicans and Wallace Democrats. The tension between national security, domestic spending, and tax cutting was acute, even though revenues expanded
with the economy.

   The shift of political power to the right made Keynesianism more attractive
to former New Dealers. To forge any winning coalition, especially in Congress,
they had to compromise. Keynesianism, as it crystallized after the war as an almost content-less prescription for spending without structural economic reform, was to a significant extent a status quo to be defended; despite defense
budget cuts, the state was much expanded by war. The requirements for a coalition to block drastic cuts were far less stringent than those for winning new capacities, as the debate over the Employment Act of 1946 showed.[49] Keynesian
theory, as interpreted by American economists, provided an intellectual basis
for treating the economy as a black box that could be regulated by adjustment
of financial inputs, such as government spending. Left-leaning Democrats thus
found virtue in the achievable, extending Keynesian logic even to the governance of technological innovation, a subject in which Keynes himself had
shown little interest.

   [49] Stephen K. Bailey, *Congress Makes a Law: The Story behind the Employment Act of 1946*
(New York: Columbia University Press, 1950).

ray full employment and Kilgore National Science Foundation (NSF) bills, which were naturally opposed by members of Congress who preferred that things revert to the prewar status quo. The death of President Roosevelt accentuated this inevitable shift of power from the executive to the legislature. Harry Truman lacked his predecessor's popularity as well as the formal authority of emergency powers once the war ended.

Congress was the arena in which conservatism had always fared best, and this tendency became more pronounced as the public registered its disgust with controls, strikes, and executive ineptitude in the 1946 midterm elections. No longer content to contain the New Deal by thwarting initiatives like Murray's and Kilgore's, the new Republican majority moved to roll it back. The Taft-Hartley Act of 1947 was the most profound of the measures that were enacted by the "do-nothing" 80th Congress. Even after President Truman's come-from-behind victory in 1948, which owed more than a little to the conservative Republicans' overinterpretation of their mandate, Congress remained a bastion of "free enterprise" rhetoric. Although the conservatives were unable to enact very much of their agenda, which included tax breaks that they hoped would free up private capital for speculative technological ventures (among other things), they remained a major obstacle to their postwar ideological competitors.

The conservative arsenal of ideas was augmented in the late 1940s by the re-emergence of anti-Communism as a potent political force. Interestingly, the rhetorical escalation against "subversives" at home was not matched, at least at first, by a comparable expansion of the national security state to defend the nation against "Soviet Russia." To be sure, military spending from 1945 to 1950, particularly for R&D, remained far above prewar levels. Demands for "normalcy," however, frustrated those who feared that the nation's international commitments were outrunning its means to fulfill them (as I describe in more detail in Chapter 7). The military and foreign aid budgets rose in this half-decade, but modestly and rarely without a fierce fight. Although national security arguments were sometimes invoked to justify new domestic programs, like the NSF, they hardly carried the day alone. And, even when such measures passed, minuscule budgets were provided to implement them.

Nonetheless, national security obligations, once the war debt and veterans' programs are included in the calculation, consumed the lion's share of the federal budget and helped dim the prospects for other new federal initiatives. As we have seen, Henry Wallace's dream of an expansive civilian technology program after the war was crushed by conservatism, anti-Communism, military demands, and tight budgets. After Wallace resigned in September 1946, there were no New Dealers left in the cabinet and few in the Congress. To get anything done at all, those who had shared Wallace's vision of an active and expert administrative state, such as Leon Keyserling, vice-chairman of the new Council of Economic Advisors (CEA), had to rethink their position, scale back their ambition, and find new allies.

CHAPTER 6

Groping toward Management

SCIENCE, TECHNOLOGY, AND MACRO- AND MICROECONOMIC POLICY, 1945–1950

AMERICANS came out of World War II with vivid memories and a powerful ⌐
to consume. Their memories encompassed not only the confusion and ⌐
strictions of wartime governance, but the deprivation of the years before
well, inspiring a yearning for "normalcy," as Alonzo Hamby has put it, m
reminiscent of the 1920s than the 1930s.[1] This was a condition easy to visu
ize but not necessarily easy to achieve, given the economic, political, and tec
nological abnormalities of the past fifteen years of depression and war. ⌐
though many postwar policy-makers shared the yearning for the prosperity a⌐
stability of the old days, they differed sharply in their interpretations of the r⌐
cent past and its implications for the nation's future. Conservatives, for i⌐
stance, viewed the period of Depression and war as an aberration to be boxe
away. National security zealots, on the other hand, saw it as a time in which th
nation came of age and global responsibilities became normal. Reform liberal⌐
and associationalists, although chastened by their failures in practice, were convinced that the best elements of their visions of the state deserved a permanent
place in an American life that had been irrevocably changed. Keynesians believed that their techniques had matured and constituted a tool kit for effective
governance in what they agreed was a new world. These differences, in turn,
led to contrasting and often contradictory policy programs. The immediate
postwar period was marked by a stalemate among partisans of these various visions; the stalemate slowly gave way as old associationalists and reform liberals found a new Keynesian common ground.

One reason for the stalemate was the return of control over domestic policy-
making to Congress, resuming a trend interrupted by the war. Members of Congress took the initiative (often to the consternation of the president) as early as
mid-1943 on domestic issues of reconversion such as contract settlement, surplus property disposition, and adjustment assistance. Congressional consideration of how to move the economy from war to peace led directly to legislative
proposals for reorganizing peacetime governance, like the reform liberal Mur-

---

[1] Alonzo Hamby, *Beyond the New Deal: Harry S. Truman and American Liberalism* (New York: Columbia University Press, 1973), 54.

A similar dilemma faced associationalists. World War II had convinced them, in a way that the NRA had not, that the state, with their participation, might play a useful role in economic management. In any case, the federal government was big and bound to stay that way and, therefore, the best had to be made of it. While this war spawned no apostles of associationalism of the stature and devotion of World War I's Herbert Hoover and Bernard Baruch, men like Vannevar Bush and Karl Compton maintained some faith in the delegation of state authority and funds to "representative" private experts, particularly in science and technology policy. Their ranks were too small, however, to achieve their ends alone.

Reform liberals and associationalists did not adapt in the immediate postwar period only because they had to build winning political coalitions; many also found flaws in their visions of the state. Defectors from the Wallace camp feared that an administrative state would be captured (as they thought the War Production Board had been) and turned to unpleasant purposes, like violating civil liberties or breaking strikes. Ex-Hooverites feared noncompliance if cooperation was voluntary and red tape and stagnation if cooperation was state-mandated. There was also the positive attraction of Keynesian macroeconomics. The Keynesian vision of the state seemed to have been vindicated by the extraordinary growth and price stability of the wartime economy. Keynes provided a new language and conceptual framework for economic governance and promised a new middle way between free market chaos and regulatory regimentation. But before Keynesianism could be put into peacetime practice, it required further specification. Would fiscal stimulus (or restraint) be targeted on consumption or investment? Would it be provided through tax reductions or increased government spending? In what realms did the market, even if aggregate inputs were properly managed, nonetheless fail?

A convergence of views on economic policy, if not the consensus that Herbert Stein has suggested, emerged out of the political battles of 1945 to 1950. Economic growth through demand management became a fundamental responsibility of the federal government, even a fetish—"growthmanship," Richard Nixon, that famous Keynesian, called it. It was to be achieved, as those whom Robert Lekachman later labeled "commercial Keynesians" (many of whom were former associationalists) wanted, mainly through indirect means such as tax reductions and "automatic stabilizers." This approach left a wide berth to management prerogatives. Yet, the reform liberal vision did not disappear entirely. "Social Keynesians" occasionally won grudging support to maintain and even marginally expand some of the microeconomic regulation and public investment measures of the New Deal.[2]

In science and technology policy, too, a convergence occurred, if not the

---

[2] Herbert Stein, *The Fiscal Revolution in America,* rev. ed. (Washington: AEI Press, 1990), 197–240; Robert Lekachman, *The Age of Keynes* (New York: Random House, 1966), 209, 287.

"postwar consensus" that Bruce Smith has hypothesized. A conducive macro-economic environment, in which private actors would have the expectation of sufficient demand to invest in R&D and technological innovation, was the essential goal of this policy. The state needed to develop the analytical capability to monitor this private investment, so that it could compensate in case of failure, although the ways and means of compensation were matters of dispute. Beyond this the government would have an investment policy in a couple of areas in which markets appeared to fail, academic science and small business start-ups. The convergence on the boundaries of market failure was slow and painful in coming. Ironically, just when it seemed to have been achieved in the spring of 1950, the Korean War erupted, subordinating the fledgling NSF and the nascent venture capital program to the demands of the national security state.[3]

FROM STAGNATION TO EXHILARATION:
THE KEYNESIAN DIAGNOSIS TRANSFORMED

Between 1938 and 1948, the conventional wisdom among American Keynesians underwent a remarkable transformation. Indeed, the Keynesian answer to the crucial question of whether corporate capitalism could generate technological innovation at a satisfactory rate completely flipped. In 1938 the Harvard economist Alvin Hansen's "secular stagnation" thesis held sway. The economy, Hansen claimed, was more dependent than ever on new technology and less capable than ever of producing it. "[D]eliberate action of a far bolder character than hitherto envisaged," he told the American Economic Association in his presidential address that year, "must be undertaken in order to make the price system and free enterprise sufficiently responsive to permit at least that measure of capital formation to which the rate of technological progress had accustomed us in the past." In 1948, with the electronic and atomic marvels of the war in mind, the Keynesian wunderkind Paul Samuelson turned Hansen's argument on its head. In a textbook that dominated Economics 101 for years, Samuelson concluded that "secular exhilaration rather than secular stagnation may be our most important worry."[4]

Hansen's Depression-era pessimism tapped an indigenous strain of economic thought and blended it with the latest from Cambridge, England. The closing of the frontier, the restriction of immigration, and the apparent saturation of the automobile market with nothing on the horizon to take its place to drive industrial development were popular themes of American writers like

---

[3] Bruce L. R. Smith, *American Science Policy since World War II* (Washington: Brookings Institution, 1990).

[4] Alvin H. Hansen, "Economic Progress and Declining Population Growth," *American Economic Review* 29 (1939): 12; Paul A. Samuelson, *Economics: An Introductory Analysis,* 2d ed. (New York: McGraw-Hill, 1951), 408.

William T. Foster and Waddill Catchings. For Hansen, these factors added up to a lack of outlets for new investment, the most volatile component of the Keynesian national income analysis. They were compounded by a technological trend toward capital-saving invention that further reduced aggregate demand. Hansen also endorsed the reform liberal thesis that the big businesses that dominated industrial R&D suppressed or restricted technological developments that would cut into their existing markets, depriving the economy of needed competition and the consumption that it would stimulate. Hansen therefore cheered on Thurman Arnold's patent campaign and advocated government-funded R&D and investment (especially for prefabricated housing), even as he sought at the same time a federal spending program that would boost consumption.[5]

Other early Keynesians involved in what Herbert Stein has termed the "struggle for the soul of FDR" during the 1937–38 recession rejected stagnation and Hansen's call for direct stimulation of investment. This group, which included Beardsley Ruml and Ralph Flanders, two of the future founders of the Committee for Economic Development (CED), which would become the most influential voice of commercial Keynesianism after the war, agreed with Hansen that the economy suffered from too much saving and too little investment. They argued, however, that the government ought to concentrate on stimulating consumer demand, which would indirectly expand investment by boosting expectations about sales. Although they were not averse to deficit spending during slumps, they were quite interested as well in tax reforms that penalized saving and rewarded consumption. Hansen's arguments may have had more influence among the young economists who would go on to staff the agencies of wartime Washington, but Ruml's views were probably more effective in winning the president's assent to a new spending program in April 1938. Consumption-oriented measures, like social welfare spending and progressive taxation, dominated the administration's economic agenda into 1940.[6]

World War II catalyzed a dramatic about-face. During the mobilization period, Keynesian "all-outers" pressed for massive defense investments; during

---

[5] Bradford Lee, "The Miscarriage of Necessity and Invention: Proto-Keynesianism and Democratic States in the 1930s," in Peter A. Hall, ed., *The Political Power of Economic Ideas: Keynesianism across Nations* (Princeton: Princeton University Press, 1989), 132–33; Hansen (above, n. 4).

[6] Stein (above, n. 2), 91–130; Henry S. Dennison, Lincoln Filene, Ralph E. Flanders, and Morris E. Leeds, *Toward Full Employment* (New York: Whittlesey House, 1938), 189–202; Alan Brinkley, *The End of Reform: New Deal Liberalism in Recession and War* (New York: Knopf, 1995), 86–105; William J. Barber, "Government as a Laboratory for Economic Learning in the Years of the Democratic Roosevelt," in Mary O. Furner and Barry Supple, eds., *The State and Economic Knowledge: The American and British Experiences* (New York: Cambridge University Press, 1990), 120–22. In my view Brinkley gives an unbalanced reading of Hansen's position, despite Hansen's reference to consumption as the "great frontier of the future" (Speech, March 15, 1940, Alvin H. Hansen papers, Harvard University Archives [hereafter "Hansen papers"], 3.10).

the war, the federal government proceeded to supply about 60 percent of the financing for industrial plant and equipment and subsidized much of the rest through tax incentives. Although the fact that the private sector did much of the R&D and operated most of the plants clouded the matter, Hansen could certainly feel vindicated by the outpouring of innovations that this public investment produced. Yet, once the United States had committed itself to total war, the priority of investment could be taken for granted. The true challenge for economic management was to restrain consumption and inflation in the face of aggregate demand bloated by massive state spending. Agencies like the Office of Price Administration (OPA) and the Bureau of the Budget (BOB) applied Keynesian theory to this task, developing quantitative estimates of such elusive concepts as the "marginal propensity to consume" to use as policy guidance. The war considerably advanced the economic managers' understanding of taxation, broadened the revenue base, and provided new instruments, such as withholding, to manipulate the fiscal effect of taxes. While some of their proposals were blocked by more conventional thinkers in the Treasury and Congress, the Keynesians emerged from the war brimming with confidence that their framework was flexible enough to be applied in periods of restraint as well as recovery—and that it worked.[7]

Wartime planning exercises for the postwar period showed that the war experience could be used to justify both the commercial and social strands of Keynesian thought. Hansen at first worked through the National Resources Planning Board (NRPB), to which the president assigned postwar planning responsibilities in 1941; after that agency was killed by Congress in 1943, he led an informal interagency working group in the development of an "American White Paper." Modeled on the recently published British White Paper, which had laid down Keynesian principles for postwar governance, the working group's drafts advocated an active fiscal policy encompassing generous social welfare spending and state-led technological development, particularly programs to aid small businesses and supply venture capital. Social Keynesians reasoned that once the stimulus of wartime spending was withdrawn, stagnation would resume, a fear widely shared by the public. The "American White Paper" was never formally promulgated, but some of its ideas were worked into the major presidential statements of early 1945. Hansen's critics claimed that his views had by this time become "an official creed."[8]

[7] Byrd L. Jones, "The Role of Keynesians in Wartime and Postwar Planning, 1940–1946," *American Economic Review Papers and Proceedings* 62 (1972): 126–28, 138–39; Robert J. Gordon, "$45 Billion of U.S. Private Investment Has Been Mislaid," *American Economic Review* 59 (1969): 226; Barber (above, n. 6), 122–33; Stein (above, n. 2), 180–93. Gregory Hooks, *Forging the Military-Industrial Complex: World War II's Battle of the Potomac* (Urbana: University of Illinois Press, 1991), 127–41, provides an interesting description and a more critical account but uses unsatisfactory figures.

[8] National Resources Planning Board, *National Resources Development Report for 1943. Part I: Post-War Plan and Program* (Washington: USGPO, 1943); Hansen to Gerhard Colm, July 11, 1944, Hansen papers, 3.10; Hansen to J. Weldon Jones, August 18, 1944, RG51, Entry 39.3, Box

But the critics exaggerated. When the NRPB was shut down, its planning responsibilities were passed to the Office of War Mobilization and Reconversion (OWMR), headed by the more cautious James Byrnes. His reports to the president in 1944 and 1945 emphasized, among other things, tax policies like accelerated depreciation that would "give a real incentive to companies to keep our industry ahead of the world technologically." Byrnes commented acidly: "We should not be stampeded into large public works projects." More importantly Congress had little interest in what Hansen had to say, as the killing of the NRPB demonstrated, and only gave slightly more credence to OWMR or the newly formed CED. The Senate Postwar Planning Committee, for instance, chaired by Georgia's Walter George, merely toyed with Keynesian ideas, whatever their stripe, stripping the 1944 reconversion bill offered by Senators Kilgore, James Murray, and Truman of most of its economic planning apparatus.[9]

The conflict came to a head in the 1946 Employment Act, which defined general principles and institutional arrangements for postwar economic policymaking. In offering the original Full Employment Act in January 1945, Senator Murray anticipated a slump and proposed that government spending along the lines of the "American White Paper," largely under the control of the president, be authorized to combat it. Although the Murray bill passed the Senate just after V-J Day in a relatively undiluted form, conservatives in the House and their allies in the business community waged a ferocious campaign against it. The economy's unexpected buoyancy added fuel to the campaign, revealing the flimsiness of the models to which Murray would have had the nation subscribe. The final bill maintained legislative control of taxing and spending authority and gave Congress a new joint committee to provide macroeconomic policymaking advice to match that of the president's new Council of Economic Advisors. Any public investment that economic conditions might seem to call for would be provided only after due deliberation. This cautious approach was congenial to the commercial Keynesians, who argued that built-in stabilizers, such as the fiscal deficits that resulted from shrinkage of the tax base during a recession, should be permitted to work before the government should be authorized to compensate with new spending programs.[10]

The Employment Act outraged conservatives by establishing a positive duty

---

71, Folder 431, 6; Gerhard Colm, draft on "Postwar Employment," October 9, 1944, Gerhard Colm papers, HSTL (hereafter "Colm papers"), Box 1, "Postwar Employment Program of Interagency Group," 11–15; Hadley Cantril, ed., *Public Opinion, 1935–1946* (Westport, CT: Greenwood, 1978), 901–4; George Terborgh, *The Bogey of Economic Maturity* (Chicago: Machinery and Allied Products Institute, 1945), 13.

[9] James F. Byrnes, *Reconversion: A Report to the President,* 78th C., 2d s., 1944, S. doc. 237; Byrnes, "War Production and VE Day," Office of War Mobilization and Reconversion pamphlet, April 1, 1945, available in Widener Library, Harvard University, 28; U.S. Senate, Special Committee on Postwar Economic Policy and Planning, *Postwar Tax Plans for the Federal Government,* 79th C., 1st s., 1945, Committee Print 7; Stephen K. Bailey, *Congress Makes a Law* (New York: Columbia University Press, 1950), 13–36.

[10] Bailey (above, n. 9); Stein (above, n. 2), 197–204.

for the federal government with respect to economic growth and bitterly disappointed social Keynesians by drastically limiting the instruments that it could use to do so. The act nonetheless codified a framework that the latter could abide by. The language of future economic policy debates would be Keynesian, ensured by the CEA, its required annual report on economic conditions, and the Congressional Joint Committee on the Economic Report. Both branches of government would develop the capacity to monitor economic developments and to offer compensatory policies should conditions demand them, whether taxing or spending, whether targeted on consumption or investment. In the eyes of the commercial Keynesians, the act's most important feature was its acknowledgement that government was not the sole curator of the nation's economic welfare. In case of a downturn, the private sector was to do its best first and be given a long chance to right things. As the CED's Ralph Flanders put it in Senate testimony, economic stability and growth were contingent on all elements of society, not just government, fulfilling their responsibilities.[11]

MONITOR, JAWBONE, AND HOPE: MANAGERIAL PREROGATIVES AND MACROECONOMIC OVERSIGHT

The boom that removed the urgency from the Employment Act debate continued unabated for more than three years, took a slight dip in 1949, and then resumed. Inflation, not recession, was the main enemy. Under these conditions of "exhilaration," rather than "stagnation," the government could cheer on private enterprise, put its books in order, and even begin to retire the war debt, as the president was inclined to do, without much fear that fiscal austerity would precipitate a slowdown. The large firms that had won the war were now winning the peace, in part, from the Keynesian perspective, by making R&D a routine component of their investment. Policy-makers did worry about whether the productivity gains of such investments would be shared with workers and consumers, thereby helping to maintain demand; the linkage of productivity and pay in the 1950 UAW-GM "treaty of Detroit," which established a national pattern for collective bargaining, ultimately resolved this concern. Although management had been ceded the prerogative of determining the pace and direction of technological change, labor had proved itself strong enough to acquire its rightful share of the fruits. With the short-term apparently assured, policy entrepreneurs in the CEA and BOB began to turn their attention to the economy's long-term potential for growth. They developed new capacities to keep track of and set goals for R&D spending and began to try to integrate the economics of technological innovation into Keynesian equilibrium analysis.

[11] U.S. Senate, Committee on Banking and Currency, *Full Employment Act of 1945,* 79th C., 1st s., 1945, 357–69.

John Kenneth Galbraith summed up the half-decade's convergence of social and commercial Keynesianism in *American Capitalism* (1952) with the statement that the large firm was "an almost perfect instrument" of technological development. Labor costs had been taken out of competition by unionization, so process improvement and product development had become the major means through which large firms could compete with one another and pursue growth. Corporate R&D laboratories routinized the innovation process. The prewar fear that big business would collude or use its legal and political power to suppress new inventions faded. As long as there were a small number of competitors in an industry, the conventional wisdom went, innovation would proceed rapidly as long as the macroeconomic environment was sufficiently expansive. Keynesians were therefore pleased that wartime administrators ended Alcoa's aluminimum monopoly, but not particularly concerned that the Big Three's grip on autos remained tight despite efforts of entrepreneurs like Henry Kaiser and Preston Tucker to establish new competitors during the reconversion period. The government's preeminent role was not to restructure the market, except in the extreme case of a monopoly like Alcoa's, but to keep buyers buying. "Adequacy of demand," Harvard's Seymour Harris put it, "will assure high levels of productivity, for it yields capacity output at low unit costs, and it can provide surplus funds to further the advancement of science."[12]

The Keynesians' new-found confidence in large firms owed something to the antitrust division's success in barring the most egregious abuses of patent power, but more to the events of the war and the postwar boom. The war redeemed the reputation of business and brought R&D unprecedented prestige. Management solidified this tentative trust by plowing profits back into new facilities, equipment, and expertise. Overall private investment consistently set records in the immediate postwar years, confounding the stagnationists and confirming the CED. R&D divisions received their due share of this corporate spending, beginning a period of "explosive growth," in the words of historian Kendall Birr. Starting from the foundation provided by wartime R&D contracts (and maintained to some extent by continued military R&D), many large firms dramatically expanded their central research laboratories, building lavish campus-like facilities to attract technical talent in some cases. In RCA and other high-technology firms, the position of research director became a stepping-stone to chief executive officer. A 1947 survey by *Business Week* found that 87 percent of firms had expanded their research since before the war and 72 percent expected to expand it further.[13]

[12] John Kenneth Galbraith, *American Capitalism: The Concept of Countervailing Power* (Cambridge: Riverside Press, 1952), 91; Seymour Harris, "The Issues," in Harris, ed., *Saving American Capitalism* (New York: Knopf, 1948), 11; Gerald T. White, *Billions for Defense: Government Financing by the Defense Plant Corporation during World War II* (University, AL: University of Alabama Press, 1980), 103–9.

[13] Kendall Birr, "Industrial Research Laboratories," in Nathan Reingold, ed., *The Sciences in*

Military spending aside, the federal government had little direct influence on corporate investments in science and technology. Large firms routinely counted their R&D spending as a current cost for tax purposes, rather than a capital expense that had to be written off over a period of years. This accounting practice provided a modest incentive for large firms to do R&D, but it long predated the war. The more general concept of public investment to spur private investment made a very brief reprise in the 1948 campaign as a presidential ploy to sway western voters, but the legislative program Truman presented after his victory made no new departures in this direction. To the contrary the January 1949 *Economic Report of the President,* written under the direction of Leon Keyserling, the feisty former aide to Senator Robert Wagner who was now asserting himself against his more conservative boss, CEA chairman Edwin Nourse, emphasized not public investment, but rather the importance of government's role in creating a positive environment for private investment decisions to stimulate growth.[14]

Keyserling's stated faith in private enterprise (albeit under the federal government's watchful eye) raised eyebrows even in centrist policy circles, where he was seen as an old-line New Dealer. It was put to the test when investment spending unexpectedly dropped during 1949. Keyserling had entered that year with the expectation that consumption was lagging and that, if there was to be a more active economic policy in the wake of the election, it ought to focus on consumption rather than investment. Early signs of the recession prompted him to reconsider. Senator Murray's antirecession bill, with which Keyserling was said to sympathize, dressed up reform liberalism in social Keynesian clothing. Perceiving an NRA-like squeeze by colluding large firms in heavy industrial sectors, such as steel, Murray proposed to authorize the federal government to conduct R&D and make direct investments in these sectors. But Keyserling refrained from endorsing this antistagnationist program. Neither the president nor Congress, he concluded, was likely to have the stomach for such measures. A winning coalition could be built instead behind a moderate fiscal stimulus provided largely by the automatic stabilizers and authorization to study the stabil-

the American Context: New Perspectives (Washington: Smithsonian Institution Press, 1979), 202; Margaret Graham, "Industrial Research in the Age of Big Science," *Research on Technological Innovation, Management, and Policy* 2 (1985): 47–79; "Industry Is Spending More for Research," *Business Week,* November 1, 1947, 58. National investment spending is tracked and assessed in the semiannual *Economic Report of the President* (and the accompanying report of the CEA), which was first presented to Congress in January 1947.

[14] J. Keith Butters, "Taxation and New Product Development," *Harvard Business Review* (Summer 1945): 451–60; U.S.House of Representatives, Committee on Ways and Means, *General Revenue Revision,* 83rd C., 2d s., 1954, 940–59; Keyserling to Clark Clifford, December 20, 1948, Leon Keyserling papers, HSTL (hereafter "Keyserling papers"), Box 8, "White House Contacts—Clark Clifford, 1946–1952"; Hamby 1973 (above, n. 1), 209–15, 294–303; Robert M. Collins, "The Emergence of Economic Growthmanship in the United States: Federal Policy and Economic Knowledge in the Truman Years," in Furner and Supple (above, n. 6), 149–50.

ity of business investment. When the recession ebbed before the year was out, Keyserling was able to share in the administration's credit-taking and to use the investment study to build momentum for a longer-term economic policy agenda, discussed below.[15]

A steady stream of corporate investments, incremental innovations, and ingenious new products were not in themselves sufficient from the Keynesian point of view to ensure continued economic growth in the long run. The division of the benefits of these advances had to be spread to workers through wage increases and price reductions if effective demand was to keep up with expanding supply. On this point the CED and the CEA agreed from 1946 on: collective bargaining ought to result in a linkage between productivity growth and wage growth. The end of the war, however, greatly curtailed federal leverage over labor/management relations, often reducing the president to little more than "jawboning." The postwar CEA sometimes feared that labor would delink productivity and wages. It claimed, for instance, that Truman's nemesis, John L. Lewis of the United Mine Workers, had set wage demands too high in 1947, contributing to inflationary pressures. More commonly the council worried that managers and shareholders, rather than labor, would hoard the gains of technological progress. The White House's exhortation on behalf of "responsible" contracts may have had some modest impact on management in high-profile labor negotiations to which the press and public paid attention. More fundamentally, though, in an expanding economy the logic of "countervailing power" (to use Galbraith's term) harnessed wages to productivity growth in many major industrial sectors. General Motors, the pacesetter, saw no sense in risking a crippling strike in the booming market of 1948, when it first offered the United Auto Workers (UAW) a raise based on the cost of living plus 2 percent for productivity growth. This deal, ratified in 1950 and hailed by *Fortune* as the "treaty of Detroit," set the pattern that other settlements followed; the principle became a pillar of postwar labor relations.[16]

[15] "Oil on Troubled Waters," *Washington Post,* January 1, 1950, 15; *Economic Report of the President* (Washington: GPO, 1950), 6; Colm to Keyserling, March 3, 1949, Keyserling papers, Box 7, "Projections"; J. Weldon Jones to Director, May 25, 1949, RG51, Entry 39.3, Box 66, Folder 398; President's radio message, July 13, 1949, Keyserling papers, Box 8, Folder "White House Contacts—Harry S. Truman—3"; William O. Wagnon, Jr., "The Politics of Economic Growth: The Truman Administration and the 1949 Recession" (Ph.D. diss., University of Missouri, 1970), chaps. 2–5; Alonzo Hamby, *Man of the People: A Life of Harry S. Truman* (New York: Oxford University Press, 1995), 499–501; Leon Keyserling, "Prospects for American Economic Growth," speech, September 18, 1949, Harry S. Truman papers, HSTL (hereafter "Truman papers"), OF 791.

[16] Melvin G. DeChazeau et al., *Jobs and Markets: How to Prevent Inflation and Depression in the Transition* (New York: McGraw-Hill, 1946), 40–44; Leon Keyserling, "Deficiencies of Past Programs and Nature of New Needs," in Harris, ed. (above, n. 12), 86–89; *Mid-Year Economic Report of the President* (Washington: GPO, 1947), 40–43; Fred Israel, ed., *State of the Union Messages of the Presidents* (New York: Chelsea House, 1966), 2972–73; Nelson Lichtenstein, *The Most Dangerous Man in Detroit: Walter Reuther and the Fate of American Labor* (New York: Basic, 1995), 270–81.

The federal government lacked the power to act on pay for productivity, and it also lacked reliable statistical information on the subject. Gerhard Colm, CEA's de facto chief of staff, initiated long-term modeling studies in late 1947 that depended crucially on productivity estimates but was forced to rely (as Keynes had been) on virtually arbitrary extrapolations of historical trends. Colm's staff worked with Ralph Flanders, who joined the Senate as a Republican from Vermont in 1946, to defend the Bureau of Labor Statistics' young productivity measurement program from the conservatives' budget axe in the 80th Congress. By early 1949 the CEA was considering projects to track technological improvements that raised productivity and to study the wage-productivity relationship more carefully.[17]

Statistics on R&D spending were also difficult to come by. In this area the Bureau of the Budget did pioneering work in the immediate postwar period. Before the war, following in the footsteps of Karl Compton's Science Advisory Board, the National Research Council's Division of Engineering and Industrial Research and the National Resources Planning Board began to compile some figures, culminating in their collaboration in the three-volume *Research—A National Resource,* published between 1938 and 1942. The promise of that title, however, could not be fulfilled without more systematic collection of statistics and a framework for their use in federal policy-making. The former was provided by BoB beginning in 1947. The initial motivation for collecting statistics was the never-ending quest to find areas of duplication that would permit budget-cutting. Its aims expanded, however, as BOB was called upon to support Keynesian demand management policies. When the bureau's director requested that his Fiscal Analysis Division supply an accounting of federal dollars spent on economic development in the spring of 1949, for instance, the new R&D figures were included, even though the staff was highly suspicious of the quality of the data. By August this budget had been renamed an "investment budget," and it was included as a special analysis in the fiscal 1951 budget presented by the president to the Congress at the beginning of 1950.[18]

[17] Colm to CEA staff, October 14, 1947, and draft "Nation's Economic Budget for 1958," May 21, 1948, both in Keyserling papers, Box 6, "Economic Budget Studies, 1946–1951"; J. C. Davis and T. K. Hitch to Keyserling, February 18, 1949 (with attachments), Keyserling papers, Box 9, "Productivity"; J. M. Keynes, "The Probable Range of the Postwar National Income," in Donald Moggridge, ed., *The Collected Writings of John Maynard Keynes* (London: MacMillan, 1973), 336–42.

[18] Karl T. Compton, "The Natural Sciences in National Planning: Is Half of One Percent of the Federal Budget Enough?" *Technology Review* 36 (1934): 344–46; National Resources Planning Board, *Research—A National Resource,* 3 vols. (Washington: GPO, 1938, 1940, and 1942); memos and correspondence, RG51, Entry 47.8A, Box 6, "Research and Development—Budget Statistics"; Willis H. Shapley, "Problems of Definition, Concept, and Interpretation of R&D Statistics," in *Methodology of Statistics on R&D,* NSF 59–36 (Washington: NSF, 1959), 8–15; J. Weldon Jones to Griffith Johnson, May 5, 1949, RG51, Entry 39.3, Box 67, Folder 403; Memo to Program Analysts, Fiscal Analysis Division, August 3, 1949, and Johnson to Director, August 17, 1951, both in RG51, Entry 39.3, Box 129, Folder 869; *Budget of the United States for Fiscal Year 1951* (Washington: GPO, 1950), 1113–20.

The BOB's R&D figures were also used by the president's Scientific Research Board, chaired by White House aide John Steelman, in its 1947 report on U.S. science policy. The Steelman report set 1 percent of national income as a goal for total public and private R&D spending ten years hence, in 1957. This numerical target was of a piece with those set for overall economic growth and for specific economic sectors, which were developed by Keyserling and Colm and published in the 1949 *Economic Report*. Such goals were hardly the result of scientific calculations, nor were they binding on Congress or the president (much less the private sector), but they did provide widely used benchmarks for policy evaluation. Within a few years Steelman's 1 percent was offered as a rule of thumb not just for the United States but for developing countries around the world.[19]

By relating national investments in science and technology to the national income, the Steelman report took a step beyond previous efforts, like those of Vannevar Bush and Harley Kilgore in 1945, which had offered only federal R&D spending goals, either in absolute terms or in relation to the federal budget. It moved toward an assessment of what Seymour Harris called "optimum expenditure in science" to be based on macroeconomic modeling, which he guessed "might well run into the tens of billions of dollars." Within the economics profession, the Keynesian approach to technological innovation soon challenged more traditional microeconomic analyses, like those that had been funded by the Rockefeller Foundation under the direction of W. Rupert MacLaurin at MIT in the early 1940s. MacLaurin's work focused on such Schumpeterian themes as industrial history, firm size, and patent control. The new wave was exemplified by Simon Kuznets, who later won the Nobel Prize for his quantification of national income. Kuznets' Committee on Economic Growth of the Social Science Research Council tried assiduously in the late 1940s and early 1950s to quantitatively describe technological change. But the high hopes of the econometricians were not fully realized. Although technological innovation took a central place in the economics of growth as it developed in the 1950s, its measurement proved extremely difficult. Robert Solow's prize-winning 1957 paper solved the problem by sidestepping it, ascribing to technology the residual of growth that could not be explained with more easily measured variables, like the growth of labor and capital.[20]

[19] President's Scientific Research Board (PSRB), *Science and Public Policy. Volume I: A Program for the Nation* (Washington: GPO, 1947), 7; John D. Morris, "Truman Board Bids U.S. Put $2 Billion a Year in Science," *New York Times,* August 28, 1947, 1; *Economic Report of the President* (Washington: GPO, 1949), 50–61; George A. Lincoln, *Economics of National Security,* 2d ed. (New York: Prentice-Hall, 1954), 360; W. Arthur Lewis, *The Theory of Economic Growth* (Homewood, IL: Richard Irwin, 1955), 176. The public record does not reveal how the Steelman Board arrived at the 1 percent goal. Vannevar Bush claimed that Steelman did not participate in the drafting of the report and may have never read it.

[20] Seymour Harris, "Should the Scientists Resist Military Intrusion?" *American Scholar* (April 1947): 224; W. Rupert MacLaurin, *Invention and Innovation in the Radio Industry* (New York: MacMillan, 1949); Carolyn Shaw Solo, "Innovation in the Capitalist Process: A Critique of Schum-

That Solow's residual rested largely on R&D spending was a matter of faith that went virtually unchallenged until the 1970s when productivity growth mysteriously slowed down in a fashion unlinked to measured R&D, and Japanese firms showed that management practices could make substantial contributions to innovation without spending much on R&D at all. U.S. science and technology policy-makers have nonetheless largely retained the faith that aggregate R&D spending is *the* critical measure for policy evaluation. This faith, propped up by the interest groups that federal R&D spending has nourished in the postwar period, is one legacy of the Keynesian influence in this policy area. As I discuss in Chapter 8, occasional efforts to revise the conceptual and policy framework inherited from the late 1940s, to incorporate new insights on the microeconomic foundations of innovation and deemphasize aggregate R&D spending, have generally been unsuccessful. The conceptual developments described above, however, were far from sufficient in themselves to catalyze federal R&D spending of the scale that the past few decades have witnessed. A spending program to compensate for the failures of the market in science and technology had to wait until a compromise was achieved on just where exactly the market failed, and even then it was but a trickle barely portending the torrent to come.

THE SCOPE OF MARKET FAILURE I: FEDERAL FUNDING OF ACADEMIC SCIENCE

The difficulty experienced by competing postwar policy entrepreneurs in settling on a mutually acceptable structure for infusing federal funds into academic science is ironic. Before World War II even ended, the two most prominent of these entrepreneurs, Bush and Kilgore, agreed that the federal government needed to do something, because the market could not be counted on. Moreover, conservatives opposed federal support for university-based research less firmly than other types of public investment, largely because they thought science had proved its worth to national security during the war. Yet the stalemate held for five long years, from 1945 to 1950. Tactical decisions and lingering attachments to prewar symbols of the associationalist and reform liberal visions of the state that would prove to have little practical import in the postwar period kept the coalitions assembled by Bush and Kilgore at loggerheads when they could have united to win over the president and Congress.

Herbert Hoover and Karl Compton had both attempted to build associational policies for the support of university research in the interwar period. Hoover

---

peterian Theory," *Quarterly Journal of Economics* 65 (1951): 417–28; "Conference on Quantitative Description of Technological Change," Simon B. Kuznets papers, Harvard University Archives, Series 10, Box 3, "April 1951"; Robert Solow, "Technical Change and the Aggregate Production Function," *Review of Economics and Statistics* 39 (1957): 312–20.

sought a privately funded National Research Endowment (NRE) in the 1920s, to be administered in the public interest by the network of expert committees that made up the National Research Council. The NRE failed to convince potential industrial sponsors that they would reap sufficient benefits from its academic beneficiaries, and the effort collapsed with the Depression. Compton's 1933 "Recovery Program for Science Progress" and 1934 "National Program for Putting Science to Work" were also to be administered by private experts, but the funds were to come from the public purse, rather than private donors. Both of Compton's programs encountered conservative fears of an intrusive state and reform liberal disdain for delegating public authority to private bodies; Harold Ickes's National Resources Board delivered the coup de grace on the latter grounds.[21]

Wartime innovations gave rise to the widely shared perception that science was of great practical use and that federal funds could make it pay off. Universities housed the laboratories that invented radar and computers; professors of physics made the atomic bomb. Academics were not always doing science (much less pure science) in these endeavors, but that was the label applied to the work. Bush wrote Hoover after the war that he had to "introduce all my people as scientists," even if they were engineers, in order to be taken seriously by the military services. *Time*'s 1944 cover portrait bore the caption "Vannevar Bush—General of Physics."[22]

While Compton and Bush were occupied with the war effort, Senator Kilgore offered a series of bills for federal support of science in war *and* peace. The first of these, drafted in the late summer of 1942, projected the government as an active investor in the development of new technology-based industries from academia through the pilot plant stage, as part of a general economic mobilization. It had little chance of passing Congress and seems to have been meant primarily to provide leverage for those in the War Production Board (WPB) who hoped to use wartime emergency powers to create a powerful new research arm within that agency that might be able to live on into the postwar period. Despite the defeat of his allies in the WPB, Kilgore's fancy had been taken by the subject, and he continued to build the reform liberal case in hear-

[21] Lance E. Davis and Daniel J. Kevles, "The National Research Fund: A Case Study in the Industrial Support of Academic Science," *Minerva* 12 (1974): 207–20; Herbert Hoover, "The Vital Need for Greater Financial Support of Pure Science Research," *Circular and Reprint Series of the National Research Council,* no. 65, December 1925; Robert Kargon and Elizabeth Hodes, "Karl Compton, Isaiah Bowman, and the Politics of Science in the Great Depression," *Isis* 76 (1985): 301–18; Science Advisory Board, *Report, July 31,1933–September 1, 1934* (Washington: National Research Council, 1934), 267–83; "Put Science To Work!" *Technology Review* 37 (1935): 133–35, 152–58. Later efforts in Congress with similar goals fared no better; see Carroll W. Pursell, Jr., "A Preface to Government Support of R&D: Research Legislation and the National Bureau of Standards, 1935–1941," *Technology and Culture* 9 (1968): 145–64.

[22] Bush to Hoover, September 27, 1945, Bush papers, LC, Box 51, File 1245; "Yankee Scientist," *Time,* April 3, 1944, 52–57.

ings in 78th Congress (1943–1944) that focused on patent abuses by large firms. Thurman Arnold and Henry Wallace played starring roles. By 1945, however, Kilgore's "Office of Technological Mobilization" had metamorphosed into a "National Science Foundation" (NSF). The real legislative opportunity that peace would bring, combined with the opposition of Congressional conservatives, business organizations, and the wartime science elite, caused Kilgore to descend from the rhetorical to the practical. S. 1297, which he offered in June 1945, obligated 90 percent of NSF's funds to defense, medical, and university research; technological development, distinct from scientific research, was ceded to Senator Fulbright's bill before the end of that year.[23]

Bush kept track of Kilgore's maneuvering and nudged him in a more congenial direction when he could. When the war was all but won in late 1944, however, Bush decided to lay down his marker, particularly on the issue that had occupied Hoover and Compton before the war, the degree to which private experts would govern the distribution of federal funds for research. In *Science, the Endless Frontier* (*SEF*), a report to the president on postwar research policy delivered in June 1945, Bush called for a National Research Foundation (NRF) to be provided with long-term funding, controlled by nongovernmental scientists, and free to support research on the basis of scientific merit alone. Regulations governing conflict of interest and mandating competitive bidding were to be waived. Where Kilgore wanted a broad range of social interests to be represented on NSF's governing board, which would be directly accountable, along with the agency's director, to the president, Bush placed great faith in the good will of scientists and academic administrators of the NRF.[24]

Although there were other points of conflict, it was these differences over the agency's administrative structure that would prove fatal to both bills. Yet the two sides agreed on the most fundamental point, that the federal government ought to invest in the nation's "scientific capital," by which both meant academic research. Such research, as the Bush report put it, in an echo of Hansen's 1938 American Economic Association address, was the nation's "one inexhaustible resource" even if population growth and geographical expansion were at an end. Bush and Kilgore both envisioned an annual budget in the neighborhood of $100–150 million. Both believed that such a program would substantially enhance national security as well as national prosperity. Both had moved

[23] U.S. Senate, Committee on Military Affairs, *Technological Mobilization,* 77th C., 2d s., 1943; U.S. Senate, Committee on Military Affairs, *Scientific and Technological Mobilization,* 78th C., 1st and 2d s., 1943–44; U.S. Senate, Committee on Military Affairs, *The Government's Wartime Research and Development, 1940–1944. Part II—Findings and Recommendations,* 79th C., 1st s., 1945, Committee Report no. 5; Carl M. Rowan, "Politics and Pure Research: The Origins of the National Science Foundation, 1942–1954," (Ph.D. diss., University of Miami, Ohio, 1985), 62–63; Daniel J. Kevles, "The National Science Foundation and the Debate over Postwar Research Policy, 1942–1945," *Isis* 68 (1977): 5–27.

[24] Vannevar Bush, *Science, the Endless Frontier* (Washington: GPO, 1945); Rowan (above, n. 23), 43–44, 52–54, 57–60.

a large distance from their original positions, Kilgore from stagnationism and Bush from Hooverian associationalism, at the cost of ruffling some feathers among their allies. And, in late 1945 and early 1946, both seemed prepared to compromise further to have a single bill that could win a majority despite rising conservatism in Congress.[25]

Indeed, Kilgore, with the White House behind him, further amended his bill during the winter. The resulting bill, S. 1850, won the endorsement of Bush and his allies, including moderate members of Congress of both parties, although Bush still hoped for further amendments on the Senate floor. The new bill provided for the scientific community to have greater input on the foundation's staffing and the membership of its board, while reserving ultimate authority to the president. The truce between Kilgore and Bush, however, sparked conservative entrepreneurship. Frank Jewett, president of the National Academy of Sciences and of Bell Telephone Laboratories, opposed any federal funding of academic science on the grounds that it would lead inevitably to political domination of research universities. He drafted a bill in January 1946, which was introduced by Senator Raymond Willis shortly thereafter, that gave the conservatives an opportunity to show "the strength of the forces which were suspicious of the whole idea of a Science Foundation" (in the words of the sociologist Talcott Parsons). They were considerable, particularly in the House, and they were fierce, bolstering their arguments with charges of socialism.[26]

The gambit paid off, splitting Bush and Kilgore once more. Although the Senate passed S. 1850, it died in the House Commerce Committee with Bush's connivance. The conservative show of strength apparently convinced Bush that he might win a bill more to his liking in the next Congress and that the odds of House passage for any science bill in the 79th Congress were low, if for no other reason than that the Republican minority, aided at times by southern Democrats, was obstructing almost all legislation in the hopes of strengthening its hand in the midterm elections. Moreover, in the interval between the development of the compromise bill in the winter and congressional consideration in the late spring, Bush had arranged for other federal patrons to fund the academic research that he believed to be most important to the nation's future. Physical scientists found that the Office of Naval Research (ONR) took Bush's research funding philosophy to heart, granting them substantial discretion. The research contracts of OSRD's Committee on Medical Research (CMR) were

[25] Bush (above, n. 24), 2, 68; Senate Military Affairs, 1945 (above, n. 23); James R. Newman to John W. Snyder, February 8, 1946, RG250, Entry 54, Box 275, "Legislation Concerning a Postwar Program for Scientific Research"; J. Merton England, *A Patron for Pure Science* (Washington: National Science Foundation, 1982), 9–24.

[26] Rowan (above, n. 23), 106–14; Talcott Parsons, "National Science Legislation, Part 1: An Historical Review," *Bulletin of the Atomic Scientists* (November 1946): 8; Jessica Wang, "American Science in an Age of Anxiety: Scientists, Civil Liberties, and the Cold War, 1945–1950" (Ph.D. diss., MIT, 1994), chap. 7.

taken over by the sympathetic Public Health Service and its National Institutes of Health (NIH). The Atomic Energy Commission (AEC), whatever its final form, looked likely to carry on the work of the Manhattan Project. The nation could afford to wait, so it did.[27]

The tables were turned in the Republican-controlled 80th Congress. Senator H. Alexander Smith advanced the Bush position but worked out a compromise with the president, BOB, and moderate opponents in the hope of avoiding a veto. The amended Smith bill gave the president the authority to appoint the NSF's director and board but allowed the board to elect an executive committee to oversee the director. It passed the Senate in May 1947. Soon thereafter, House Republicans, urged on by Jewett and by Senator Robert Taft, the preeminent congressional conservative, deleted the amendments, and it was the House bill that emerged from conference and was sent on to the president. Although nearly all interested groups outside the government and even some in the administration endorsed the bill as better than nothing, Truman was persuaded that it set a bad precedent. "It would," his veto message of August 6 read, "vest the determination of vital national policies, the expenditure of large public funds, and the administration of important governmental functions in a group of individuals who would essentially be private citizens."[28]

The continuing stalemate delighted conservatives and frustrated President Truman, Senator Smith, and Senator Kilgore. In the winter of 1948, they worked out yet another compromise, and the two Senators jointly introduced the bill. The new administrative formulation called for a presidentially appointed director to share authority with a policy-making board. As in 1946, the bill passed the Senate and died in a House committee, this time Rules. This time, too, conservatives in Taft's corner were responsible, objecting to the NSF as wasteful spending and red-baiting some of Kilgore's allies. The 1948 elections changed the situation just enough for a bill to be enacted. Kilgore and Bush held their forces together in the 81st Congress, despite even more rancorous attacks from the right. When the bill was bottled up in the House Rules Committee, they were able to extricate it thanks only to a parliamentary procedure that allowed another committee chairman to call up a bill on the second or fourth Monday of the month if it had been held in Rules for more than 21 days.[29]

On May 10, 1950, President Truman finally signed the National Science

[27] Rowan (above, n. 23), 115–23; Harvey Sapolsky, *Science and the Navy* (Princeton: Princeton University Press, 1990), 9–36; Daniel M. Fox, "The Politics of the NIH Extramural Program, 1937–1950," *Journal of the History of Medicine and Allied Sciences* 42 (1987): 454–59; Richard G. Hewlett and Oscar E. Anderson, *The New World: A History of the United States Atomic Energy Commission, Volume I, 1939–1946* (1962; rpt. Berkeley: University of California Press, 1990), 633–38.

[28] Rowan (above, n. 23), 124–48; England (above, n. 25), 61–82; "Memorandum of Disapproval of the National Science Foundation Bill," *Public Papers of the President: Harry S. Truman, 1947* (Washington: GPO, 1963), 369.

[29] Rowan (above, n. 23), 156–82; England (above, n. 25), 92–106.

Foundation Act. The bill provided that he appoint members of the National Science Board (NSB) after considering recommendations from educational and scientific organizations; the NSB was then to recommend a director to be appointed by the president, with whom it would share power. Groups with a wide variety of ideological and material interests advanced names for the board; Truman chose not only scientific establishment types like James Conant, the president of Harvard University, but also blacks, women, Catholics, midwesterners, and social scientists. After sidestepping legislative intent by giving the NSB a diverse membership, the president ignored the law entirely by offering the NSF directorship to Frank Graham, the reformist former president of the University of North Carolina. In this case, however, the president was forced to renege when the establishment members of the board objected. The first director of NSF turned out to be Alan Waterman, the chief scientist of ONR.[30]

Despite this inauspicious start, Bush's fear that a broadly based board and a director accountable to the president would exercise dictatorial control proved groundless. If anything, Waterman accommodated academic scientists even more than Bush liked, deferring to disciplinary peer review committees and not setting out multidisciplinary problems to focus scientific attention as Bush's wartime organizations had done. (Of course, without jurisdiction over defense, medical, or industrial research, NSF's problem-solving turf was highly constrained.) Waterman's NSF more closely approximated the vesting of public functions in private individuals to which Truman's 1947 veto message had objected than almost any other arm of the federal government. But it had little money to distribute to fulfill those functions. A tight budget cap on NSF had been accepted to pacify House conservatives in the final negotiations. With the coming of the Korean War, they moved to zero out NSF altogether in fiscal 1952; only by playing up NSF's contribution to national security did the president and NSF director secure a measly $3.5 million.[31]

This "puny partner" (as Daniel J. Kevles has characterized the early NSF) surely did not live up to Harley Kilgore's initial "grand vision" (to borrow Daniel Kleinman's phrase).[32] That vision had been abandoned when Kilgore got serious about legislating in 1945; he left technological development to Senator Fulbright and Secretary Wallace. What remained, federal funding of academic science, was an avenue for public investment that would redound through unspecified channels to the benefit of the entire economy. In the social Keynesian vision, as expressed, for instance, in the "American White Paper," it was

[30] England (above, n. 25), 113–28; Rowan (above, n. 23), 185–91.

[31] England, (above, n. 25), 141–80; Joel Genuth, "The Local Origins of National Science Policy" (Ph.D. diss., MIT, 1996); "Memorandum for the Record," September 6, 1950, Frederick J. Lawton papers, HSTL, Box 6, "Meetings with the President."

[32] Daniel J. Kevles, *The Physicists: The History of a Scientific Community in Modern America* (New York: Knopf, 1977), 358; Daniel Lee Kleinman, *Politics on the Endless Frontier* (Durham: Duke University Press, 1995), 145.

one of many such avenues. When forced by political realities to make choices among these avenues, however, social Keynesians did not rank science very high. Its impact was indirect and long-term, and the amounts involved (even in the best case, much less the actual FY52 outcome) were modest. Nor did it deeply engage the social constituencies, such as labor, that subscribed to this vision of the state. Nevertheless, the convergence between Bush and Kilgore in 1945–1950 fits neatly with the convergence between commercial and social Keynesians that occurred during the same five years. Science, like the economy, was seen as a system that could be managed from the outside through the manipulation of funding; its internal institutions functioned satisfactorily. Kilgore made his peace with the elite universities, just as Keyserling made his peace with the big corporations. What remained to be done was to make federal R&D spending big enough that it could be a useful tool for economic growthmanship. National security concerns (in the form of Sputnik in 1957) ultimately proved to be the critical catalyst for NSF's remarkable long-term growth.

THE SCOPE OF MARKET FAILURE II:
SMALL BUSINESS FINANCE AND VENTURE CAPITAL

The story of nonmilitary federal financial assistance to high-technology start-up firms in the 1930s and 1940s is similar to that of NSF. Prewar association-alists and reform liberals generally agreed that the market left an "institutional gap" in the provision of venture capital to small enterprises. Keynesian economics provided a language through which the two groups could find common ground on this issue, yet they spent the first postwar half-decade squabbling over the exact means through which the state should try to rectify the market failure that they agreed existed. The postwar boom and the rehabilitation of big business among the old New Dealers made the delay in establishing a policy more acceptable, while conservatives who were skeptical that the market failed at all made the delay more certain. The slackening of investment and the consequent recession in 1949 injected a new urgency into the policy debate. Even though the economy bounced back within a year, the downturn prompted a convergence of effort, led by the CEA's Leon Keyserling, around indirect federal measures to bolster private venture capitalists. When the Korean War erupted, however, this program was even more embryonic than nonmilitary federal funding of academic science. The fruit of Keyserling's entrepreneurship would not fully ripen for nearly another decade, with the Small Business Investment Act of 1958 and the Kennedy administration's aggressive implementation of it.

The reform liberal critique of the banking system during the Depression was wide and deep; the view that American bankers were too timid to fund new ventures that could give the economy vitality was but one aspect of it, associated with such figures as Adolph A. Berle, Jr., and Rexford Guy Tugwell, both members of Roosevelt's original 1932 Brains Trust. The braintrusters wanted the Reconstruction Finance Corporation (RFC), which had been propping up banks and railroads, to take up the slack. Although few of the New Dealers shared the writer David C. Coyle's intense enthusiasm for agile, technologically innovative small firms, they hoped that the RFC might fund some firms of this type along with less risky industrial ventures. The president requested authority for the RFC to make direct loans to industry in 1934, and Congress granted it in 1935. However, Congress restricted this lending program (and similar authority granted to the Federal Reserve Banks) to working capital and made it subject to the influence of participating private banks and industrial advisory committees, greatly limiting the possibility that high-risk ventures would receive government funds. Moreover, Jesse Jones, the czar of the RFC, despised the reform liberals as much as he hated Wall Street, and he opposed using the state to restructure the economy. Jones's RFC loosened standard banking criteria somewhat, opening the financial tap to a parched market rather than digging deep and turning the ground over. Not surprisingly, the agency never lent industry close to the full amount authorized.[33]

The reform liberal critique of banking resonated in some associationalist circles, although their response was characteristically more restrained. The Boston retailer Lincoln Filene, one of Ralph Flanders' co-authors on *Toward Full Employment* (1938), for instance, produced an influential 1939 study demonstrating that small businesses had substantial difficulty getting access to long-term financing. Filene's report refrained from endorsing federal action, however, envisioning the liberalization of traditional banking practices and the private organization of small business investment trusts as the most appropriate steps. MIT President Compton dissented mildly from Filene's analysis, viewing small high-technology firms as "not hampered so much by the lack of venture capital . . . as by the [investors'] need for organization and techniques to appraise opportunities." With Flanders and others connected with the New England Council, Compton organized the "quasi-public" New England Industrial Research Foundation to perform this function in 1941. Lawrence Bass was recruited from the Mellon Institute of Pittsburgh to run it. The council's hope was

[33] A. A. Berle, Jr., "High Finance: Master or Servant?" *Yale Review* 23 (1933): 20–42; "Banks for Industry," *Business Week,* February 24, 1934, 7; Science Service press release, February 2, 1935, in National Academy of Sciences (NAS) Archives, Executive Board, Science Advisory Board, Committee on Relation of the Patent System to the Stimulation of New Industries, "1934–1935"; David C. Coyle, *The American Way* (New York: Harper and Bros., 1938), 35–44; Roosevelt to Senator Henry P. Fletcher, March 19, 1934 (with commentary), in Samuel J. Rosenman, ed., *FDR-PP,* vol. 3, 152–55; James S. Olson, *Saving Capitalism: The Reconstruction Finance Corporation and the New Deal, 1933–1940* (Princeton: Princeton University Press, 1988), 111–16, 153–74; Jordan A. Schwarz, *The New Dealers* (New York: Knopf, 1993), 77–85.

that innovative small companies on MIT's "research row" and elsewhere would become a major new source of economic growth for the Boston area.[34]

As the war approached, the legislative initiative with the most momentum in this field was probably Senator James Mead's bill to establish a Federal Industrial Loan Corporation to be overseen by the Federal Reserve Board. The chairman of the Fed, Marriner Eccles, was widely seen as the bill's guiding spirit. Eccles was an ardent Keynesian, whose expansionist views on fiscal and monetary policy predated Keynes' *General Theory;* he was the individual most responsible for bringing the Keynesian vision of the state to the center of economic policy debate during the New Deal. For Eccles, the Mead bill's most important promise was the injection of additional liquidity into the economy. It authorized the Fed to make equity investments in small businesses and to guarantee bank loans to them in a manner similar to the guarantee provided on mortgage lending by the Federal Housing Authority. The Mead bill promised to make good on Alvin Hansen's claim that "[t]he government is becoming an investment banker." It was taken by associationalists, as one put it, to be a combination of gesture, threat, and "invitation to private capital to wake up."[35]

The mobilization preempted debate on Mead's initiative, channeling entrepreneurial energy on behalf of small business into the governance of defense contracting. Military procurement officers were biased in favor of large firms, viewing them as more reliable, more technologically sophisticated, and easier to deal with than small firms; civilian defense officials, often dollar-a-year big businessmen, typically shared this bias. The Smaller War Plants Corporation (SWPC), formed at the behest of Senator Murray in 1942, tried to serve as the collective agent of small business in the war effort, but it was weak and disorganized from the get-go. Under Maury Maverick's leadership beginning in 1944, the SWPC became more aggressive and turned its attention to the technological competitiveness of small business in the reconversion and postwar periods. These efforts, as we have seen, were ultimately incorporated into the failed technology policy of Secretary of Commerce Henry Wallace.[36]

While the SWPC and the Department of Commerce pressed during the war

---

[34] "Memorandum on Semi-Fixed and Permanent Capital for Small Business," Lincoln and Therese Filene Foundation, December 1939, pamphlet in Baker Library, Harvard University; "Preliminary Prospectus," April 15, 1941 (quote from 2) and "New England Industrial Research Foundation, Inc.," August 26, 1941, both in Karl T. Compton papers, MIT Archives, AC4 (hereafter "Compton papers), Box 158, Folder 9.

[35] Rudolph Weissman, *Small Business and Venture Capital* (New York: Harper and Bros., 1945), 68–71; Harmon Ziegler, *The Politics of Small Business in America* (New York: Public Affairs Press, 1961), 88–89; Alvin H. Hansen, *Full Recovery or Stagnation?* (New York: Norton, 1938), 318; Patrick R. Liles, "Sustaining the Venture Capital Firm," unpub. ms., Management Analysis Center, Cambridge, MA, 1977, 17.

[36] Ziegler (above, n. 35), 93–100; Jonathan J. Bean, "World War II and the 'Crisis' of Small Business: The Smaller War Plants Corporation, 1942–1946," *Journal of Policy History* 6 (1994): 223–30.

for microeconomic reform to aid small business, the Bureau of the Budget took a macroeconomic perspective. BOB staff focused on federal financial, rather than technical and managerial, assistance to small business (although it also endorsed the latter), in part because in economic downturns such assistance "becomes one type of fiscal stimulus to the economy, more economical of public funds, than some alternatives." In short it had the makings of an automatic stabilizer. Picking up where Berle had left off in the 1930s, BOB proposed that RFC make and guarantee loans to small businesses. A competing plan, drafted by A.D.H. Kaplan of the CED and supported by the Investment Bankers Association of America (IBAA), built on and modified the prewar Mead bill in important ways. It proposed that private investors be permitted to form small business investment companies; the Federal Reserve Banks would then triple this investment. Although the Fed would supervise them, these investment companies would be operated by their private partners. Neither bill got out of the Senate Banking Committee in the 79th Congress. The advocates of direct RFC loans, such as the members of the Senate Small Business Committee, retained a deep suspicion of the "money trust"; backers of the IBAA plan, like Jules Bogen of the American Enterprise Association, considered RFC lending to be "a step toward State Socialism." As in the case of the NSF Act, many members of Congress, and many small business owners as well, saw no need for any federal action. Any small business loan act was doomed to fail without a settlement among those who agreed that there was in fact a market failure.[37]

Deadlocked, the two sides did what they could in lieu of legislative action. The RFC made a number of loans to technologically innovative, if not necessarily small, ventures, like Kaiser-Frazee in automobiles and Lustron in prefabricated housing. These loans were intended to challenge the prewar status quo, but they failed miserably. Lustron, in particular, became an albatross; the firm's only apparent competence was securing loans through political connections, notably Senator Joseph McCarthy. The RFC's postwar program for "blanket participation" in bank loans to small business was equally ill-fated. Its explosive growth rapidly outstripped the agency's oversight capacity, precipitating scandals and a shutdown in January 1947. Congressional investigators, both Democratic and Republican, dogged the RFC with allegations of cronyism throughout President Truman's second term.[38]

[37] J. E. Reeve, "Government Credit Aids to Small Business," January 8, 1945, 13; Reeve to George Graham, April 26, 1945; Dewey Anderson to Reeve, October 29, 1945, all in RG51, Entry 39.3, Box 98, Folder 634; Investment Bankers Association of America, "Capital for Small Business," pamphlet, April 5, 1945, and Jules Bogen, "The Market for Risk Capital," American Enterprise Association pamphlet, August 1946 (quote from 27), both available at Baker Library, Harvard University; Lincoln Filene to Truman, January 9, 1946, Truman papers, PSF, Box 136, "Small Business."

[38] Mark S. Foster, "Henry John Kaiser," in *Encyclopedia of American Business History and Biography: The Automobile Industry, 1920–1980,* 224–31; Richard O. Davies, *Housing Reform during the Truman Administration* (Columbia: University of Missouri Press, 1966), 70–72; Addison

Meanwhile, the founders of the New England Industrial Research Foundation acted upon the widely discussed idea of pooling private resources for venture capital. Ralph Flanders, who had become chairman of the Boston Federal Reserve Bank and chairman of the CED research and policy committee during the war, was persuaded by the work of Kaplan and his colleagues that the availability of venture capital funds was indeed a problem, particularly in an era in which risk-averse institutions like insurance companies were playing an everbigger part in financial markets. Flanders, in turn, helped change Karl Compton's mind on this point. With sympathetic financiers, they approached Donald David, the dean of the Harvard Business School (HBS), and General Georges Doriot, an HBS professor recently released from wartime service in the Quartermaster Corps, in the winter of 1945–46 for assistance in organizing what they at first called the "Development Capital Corporation" but later renamed the American Research and Development Corporation (ARD). ARD screened new high-technology business opportunities, recruited funds for them, and participated in their management. Flanders served as ARD's president from its incorporation in June 1946 until his election to the Senate in the fall of 1946, after which Doriot took over and ran the firm; Compton and other MIT faculty served as advisors. Upon securing a special exemption from the Securities Exchange Commission, ARD made a public stock offering on August 9, 1946.[39]

Attempting to keep the associative tradition alive, ARD was consciously intended to fulfill a public mission and serve as a national example to other public-spirited private groups. "Capitalists," said General Doriot, "need to be awakened." This theme was featured prominently in its publicity. It won good press and helped to make ARD a widely cited model in policy debates. What it didn't do was sell stock; the company's initial subscription of $3.4 million (including $225,000 from several universities) fell well short of the hoped-for $5 million. ARD's early financial performance failed to kindle investors' enthusiasm, either, which was not surprising since the start-up companies into which it put its funds were bound to take many years to make money. Not until the firm dropped its public missionizing and organized its marketing exclusively around the profit potential of its holdings in the mid-1950s did its finances stabilize. No other groups followed ARD's example in this period; in his 1961 au-

W. Parris, *The Small Business Administration* (New York: Praeger, 1968), 8–18; Douglas R. Fuller, *Government Financing of Private Enterprise* (Stanford: Stanford University Press, 1948), 97–104.

[39] "The Winning Plans in the Pabst Postwar Employment Awards," Pabst Brewing Company pamphlet, 1944, Widener Library, Harvard University, 32; Liles (above, n. 35), 21–35; Merrill Griswold and William C. Hammond to Doriot, October 25, 1945, Compton papers, Box 103, Folder 4; Compton to Horace Ford, March 22, 1946, Compton papers, Box 89, Folder 6; Compton to Doriot, April 24, 1946, Compton papers, Box 74, Folder 6; Henry Etzkowitz, "Enterprises from Science: The Origins of Science-Based Regional Economic Development," *Minerva* 31 (1993): 343–48. Vannevar Bush was also invited to join the advisory board, but he reluctantly refused ("I will have to be a sister but not accept marriage."), citing his other responsibilities. Bush to Compton, March 6, 1946, Compton papers, Box 42, Folder 13.

tobiography, Flanders lamented that ARD "remains the only publicly financed institution of its kind." ARD returned about 7 percent per year in its first twenty years, a performance that the firm's historian, Patrick Liles, labels not "brilliant," but not "disastrous." Its investment in Digital Equipment Corporation led ultimately to its enormous success in the late 1960s.[40]

Neither RFC nor ARD satisfied their proponents. Yet, with investment running at record levels in 1947 and 1948, the economic situation did not impel entrepreneurship on behalf of a federal small business program. Nor was the political climate promising; the public was fed up with government meddling. Indeed, with the Republican congressional victory in 1946, conservatives took the initiative. HR 1 in the 80th Congress called for a 20 percent reduction in the personal income tax. The conservatives argued that the measure would, among other things, stimulate venture capital formation, since friends and family remained the primary financial source for new enterprises. In fact, as Herbert Stein notes, they suggested that the tax cuts would ultimately pay for themselves through investment-led growth. There was no reason to think, however, that any new investment stemming from income tax cuts would be channeled to small business in particular, much less high-technology start-ups. Truman vetoed the bill in June 1947. One reason was the sufficiency of investment. If anything, Keyserling and other Keynesians in the administration thought a consumption-oriented tax cut might be economically sensible; they considered briefly and then dropped tax incentives for private R&D. Although Senator Flanders and the CED were sympathetic to tax cuts, they too preferred a program that was more justifiable in the Keynesian paradigm. Rather than attempting to force spending down by cutting taxes first, as the conservatives wanted, the commercial Keynesians preferred to set tax rates so that there would be a modest surplus when unemployment was low and to bring down both taxes and spending gradually. The conservatives had to make substantial concessions to these views in order to win enough moderate support to override Truman on the tax bill, which they finally did on their third try in April 1948. This bill failed to include (for reasons that are unclear) the one proposed measure aimed specifically at stimulating technological innovation in small firms, which would have allowed them to deduct rather than capitalize R&D spending, just as large firms with R&D divisions did.[41]

[40] Doriot to Flanders, February 16, 1949, Ralph Flanders papers, Syracuse University Library, Box 100, "AR&D Corporation–1949"; Liles (above, n. 35), 75; CED, "Meeting the Special Problems of Small Business," pamphlet, 1947, Baker Library, Harvard University, 36; Fuller (above, n. 38), 165–66; Ralph E. Flanders, *Senator from Vermont* (Boston: Little, Brown, 1961), 189.

[41] Ronald F. King, *Money, Time, and Politics: Investment Tax Subsidies and American Politics* (New Haven: Yale University Press, 1993), 124–26; Stein (above, n. 2), 206–32; Keyserling to Truman, June 13, 1947, Keyserling papers, Box 8, File "White House Contacts—Harry S. Truman—2"; Ralph E. Flanders, "A Federal Tax System to Encourage Business Enterprise," pamphlet, June 15, 1944, available at Littauer Library, Harvard University; CED, "Monetary and Fiscal Policy for Greater Economic Stability," pamphlet, 1948, available at Widener Library, Harvard University,

The first postwar recession in 1949 provided the Keynesians with an opportunity to act on their nagging concern about the adequacy and stability of venture capital. The president took the course of least resistance as the downturn was felt, which was to hope that the automatic stabilizers worked in the short term (they did) and to use the opportunity to develop new policies to address the recession's causes over the long term. CEA figures showed that private investment had fallen 18 percent in 1949, confirming (as the CEA's staff liaison to the newly formed interagency working group on investment put it) that "the instability of the American economy is basically instability of private investment." At its first meetings in November 1949, the working group agreed that the economic outlook for the next few years was deflationary and that federal policy should stimulate investment as well as consumption. The group took as its central policy focus small-business capital spending, which new estimates suggested could contribute an additional 15–20 percent to total investment. Their interest was not merely in reviving aggregate demand, however, but in ensuring that new ideas, including new technological ideas, were brought into the economy, by small businesses themselves and through their competitive effects on big business. By January 1950 the administration had agreed on some modest tax incentives for small and medium-sized businesses, and the president's state of the union message promised a more aggressive program.[42]

The Congressional Joint Committee on the Economic Report, which held extensive hearings on investment in December 1949, featuring ARD officers among others, placed pressure on the administration. The committee endorsed A.D.H. Kaplan's plan, prepared for the CED, for a nationwide network of private investment companies to make loans to and buy the stock of small businesses under the supervision of the Federal Reserve. The CEA-led working group constructed a similar package of guarantees, tax incentives, and regulatory supervision for such companies, but preferred to place oversight in the Commerce Department, a view that the president, who had a constitutional suspicion of bankers, strongly endorsed. When push came to shove, however, as the proposed program reached its final stage, the president relented to congressional opinion and gave the Fed the job. The administration package also included a provision that, if private enterprise failed to meet small business's cap-

---

38–44; U.S. House of Representatives, Committee on Ways and Means, *Revenue Revisions, 1947–1948,* 80th C., 1st s., 1948, 1355–72; C. V. Kidd to Steelman, June 2, 1947, Truman papers, OF 192, Box 677, "1945–August, 1947"; draft of "Nation's Economic Budget for 1958–An Exploratory Study," May 21, 1948, Keyserling papers, Box 6, "Economic Budget Studies, 1946–1951," 12.

[42] Edgar M. Hoover, "Capital Accumulation and Progress," October 1949, Keyserling papers, Box 7, "Investment," 1; Reeve to G. G. Johnson, December 6, 1949; W. D. Carey to Reeve, December 8, 1949; and Investment Policy Group to Tax Policy Group, December 8, 1949, all in RG51, Entry 39.3, Box 98, Folder 634; William F. Butler, *Business Needs for Venture Capital* (New York: McGraw-Hill, 1949), 75–77; "President's Message to Congress," January 23, 1950, Keyserling papers, Box 8, "White House Contacts—Harry S. Truman—3."

ital needs, the RFC would be authorized to do so. Such RFC lending, markedly scaled down from the proposals of 1945–46 and fenced in statutorily, was intended to be a modest discretionary tool for the executive to use in case recession threatened. On May 5, 1950, the president sent the small business message to Congress and made it a "top 10 priority," citing a wide variety of contributions that small business made to the nation's economic stability and growth, including its pioneering of new techniques and stimulation of new technology through competition.[43]

Keyserling and Kaplan, CEA and CED, had finally converged on federal action to rectify the market failure in venture capital. They agreed that the public sector ought to compensate for deficiencies in investment that might derive from this market failure. The public sector would facilitate a private response, restructuring the capital market to serve small businesses better. Public capital would stand ready to be tapped for private needs in a countercyclical fashion, but under strict conditions. The small business message epitomized what Craufurd Goodwin pictures as a "brief, golden halcyon period when the problems of the previous four years could be examined calmly and creatively." Goodwin's optimism must be tempered, however, by the congressional outlook for the small business bill, which was not bright, even though it proposed few if any net expenditures. House Small Business Committee chairman Brent Spence, its logical champion, evaded responsibility for it. Worse, the administration itself seemed hesitant and divided, and Commerce Secretary Charles Sawyer appeared ill-informed and foolish as its main proponent. Such problems might have been overcome with time, but there was no chance. When the Korean War began on June 25, the administration suddenly had an entirely new set of problems and legislative priorities. The small business bill faded.[44]

A few of the ideas in the peacetime small business bill were ultimately

---

[43] Joint Committee on the Economic Report, *Volume and Stability of Private Investment,* 81st C., 1st s., 1950, 446–91; CED, "Meeting the Special Problems of Small Business" (above, n. 40); "Money Talks," *Fortune,* March 1950, 19–20; Burton Klein, "Memorandum on the Establishment of Investment Companies . . . ," January 30, 1950, RG51, Entry 39.3, Box 98, Folder 634; Charles S. Murphy to president, February 7, 1950, Truman papers, PSF, Box 136, "Small Business"; Spingarn, Memo to File, May 9, 1950, Stephen J. Spingarn papers, HSTL (hereafter "Spingarn papers"), Box 28, "Small Business"; draft bill, March 17, 1950, RG51, Entry 39.3, Box 98, Folder 634; president's message to Congress on small business, May 5, 1950, Keyserling papers, Box 8, "White House Contacts—Harry S. Truman—3"; Spingarn to Frederick J. Lawton, May 19, 1950, RG51, Entry 39.3, Box 98, Folder 634. The message also proposed a self-financing plan for insuring very small loans and the technical information clearinghouse for the Department of Commerce discussed in Chapter 5.

[44] Craufurd D. Goodwin, "Attitudes toward Industry in the Truman Administration: The Macroeconomic Origins of Microeconomic Policy," in Michael J. Lacey, ed., *The Truman Presidency* (New York: Woodrow Wilson International Center for Scholars and Cambridge University Press, 1989), 127; Spingarn to President, June 28, 1950, Truman papers, PSF, Box 136, "Spingarn"; Wagnon (above, n. 15), 205–11; Robert L. Branyan, "Anti-Monopoly Activities during the Truman Administration" (Ph.D. diss., University of Oklahoma, 1961) 196–207.

worked into the legislation that set up the Small Defense Plants Administration (SDPA) in 1951, but the SDPA was even more pathetic than World War II's weak SWPC. The 1952 election campaign brought more dramatic changes. The second C in the Republican slogan "K_1C_2" (which stood for Korea, Communism, and Corruption) signaled the demise of the RFC. In order to win votes to terminate the RFC's $1 billion lending program, however, the Eisenhower administration reluctantly agreed to create in its place an independent Small Business Administration (SBA) with a $275 million loan fund. SBA could not provide long-term credit, however, and did nothing to assuage concern about a venture capital shortage. This concern intensified during the tight money period of 1955–57, culminating in a series of studies by the Federal Reserve, published during the recession that followed, which substantiated the existence of an "equity gap." In 1958 Congress passed the Small Business Investment Act, which was similar to the administration proposal of 1950 but vested oversight and support of the new Small Business Investment Companies (SBICs) in the SBA.[45]

Under the Eisenhower SBA, few SBICs organized, but President John F. Kennedy's mandate to "get America moving" changed that. Aggressive promotion by Kennedy appointees sparked an SBIC boom in the early 1960s. Although only about 10 percent of SBIC funds were invested in high-technology start-up firms, according to management analyst Edward B. Roberts, they provided the basis for the modern venture capital industry. The First National Bank of Boston (now BankBoston), for instance, created the first SBIC to channel funds to New England high-technology firms, and the cadre of bankers involved in this effort formed the core of the Boston venture capital community that developed in the 1960s. Of course, many of the budding firms that these investors found so promising in Boston (and in the future Silicon Valley near San Francisco) were developing defense technology. The national security state played as important a role in catalyzing nonmilitary federal assistance to high-technology start-up firms as it did catalyzing nonmilitary federal funding of academic scientific research.[46]

THE POSSIBILITIES OF 1950

In the first half of 1950, something like a "vital center," to appropriate the term coined by Arthur M. Schlesinger, Jr., had emerged in civilian science and technology policy. The productivity bargain, the establishment of NSF, and the development of small business legislation suggested that the federal government

[45] Ziegler (above, n. 35), 104–15; Parris (above, n. 38), 7–25, 150–58.

[46] John Dominguez, *Venture Capital* (Lexington, MA: D. C. Heath, 1974), 3–5; Richard Florida and Mark Samber, "Capital and Creative Destruction: Venture Capital, Technological Change and Economic Development," May 1994, unpub. ms., 25–43; Edward B. Roberts, *Entrepreneurs in High Technology* (New York: Oxford University Press, 1991), 137–38.

would now play a modest but constructive role in supporting the development and diffusion of new technologies that could contribute to economic growth. The convergence of the old associationalists and the old reform liberals on the meaning of market failure in science and technology and the appropriate federal response to it emerged from equal parts reeducation and exhaustion. Both groups had learned to speak the new Keynesian language of demand management, investment, and consumption, and they learned that if they wanted to influence these variables they would have to unite against those who preferred to do nothing.

For the commercial Keynesians, the transition was easier, and not only because they got much of what they wanted. Although they were willing to live with the state that the New Dealers had built, Vannevar Bush, Senator Ralph Flanders, Karl Compton, and the CED preferred to address unsolved problems by first trying private remedies informed by public spirit, like the ingenious if impecunious ARD. Gridlock in Washington was not edifying nor ideal, but their program did not require the public sector to make dramatic departures from the status quo, as long as economic growth remained satisfactory. The lack of an NSF and federally guaranteed SBICs was bothersome, but it was preferable to overly ambitious and potentially corrupt policies like those of the RFC. And, on some issues, like tax reform, the conservatives were the logical partners to provide the legislative heft and ideological fire to move policy in a direction congenial to commercial Keynesianism.

The stalemate was much more frustrating to reform liberals who turned to social Keynesianism. By 1950 Alvin Hansen was again an academic economist with little influence in the high councils of Washington. Secular stagnation and postwar depression had been shown to be myths, shattering the credibility of the economic models on which he had hoped to base policy. Business-led prosperity had to be reckoned with. Senator Harley Kilgore, Leon Keyserling, and others in CEA and BOB acknowledged economic as well as political reality in advocating that public policy defer to private economic decision-making. They were far from complacent, however, about the market's capacity to maximize economic growth. When circumstances allowed, as in 1949, they continued to push investment policies that would advance science and technology to this end. More often than not, they had to settle for indirect measures, implemented by the corporate and academic sectors, that only partially acheived their goals. Yet one cannot speak sensibly of a vital center without Korea and Communism, without Senator Joseph McCarthy. In the late 1940s the left wing of American politics was demolished, a process symbolized by Henry Wallace's arc from the pinnacle of power to oblivion. Where Bush's tacit alliance with Senator Taft provided leverage, Kilgore's with Wallace was costly. Genuine public discontent with the state mixed with and was fed by anticommunist fear and intimidation. The result was a common denominator much closer to the original position of the CED than Keyserling's CEA.

There was to be one huge exception, however. National security would prove to be a potent justification for investments in science and technology and much else besides. The Office of Naval Research in the late 1940s was a premonition of what was to come. ONR's renowned generosity and flexibility with respect to academic scientists bore little relation to the navy's apparent needs. When defense management was loose enough, national security provided a convenient pretext to move ahead with policies designed primarily to serve other ends. NSF, too, benefited from the belief that it would help to win future wars. Over time, advocates of the national security state would vehemently contest such figurative and monetary appropriations. Yet, the establishment of the military as a patron worth having and national security as a label worth fighting for did not occur automatically or immediately after the victory in World War II. The immediate postwar period was one of frustration and bitterly won incremental gains for proponents of the national security state. It took the Korean War to break this bottleneck.

CHAPTER 7

"The Crescendo of Hideous Invention"

THE NATIONAL SECURITY STATE COMES OF AGE, 1945–1953

THE DOMINANCE of pocketbook issues in the late 1940s came as a welcome relief to most Americans. After years of waiting impotently for news from faraway places with funny-sounding names, struggles over the boundaries of market failure returned them to a familiar political universe. For most citizens, whether they leaned left or right politically, the rest of the world was but an irritation, an unwelcome intrusion on domestic squabbles. Such parochialism infuriated those, like James Forrestal, the first Secretary of Defense, who worried that the international commitments of the United States were outrunning its means of redeeming them. Their fears were expressed most vividly in NSC-68, a secret 1950 policy document advocating a massive military buildup. But despite foreign policy crisis after foreign policy crisis, from Greece to Czechoslovakia to Berlin to China, prosperity usually trumped security.

While the size of the defense budget remained relatively fixed in the late 1940s, its composition began to shift. Faintly, the outlines emerged of a force structure skewed in favor of the air force and dependent on extraordinarily complex machines and weapons that were supposed to deliver an immediate knockout punch to the Soviet Union. The explosion of the Korean tinderbox on June 25, 1950, ratified NSC-68 and prompted a wide-ranging rearmament program that ultimately cast these faint outlines of a high technology force into bold relief. At first, the lifting of the budget cap precipitated an expansion of the army and navy as well as the air force. Once the peak of the crisis passed, however, the services' appetite for funds quickly bumped up against domestic political constraints. New caps were installed in the early 1950s (albeit at much higher levels than in the late 1940s) that reproduced the effects of the old ones in an exaggerated fashion. The composition of the defense budget shifted dramatically in favor of the air force and the dedicated scientific and industrial base needed to develop and support its jet bombers and their atomic ordnance. By 1953, when President Dwight D. Eisenhower took the oath of office, military R&D spending made up 90 percent of federal R&D spending and over 50 percent of all R&D performed in the United States.[1]

---

[1] Office of the Secretary of Defense, "The Growth of Scientific Research and Development," RDB 114/34, July 27, 1953, 1; *Budget of the U.S. Government for Fiscal Year 1955* (Washington: GPO, 1954), 1157.

The scale of the postwar national security state and its high-technology orientation were not determined by the technological opportunities generated by World War II nor by the actions of the Soviet Union. Certainly, the "technical sweetness" (as J. Robert Oppenheimer put it) of weapons work attracted brilliant minds and contract-hungry entrepreneurs. Just as surely, the Soviets aggressively acquired German military technology, spied on the United States and its allies, and embarked on crash weapons development programs. But domestic political processes translated technical opportunity and external provocation into a science and technology policy oriented toward the military. It took a peculiar resolution of the multifaceted conflicts among advocates of the national security state and between them and supporters of other visions of the state to ensure that the 1950s would see what Joseph and Stewart Alsop called "the crescendo of hideous invention."[2]

The deepest fault line among national security thinkers pitted a "mobilization" strategy against a "deterrence" strategy, to use Samuel Huntington's labels.[3] General George C. Marshall and many in the army, along with most of the industrial and scientific establishment, including Vannevar Bush, called for a national security state that would rely heavily on the civilian resources of the nation, adapting these resources through such programs as Universal Military Training (UMT) so that they could be rapidly mobilized in case war threatened. "Mobilization" echoed in interesting ways Bernard Baruch's associationalist "preparedness" vision of the interwar period. On the other hand, General H. H. Arnold and the air force, the aircraft industry, and a new breed of "defense intellectuals," like Caltech's Theodor von Karman, expected permanently mobilized forces-in-being, notably a 70-group air force, to actually win the next war. These forces required continual modernization in order to deter what their champions took to be an ever-present threat. The air force's proposed program had a navy counterpart, with "supercarriers" at its core.

The conflict between advocates of "mobilization" and "deterrence" over the shape of the national security state might not have become so bitter had the budget for national security not been so limited at first. But either strategy, much less the two together, required spending more money on the new Department of Defense (DOD) than most in late 1940s Washington wanted to spend. Reform liberals, such as White House staffer James Newman, saw military expenditures squeezing social spending and civil liberties and shackling the economy to big business. For Keynesians like Leon Keyserling of the Council of Economic Advisors, the economic stimulus of military spending either made an overheated economy worse or displaced the more effective and more just

[2] Robert Jungk, *Brighter Than a Thousand Suns: A Personal History of the Atomic Scientists,* trans. James Cleugh (New York: Harcourt, Brace, Jovanovich, 1958), 296; Joseph and Stewart Alsop, "Are We Ready for a Push-Button War?" *Saturday Evening Post,* September 6, 1947, 19.

[3] Samuel P. Huntington, *The Common Defense: Strategic Programs in National Politics* (New York: Columbia University Press, 1961), 25–27.

stimulation that could be provided by welfare programs or tax cuts. Senator Robert Taft and his conservative allies thought military spending interfered with tax cuts, too, although they wanted to shrink the New Deal state even more than the national security state. If the conservatives often tied together anti-statist and national security rhetoric in red-baiting, security for them typically stopped at the ocean's edge. National security advocates were powerful enough to fend off an effort by Newman and Atomic Energy Commission (AEC) chairman David Lilienthal to convert the AEC into a government-led industrial development program, but they had modest success at busting the budget caps that all of these strange bedfellows agreed upon before 1950.

Their first major success, in the fight over the supplemental fiscal 1949 budget, was a harbinger of victories to come. Within a size limit established by the president, congressional conservatives shaped a budget that favored the air force. If large sums were going to be spent, conservatives preferred "deterrence," which promised security for the American continent and minimized the national security state's intrusions on personal liberty (at least for citizens who were not and had never been alleged to be Communists). Korea shattered the budget caps, a necessity made into a virtue by Keyserling's framing of military spending as a spur to economic growth, growth that would be provided in part by technological "spillovers" from military R&D. The "stretch-out" and retrenchment ultimately labeled the "New Look" by President Eisenhower sparked a renewed alliance between conservatives and "deterrence" enthusiasts. For the new president, as for Truman, the domestic political path of least resistance was investment in high-technology weapons, which promised (in Melvyn Leffler's words) "to achieve U.S. security objectives on the cheap."[4]

The triumph of "deterrence" had profound consequences for science and technology policy. R&D and procurement of advanced systems absorbed a rapidly increasing share of military resources. General Curtis LeMay, who built the new U.S. Air Force's new Strategic Air Command (SAC) into a fearsome unit, epitomized successful policy entrepreneurship in the period. Although the "supercarrier" went down in the budget wars of the late 1940s, the navy found a counterpart for LeMay in the submariner Captain (later Admiral) Hyman Rickover. Even the army ultimately got on the high-technology bandwagon, ordering up tactical nuclear weapons and developing ballistic missiles.

VISIONS OF THE NATIONAL SECURITY STATE

By virtue of having troops on the ground in Europe and Asia, the United States inescapably inherited a substantial foreign policy agenda after World War II. The aspirations of President Roosevelt, however, had gone far beyond coping

---

[4] Melvyn P. Leffler, *A Preponderance of Power: National Security, the Truman Administration, and the Cold War* (Stanford: Stanford University Press, 1992), 97.

with these immediate demands. His administration at times had resurrected Wilsonian rhetoric of collective security and prosperity through such new international institutions as the United Nations (UN) and the International Monetary Fund (IMF). At other times FDR had engaged in realpolitik to create a bipolar world order that "contained" the Soviet Union's sphere of influence. President Truman adopted and held to Roosevelt's global ambitions. At first his administration also maintained his predecessor's ambivalence between international cooperation and confrontation. By early 1946, though, containment dominated U.S. foreign policy.[5]

Pursuing the goal of containment, the Administration quickly incurred a series of overseas commitments. Western Europe, the Middle East, Japan, South Korea, and Southeast Asia were pulled or pushed under the U.S. security umbrella by 1947. These policies prompted pressure for resources that would ensure that the promises made in these places were credible. Although they agreed on the goal of containment, U.S. foreign and military policy-makers divided sharply over the scale and type of military forces that would be most appropriate and effective in pursuit of it. General Arnold, the godfather of the modern air force, saw military forces-in-being as a first line of defense, to deter American adversaries from taking risks by threatening them with utter destruction. General Marshall, the architect of the recently won victory, stressed political and economic aid and foreign military assistance, if necessary; U.S. military power stood in reserve, of course, but only to be mobilized as a last resort in crucial locations. The civil war over the shape of the national security state was complicated further by conflicts with outside forces. Both conservatives, particularly in Congress, and Keynesians, especially in the White House, found the call for greater military spending disturbing.

"Deterrence" grew out of the strategic bombing experience of World War II. The air force concluded that it had won the war; indeed, Japan had surrendered without an invasion. The ability to wage "an independent air campaign . . . directed against the essential war-making capacity of the enemy," Air Force Chief of Staff Carl Spaatz declared in 1946, had been and would remain militarily decisive. Although the basic tactics for such a campaign were forged by General LeMay in the March 1945 firebombing of Tokyo, atomic bombs strengthened the logic of LeMay's approach. If hundreds or thousands of A-bombs could be delivered within hours, a war would be over almost before it started. Upon taking command of SAC in 1948, LeMay set the goal that his flyers be able to deliver 80 percent of their ordnance in one mission. The capacity to wreak quick and utter destruction, LeMay suggested, would so intimidate potential aggressors that they would keep the peace. The RAND Corporation, set up by Arnold and MIT's Edward Bowles in 1945 and delegated to LeMay's care, developed

---

[5] John L. Gaddis, *Strategies of Containment* (New York: Oxford University Press, 1982), 3–24; Daniel Yergin, *Shattered Peace: The Origins of the Cold War and the National Security State* (Boston: Houghton Mifflin, 1977), 42–86; Leffler (above, n. 4), 25–140.

the delicate psychological assumptions on which deterrence would be based, even as it identified atomic targets in the event that deterrence failed. RAND was intended to bring intellectual vigor to the air force, harnessing academic consultants and nourishing a cadre of in-house gadflies. It became the ideologist of the national security state, dreaming up new capacities and conceiving how to use them so that they would never be used.[6]

While RAND speculated about geosynchronous satellites and intercontinental ballistic missiles (ICBMs), the armed services set about making the prototypes of the last war into the weapons of the next. These included not just Allied inventions like fission bombs and radar sets, but the jet engines and missiles that Germany had developed. Every year the military men went to BOB and congressional appropriations committees and called for "high pressure" and "aggressive" R&D programs that required $1 billion or more. The technological challenges they faced were stunningly difficult. The air force's commitment to heavy bombers, for example, demanded not only engines that could power them to the heartland of Eurasia and airframes that could take the punishment of such a trip, but weapons that could be carried and dropped and electronics and armament for defense along the way. These subsystems, exceptionally complex in themselves, had to be integrated into even more complex machines that could be operated by a few lonely officers in the stress of combat. Not surprisingly, the development costs of bombers shot up.[7]

The performance requirements for military innovations were continually raised. To be sure, R&D revealed new possibilities that needed to be explored and intelligence estimates of Soviet capabilities were given worst-case interpretations that demanded a U.S. response. But competition among the services and among weapon systems made its contribution, too, to the "crescendo." The navy's program to develop aircraft carriers that could launch atomic bombers capable of reaching Moscow, for instance, emerged from the admirals' acceptance of the logic of deterrence and their fear that it made their beloved service obsolete. The advantage of sea-based bombers was that they were closer to the targets than were bombers at domestic air force bases, but they required huge

[6] Carl Spaatz, "Strategic Air Power: Fulfillment of a Concept," *Foreign Affairs,* April 1946, 388; Michael S. Sherry, *The Rise of American Air Power* (New Haven: Yale University Press, 1987), 264–82; Walton S. Moody, *Building a Strategic Air Force* (Washington: Center for Air Force History, 1996), 231; Richard Rhodes, *Dark Sun: The Making of the Hydrogen Bomb* (New York: Simon and Schuster, 1995), 345–49; Fred Kaplan, *The Wizards of Armageddon* (New York: Simon and Schuster, 1983), 50–63.

[7] U.S. House of Representatives, Committee on Appropriations, *First Supplemental Appropriation Rescission Bill, 1946,* part 2, 79th C. 1st s., 1945, 623, 493; Chart, December 29, 1946, Budget Section, Programs Division, RDB, RG330, Entry 341, Box 489, Folder 6; Charles D. Bright, *The Jet Makers: The Aerospace Industry from 1945 to 1972* (Lawrence: Regents Press of Kansas, 1978), 106–10; Michael E. Brown, *Flying Blind: The Politics of the U.S. Strategic Bomber Program* (Ithaca: Cornell University Press, 1992), 69–148. Rhodes (above, n. 6), brilliantly describes the complexities of the hydrogen bomb; the Alsops (above, n. 2), do the same for missiles.

ships and all the accoutrements that went with them. The army's top brass rejected "deterrence," but the Army Ordnance Department nonetheless worked
on replicating and refining the German V-2 with the notion of extending the
range of artillery to a strategically meaningful distance. Closing the circle, the
threat of army control of "the new push-button warfare," *Business Week* reported in October 1946 prompted air force fears that it would be "reduced to
the status of aerial truckdriver."[8]

"Deterrence" in its various manifestations thus prompted scientific and technological efforts across a broad front, from the sublime to the ridiculous, from
the miniaturized genius of inertial guidance systems to the clunking hulk of the
prototype nuclear aircraft engine. These efforts had to be managed by the military users themselves; there was no "civil counterpart" to bear a portion of the
cost, as Boeing had had in the case of the B-17 in the 1930s. And they would
ideally engage the nation's best talent, regardless of whether it resided in the
academic, corporate, or public sector. "Deterrence" advocates were organiza-
tionally creative to this end. In addition to founding RAND, for instance, the
air force aggressively used the R&D contracts pioneered by Bush in World War
II, established a Scientific Advisory Board, and secured increased discretion for
procurement officers. Through such devices, scientists like Ivan Getting were
made (in his words) "a part of the Air Force family," and contractors came to
depend on the military as a major or even dominant source of revenue.[9]

General Marshall learned a different lesson from World War II than did General Arnold. He had had to train the green troops, construct a globe-girdling
pipeline to supply them, and see that the nation's industries filled it up. For Marshall (whom Truman called back to service as Secretary of State in 1947 and
Secretary of Defense in 1951), modern war was not an atomic blitzkrieg, but
the process of putting the country's full productive potential to work for the military when it was called on to fight. The Joint Chiefs of Staff (JCS) needed to
have the raw materials at hand to forge a fighting machine quickly—more
quickly than the two plus years the United States had had before Pearl Harbor—
but they did not need to have it built and rigged on a hair trigger.[10]

The raw materials that "mobilization" required included people, plants, and
ideas. Marshall advocated UMT, so that no successor would have to go through

[8] Bright (above, n. 7), 47–52; Edmund Beard, *Developing the ICBM: A Study in Bureaucratic
Politics* (New York: Columbia University Press, 1976), 24–44; "Industry Has Stake in Fight for
Control of New Weapons," *Business Week,* October 19, 1946, 7.

[9] Remarks by General Eaker to National War College, June 5, 1947, James Webb papers, HSTL
(hereafter "Webb papers"), Box 9, Folder "Air Force"; "Industry-Military Link Forged," *Business
Week,* November 16, 1949, 20–22; Nick A. Komons, *Science and the Air Force* (Arlington, VA:
Office of Aerospace Research, 1966), 1–6; Allen Kaufman, "In the Procurement Officer We Trust:
Constitutional Norms, Air Force Procurement and Industrial Organization, 1938–1947," paper presented at the Hagley Museum, October 1995, 56–62; Jacob Neufeld, ed., *Research and Development in the U.S. Air Force* (Washington: Center for Air Force History, 1993), 44.

[10] Huntington (above, n. 3), 44–47.

the agony that he endured raising troop strength in 1940. As the Cold War deepened, "mobilization" enthusiasts expected Western Europe to contribute people, too, and supported foreign military assistance so that this burden would be shared. Marshall put his own name on the plan designed to ensure, among other things, that Europe's industrial resources would be denied to the Soviets and available to the Americans. At home, DOD maintained industrial plants and machine tools worth an estimated $5 billion to shorten the time in which a surge of war goods could be produced; it also stockpiled critical materials. Ferdinand Eberstadt, the wartime architect of the Controlled Materials Plan, crafted a provision of the National Security Act of 1947 to establish a National Security Resources Board (NSRB) that would coordinate government and business in planning industrial mobilization.[11]

"Mobilization" strategists realized that technological advances made it impossible to simply refight World War II. Marshall and Eisenhower, who became Army Chief of Staff after the war, were far more open to Bush and his fellow scientists than the interwar military leadership had been. Eisenhower, for instance, issued an order in April 1946 calling on the War Department to incorporate civilian scientists into military planning and to separate R&D from other logistical functions. But Bush's reading of the technological tea leaves was a far cry from RAND's. Bush thought bombers to be ineffective and ICBMs implausible. The next war "would be no affair of pushbuttons," Bush wrote in 1949. "For war in the middle future . . . the ultimate advantage will lie with that nation which has scientific and technical capability widespread among its people, industrial capacity and versatility, and a determined will to prevail."[12]

Bush did not intend a return to the boom and bust military appropriations of the years prior to World War II nor to the technological complacency that had accompanied them. The "mobilization" program would cost money. However, it would spend less of this money on R&D and procurement of advanced weapons systems than "deterrence" would. The army spent less on R&D than either the navy or the air force between World War II and the Korean War, even though it had a larger overall budget. For "mobilization," it was at least as important for the military to maintain access to and communication with the best scientists and engineers in civilian institutions as to have them working directly on military projects in strict secrecy. In addition to directing the development of purely military arts, like the design of atomic weapons, the national security

[11] Leffler (above, n. 4), 141–219; Robert J. Gordon, "$45 Billion of U.S. Private Investment Has Been Mislaid," *American Economic Review* 59 (1969): 221–38; William S. Hill, Jr., "The Business Community and National Defense: Corporate Leaders and the Military, 1943–1950" (Ph.D. diss., Stanford University, 1979), 71–75; Jeffery M. Dorwart, *Eberstadt and Forrestal: A National Security Partnership, 1909–1949* (College Station: Texas A&M University Press, 1991), chap. 8.

[12] Eisenhower to War Department managers and officers, April 30, 1946, Stuart Symington papers, HSTL (hereafter "Symington papers"), Box 11, "Research and Development"; Vannevar Bush, *Modern Arms and Free Men* (Simon and Schuster: New York, 1949), 115, 122.

state needed the capability to monitor advances in pure science and in civilian industrial sectors. Freedom from military strictures would maximize technical creativity. It would also maintain the good will of the scientific leadership that the military would need to convert the expected peacetime advances to military ends if war threatened, just as Bush's Office of Scientific Research and Development (OSRD) had done in World War II.[13]

Bush and his colleagues put forward a number of organizational plans to implement this strategy, among them the Research Board for National Security, the military division of the National Research Foundation, and the Joint Research and Development Board attached to the JCS. They typically called for civilians to be in charge of committees that included military, academic, and industrial members and for R&D funds to be managed by civilian rather than military entities. Civilians would rein in the excesses of military technological enthusiasm and guarantee that technical resources, particularly "scientific manpower," would be available to contribute to economic growth and higher living standards that underlay the entire security structure. Bush's postwar experience was rich in irony and frustration. From butting heads with stick-in-the-mud generals and admirals before and during the war, he had come full circle, pleading for a "well-rounded national scientific program" that would support something besides military R&D.[14]

These battles between advocates of "deterrence" and "mobilization" over the internal structure of the national security state inevitably intersected with external political events, because both strategies demanded substantial funds and legal authority. Proponents of other visions of the state, who thought the threat of economic instability more pressing than the threat of Soviet aggression, preferred to use national resources differently. Between V-J Day and the beginning of the Korean War, and especially in the first two postwar years, a "baptist-and-bootlegger" coalition of conservatives and Keynesians, aided by military disunity, kept a tight lid on the defense budget. In political scientist Edward Kolodziej's words, "The military was unified less by a common set of strategic concepts than by the shared experiences of having had to shape their respective budgets to conform to the President's spending ceiling."[15]

Conservatives, led by Senator Taft, still found the intrusions of a large military on domestic liberty disturbing in the wake of World War II. A standing army, they thought, promised foreign entanglements that could justify police state measures at home. Big spending, whether for troops, weapons, or allies, interfered with tax cuts, the conservatives' highest policy priority throughout

[13] Service expenditures taken from *Budget of the U.S. Government,* various years; R&D expenditures from "Federal Expenditures for Research and Development—Fiscal Years 1940–1950," August 15, 1951, RG51, Series 47.8A, Box 6.

[14] U.S. House of Representatives, Committee on Military Affairs, *Research and Development,* 79th C., 1st s., 1945, 2–6.

[15] Edward A. Kolodziej, *The Uncommon Defense and Congress, 1945–1963* (Columbus: Ohio State University Press, 1966), 91.

the immediate postwar period. "During the war," stated Representative Charles Plumley, chairman of the Naval Appropriations Subcommittee in the 80th Congress, "Congress was forced to be very liberal. . . . We must now return to good business practices as of peacetime. . . . to the end that eventually the burden of the individual taxpayer may be reduced." At times, conservatives even argued that advocates of the national security state were dupes in a devious Soviet plot to subvert the American way of life through big government and big spending. Conservative business groups, such as the National Association of Manufacturers and the U.S. Chamber of Commerce, steadfastly supported Taft's priorities.[16]

Keynesians (and the few remaining reform liberals) also had better uses for the public's money than spending it on the army, navy, or air force. If macroeconomic conditions required more government spending, it ought to replenish the nation's housing stock, its schools, and its highways, which had been depleted by the war, or else it should supplement the meager consumption of the poorest Americans. The DOD was not the proper vehicle for a fiscal stimulus. "Military expenditures," the BOB fiscal division's national security specialist stated when recession loomed in 1949, "are basically a waste of social resources and should be kept at a minimum consistent with security needs. Therefore, a policy of increasing national defense expenditures to avert a depression is not recommended." The Keynesian businessmen of the Committee for Economic Development and the labor movement agreed on this point, whatever their disagreements over the appropriate way to supply such a stimulus.[17]

In any case the economy did not lack stimuli from 1946 to 1949; inflation was economic enemy number one. Rearmament, conservatives and Keynesians agreed, would make it worse. With unemployment low (unlike 1939–40), Keynesian analysis suggested that increased military spending would quickly bottleneck key industrial materials and bid up wages. More traditional economists, like Edwin Nourse, the first chairman of Truman's Council of Economic Advisors (CEA), expected that military spending would make wage and price controls inevitable, leading to increased government ownership. President Truman's repeated requests for standby control authority made this fear tangible. At the end of his term in September 1949, Nourse advised the National Security Council (NSC) that a rise in the deficit to pay for military spending would likely be more detrimental to "total national security" on account of its economic side effects than it would contribute to national security conventionally understood.[18]

---

[16] Lynn Rachele Eden, "The Diplomacy of Force: Interests, the State, and the Making of American Military Policy in 1948" (Ph.D. diss, University of Michigan, 1985), 185–93; Kolodziej (above, n. 15), 67–68; Hill (above, n. 11), 128–57.

[17] Edwin G. Nourse, "The Impact of Military Preparedness on the Civilian Economy," *Vital Speeches of the Day,* May 1, 1949, 429–32; M. S. March, draft suggestions for antirecession proposal, April 27, 1949, RG51, Entry 39.3, Box 67, Folder 403; Hill (above, n. 11), 128–57.

[18] "Economic Consequences of a Third World War," *Business Week,* April 24, 1948, 19–23;

Postwar defense policy and its science and technology component, then, were the objects of a two-front war. The overall size of the national security state was fought over in the White House and in Congress, and the impact of defense spending on the domestic economy weighed heavily in the struggle. These concerns, in fact, stifled the expansion of the defense budget before the Korean War. The extent to which the military, whatever its size, would rely on science and technology, was the subject of contention within the Pentagon as well, a contest that grew almost cannibalistic the tighter the defense budget ceiling was clamped down. In this contest the air force slowly gained the upper hand, laying the groundwork for its rise to dominance in the 1950s.

BUDGETS, BOMBERS, AND BOMBS:
DEFENSE TECHNOLOGY POLICY TO 1950

On V-J Day the prospect of a permanent defense economy seemed remote. While more orderly than the mess that followed World War I, demobilization was nonetheless a pell-mell rush. Fiscal 1946 military appropriations were rescinded; fiscal 1947 requests slashed. When the first impulse to bring the boys home had passed a year after the Japanese surrender, the U.S. military found its premier technology programs in a shambles. Funds to develop new strategic bombers were scarce; the atomic weapons complex was ramshackle. The stalemate that led to this austerity, from the military's perspective, was broken only by the crisis atmosphere that followed the coup in Czechoslovakia in early 1948, and then only temporarily. Once the president had conceded that defense spending would rise (although not as much as the Pentagon wanted), congressional conservatives backed the air force, and the air force in turn favored LeMay's bomber program. "Deterrence" made steadier gains in the atomic arena. Dashing the hopes of reform liberals who wrote the 1946 Atomic Energy Act, the Atomic Energy Commission became virtually an off-budget subsidiary of the air force and the navy, a process that culminated with the establishment of the hydrogen bomb development program in 1950.

From the national security perspective, the ceilings that characterized this period of defense budgeting were arbitrary. The numbers were driven by domestic concerns, such as fear of inflation and pressure for tax cuts and nonmilitary spending. The crudest way ceilings were set was the "remainder." The administration would estimate revenues, deduct domestic and foreign aid programs and interest payments, and allocate the remainder to the military. For fiscal 1948

Nourse speech to Chamber of Commerce, April 27, 1948, Edwin G. Nourse papers, HSTL (hereafter "Nourse papers"), Box 9; Craufurd D. Goodwin and R. Stanley Herren, "The Truman Administration: Problems and Policies Unfold," in Goodwin, ed., *Exhortation and Controls: The Search for a Wage-Price Policy, 1945–1971* (Washington: Brookings, 1975), 30–60; Nourse to NSC, September 30, 1949, Nourse papers, Box 8.

this meant a defense budget request of $11.1 billion, down from about $80 billion in fiscal 1945. The three services asked for over $1.1 billion in R&D spending at the beginning of the budget process that year, but by the time BOB was finished, less than $430 million remained in the request. The cuts left von Karman's five year R&D plan for the air force in ruins; foreign powers, Air Force Secretary Stuart Symington was informed, were racing ahead while the United States dawdled.[19]

If anything, the ceilings got tighter with the Republicans in control of Congress. Powered to a midterm victory in 1946 by the twin issues of decontrol and tax reduction, House Republicans knocked the administration's 1948 defense budget down further. Although the Senate restored most of these funds, the military's real purchasing power was dwindling fast due to double-digit inflation. Military R&D suffered particularly from fierce competition with civilian sectors for scientific manpower as private R&D spending boomed. The BOB directive for the FY49 military budget required the services to estimate the impact of a budget ceiling of about $10 billion, another $1 billion cut, a prospect that evoked howls and portended disproportionately deep cuts in investments in military innovation in order to preserve a modicum of readiness.[20]

Although the FY48 military R&D appropriation was enough to support some 13,000 projects, which provided a "fair margin of superiority in practically every technical area of weapon development," according to the Pentagon's publicly stated view, war raged within those five walls. Antagonism between the services reached epic proportions. One step below interservice rivalry, operations, procurement, and R&D accounts within each service were pitted against one another in the budget process. General LeMay's initial postwar job as Deputy Chief of Staff for R&D, for example, was eliminated in 1947; as he later explained, "about the only thing I got done was to forget about R&D programs and try to put all the money we could lay hands on into the basic tools that we would need for a big R&D program [later]." The air force's long-range missile program was shut down entirely; limited R&D funds were focused on bombers.[21]

[19] Huntington (above, n. 3), 221; Koldoziej (above, n. 15), 57; Chart, December 29, 1947, Budget Section, Programs Division, RDB, RG330, Entry 341, Box 489, Folder 6; unsigned memorandum to Symington, December 30, 1946, Symington papers, Box 2, "Budget."

[20] Kolodziej (above, n. 15), 56–70; Compton to Truman, November 2, 1949, Harry S. Truman papers, HSTL (hereafter "Truman papers"), OF 1285h; Ralph Clark to Executive Council, JRDB, September 23, 1947, RG330, Entry 341, Box 489, Folder 5. The exact impact of inflation on the R&D budget is impossible to pin down. According to Steven L. Rearden, *History of the Office of the Secretary of Defense. Volume I: The Formative Years, 1947–1950* (Washington: Historical Office, Office of the Secretary of Defense, 1984), 310, consumer inflation for 1947 was about 14 percent and wholesale inflation about 25 percent.

[21] *First Annual Report of the Secretary of Defense* (Washington: GPO, 1949), 15, 119; Beard (above, n. 8), 52–62, 112; Thomas M. Coffey, *Iron Eagle: The Turbulent Life of General Curtis LeMay* (New York: Crown, 1986), 255; James E. Hewes, Jr., *From Root to McNamara: Army Organization and Administration, 1900–1963* (Washington: Center for Military History, 1975), 172.

Even the heavy bomber program, the air force's flagship, encountered turbulence. Total military aircraft procurement expenditures, which had been $11.5 billion in the last year of the war, declined to only $700 million in 1948. Three-quarters of the air force portion of these funds went to bomber manufacturers, but even this concentration of investment in an industry with extremely high development costs was far too meager to induce the fanatic private efforts through which aircraft entrepreneurs had advanced military technology during the previous peacetime. Only "entirely fortuitous and unforeseen technological windfalls" (in the words of analyst Michael Brown), extracted as part of the "intellectual reparations" program from Germany, allowed the development of a functional jet bomber, the Boeing B-47. "By the latter part of 1947," states industrial historian Charles Bright, the aircraft industry "had run out of money, ideas, courage and hope."[22]

Military resistance to the ceiling rose markedly in late 1947 as the FY49 budget was being prepared. The air force had finally been granted a new, powerful venue to push its case once its independence was finally guaranteed by the passage of the military unification bill in July. President Truman appointed an Air Policy Commission, chaired by Thomas K. Finletter, which proceeded to develop (to the president's dismay) the notion of "unbalanced" funding among the services to recognize that air power was now the most vital element of national security. Naval aviators used the Finletter commission's hearings to advance their carrier-based vision of deterrence. Both air services asked that research and development (particularly development) be accelerated dramatically. Even the army found its voice, faced with a projected 54 percent drop in real R&D spending (compared to its initial proposal to BOB) under the $10 billion ceiling. "The loss of morale," it argued, would be "incalculable"; "the loss of confidence . . . may well be fatal." The National Military Establishment prepared what it called a "compromise" budget that preserved R&D spending (among other things) as a "sort of last stand" to make its case to BOB.[23]

The budget bureau rejected these efforts; "hold the line," was the watchword of the Budget Message delivered in January 1948. Domestic issues outranked national security, and the Marshall Plan took precedence over the military in the administration's spending calculus. With the publication of the Finletter report, *Survival in the Air Age,* in the same month, political conflict over the size and composition of the defense budget became more open and more intense than it had been since before the war. As the air force and aircraft industry mobilized support for "deterrence," President Truman and Secretary Marshall were forced to wage a campaign to secure aid to Europe from tax-cutting con-

[22] Hill (above, n. 11), 201, 224; Brown (above, n. 7), 86; Bright (above, n. 7), 13.

[23] Hill (above, n. 11), 204–31; Rearden (above, n. 20), 313–16; RDB Committee on Aeronautics, February 5, 1948, RG330, Entry 341, Box 523, Folder 1; Clark to Executive Council, October 1, 1947, and "List of Questions Prepared by the Bureau of the Budget for Research and Development Board Hearing," October 29, 1947, both in RG330, Entry 341, Box 489, Folder 5.

gressional conservatives. The president also faced a new political threat on the left, Henry Wallace's emerging candidacy, which trumpeted a renewal of FDR's ideal of international cooperation. Truman's response was to harden his Cold War line, giving the worst possible interpretation of Soviet actions that winter, particularly the Czech coup in late February, to win support for his embattled legislative package and to isolate Wallace. On March 17, what Frank Kofsky has accurately labeled a "war scare" culminated in two presidential speeches. One called on Congress to support the Marshall Plan, UMT, and the draft; the other painted Wallace as a friend of the Communist enemy. The Marshall Plan quickly sailed through Congress. Ironically, Wallace was for the moment unscathed, though Truman's anticommunist rhetoric would eventually weigh heavily in the election.[24]

But the president had unleashed forces beyond his control. The war fever gripping the nation offered grand opportunities for national security entrepreneurship. The Joint Chiefs pressed for a $9 billion supplemental budget, a 90 percent boost; Secretary of Defense Forrestal was less hawkish but thought $3.5 billion might get through. After an extended battle within the administration in April and May, the president proposed a supplemental appropriation of about $3 billion over the objections of his inflation-conscious budget director, James Webb. Although Congress accepted the new ceiling, it altered the supplemental budget's priorities. In authorization hearings, Air Force Secretary Symington publicly broke ranks with the administration; relying on the Finletter report, he called for an additional $850 million in air force funding. Senator Taft seized on Symington's proposal as an alternative to UMT, which he thought to be ineffective, an infringement on domestic liberty, and inappropriate to the defense of the continental United States. If the circumstances required the expansion of the national security state, Taft preferred to see the air force gain. Senator Arthur Vandenberg, the Republican whose support had been the key to the Marshall Plan's legislative success, conceded this issue to Taft, in part because other matters in which he needed Taft's acquiescence were pending. Congress thus added $822 million for aircraft procurement and refused authority and funding for UMT.[25]

The president was able to insert a rider on the aircraft procurement bill stip-

[24] Bush to RDB, January 2, 1948, RG 330, Entry 341, Box 489, Folder 6; Frank Kofsky, *Harry S. Truman and the War Scare of 1948,* paperback ed. (New York: St. Martin's, 1995), 84–141; "Price of Mobilizing America to Defend Democratic Nations," *U.S. News and World Report,* March 26, 1948, 13–15; Alonzo L. Hamby, *Beyond the New Deal: Harry S. Truman and American Liberalism* (New York: Columbia University Press, 1973), 223. Kofsky's account, while persuasive in many respects, allots too much power and importance to the aircraft industry and underestimates the sincerity with which Marshall and Truman sought UMT.

[25] Kofsky (above, n. 24), 172–82; Lynn Eden, "Capitalist Conflict and the State: The Making of U.S. Military Policy in 1948," in Charles Bright and Susan Harding, eds., *Statemaking and Social Movements: Essays in History and Theory* (Ann Arbor: University of Michigan Press, 1984), 245, 253; Rearden (above, n. 20), 321–30.

ulating that his direct approval would be needed to spend these additional funds, and he refused to supply this approval during fiscal 1949. Even without the additional $822 million, however, spending on military aircraft rose substantially. Aircraft production rose 88 percent in the second half of calendar 1948 (the first half of fiscal 1949), the industry returned to profitability, and its order books were filled for future years. The supplemental appropriation increased the military R&D budget by $144 million (or about one-third), of which $80 million was allotted to the air force and $35 million to the Naval Bureau of Aeronautics. Projects in support of strategic air, air defense, and combat air dominated the National Military Establishment's R&D program. Most importantly, the debate over the supplemental appropriation in the spring of 1948 revealed that conservatives would find common ground with "deterrence" advocates in a perceived crisis of national security. The victory of this new coalition, symbolized by the fact that the air force's appropriations temporarily surpassed the army's, was a harbinger of what would later be termed "massive retaliation," an unbalanced force structure that relied primarily on strategic bombing with atomic weapons.[26]

After the war scare subsided, military spending leveled off at a new plateau of about $13 billion. Domestic programs and inflation-fighting regained presidential favor for fiscal years 1950 and 1951. Stymied in their crusade for "defense first, economy second," as Symington put it, the services resumed their civil war. The appeal of the air force relative to the other services was graphically demonstrated when Congress endorsed the decision of the new Secretary of Defense, Louis Johnson, to maintain the bomber program at the expense of the navy's "supercarrier" version of "deterrence." But the air force's success was largely defensive; at best, it avoided cuts imposed on the other services. Within the air force, R&D suffered disproportionately as planes were rushed into production in an effort to guarantee future funding. Even the establishment of a new Air R&D Command (ARDC) and reestablishment of LeMay's old job of Deputy Chief of Staff for R&D in 1950, which left "lots of blood on the floor" (as one participant later stated), were pyrrhic victories, since neither could gain authority over actual projects.[27]

[26] John B. Rae, *Climb to Greatness: The American Aircraft Industry, 1920–1960* (Cambridge: MIT Press, 1968), 174–92; Hill (above, n. 11), 268, 361; Symington to W. J. McNeil, April 30, 1948, RG330, Entry 341, Box 489, Folder 6; "Major Stages in Development of R&D Budgets FY1949 and 1950," undated, RG330, Entry 341, Box 489, Folder 6; "FY51 RDB Budget Presentation before JCS Budget Advisory Committee, 15 July 1949," RG330, Entry 341, Box 493, Folder 1; "Pattern for Arms Spending: New Emphasis on Air Power," *U.S. News and World Report,* June 4, 1948, 11–13; Samuel R. Williamson, Jr., and Steven L. Rearden, *The Origins of U.S. Nuclear Strategy, 1945–1953* (New York: St. Martin's, 1993), 96.

[27] Rearden (above, n. 20), 335–84; George M. Watson, Jr., *The Office of the Secretary of the Air Force, 1947–1965* (Washington: Center for Air Force History, 1993), 99; Leffler (above, n. 4), 272–77; Beard (above, n. 8), 83–97, 107–20; Neufeld (above, n. 9), 39. See also Warner R. Schilling, "The Politics of National Defense: Fiscal 1950," in Schilling, ed., *Strategy, Politics, and Defense Budgets* (New York: Columbia University Press, 1962), 1–266.

Although their progress on the aircraft front was a matter of two steps forward and one step back from 1947 to 1950, "deterrence" forces came to dominate atomic R&D once the extended debate over the Atomic Energy Act (AEA) of 1946 was finally played out. This was not what the drafters of the AEA, James Newman and Byron Miller, intended. They had hoped that the AEC would carry on the reform liberal tradition of the Tennessee Valley Authority (TVA), and even serve as a base from which that tradition's depleted defenders could regroup and begin to transform "the structure of society itself." Although the AEC resembled the "island of socialism" that Newman and Miller pictured, it produced weapons of mass destruction rather than electric power too cheap to meter.[28]

Newman and Miller's vision reflected the fear that civilian technology had stagnated, a fear that had helped to motivate the TVA and other public power projects in the 1930s. In 1945 Alan Sweezy, an economist who had been affiliated with the National Resources Planning Board, a defunct bastion of reform liberal thinking, identified atomic energy and housing as the two industries in which a "technological revolution" seemed most likely to provide substantial investment opportunities into the next decade and beyond. Just as the World War I–vintage Muscle Shoals plants had formed the core of the TVA, this line of thought went, the Manhattan Project would metamorphose into an AEC that would shake up entrenched utilities and lift up backward regions. Three-quarters of Americans polled in September 1945 agreed that the government, rather than industry, ought to take charge of the development of atomic energy.[29]

The AEA debate in 1945–46 involved many significant issues, including civilian control of the military and the prospects for international control of nuclear weapons. For Newman and Miller, who worked in both the executive and legislative branches during this period, the promise of civilian applications of atomic energy was among the most compelling motives for their version of the legislation. They wrote into the act and saw through to passage provisions that empowered the AEC not only to conduct a wide-ranging R&D program, but to license broadly all possible uses of the technologies it developed. Further, like TVA, the new agency was given the power to compel licensing of patents on atomic technologies owned by firms. "The regulatory position of the Commission and its monopoly of fissionable material," the drafters concluded, "are thus to be used in order to force the widest possible dissemination of technical information and the greatest possible number of participants in the productive process."[30]

[28] James R. Newman and Byron S. Miller, *The Control of Atomic Energy: A Study of Its Social, Economic, and Political Implications* (New York: Whittlesey House, 1948), 4, 21.

[29] Alan Sweezy, "Declining Investment Opportunity," in Seymour E. Harris, ed., *The New Economics* (New York: Knopf, 1947), 431; Hadley Cantril, ed., *Public Opinion, 1935–1946* (Westport, CT: Greenwood, 1978), 27.

[30] Richard G. Hewlett and Oscar E. Anderson, Jr., *The New World, 1939/1946* (University Park, PA: Pennsylvania State University Press, 1962), 408–530; Newman and Miller (above, n. 28), 132.

The reform liberals acknowledged that the legislators who passed the AEA did not necessarily share their expansive vision of state-led economic development. "To one who likes his history seasoned with paradox," Newman and Miller wrote, "the spectacle of a predominantly conservative Congress under the goad of the powerful conservative instinct of security enacting a thoroughly radical piece of legislation must provide considerable satisfaction." Their satisfaction was enhanced by the act's initial implementation, which suggested that their interpretation would govern. The president appointed the TVA's David Lilienthal to chair the AEC and supported him despite Senator Taft's effort to block his confirmation. In his January 1947 Budget Message, Truman hailed his administration's civilian goals for atomic technology, and the AEC was placed in the budget category of "resource development," the same as the TVA.[31]

While the AEA was being fought over, the remnants of the Manhattan Project were orphaned. The scientists and engineers who had made it work departed in droves. The army, under whose nominal care it fell, was saddled with occupation duty and besieged by budget economizers and by the other armed services. General Leslie Groves, the project's lame-duck caretaker, struggled half-heartedly to stem the decay. By the time the AEC made its first report to the president in March 1947, there was not even a single usable atomic weapon. There were enough parts to build a few A-bombs, but the expertise to assemble them, a difficult and laborious job, had largely dissipated. Groves had always intended on mass-producing atomic weapons with "idiot-proof" interchangeable parts, but the Los Alamos laboratory, brought back from the brink of collapse by its new director, Norris Bradbury, had just begun to tackle this job. Despite its trial run at Hiroshima and Nagasaki, atomic warfare remained in the prototype phase, its products hand-crafted, its raw material pipeline in chaos, and its plant and equipment requiring massive infusions of cash to make the transition to technological maturity.[32]

Lilienthal's discovery of the decrepit state of the atomic weapons program coincided with his shocked realization that atomic power plants were considered by most experts to be decades away. The AEC had little choice but to devote the biggest part of its budget to the production of fissile material and weapons; the renovation of the Hanford works begun in 1947 was the biggest peacetime construction job in history. Military pressure diverted the reactor development program from research and electricity to naval and aircraft propul-

[31] Newman and Miller (above, n. 28), 4; Hamby (above, n. 24), 183; *Budget of the U.S. Government for Fiscal Year 1948* (Washington: GPO, 1947), M8.

[32] Rhodes (above, n. 6), 211–13, 277–84; David Alan Rosenberg, "The Origins of Overkill: Nuclear Weapons in American Strategy," *International Security* 7(4) (1983): 14–15; Richard G. Hewlett and Francis Duncan, *Atomic Shield: A History of the U.S. Atomic Energy Commission, Volume II, 1947–1952,* paperback ed. (Berkeley: University of California Press, 1990), 42–48, 57–62; Hewlett and Anderson (above, n. 30), 624–33.

sion. If such projects seemed far out to some, at least there was a ready customer for them, notably the formidable submariner, Captain Rickover. The navy's enthusiasm was a stunning contrast to the pessimism of the electric utilities. The new congressional Joint Committee on Atomic Energy (JCAE), the legislative counterpart of the AEC, also began exerting leverage for enhanced security and greater military production, first under the chairmanship of the Republican Senator Bourke Hickenlooper in the 80th Congress and then the Democrat Brien McMahon, Newman's former patron, in the 81st. By the summer of 1949, Chairman Lilienthal was besieged by charges of "incredible mismanagement" for failing to protect atomic secrets well enough and to build atomic weapons fast enough.[33]

The "crescendo of hideous invention" reached its climax in the case of the AEC with the Soviet atomic test on August 29, 1949, and the presidential decision to establish a hydrogen bomb R&D program on January 31, 1950. The Soviet test shocked the president, who had anticipated that the U.S. nuclear monopoly would continue for some years to come. It guaranteed that the AEC's civilian goals would be set aside and that its resources would be devoted almost completely to national security purposes. What was debated in the wake of the test was what fraction of these resources would be committed to a strategy of continual modernization, represented by the H-bomb, as opposed to stockpiling fission bombs, which could now be mass-produced. H-bombs were a natural extension of the air force's vision of the national security state, and, as in the fiscal 1949 defense budget debate, the air force got its way. (General LeMay even put Edward Teller, the H-bomb's most ardent scientific advocate, on an air force contract when Teller got fed up with AEC, violating the spirit of the AEA and threatening to break the agency's monopoly on nuclear weapons development.) Even if the military efficacy of the H-bomb was dubious, as Army Chief of Staff Omar Bradley initially argued, it would certainly serve as a terrifying symbol of American power. In the end, it was concern about the "psychological balance" of power, as the Joint Chiefs of Staff (JCS) called it, that impelled the president to authorize a serious investigation of the feasibility of thermonuclear weapons, indeed, making the final decision to build them little more than a foregone conclusion.[34]

The president's appointment of Gordon Dean to replace David Lilienthal as chairman of the AEC in the wake of the H-bomb decision symbolized not

[33] Rebecca Lowen, "Entering the Atomic Power Race: Science, Industry, and Government," *Political Science Quarterly* 102 (1987): 459–79; Hewlett and Duncan (above, n. 32), 96–102, 114–21, 127–32, 145–47, 172–219, 323–32, 354–61; Brian Balogh, *Chain Reaction: Expert Debate and Public Participation in American Commercial Nuclear Power, 1945–1975* (New York: Cambridge University Press, 1991), 86–94.

[34] Herbert York, *The Advisors: Oppenheimer, Teller, and the Superbomb,* 2d ed. (Stanford: Stanford University Press, 1989); Rhodes (above, n. 6), 381–408; Neufeld (above, n. 9), 45; Gregg Herken, *The Winning Weapon: The Atomic Bomb in the Cold War, 1945–1950* (New York: Knopf, 1980), 317.

merely the agency's endorsement of the preeminence of national security among its missions, but its acceptance as well of an urgent responsibility to push the technological envelope as rapidly as possible in pursuing that mission. Its laboratories would generate and test ideas for nuclear weapons (and propulsion systems), and its facilities would produce them, much as Boeing made bombers and General Electric made jet engines. Although the AEC was in nominal control of the stockpile, it was only a matter of time before atomic weapons were given over to the physical custody of the military in the same way as a bomber. The AEC was adapting to the role that LeMay and Rickover had sought for it, that of a supplier subject to ever-escalating military requirements. It had no authority and little influence over those requirements and often had little understanding of how they were established. Yet, like the contractors, the commission thrived financially. Its expenditures, now classified as "major national security" rather than "resource development," tripled to nearly $2 billion between fiscal 1949 and fiscal 1952.[35]

On June 6, 1950, six years after the invasion of France under the command of General Eisenhower, SAC carried out a simulated nuclear air strike on the Soviet Union under the command of General LeMay. As Richard Rhodes relates, LeMay's troops performed to the satisfaction of their demanding leader, something they most assuredly had not done when he had first reported for duty two years earlier. He had molded SAC into a vigorous elite unit, imbued with the heady notion that it could win wars by itself. The bulky apparatus that Eisenhower had had to rely on to win his war, the naval bombardment, the landing craft, the tanks, the infantry, the close air support and the logistical wherewithall to make them run—all this would become obsolete if the president would let SAC do its job. SAC's esprit de corps in this exercise was a measure of the success of the "deterrence" conception of national security during the previous two years. With the aid of congressional conservatives, the air force had become the richest and most powerful service. Led by the air force, the services had begun to establish a dedicated, technologically sophisticated supply chain that encompassed not only the AEC and major firms, but elite universities as well. Like the AEC, the scientists were increasingly on tap, not on top. The peculiar leverage that Bush had had in mobilizing civilian science for World War II evaporated as entrepreneurial scientists and administrators pursued deals with military funders on mutually agreeable research projects.[36]

SAC's ability to deliver what it promised on this date, however, was still

---

[35] Hewlett and Duncan (above, n. 32), 410–84; *The Budget in Brief* (Washington: GPO, 1957), 52.

[36] Rhodes (above, n. 6), 438–39; Rosenberg (above, n. 32), 15–21; Paul Forman, "Beyond Quantum Electronics: National Security as a Basis for Physical Research in the United States, 1940–1960," *Historical Studies in the Physical and Biological Sciences* 17 (1987): 150–229; Harvey Sapolsky, *Science and the Navy* (Princeton: Princeton University Press, 1990), 37–56.

jeopardized by inadequate science and technology. Its most modern long-range bomber, the Convair B-36D, was a propeller plane to which jet engines had been added in 1949, charitably characterized as a "10-engined monster" by John Rae. The combat effectiveness of the B-36 was highly uncertain, as the navy had pointed out in trying to salvage its even more dubious "supercarrier." In any case most of SAC's force consisted of less capable B-29s left over from World War II. SAC's atomic cupboard was no longer bare, as it had been when LeMay took command, but it was far from the thousands of atomic weapons that "deterrence" advocates believed were required to win a modern war. Similarly, although SAC crews were gaining the capacity to handle atomic weapons, the routines for their production, assembly, storage, and delivery by AEC to SAC remained rudimentary at best.[37]

"Deterrence" had been given organizational content and advocates of the national security state had won a somewhat larger chunk of the federal budget by June 1950, but they were far from triumphant. The president's go-slow attitude toward NSC-68, intended by Secretary of State Dean Acheson to be a "bludgeon" with which to override conservatives and Keynesians who placed domestic programs first, demonstrates this point. Drafted by Paul Nitze, George Kennan's successor as the head of the Department of State's Policy Planning Staff, in the spring of 1950, NSC-68 argued in shrill terms for "more, more, and more money" (as Melvyn Leffler puts it) for defense, particularly to provide for military hardware. "More, more, and more money" was not available under the caps that were the cornerstone of the administration's budget policy. Truman therefore referred the document back to the NSC for a cost estimate (which its authors had conveniently omitted) and specified that BOB, CEA, and the Economic Cooperation Agency (which ran the Marshall Plan) be included in the process. The structure of this review ensured that policy-makers committed to visions of the state other than the national security state would be heard from before the administration put itself on the line. In the meantime the FY52 budget process continued, with the possibility of an even tighter ceiling being explored by BOB. Samuel Wells, Jr., speculates that, as in 1948, an increment of $3 billion in additional military spending might ultimately have been provided if the peace had held. But nineteen days after the SAC simulation, before the costing of NSC-68 was finished, the Korean War began.[38]

[37] Rae (above, n. 26), 181–84; Brown (above, n. 7), 136–40; Hewlett and Duncan (above, n. 32), 172–84; David Alan Rosenberg, "US Nuclear Stockpile, 1945–1950," *Bulletin of Atomic Scientists* (May 1982): 25–30.

[38] Leffler (above, n. 4), 355–60; Samuel F. Wells, Jr., "Sounding the Tocsin: NSC 68 and the Soviet Threat," *International Security* 4 (1979): 116–58; Forman (above, n. 36), 157–58 (notes 12–13); Gaddis (above, n. 5), 90–109; Paul Y. Hammond, "NSC-68: Prologue to Rearmament," in Schilling, ed. (above, n. 27), 326–49.

MAKING A VIRTUE OF NECESSITY: KOREA, "TECHNOLOGICAL SPILLOVER," AND THE "NEW LOOK"

The Korean War exploded the barriers to the expansion of the national security state. Across the political spectrum, even to Henry Wallace, Americans joined in supporting an armed response to Communist aggression. For those in the know, the conflict confirmed Nitze's view of Soviet aspirations; the U.S. response, therefore, could not be confined to the immediate crisis in Korea but had to be global and prolonged. Although the hot war on the ground appeared to offer a splendid opportunity for the army and "mobilization" thinking to reclaim some of the ground lost in the late 1940s, the "NSC-68 mentality" (to use Daniel J. Kevles's phrase) was premised on "deterrence." Even as the conventional battle stalemated in Korea, the United States committed itself fully to military technological superiority, especially in strategic weapons, in the Cold War. The new reality that national security would be a very large commitment over the "long haul" forced Keynesians and conservatives to accommodate. Keynesians did so by citing the stimulative effect of military spending on the economy and developing the notion of "technological spillover" to describe one of the main channels for this effect. The conservative accommodation took the form of favoring the air force and "deterrence," as it had in fiscal 1949. When the crisis eased, the two groups helped to impose defense budget ceilings once again, at a level of about $40 billion or three times the pre-Korea ceiling, of which the air force took nearly half.[39]

The fiscal 1951 budget, with a ceiling of about $13 billion for the military, was under congressional consideration when the war started. The first supplemental budget, submitted in July 1950, financed the surge of troops and ammunition that was supposed to win the quick victory that everyone in Washington expected. The $11.6 billion appropriation paid the draftees and put into motion the mobilization of the industrial reserve of plants and equipment that had been maintained since the previous war. However, even at this early date, about half of the new spending was intended not to support the troops in Korea, but to implement the global ambitions of NSC-68. The first supplemental, for example, furnished the navy, which had been denied a role in "deterrence" the previous year, with funds for a new class of aircraft carrier. The second supplemental budget of $17 billion, offered in December, advanced "deterrence" further. It boosted DOD R&D spending by $410 million on top of the approximately $500 million already allocated. Similarly, military analyst Paul Hammond notes, "Although 99% of the Air Force effort in the Korean War was de-

---

[39] Hamby (above, n. 24), 403–8; Daniel J. Kevles, "K$_1$S$_2$: Korea, Science, and the State," in Peter Galison and Bruce Hevly, eds., *Big Science* (Stanford: Stanford University Press, 1992), 327; Kevin N. Lewis, *The U.S. Air Force Budget and Posture over Time* (Santa Monica: RAND Corporation, 1990), 14.

voted to tactical uses, the major procurement expenditures for expansion were going for an increase in strategic air power—for relatively long-range air-atomic capabilities, rather than for ground support fighters." In February 1951 the air force signed the first production contract for the B-52, even though flight testing on the aircraft had not begun and even though a longer conventional war on the ground in Korea was clearly in prospect because of the Chinese intervention there.[40]

With an additional $6 billion in a third supplemental budget, the final figure for FY51 defense appropriations ballooned to $48.2 billion. The next year's budget surpassed $60 billion. All the services shared in the cornucopia, as did the European allies, but the air force did best, receiving $23 billion, including an extra $1 billion for aircraft procurement kicked in by the Senate. In FY53 the pattern was confirmed; even though the president imposed a "stretch-out" that reduced the defense budget to under $50 billion, the air force budget remained virtually unchanged, imposing the brunt of the cuts on the other services, particularly the army. The three Korean War budgets, taken together, marked what one military historian calls a "momentous shift" from a "balanced" force structure in which the army bulked largest to one in which the air force absorbed the lion's share. Within the air force, SAC was the biggest beneficiary of the shift, maintaining its priority over the tactical and air defense missions. President Truman also approved a massive expansion of the AEC's military programs, doubling the agency's budget again, to $4 billion in fiscal 1953. The United States, the JCS argued, could never have too many nuclear weapons, and the president concurred.[41]

Military R&D spending benefited from a rearmament program that emphasized high-technology weaponry. It more than tripled during the Korean War, stabilizing at about $1.8 billion. The proportion of R&D conducted in U.S. industry that was motivated or paid for by the military doubled from about a quarter to about half, with exceptional growth in aircraft and electronics. Academic physical science and electrical engineering research was even more dominated by military funding, with organizations like MIT's Research Laboratory for Electronics and Stanford's Electronics Laboratory growing geometrically thanks to the services' patronage. Even when service budgets declined, as the army's did in 1953, military R&D spending continued to track upward. "Deterrence" had conquered; like the navy, the army now sought strategic forces and their continual modernization.[42]

[40] Hammond (above, n. 38), 350–59; Kolodziej (above, n. 15), 129–39; "Federal Expenditures for Research and Development—Fiscal Years 1940–1950," August 15, 1951, RG51, Series 47.8A, Box 6; Brown (above, n. 7), 147–49.

[41] Kolodziej (above, n. 15), 140–66; Moody (above, n. 6), 392; Watson (above, n. 27), 104–20; Hewlett and Duncan (above, n. 32), 561–78.

[42] *Budget of the U.S. Government for Fiscal Year 1957* (Washington: GPO, 1956), 1151; RDB 114/34 (above, n. 1), 9–10; Forman (above, n. 36), 152–55; Kevles (above, n. 39), 314–15, 329;

"Mobilization" was never really tested. Congress refused to pass UMT. The industrial reserve of plant and equipment performed miserably, much of it having become obsolete since V-J Day. The idea of a "new OSRD," which had been floated by Bush's allies as early as 1948, generated little enthusiasm in 1950. After canvassing the scientific establishment (including Bush himself) on this matter for BOB, William Golden, an investment banker with ties to AEC Commissioner Lewis Strauss, recommended only that planning for such an agency be authorized. His reports suggested that military R&D was so vast that mobilizing civilian scientists would serve little purpose. Golden did advocate that the president appoint scientific advisors who might filter out some of the services' technological enthusiasm, but even this modest initiative was shunted aside. A scientific advisory committee to the director of defense mobilization was established instead, and it did nothing important while Truman was president.[43]

The triumph within the national security state of General LeMay and other enthusiasts of "deterrence" owed much to their groundwork in the lean years since 1945 and to the uncanny timing of the Korean War. They had a terrifying message and tight control over information that might refute it. Their weapons were continually improving, as "Mike," the prototype H-bomb, exploded in November 1952, showed. "Deterrence" advocates also benefited from a renewal of their alliance with conservatives that had appeared briefly during the war scare of 1948. There was, of course, the McCarthyite apparatus of intimidation that went so far as to impugn the patriotism of General Marshall before it was dismantled. Beyond this, Senator Taft's congressional bloc provided leverage at critical moments to secure substantial resources. The additional funding provided to the air force in FY52, for instance, was at least in part an effort to appease Taft's criticism of the administration's commitment to European defenses. More significantly, the air force's dominance of the "stretch-out" begun in FY53, too, reflected the conservatives' belief that "deterrence" was the most economical and least intrusive military strategy.[44]

The "stretch-out" itself was an illusion in part. Huge sums carried over by the armed services from prior-year appropriations meant that fiscal 1953 was

---

Lawrence P. Lessing, "The Electronics Era," *Fortune,* July 1951, 78–83, 132–38; Stuart W. Leslie, *The Cold War and American Science: The Military-Academic Complex at MIT and Stanford* (New York: Columbia University Press, 1993), 44–75. As Forman and Kevles note, figures on R&D spending can only be approximated, given variations in definition over time and across agencies.

[43] Bright (above, n. 7), 61–65; Kevles (above, n. 39), 321–27; Golden to Truman, December 18, 1950, William T. Golden papers, HSTL. This memo and others (but not all) from Golden's study have now been reprinted in William Blanpied, ed., *Impacts of the Early Cold War on the Formulation of U.S. Science Policy* (Washington: American Association for the Advancement of Science, 1995). The memos suggest considerable variance in policy-makers' interpretation of the ideas for organizations and policies that Golden was circulating.

[44] Rosenberg 1983 (above, n. 32), 21–27; Moody (above, n. 6), 385–92, 446–54; Gaddis (above, n. 5), 118–21.

the peak year of actual expenditures. But military spending (though not military R&D spending) did decline thereafter, to approximately $40 billion, about 9 percent of the gross national product (GNP). The cuts stemmed from a reassertion of the Keynesian as well as the conservative vision of the state. But, although they became more vocal and active by the end of the Korean War, adherents of both of these visions had learned to live with the bigger, bolder national security state.

As they had in 1940, the Keynesians made a smooth transition to become "all-outers" for defense in 1950. Other things being equal, Leon Keyserling (who acceded to the chairmanship of the CEA in the fall of 1949) and his allies would rather have spent money on social instead of military programs, a preference that motivated their support for the pre-Korea defense budget ceilings. But Keynesianism was in theory neutral between the two. When faced with the inevitability of large supplemental defense budgets, Keyserling was well equipped to provide optimistic advice to the war's managers. The United States need not become a "garrison state," a prospect feared by liberals and conservatives alike, but with proper policy could have (as the editors of *Fortune* emphasized) "guns *and* butter." Not only that, it could have both better guns and better butter.[45]

Sumner Slichter, the chairman of the CED's Research Advisory Board, half-jokingly anticipated this chain of reasoning in October 1949. "[T]he cold war," he stated, "increases the demand for goods, helps sustain a high level of employment, accelerates technological progress, and helps the country raise its standard of living. . . . So we may thank the Russians for helping make capitalism in the United States work better than ever." Slichter was thinking of defense budgets in the $10–15 billion range. Keyserling was characteristically more expansive and, in his meetings with Nitze during the drafting of NSC-68, stressed that $40 billion could be afforded, if necessary. Nitze noted that "Keyserling . . . wanted to spend the money on other programs," but his report nonetheless employed the CEA chairman's argument that vastly expanded military spending would not damage the economy, particularly given the dismal medium-term outlook that government economic models yielded.[46]

When the Korean War overrode all doubts about the necessity of such spending, the president quickly approved NSC-68, which included an economic chapter drafted by CEA chief of staff Gerhard Colm. Keyserling, drawing directly on pre-Korean War Keynesian initiatives, took the lead in drafting the Defense Production Act to govern the rearmament, pressing for expanded investment, rather than direct controls, as the major economic management tool. CEA's *Report to the President* at the beginning of 1951 claimed that the nation could afford to spend up to 25 percent of GNP on national security if it had to,

[45] "America's Commitment," *Fortune,* August 1950, 53–59.

[46] Hill (above, n. 11), 382 (citing *Commercial and Financial Chronicle,* Oct. 27, 1947); Gaddis (above, n. 5), 92–95.

while maintaining its fundamental economic strength. Expansion of productive capacity would limit the danger of inflation, and tax and credit policies could do the rest. The clear implication was that Cold War investment would lead ultimately to a peacetime boom like that which had followed World War II. Slichter and the CED fundamentally agreed, although not surprisingly they were less optimistic about the pace of growth and more inclined to impose austerity on consumers and on nondefense programs in the short run to free up capacity for the military effort.[47]

Neither the war nor the CEA's plan for managing the home front conformed to these initial expectations. The Chinese intervention and a burst of inflation at the end of 1950 caused the president to declare a state of emergency and impose some economic controls, which he delegated to a new Office of Defense Mobilization (ODM) under Charles E. Wilson. In early 1951 the Federal Reserve Board assumed a more independent and more constrictive stance on interest rates than CEA preferred, limiting the impact of federal spending on investment. Nonetheless, the Korean War years proved to be a period of strong investment, low inflation, and rapid growth. Full-scale World War II-style price, production, and materials controls were never imposed (although griping about Korean War controls reached World War II levels). The experience confirmed the Keynesians in their belief that the expansion of productive capacity ought to be the central approach to rearmament. They could see no economic reason, for instance, to justify the fiscal 1953 "stretch-out." As a report co-authored by Colm put it, "[t]he productivity of the American economy is so immense that the U.S. need not be afraid of adopting sizable additional national security programs if they are found to be advisable in support of the cause of security and liberty in the free world."[48]

Keynesians increasingly identified the crucial source of this stunning productivity growth to be investments in new technologies made possible by research and development, regardless of whether they were made for military or

[47] Edward S. Flash, Jr., *Economic Advice and Presidential Leadership* (New York: Columbia University Press, 1965), 36–39; *Mid-Year Economic Report of the President* (Washington: GPO, 1950), 9–12, 37–39; *Economic Report of the President for 1951* (Washington: GPO, 1950), 13–14, 57–64, 82; Committee for Economic Development, "Economic Policy for Rearmament," pamphlet, September 1950, available in Widener Library, Harvard University; Sumner Slichter, "Business and Armament," *Atlantic,* November 1950, 38–41; Robert M. Collins, "The Emergence of Economic Growthmanship in the United States: Federal Policy and Economic Knowledge in the Truman Years," in Mary O. Furner and Barry Supple, eds., *The State and Economic Knowledge: The American and British Experiences* (New York: Cambridge University Press, 1990), 153.

[48] Flash (above, n. 47), 40–99; Alonzo Hamby, *Man of the People: A Life of Harry S. Truman* (New York: Oxford, 1995), 575–98; Herbert Stein, *The Fiscal Revolution in America* (Chicago: University of Chicago, 1969), 241–80; Keyserling speech to ADA, "The Role of Liberals in the Defense Program," May 18, 1951, and Keyserling, "Security and the National Economy," November 23, 1953, both in Leon Keyserling papers, HSTL (hereafter "Keyserling papers"), Box 19; National Planning Association, "Can We Afford Additional Programs for National Security?" pamphlet no. 84, October 1953, iv.

nonmilitary purposes. The idea that military innovations would have civilian benefits had been an article of faith at the end of World War II. Harry Hopkins, for instance, provided Vannevar Bush with the entreé in 1944 to write the famous letter to the president requesting *Science, the Endless Frontier* largely in the hope that it would assist in the conversion of wartime R&D into technologies that would advance living standards. Despite scattered examples, however, precious little systematic evidence was adduced in the immediate postwar period that this was the case. During wartime, stated Solomon Fabricant, the productivity specialist at the National Bureau of Economic Research, "attention is diverted from the mainsprings of progress." Like general military expenditures, military R&D expenditures were seen largely as a waste of social resources that could be much more usefully invested (in the absence of a security threat) by civilian agencies like NSF.[49]

The claims that the distinction between military and nonmilitary research was "somewhat arbitrary and not altogether significant" and that the benefits of military research would "nearly always" spill over to the economy (as an official of the DOD Research and Development Board argued in January 1950) were therefore offered only occasionally before the Korean War, even by advocates of military R&D. By the end of the war, however, these claims were widely accepted. The Twentieth Century Fund's *America's Needs and Resources,* for instance, a Keynesian analysis that Colm had taken as the model for CEA's long-term growth studies in 1947, added two new chapters in its 1955 revision, on technological change and productivity. "Technology," it proclaimed, was the "Primary Resource." The study's authors credited the extraordinary and unexpected advances of the previous decade, which had caused their earlier model's predictions to go awry, to industrial research and to freedom. It lumped all industrial research together and completely ignored the military's important role in it.[50]

The 1954 *Economic Report of the President* gave this bit of conventional wisdom official imprimatur: "Although most Federal research and development funds are now devoted to projects sponsored by the Department of Defense and the Atomic Energy Commission, it would be a mistake to assume that the results will not be largely applicable, sooner or later, to civilian purposes." This "spillover" (or "spinoff," as NASA later dubbed it) did not motivate military

[49] Daniel J. Kevles, "FDR's Science Policy," *Science* 183, March 1, 1974, 798–800; "Reconverting War Research," *Business Week,* January 10, 1948, 56–59; Solomon Fabricant, "Armament Production Potential," in Jules Backman, ed., *War and Defense Economics* (New York: Rhinehart, 1951), 30.

[50] S. D. Cornell, speech to Navy Postgraduate School, January 12, 1950, RG330, Entry 341, Box 597, Folder 2; J. Frederic Dewhurst and Associates, *America's Needs and Resources* (New York: Twentieth Century Fund, 1947); Colm to staff, October 14, 1947, Keyserling papers, Box 6, "Economic Budget Studies, 1946–1951"; J. Frederic Dewhurst and Associates, *America's Needs and Resources: A New Survey* (New York: Twentieth Century Fund, 1955), 834–944; Sumner H. Slichter, "Productivity: Still Going Up," *Atlantic,* June 1952, 64–68.

R&D spending any more than a desire for countercyclical fiscal stimulus motivated general military spending. Given a permanent state of semimobilization,
however, the concept not only had some empirical validity but made political
sense. The national security state had won a substantial place in the governance
of science, technology, and the economy in the U.S., and Keynesians wanted to
continue to be relevant.[51]

Although reconciled to large-scale military spending, many Keynesians still
hoped to see a revival of social programs, especially once the fighting in Korea
wound down. Conservatives, however, had more difficulty with the fact of
spending than with its purposes. The "stretch-out" and subsequent decline in
the defense budget stemmed primarily from their influence, and it fell to the
new occupant of the White House in 1953 to try to broker a settlement between
the conservative wing of his party and advocates of the national security state.
After some tentative moves in an alternative direction, President Eisenhower
accomplished this task by hewing to the path of "unbalanced forces" laid out
by his predecessor. "Technology," Huntington says, "mediated between conflicting political goals." Or, to put it in the less polite phrase of the time, strategic programs promised "more bang for the buck." This resolution, ironically,
strengthened the logic of spinoff and the nexus between the national security
and Keynesian visions of the state.[52]

Eisenhower ran on the platform of "security and solvency." He was no Robert
Taft, but he was committed to further defense reductions in order to balance the
federal budget and perhaps provide a tax cut. Taking the Administration's first
crack at the problem, the revision of the $40 billion defense budget for fiscal
1954, Deputy Secretary of Defense Roger Kyes attempted to meet an ambitious
budget target by making technical adjustments, like requiring the services to
spend funds carried over from prior appropriations, without pronouncing on
strategy or force levels. This tactic inflamed the air force yet yielded an impressive $5 billion saving because of that service's huge backlog. But it could
not be repeated. NSC 162/2, which guided the fiscal 1955 budget, was the air
force's revenge. It reconciled security and solvency by making atomic bombs
a "weapon of first resort," in the words of historian David Alan Rosenberg.
Large-scale ground wars were ruled out; anything larger than a "brushfire" was
supposed to prompt a nuclear response. The air force was thus placed back on
its track of expansion. The new policy mollified tax- and budget-cutters like
Treasury Secretary George Humphrey by painting a bulls-eye on the army (and
navy, to a lesser extent). And it rubbed salt in the wounds by requiring the army
to contribute more of what little it had left to continental air defense, a new

[51] *Economic Report of the President for 1954* (Washington: GPO, 1954), 162; Herbert Striner
et al., *Defense Spending and the U.S. Economy,* 2d ed., vol. 1 (Baltimore: Johns Hopkins University, 1959), 16–28; John G. Welles and Robert H. Waterman, Jr., "Space Technology: Payoff from
Spinoff," *Harvard Business Review* (November-December 1963): 106–18.

[52] Huntington (above, n. 3), 74.

strategic thrust. On January 12, 1954, Secretary of State John Foster Dulles publicly announced the "New Look" policy, making explicit the doctrine of massive retaliation that the Truman administration had long danced around.[53]

Massive retaliation demanded massive R&D. Military R&D spending continued to rise under the New Look (albeit at a slower rate than during the first three years of the buildup), even as the full defense budget declined. The bomber and nuclear weapons development programs continued to sail along; LeMay got his way. In fact, he indirectly spawned his own competition. RAND and ARDC, organizations that LeMay had helped to set up, had kept the idea of the ICBM alive, despite severe budget cuts and the disdain of scientific skeptics and bomber fanatics. A series of scientific and technological breakthroughs, notably the crafting of an H-bomb that would fit on top, increased the ICBM's plausibility, and it fit perfectly into the New Look doctrine. In General Bernard Schriever, who was appointed to build up the air force's Atlas program in 1954, it acquired a champion to equal LeMay. From a paltry $14 million in fiscal 1954, Atlas grew into a $2.1 billion behemoth in fiscal 1958. In the same period, Admiral Rickover's nuclear submarine sprouted an ICBM development program under Admiral William Raborn, leading toward a system that would ultimately assure the navy a role in massive retaliation under the name Polaris.[54]

Continental air defense had long been a pet project of scientists who found the bigger and better bombs promoted by Edward Teller to be distasteful or even immoral. Like the ICBM, it offended the air force brass and posed technical challenges of a budget-busting magnitude. Air defense concepts were nurtured through the lean years of the late 1940s and early 1950s by MIT physicists and engineers; the Soviet H-bomb test in August 1953 secured their place in the New Look. For FY55 the program received an additional $1 billion, and it soon grew into the largest military R&D project since Manhattan, centered at MIT's Lincoln Laboratory. Aircraft, missiles, and air defense all relied heavily on electronics, rocketing that industry's military R&D and military sales into the stratosphere.[55]

The New Look embellished the organizational achievements as well as the doctrine of "deterrence." The air force and navy ICBM programs were powerful special commands that integrated R&D with procurement. The major aerospace and electronics contractors that had grown up dependent on the military,

---

[53] Glenn H. Snyder, "The 'New Look' of 1953," in Schilling (above, n. 27), 393–99, 418–503; Moody (above, n. 6), 454–61; Koldziej (above, n. 15), 166–203; Rosenberg 1983 (above, n. 32), 28; Lewis (above, n. 39), 9–15.

[54] Walter A. McDougall, . . . the Heavens and the Earth: A Political History of the Space Age (New York: Basic, 1986), 105–29; Harvey M. Sapolsky, *The Polaris System Development: Bureaucratic and Programmatic Success in Government* (Cambridge: Harvard University Press, 1972), 11.

[55] Huntington (above, n. 3), 326–41; Kenneth Flamm, *Creating the Computer* (Washington: Brookings, 1988), 53–58; Leslie (above, n. 42), 31–37; Forman (above, n. 36), 161–66.

like Martin, stabilized financially. Military contractors that served civilian markets as well, like General Electric, began to establish specialized divisions to service their military patrons exclusively. The services, particularly the air force, also cultivated a stable of small, entrepreneurial firms to perform highly sophisticated technological tasks. They often funded such firms, like Tracerlab (which had shocked both Teller and Oppenheimer by developing techniques to detect nuclear tests at a great distance), even though the assets of these start-ups were only people and ideas. These contracts in turn encouraged investors, like the nation's first venture capital firm, American Research and Development, which financed Tracerlab, to underwrite the risks.[56]

Government laboratories dedicated to the military effort also multiplied. The most notable new one was the second nuclear weapons design laboratory at Livermore, California, the brainchild of Teller, which was established by the AEC in 1952 under heavy pressure from the air force and JCAE. Conservatives tried to ensure that such government military R&D did not slide down the slippery slope to government civilian enterprise. A gratuitous complaint against the National Bureau of Standards regarding the battery additive AD-X2, for example, unrelated to the bureau's pioneering electronics research and production program, which was being conducted under military auspices but promising significant civilian applications, precipitated the transfer of that program to DOD. Finally, the academic scientists kept on tap by the military not only promoted projects but were increasingly called upon by President Eisenhower to adjudicate the technological rivalries to which these projects led. The moribund scientific advisory committee of the Truman administration was revived for this purpose; its Technological Capabilities Panel, chaired by MIT President James Killian, helped the missile programs fend off their critics and secure funding priority in the mid-1950s.[57]

[56] Neufeld (above, n. 9), 53–60; Sapolsky 1972 (above, n. 54), 64–90; James F. Nagle, *A History of Government Contracting* (Washington: George Washington University, 1992), 472–73; Merton J. Peck and Frederic M. Scherer, *The Weapons Acquisition Process: An Economic Analysis* (Boston: Harvard Business School, 1962), 128–30; Rhodes (above, n. 6), 368–71; American Research and Development Corporation, *First Annual Report* (Boston: American Research and Development Corporation, 1946), 2; Susan Rosegrant and David Lampe, *Route 128: Lessons from Boston's High-Tech Community* (New York: Basic, 1992), 119–20, 154–55.

[57] Hewlett and Duncan (above, n. 32), 581–84; Nelson R. Kellogg and Stuart W. Leslie, "Civilian Technology at the National Bureau of Standards" (Johns Hopkins University, Baltimore, 1990, photocopy), 15–23; Churchill Eisenhart, "Chronology of AD-X2 Case," in Finding Aid Binder, RG167; Sinclair Weeks to Charles E. Wilson, March 25, 1953, and press release, July 23, 1953, both in RG330, Entry 341, Box 523, Folder 3; Flamm (above, n. 55), 71–75; Kevles (above, n. 39), 329–32. Brian Balogh (above, n. 33), 95–119, interprets the New Look as providing a national security justification for civilian nuclear power development under the guise of "international prestige," thus anticipating the civilian space program.

CONCLUSION: THE IRONIES OF OVERKILL

The world of atomic weapons was a "new world," as Enrico Fermi intuited upon achieving a self-sustaining chain reaction in 1942. The two superpowers were locked in an arms race, "multiplying gadgets specialized to acts of violence," to use the prescient 1941 phrase of political scientist Harold Lasswell. The technological and international logic of "deterrence" were potent motivations for the arms race. The managerial competence and scientific insights of the advocates of "deterrence," such as LeMay's ability to shape up SAC and the Teller-Ulam design for the H-bomb, undergirded their case as well. So did the failures of "mobilization" in practice. But they needed a political logic, too, to expand the military budget and to acquire a satisfactory share of it to realize their vision of the national security state.[58]

The conservative reaction to the Korean rearmament solved the political puzzle for "deterrence." Between 1945 and 1950, Senator Taft and his allies were largely unwilling to support increased military spending and the "high-pressure" R&D program that went with it; they wanted to shrink the budget and cut taxes. They feared Lasswell's "garrison state," though not as much as Communism. As the threat of the latter grew, first with the war scare of 1948 and then with the Korean War, conservatives took comfort that they could still avoid the inflation and controls of the former by getting the biggest bang for every tight buck. Reliance on air power and atomic weapons also avoided the restrictions on individual liberty that UMT portended. The delegation of national security to military professionals, technical experts, and their gadgets had its counterpart in the segregation of the institutions that supplied these gadgets from those that served civilians. Red tape and secrecy interlaced to build the wall between state and market that conservative ideology required. Even universities found themselves "polarized," as the historian Stuart Leslie states, into military and nonmilitary spheres. "Deterrence" thus provided a way for conservatives to become more comfortable spending "more, more, and more money" on national security as NSC-68 demanded.[59]

In the process of settling in the mid-1950s at about 9 percent of GNP and some two-thirds of the federal budget, military spending inevitably attracted intense attention from Keynesians, whose central dogma linked state and market through monetary flows. Once they accepted that the security situation dictated this level, their models allowed them to come to terms with it. They predicted that the economic stimulus provided by such spending would permit the nation

---

[58] Fermi's exact message to James Conant was "Jim, you'll be interested to know that the Italian navigator has just landed in the new world." Hewlett and Anderson (above, n. 30), 112; Harold D. Lasswell, "The Garrison State," *American Journal of Sociology* 46 (1941): 465.

[59] Leslie (above, n. 42), 14.

to spend even more in the future, in a virtuous circle. The national security state's heavy emphasis on science and technology was an added bonus. By the end of the Korean War, the Keynesian calculus did not distinguish between military and nonmilitary R&D spending any more than it distinguished between military and nonmilitary spending of other sorts. What mattered was the aggregate amount of R&D spending, which quickly surpassed the target of 1 percent of GNP that had been set by the Steelman report in 1947. The concept of technological spillover gave this macro-model a microeconomic underpinning. Even if R&D funds were spent in institutions cordoned off from the rest of society, as the conservatives and the military preferred, their benefits would nonetheless diffuse into civilian products and productivity growth.

During the Eisenhower administration, the hopes of both the conservatives and the Keynesians, not to mention the air force, were borne out. Despite the high levels of military spending, the United States did not become a "garrison state." Economic controls proved to be unnecessary, inflation remained modest, and the economy grew rapidly. The awesome technological achievements of the national security state sparked new civilian growth industries. Boeing's 707 passenger jet, for instance, borrowed much of its design from the military KC-135 tanker. IBM's business computers, which were initially spun off from the 701 Defense Calculator, benefited enormously from advances originally developed in defense projects like the SAGE air defense system. High-technology start-ups and venture capitalists sprouted around these projects, too. The president's fears of a "military-industrial complex" and "scientific-technological elite," voiced in his farewell address in 1961 (which might have been Taft's words in 1949) still referred to a future of fine-tuning gone awry, economically and militarily, not to a recent past that would soon be canonized as a golden age.[60]

Eisenhower sensed that the appearance of consensus forged by Korea contained the seeds of its own destruction. The Alsops' "crescendo of hideous invention" proved not to be nearly as cheap in the long run as "the congressional economizers" hoped. Their 1947 prophecy that "[t]he expense of exploring this particular patch of scientific ignorance is quite likely to become a major issue of national politics" would come true before the decade of the 1960s was out. The gospel of "spinoff," too, far outran its actual payoff as the technologies of "deterrence" grew ever more esoteric. "Overkill," as a later generation of detractors would label the doctrine, required gadgets so specialized that they cost a fortune and were not much use to anyone outside the defense sector.[61]

That nuclear weapons were never used for their intended purpose after Na-

---

[60] David C. Mowery and Nathan Rosenberg, *Technology and the Pursuit of Economic Growth* (New York: Cambridge University Press, 1989), 185–86; Flamm (above, n. 55), 61–65, 86–95. Aaron Friedberg, "Why Didn't the U.S. Become a Garrison State," *International Security* 16 (1992): 109–42, independently reaches much the same conclusion as I do, but for different reasons.

[61] Alsop and Alsop (above, n. 2), 99; Mowery and Rosenberg (above, n. 60), 147–50.

gasaki is an achievement for which all people owe some debt of gratitude to the advocates of "deterrence." Yet the triumph of the "deterrence" vision of the national security state nonetheless had tragic military consequences as well as ironic economic consequences. The Korean War proved that nuclear weapons would not be used in a limited war, even one presumed to have been started at the behest of Moscow. Although they were willing to pulverize North Korea with vast quantities of conventional ordnance, American leaders feared (among other things) that an atomic attack would be a psychological dud, failing to bring victory in the war on the ground and thereby compromising the utility of nuclear weapons as a deterrent against the Soviet Union.[62] But this lesson in the limits of technology was not taken to heart. Indeed, after Eisenhower faded away, confidence in American technology induced his successors to take unwarranted risks. In Vietnam that confidence would cost the lives of millions of Vietnamese and tens of thousands of Americans and open a new chapter in the long-running debate over the nation's science and technology policy.

[62] Rhodes (above, n. 6), 442–52.

CHAPTER 8

The Past in the Present

THE "HYBRID" IN THE COLD WAR AND BEYOND

THE INNOVATION SYSTEM of the United States in the 1950s was a far cry from what it had been in the 1920s. It was much bigger, more complex institutionally and more diverse in its objectives. Above all, the federal government was more prominent. Federal funding made the "Big Science" of particle accelerators and the "Big Technology" of ballistic missiles possible. It also expanded dramatically the scale and scope of "Little Science," research projects conducted by individual academic investigators. Military procurement induced the growth of corporate as well as academic R&D. Firms across the country invested in new technology, often with the generous assistance of Washington. Federal facilities, especially those of the Atomic Energy Commission (AEC), evoked public mystery and enthusiasm in the 1950s, much as the General Electric "House of Magic" had in the 1920s.

The very prominence of these federal endeavors, however, has tended to obscure the more subtle ways in which public policy shaped the governance of technological innovation in the postwar United States. A broad array of industries, some technologically innovative like electric power and others stagnant like railroads, were regulated for economic reasons, usually with at least some loose coordination at the federal level. Federal intellectual property and anti-trust law influenced the technology strategies and R&D behavior of corporations, large and small. Federal initiatives restructured the financial markets, particularly for mortgages and venture capital. Macroeconomic stabilization policies aimed at bolstering confidence in business investment over the long term. It was the combined effect of all these threads of government activity, all intended at least in part to influence the pace and direction of technological innovation, that constituted the postwar policy.

This web of science and technology policy was not spun from a master design. Vannevar Bush was brilliant and effective in mobilizing the nation's scientific and technological resources for World War II, but *Science, the Endless Frontier* is better seen as a political tactic than as an original blueprint. Bush himself tacitly acknowledged as much, nearly passing over the report in his memoirs. The institutions of American government and the style of American politics precluded the dominance of any single vision of the state, even in an area of public life apparently so esoteric as science and technology policy. Most components of the policy reflected several visions at once. The impressive technological capabilities of the air force, for instance, were the manifestations not merely of the relentless promotion of national security concerns by General Curtis LeMay and his chums, but owed debts as well to Bush's associationalism, presidential economic advisor Leon Keyserling's Keynesianism, and Senator Robert Taft's conservatism. The hybrid political roots of other distinctive features of postwar federal science and technology policy can be traced in a similar fashion.

Thinking about science and technology policy as the product of multiple entrepreneurs pursuing competing visions of the state in multiple venues is useful. It links this policy area to the rest of American politics, since policy entrepreneurs often draw inspiration and seek allies elsewhere in the political system. It allows us to think through some of the complex connections between ideas, interests, and institutions that characterize the policy process. It helps us to imagine counterfactuals more clearly and to appraise them more realistically. It provides a conceptual framework that can profitably be extended forward through the rest of the twentieth century. It might even give us a glimpse of what lies beyond, as the post-Cold War era unfolds.

CASTING A BROADER EMPIRICAL NET: THE GLEANINGS

The conventional wisdom—that there was a "postwar consensus," galvanized initially by the Bush report, that dominated science and technology policy for decades—rests on a historiography that, although it contains a few outstanding studies, is rather thin and has been too much under the influence of former and contemporary practitioners. The major thrust of my research has been to broaden the scope of our knowledge of this policy history in order to build a deeper understanding of it. Postwar debates in other policy areas were deeply influenced by legacies and memories of 1920s "normalcy" and the Great Depression as well as World War II, and it was my instinct that science and technology policy would not prove to be the exception. I also pushed to supplement analysis of direct federal R&D spending with studies of regulatory and legal instruments that the American state can use to influence private behavior. This strategy entailed going beyond the presidency, which has been the institutional focus of most work in this tradition, and Congress, to which modest (but much too little) attention has been paid, to the courts, federal agencies, and civil society. I delved into policy proposals that failed to win approval as well as those that were actually put in place, the better to understand the alternatives that were perceived at the time. The results of this effort have been presented at length in the previous chapters but are worth recapping here.

Technological innovation in the Roaring Twenties was dominated by giant corporations. The development of new products and improved processes by a rapidly growing group of corporate research laboratories was facilitated by conservatives in the administration who believed that the government ought to do little with regard to science and technology besides ensure property rights and get out of the way. Old Guard Republicans carried forward the loose antitrust and tight patent policies of the pre-World War I era, which encouraged firms to acquire their technological competitors and make long-range investments in their own R&D. Treasury Secretary Andrew Mellon's flagship policy of tax cuts aimed at releasing venture capital to finance private inventive activity, among other things. Although the nation's research universities engaged in an aggressive effort to expand their base of support, they neither turned to the federal government nor were encouraged to, beyond long-established programs in agriculture and other applied fields. A few elite universities found private patrons, notably the Rockefeller foundations, to advance their quest for autonomy and excellence; others drew closer to industrial patrons, shaping research and education to suit their needs. The growth of corporate and academic R&D begun in the 1920s, largely under private auspices, continued with little respite right through the Depression and into the war.

The main counterpoint to Mellon's conservative vision in the 1920s was Herbert Hoover's associationalism. This conception of the political economy was derived from the cooperation among firms and between industry and government brought about by World War I. Although that war left a modest institutional legacy in the form of the National Research Council (NRC) and the National Advisory Committee for Aeronautics (NACA), its ideological legacy was more powerful. American capitalism's weaknesses, the associationalists claimed, stemmed from an excess of competition. Too much competition induced irrational and myopic behavior, leaving business executives without adequate information to act on the general interest as well as their own self-interest. Such failures stymied technological innovation, one of capitalism's signal strengths to Hoover's mind, particularly in very mature and very immature industries. As Secretary of Commerce from 1921 to 1928, Hoover undertook initiatives to build voluntary associations for cooperation in industrial R&D in such industries as textiles, construction, radio, and aviation through the Bureau of Standards and other elements of his department. The associationalist vision also inspired other groups, such as the Division of Engineering and Industrial Research of the NRC, to undertake similar efforts outside the formal structure of government.

The crucial arena of contention for conservatism and associationalism was the court of business opinion. Although Secretary Hoover sought larger budgets for his department and fought some internal battles to get them, neither his vision nor Mellon's asked too much of the federal government. Associationalists, however, asked competitors to cooperate with one another and with government technical bureaus in the creation of industrywide research programs and patent pools. They even asked all of industry to unite in a grand association to support academic science. It was an uphill climb. Few firms perceived the cooperative interest that the secretary and his minions identified, despite vigorous proselytizing. Nonetheless, a seed was planted that would bear fruit in the next decade.

The Crash of 1929 suggested to most Americans that Hoover had substantially underestimated the defects of capitalism. A system that suddenly left a quarter of its workforce unemployed seemed to require a thorough overhaul, rather than tinkering at the margins. Although Hoover himself was unable to accept this common wisdom, many associationalists proved willing to stretch the Hooverian vision in response to the crisis. They gave their best effort in the implementation of early New Deal legislation, such as the National Industrial Recovery and Emergency Railroad Transportation Acts of 1933, in which Congress delegated extraordinarily vague and broad authority to the executive branch. The new, improved associationalism called for the government to organize industrial associations and to give them coercive power to coordinate economic activity. Science and technology policy entrepreneurs, such as MIT President Karl Compton and the NRC's Maurice Holland, attempted to use this framework to require participation in cooperative research and information exchanges. They believed that such mandates would help suppress short-sighted wage-cutting competition and encourage firms to engage in technological competition, leading to new jobs, higher wages, and improved productivity over the long term.

To others, however, including both business and labor in "sick" industries like railroads, iron and steel, and textiles, technological innovation tended to devalue fixed capital and displace workers. Hence, they sought to use associational authority sub rosa to retard the pace of innovation and protect themselves. Although the associationalist phase of the New Deal was short-lived and the coverage of its economic policy was very spotty, the evidence suggests that the protectionists accomplished their ends more fully than Compton and the progressives. Certainly that was the popular perception; when the National Recovery Administration (NRA) collapsed in 1935, the notion that the state ought to be used to slow the pace of innovation was largely discredited with it. Some "little NRAs" nonetheless emerged intact from the rubble to regulate particular industries for another several decades. The railroad industry, for instance, found protection from its technological competitors in regulation, staving off collapse if not decline.

This protectionist thread had a counterpart within reform liberalism, associationalism's major competitor in the early New Deal executive branch. Reform liberals were much more hostile to conservatism than associationalists were; they placed the blame for the economic catastrophe squarely on the shoulders of capitalists themselves. Firms, they maintained, would not and could not act in the public interest when their self-interest diverged from it, as was typical. Instead, the state had to step in to act on behalf of the public interest, not to displace the market but to make it function up to its potential. The state they had in mind would be flexible and expert, applying different solutions in different industrial sectors. As noted above, some reform liberals feared technological unemployment and included among their preferred solutions to the Depression the use of state power to regulate the pace of innovation to ease the "adaptation" process (as the sociologist W. F. Ogburn termed it). Heavy-handed protectionist schemes like the machine tax never progressed very far, but this sentiment did contribute to the regulation of wages and hours to spread around the work that machines left people to do.

A more significant thread in reform liberal thought focused on creating new jobs, rather than sharing the old ones, by using the state to accelerate the pace of industrial innovation. New industries based on technological breakthroughs, they imagined, would absorb workers displaced by process improvements in mature sectors. The Tennessee Valley Authority (TVA) was an early expression of this vision of the state, and its "phosphate philosophy," which was said to have created a new fertilizer industry and to have given poor farmers greater market power, made its promise vivid. In the wake of the "Roosevelt recession" of 1937–38, reform liberalism reached the apex of its influence as the president countenanced an investigation into the concentration of economic power. Thurman Arnold, Assistant Attorney General for Antitrust, implemented this program, attacking both the controlling patent positions of the great firms that did most of the nation's R&D and obstacles to modernization in the construction industry, particularly those presented by the craft unions.

Paralleling the rise of reform liberalism in the administration, however, was a resurgence of conservatism in Congress. The bitter recriminations that accompanied the death of the NRA in 1935, the strident tone of the 1936 campaign, and the court fight of 1937 prepared the ground for conservatives to blame the New Deal when economy turned down at the end of 1937. Congress in 1938, unlike in 1933, refused to delegate authority to the president. Reform liberal legislation, such as Arnold's patent bill, stalled in the face of ideological polarization. Frustrated by congressional intransigence, exemplified by the impotent proceedings of the Temporary National Economic Committee, Arnold took his policy entrepreneurship to the courts, which were being repopulated by "New Dealers" (as the reform liberals took to calling themselves). Using innovative legal and political tactics, Arnold managed to expand the antitrust division and began to win cases against large patent-holders, attacking such alleged practices as suppression and restrictive licensing. The mobilization for World War II interrupted his offensive, as the military authorities gained exemptions for their large contractors, many of whom Arnold had targeted. Yet, when the fighting began to die down, Arnold's successor, Wendell Berge, was largely able to complete his mentor's project of establishing the preeminence of the public interest in technological competition over the property rights that inhered in patents. Over the next several decades, U.S. high-technology companies responded to the new legal environment by relying less on patents and external acquisition of technology and more on being the first mover and conducting in-house R&D, leaving new niches for innovative small firms in the process.

Arnold's attack on the construction trade unions (and on materials manufacturers, distributors, and contractors) was part of a larger reform liberal effort to remake housing as an innovative, low-cost, high-employment, mass-production industry like automobiles. To prepare the way for housing's Henry Fords, Miles Colean of the Federal Housing Authority argued, the government should conduct R&D, restructure the mortgage market, and serve as an intelligent large-scale buyer of innovative housing products as well as break monopolies and cozy deals. Colean's ideas for housing finance reform and public housing projects coincided with Harvard economist Alvin Hansen's notion that the federal government needed to become an investment banker. Aggressive public investment, particularly in sectors like housing, in which rapid technological innovation seemed to be stifled, was a logical consequence of Hansen's interpretation of the new Keynesian analysis. The investment shortage, in the Keynesian view, stemmed not from corporate malevolence, but from mechanical malfunctions that the state could compensate for. However, like patent reform, the late New Deal housing program, with the exception of financial changes, was stalled by congressional conservatives and by the war. More surprisingly, Arnold's construction antitrust cases came to grief; the same New Deal justices who saw a public interest in weaker patent laws saw a public interest in stronger labor protection laws, even if unions retarded the pace of technological innovation. Yet the postwar period ushered in a technological transformation of home-building nonetheless, thanks largely to government-led innovations in housing finance as well as the general buoyancy of the economy. Such successes, in conjunction with their wartime experiences, encouraged Keynesians to renounce the restructuring of economic institutions that stood at the center of reform liberalism.

The war, of course, changed far more than Keynesian policy preferences. Many U.S. military officers emerged from the war with a zeal for new devices and a strong desire to build a national security state that could design, produce, and deliver them. These views marked an astonishing turnabout. The interwar military was small and technologically backward. When President Roosevelt shifted his focus from economic recovery to preparation for war after Munich, he found a military establishment that badly lagged behind the civilian economy. Into this breach, ironically, stepped associationalists who had drifted toward conservatism when the New Deal had lurched to the left. Vannevar Bush, president of the Carnegie Institution of Washington, shared Roosevelt's activist pro-British sentiments; Roosevelt recognized Bush as a creative and capable administrator who could secure the enthusiastic cooperation of the nation's leading academic and corporate laboratories for the military effort. As congressional objections to presidential power diminished after France fell and disappeared in the wake of Pearl Harbor, Bush, acting on the president's behalf, became the key decision-maker in science and technology policy. Rejecting reliance on the heavy-handed military technical bureaus, Bush's entrepreneurship led to the creation of committee-based, public-private partnerships, exemplified by organizations like the National Defense Research Committee (NDRC) and the synthetic rubber research program, both of which owed much to the associationalist vision. The pooling of private technical resources and intellectual property, force-fed by state-financed capital investments, produced an extraordinary burst of scientific and technological progress in such major industries as chemicals and electronics.

While Bush kept at bay crusty military traditionalists who resented civilian influence on the one hand, he also firmly rejected reform liberal attempts to use the war to establish large state-led technology development projects that were not clearly tied to military products. Vice-President Henry Wallace tried to fight a "two-front war" at home and abroad. His vision encompassed the establishment of government technological capacities to support peacetime economic growth as well as the military effort. Reform liberal efforts, like the War Production Board (WPB) Office of Production Research and Development (OPRD), met resistance not only from Bush, but also from the dollar-a-year men on loan from industry who dominated the WPB, from congressional conservatives, and from the military establishment. Secretary of Commerce Wallace's postwar initiatives to make OPRD and similar organizations permanent met an even more devastating fate. With the lapsing of the war emergency, Congress once again became the main arena for science and technology policy-making. Appropriators slashed the Commerce budget, while authorizing legislation never quite came to a vote.

The immediate postwar experience of Bush's military adversaries was more satisfying than Wallace's, but only somewhat so. NDRC's wartime successes had helped to inspire military enthusiasm for technological projects of a scale and complexity that went far beyond what Bush thought necessary and that gave the military more control than he thought appropriate. The air force and the navy gained virtual control by 1950 of the Atomic Energy Commission (AEC), crushing reform liberals who had hoped that a state-led civilian atomic power industry would replicate the prewar successes of TVA. But other initiatives of advocates of the national security state bumped up against a rigid budget ceiling budget imposed by President Truman, with the support of conservatives as well as Keynesian advocates of domestic programs. The long-range missile and the supercarrier, for example, remained on the drawing board, victims of the budget crunch and the vicious internecine conflict that it spawned in the Pentagon. Even the Strategic Air Command of General LeMay, the highest priority of the air force, was left short of cash. The fiscal squeeze was relaxed just once before the Korean War, following the "war scare" in the spring of 1948. In this instance congressional conservatives, led by Senator Taft, demonstrated that if they felt they had to spend money on defense, they would rather spend it on high technology than on boot camps. Mostly, however, they preferred not to spend at all, sending the military brass into paroxysms of rage.

Bush's own postwar experience also consisted of more pain than pleasure. He was superseded in the military sphere, and his plan for a government agency to sponsor academic research that was controlled by nongovernmental experts, presented in *Science, the Endless Frontier,* was thwarted. The stalemate on the National Science Foundation (NSF), while made less painful by the generous patronage of universities by the Office of Naval Research, the AEC, and the National Institutes of Health, was not broken until 1950. Bush's associationalist vision for the NSF was compromised (on paper, if not in practice) in the final administrative arrangements, although the resulting agency was also a far cry from the reform liberal vision that had motivated Bush's chief competitor, Senator Harley Kilgore. The compromise on NSF, in which old associationalists and old reform liberals eventually found a new common ground, had a parallel in the venture capital program advanced by the administration in the spring of 1950. Both groups agreed after the war that there was a gap in the provision of capital to small high-technology businesses, but they disagreed about how to close it; consequently, the conservative status quo was maintained. This stalemate, too, was less painful than it might have been, because of the postwar economic boom. A sharp fall in investment in 1949 finally motivated action. The CEA's Leon Keyserling dropped the public investment idea that had been at the core of the reform liberal vision and advanced a plan to close the small business capital gap by stimulating private investment activity with loan guarantees, tax breaks, and deregulation. Such a package, couched in Keynesian terms, appealed to those, like Senator Ralph Flanders, who had moved away from associationalism toward a moderate "commercial Keynesian" position in the late 1930s and 1940s. Flanders preferred that the government react cautiously to economic changes and favored tax cutting over spending when stimulus was truly necessary. This stance did not preclude activism but relied on careful monitoring of economic conditions and on "jawboning" the private sector first.

Flanders and Keyserling agreed, in particular, on jawboning labor negotiations to link productivity to wages. This linkage ensured that the benefits of technological change would be shared among consumers, investors, and workers and that a healthy macroeconomic environment for investment, including investment in R&D, would be maintained. The 1950 agreement between the United Auto Workers and General Motors codified such a productivity bargain and was widely imitated. This labor/management accommodation, combined with growing agreement on the scope of market failure in academic scientific research and venture capital in the face of conservative opposition, suggested that the first half of 1950 might mark the beginning of a period of "secular exhilaration," in which firms capitalized on the civilian technological opportunities turned up by wartime and postwar R&D. Alvin Hansen's fear of "secular stagnation," which was voiced by some even in the late 1940s, faded away and with it the justification for structural economic reform.

The Korean War abruptly changed the picture. Early in 1950 national security state advocates had begun to make a vigorous argument, summarized in NSC-68, for more defense spending; the Korean War made their case far more successfully than they could have imagined. The military budget ceiling was lifted with a vengeance, as spending rose from $13 billion in fiscal 1950 to over $60 billion in fiscal 1952, settling ultimately at about $40 billion. This new ceiling, like the old one, was imposed by conservatives who would rather not have spent at all and Keynesians who wanted to find funds for domestic programs. But both groups adapted their ideals to take into account the new reality that the massive military budget represented. As they had in 1948, conservatives pressed for the U.S. defense posture to favor strategic weapons. Such a strategy seemed to them to yield more bang for the buck and to pose less of a threat of foreign entanglements and restrictions on domestic liberty than did larger ground combat forces. Codified by Secretary of State Dulles in the doctrine of "massive retaliation," this approach relied on ambitious technological efforts to develop air defenses and intercontinental ballistic missiles as well as B-52s and H-bombs. Keynesians, too, resigned themselves to the necessity of military spending and found virtue in it. The defense budget, they claimed, paid off serendipitously by supplying a demand stimulus to the economy; defense R&D paid off serendipitously through scientific and technological spillovers to civilian industry.

By the end of the Korean War, the air force was the most important organization in the U.S. national innovation system. It exercised significant influence over the atomic energy program and academic research in a range of physical science and engineering disciplines as well as over an array of large and small contractors in aviation, electronics, and a host of lesser industries. Its path to power, however, was not a steady climb to greatness, but a roller-coaster ride buffeted as much by domestic economic and political considerations as by the Soviet threat or by exogenous technological breakthroughs. It owed its preponderance in the defense budget to Senator Taft's conservative coalition. Its cooperative technical relationships with contractors and academic scientists reflected Bush's wartime associationalism. It drew on Keynesian analysis and the idea of spillover to legitimate the scale of its spending, particularly on science and technology.

THE THEORETICAL ARGUMENT REVISITED

This rendition of the history of science and technology policy from normalcy to the New Look raises the bar for theoretical explanation. Neither transaction cost economics nor liberal society analysis, the two traditions that have dominated the study of change in the governance of technological innovation in the U.S., measure up. Both are constructed around the conventional historical account. They identify simple causes for the simple patterns they see; both exude an air of inevitability. Neither is well-suited to explain the confusing and even contradictory patterns that mark the fuller historical narrative. They share a common flaw, giving too little credence to political institutions and political processes. My own approach, which nests our understanding of this policy area in larger claims about American political development, goes a bit further. Although it is far from complete, it helps us in particular to understand the hybrid nature of the outcome. In doing so, it provides a more satisfactory assessment of what might have been, the alternative possibilities envisioned by the entrepreneurs who tried to reshape science and technology policy in these tumultuous decades.

Transaction cost economics claims that efficiency determines governance structure. U.S. firms' reliance on central corporate laboratories rather than outside contractors for research, for example, is attributed by scholars in this tradition to the greater efficiency of central labs. Such arguments work well when a variety of institutional forms are tested against one another by rigorous, competitive markets. When, as in the case at hand, the generation of alternative institutions is constrained and selection pressures are not strong, efficiency is a less compelling explanation. The constraints on institutional experimentation flow from the decentralized nature of the state and the strength of civil society in the United States, which make it highly unlikely that any vision of the state will be tried out in its pure form. Associationalism, for instance, was not instituted in very many industries, due to both political and economic opposition; the "fitness" of this institutional form, therefore, was never really tested. The selection environment for science and technology policy also deviates from transaction cost assumptions, because so many factors other than efficiency operate in it. One might argue, for instance, that World War II "selected" the policies that contributed to the Allied victory. Yet, when the war was over, all of the participants in the military innovation system, including the three armed services, sought extensive institutional changes, often for parochial bureaucratic reasons. Even when policy-makers seek to make decisions on efficiency grounds, they may disagree about what efficiency means. Harley Kilgore thought that state enterprises would make vast contributions to the economy and that private influence on federal R&D programs would slow them down; Vannevar Bush thought scientists in the civil service could not keep pace with the state of the art and that only if private sector decision-makers had a substantial say over the public research agenda would it be relevant to economic needs. Their judgments are prospective, and the feedback that might let them reassess these judgments is far from comprehensive.

Liberal society analysis argues that American political culture will sustain only a minimal role for the state. The "conservative consensus" of the 1920s and the "postwar consensus" of the 1950s are in this view merely two variants of the same phenomenon. Given the differences between the two "consensuses" and the range of approaches that policy entrepreneurs construed to be compatible with a market-based economy in between, the liberal society analysis does not explain very much. Policy experiments that appalled pre-Depression conservatives were made, and important and enduring state capacities for governing technological innovation were created between 1921 and 1953. Thurman Arnold's antitrust offensive, for instance, helped catalyze large changes in business practice and industrial organization. The national security state acquired an extraordinary set of scientific and technological assets, such as the national laboratories and dedicated contractors, during the early Cold War. The liberal society analysis, ironically, is the mirror image of the conservative vision of the state to which it attributes so much power. Conservatives are obsessed with the power of the state that exists and ignore the many powers that the state has foregone, while liberal society analysts see only the shadow of the state that never came to be and miss the considerable heft of the state that actually exists.

Like the conventional empirical account, the received theoretical wisdom of transaction cost economics and liberal society analysis provides a good starting point for understanding the history of U.S. science and technology policy. A theory that purported to make sense of this history, but ignored either economic experience under particular policies or faith in the free market, would not go very far. But the received wisdom must be refined and extended. Economic experience is usually susceptible to a range of interpretations, all the more so when the factors at play in the market, both policy and nonpolicy, are very complicated. The free market, too, is an ambiguous concept in an economy in which private organizations have accumulated great power and in a world in which foreign threats are ever-present.

Drawing on the liberal society analysis, my approach begins with ideas but rejects the view that there is a hegemonic consensus. It is true that none of the figures who had a serious influence on the development of science and technology policy in the mid-twentieth century United States proposed that the state could organize the economy better than the market. Only the most conservative of them, however, thought that the institutions that the market had produced to generate new scientific knowledge and new technologies could not be improved upon. They fought battles over how policy could make the market work better and over how policy could help the market system protect itself adequately from external enemies without damaging itself. To the extent that there was a liberal consensus, it was so vague that it provided little authoritative guidance for coping with these challenges. The conflict over the development of atomic power is a paradoxical case in point. National security advocates and conservatives perceived military implications in civilian reactor research that made it too dangerous to leave this aspect of technological development to the private sector; reform liberals agreed that the government ought to conduct this research but wanted the findings to be disseminated as broadly as possible so that manufacturers and utilities would take them up and refine them through competition with one another. On patents, too, the consensus was virtually meaningless. Conservatives saw intellectual property rights as the sacred joining of individual and social interest; associationalists argued that only mandatory patent pools that abridged those rights would maximize both sorts of interest.

There are, then, a variety of conceptions of liberalism in the United States. I have identified five of these in the 1920s, 1930s, 1940s, and 1950s: conservatism, associationalism, reform liberalism, Keynesianism, and the national security state. The causal stories the adherents of each brand of liberalism relied upon to interpret changes in the economy and the international system were different. These interpretations, in turn, led these policy entrepreneurs to endorse distinctive science and technology policy proposals. Keynesians, for example, understood the "Roosevelt recession" of 1937–38 to be the result of insufficient aggregate demand that required an expansion of federal investment spending, including investment in science and technology. Conservatives, by contrast, considered the recession to be the product of too much government meddling and demanded that the budget be shrunk in order to restore business confidence. Reform liberals, meanwhile, saw the recession as the product of corporate greed. Reform liberal proposals for vigorous oversight of the technological activities of large corporations and for public investment in new technologies were compatible with Keynesian deficit spending, but as the divergence of the policy proposals of the two camps just after World War II showed, the causal stories attached to the two visions were not interchangeable. Reform liberals thought that the postwar inflation, like the prewar recession, was caused by corporate bottlenecks and myopia and considered the expansion of the government's technological capacities to be an appropriate response. Many Keynesians, by contrast, saw the inflation as the result of pent-up demand and advocated restraint in all federal spending, whatever its specific purpose.

This diversity of ideas is fostered by and in turn reinforces the decentralized structure of American political institutions, which offers so many opportunities for policy entrepreneurship. The people that I studied pursued the full range of opportunities. The president's favor, not surprisingly, was coveted. Bush quite rightly attributed the lion's share of his success to Roosevelt's firm support of his judgment; Wallace ultimately lost the confidence of both presidents he served. Winning Congressional support, especially that of leaders of party factions, such as Senator Wagner or Senator Taft, was even more valuable at times. LeMay's courting and winning of congressional conservatives helped to open the budget floodgates for the air force's high-technology programs, despite the objections of the president; Arnold's patent bills, on the other hand, never won the sponsors and majorities that they needed to get through, despite the support of the president. Arnold turned to the courts for assistance, with mixed success. His Justice Department persuaded federal judges to strike down the patent law doctrine to which his congressional antagonists had so firmly held, but the cases against construction craft unions were thrown out by the Supreme Court. The regulatory agencies also allowed scope for policy entrepreneurship, such as Compton's effort to induce the NRA code authorities to mandate joint technological activities. Science and technology policy entrepreneurs sought to persuade private elites and the public, too, and not only as an element of strategies to bring elected officials around. If private scientific and technological resources could be put to public purposes through private decisions, so much the better. Hoover's Bureau of Standards, for instance, waged a public relations campaign for voluntary cooperation in industrial research.

In order to advance their ideas in particular political institutions, science and technology policy entrepreneurs mobilized allies whose interests were compatible with their policy proposals. These interests could be ideological; often, science and technology policy proposals were part of a larger domestic or foreign policy package that derived from a shared conception of liberalism and was backed by a coalition that spanned many policy areas. Hooverites applied the associative philosophy to agriculture, trade, and even moral issues, for instance, as well as the organization of science and technology. An alliance might be built on material interest as well. Although many academic scientists were undoubtedly concerned about national security in the late 1940s, for example, it seems likely that most sought the support of military patrons primarily to secure research funds that would move their careers forward. Material interests in science and technology policy are not necessarily obvious, and policy entrepreneurs therefore did missionary work to persuade potential allies that their material interests would be furthered by the proposals. The Committee for Economic Development, for instance, tried to convince executives that a cautiously active state would be good for business, particularly if it compensated for market failures, as in the provision of capital to innovative small firms. Policy entrepreneurs tapped and tried to mold political and bureaucratic interests, too. President Truman's support for increased military spending in 1948 stemmed in part from his desire to isolate Wallace to his left; the army opposed the "deterrence" strategy of the air force and navy in part because its commanders feared they would lose both appropriations and missions if "deterrence" was adopted.

There is no simple formula that will specify the ideas, interests, and institutions that distinguish success from failure in science and technology policy entrepreneurship. Some idiosyncracies of personality and timing seem to have been important. Bush's ability to bond with Harry Hopkins and then with Roosevelt in 1940 strikes me as the most profound of these unique chains of events, with the coincidence of NSC-68 and the Korean War a close second. Tactical choices, such as those that prevented a compromise from being worked out on the National Science Foundation Act in 1946, played a role on occasion. Not everything, however, was sheer accident. Congress, for instance, showed a marked conservative bias. Only at moments in which most members of Congress perceived a grave crisis, such as in 1933, 1940, 1948, and 1950, did science and technology policy entrepreneurs of other persuasions find the legislative branch to be very congenial to their causes. One reason for this affinity might be congressional voting and seniority rules, which favored the status quo. Another might be the fact that scientific and technological organizations, both academic and corporate, were highly concentrated in the Northeast and Midwest in this period, whereas Congress is more likely to be receptive to proposals in which the benefits are more obviously geographically dispersed. A third possibility is that members had difficulty acquiring sufficient information in this complex policy area and were reluctant to take action as a result. Such speculations lead toward a more sophisticated formulation of the liberal society analysis in which particular features of governmental institutions interact with political culture to bias policy outcomes in a conservative direction.

The president, on the other hand, was more likely than Congress to be persuaded that the state ought to do something about science and technology. Presidential leadership in national security matters, of course, is unremarkable and grew much stronger between the 1920s and the 1950s. The president, too, could not avoid being judged by voters on the state of the national economy and was perhaps more willing to take risks in pursuit of economic stability and growth as a consequence. President Hoover's paralysis is an interesting counterexample that might be explained by his initial misperceptions of the depth of the crisis and the weight of conservatives in his political coalition. The courts, not surprisingly, seemed to follow the president with a lag. The long spell of Democratic control of the presidency from 1933 to 1953 slowly produced a judiciary that presented reform liberal entrepreneurs with an appealing alternative to slogging through Congress when no federal funds were required for their programs. The regulatory agencies varied. In some cases, such as railroads, they acted like trade associations and responded to the interests they regulated; in electric power, however, reform liberals and national security enthusiasts pushed the pace of technological development and eventually induced the private sector to adopt innovations made with federal funds.

The affinity of any political institution for a particular set of ideas reflects the requirements for building a winning coalition in that institution, the weight of societal interests in such a coalition, and the compatibility between interests and ideas. It was difficult, for example, to get a bill through Congress, and members were usually strongly influenced by business opinion. Business views on science and technology policy, though not monolithic, tended to be conservative. There were, however, moments in which other visions of the state seemed much more likely to advance business interests. In 1933, for instance, even Frank Jewett of Bell Laboratories, normally a rigid conservative, countenanced associationalism; in 1940 he was a leader in the technological mobilization for war. Such shifts were provisional and depended on reinforcement by experience under the policy. In Jewett's case, the failure of the emergency legislation of 1933 and the shift to the left that followed soured him on the associational experiment. The war was a more gratifying experience and, although Jewett opposed the National Science Foundation, Bell Labs remained a major military R&D contractor in the early Cold War. Labor was usually more influential within the executive branch, at least in peacetime, than it was in Congress. Like business interests, labor interests in science and technology policy were neither monolithic nor firmly fixed. They tended to accord with reform liberalism, particularly in the CIO. Walter Reuther of the United Auto Workers, for example, endorsed the reform liberal housing program, in part because he thought auto workers could assemble houses. The UAW had organized aircraft workers during the war and expected that prefabricated houses could be built in the same plants. As the fortunes of reform liberalism declined in the late 1940s, however, Reuther became a Keynesian, endorsing vigorous government R&D spending and ignoring rank-and-file concerns about technological unemployment.

The policy consequences of winning the support of any particular interest depended not only on the weight of that interest within a particular institution, but also the authority of that institution with respect to others. The president was at times virtually unchallenged by Congress and at other times almost irrelevant to its proceedings. Presidential authority waxed during wartime and in the depths of the Depression, giving reform liberals and national security advocates their best chances at making a difference. Congress asserted itself after the recession of 1937–38, World War II, and the stalemate in Korea, establishing conservatives in a powerful blocking position. In some areas of policy, the courts and regulatory agencies exercised great authority, to which the executive and legislative branches deferred. Congress and the president had the power to overturn the postwar rulings relating patent and antitrust law but did not. Similarly, both supported, at least for a while, the effort of the NRA to bring about economic recovery; it was the Supreme Court that finally put an end to it.

In sum, the science and technology policy-making process was much more fluid and intricate than the received wisdom can accommodate. Many entrepreneurs sought the support of an assortment of interests in multiple arenas of varying receptiveness and power. I do not mean to say that the situation was completely unstructured and that anything was always possible. There were moments of greater openness and long periods of substantial stalemate. Beyond this, the very complexity of the process militates against the view that one vision of the state might have secured a complete victory. If one thinks of the process as a selection environment, the forms that it selects among are themselves hybrids, with the alternatives including a little more of one vision here, a little more of another there.

In light of such considerations, one should question the counterfactual that if the national security state had not been so large and powerful, the federal government would have embarked on a significant civilian technology development program. For one thing, Henry Wallace's reform liberal program was rejected well before the explosion of military R&D spending that followed the outbreak of war in Korea. Keynesians would certainly have mounted initiatives to expand federal spending, but without examples of military spillovers, it is far from clear that they would have placed much weight on R&D within these initiatives. Congress would have weighed more heavily in making a domestically oriented science and technology policy than it did in making one that emphasized national security, further reducing the prospects for an outcome that deviated dramatically from the status quo. There are societal interests that might have been mobilized on behalf of a civilian technology policy, particularly groups that would have been cut adrift from military spending in this scenario, such as the aircraft industry (which did press for a government-funded passenger aircraft program in the 1940s) and academic scientists. It is difficult, however, to see in these interests a coalition broad enough to sway Congress. It might be that the military expenditures of the early 1950s staved off a recession that would have produced a resurgence of support for federal microeconomic initiatives. But if one imagines that there had been no hot war in Korea and thus a much smaller national security state, the most plausible hybrid is one that is simply more conservative with respect to R&D spending.

Another counterfactual worth contemplating is the absence of Vannevar Bush. Bush was able to forge such a strong bond with the president and to handle the military and Congress so smoothly that he was given carte blanche to build an agency that burst established convention, spent hundreds of millions of dollars, and smothered its competitors. It is hard to imagine Karl Compton, James Conant, or Frank Jewett replicating these feats. Certainly a reformer like Henry Wallace would have had grave difficulty in securing the militarily significant scientific and technical results that Bush was able to get because of his place within the scientific establishment. Had Bush died in 1939, I think it likely that the military technical bureaus would have developed more fully than they did, without nearly as close a relationship with academic and industrial scientists and engineers. Although such a system probably would not have been as productive as the one that Bush engineered, the Allies would still have won the war, as they did anyway, by dint of the overwhelming industrial output of the United States. A more hierarchical and less effective postwar national security state appears to be the likely outcome of such a scenario.

A MODEST GENERALIZATION: THE FURTHER EVOLUTION
OF THE POSTWAR HYBRID

Putting aside such counterfactual speculations, the utility of my approach to the history of science and technology policy may also be demonstrated by extending it through the postwar period to the present. Such an account must be little more than a brief sketch, resting on secondary sources. Even so, it shows that the ideas that motivated science and technology policy entrepreneurs in the mid-century United States have endured to the end of the century, that the legacies of these entrepreneurs have proved to be useful resources to their successors, and that the processes by which ideas become policies have changed less than one might suppose. As the post-Cold War world took shape in the 1980s and 1990s, the decades on which I concentrate here, some of the avenues closed off earlier in the century have been reopened. Although there are important new elements, recent science and technology policy debates should be read less as a shattering of the "postwar consensus" than as a resumption of old conflicts under new conditions.

The halcyon days of the national security state lasted about a decade and a half. The Soviet launch of Sputnik in 1957 was a shock, like the Korean War, that further extended the influence of the national security state vision. In its wake the president acquired a science advisor, initially to adjudicate technical disputes among the armed services, and Congress set up science committees to push the new space program. Although it was a civilian agency, the National Aeronautics and Space Administration (NASA) leaned heavily on the national security justification, heartily embraced the concept of spillover (which it termed "spinoff"), and employed many of the same public and private entities that conducted defense R&D. National security in the late 1950s and early 1960s justified not merely NASA, but also a large expansion of NSF and much else besides. Within the Department of Defense (DOD) proper, the Advanced Research Projects Agency (ARPA) was set up to look beyond the parochial service interests to capitalize on technological opportunities on the far horizon. This and other centralizing steps did little to reduce the "follow-on" imperative (as James Kurth labels it) or "technology pork barrel" (Linda Cohen and Roger Noll's term) that continually generated new weapons systems that made military officers, defense contractors, and members of Congress happy. With the coming of the Kennedy and Johnson administrations and the expansion of the Democratic congressional majority, conservative influence over the composition of the defense budget waned. The army and navy eroded air force dominance, but they were by this time equally enthusiastic about science and technology. The disastrous war in Vietnam had many causes; one was a belief prevalent throughout the U.S. military establishment that technological superiority was the most important (and perhaps even the only) attribute a fighting force needed to have. The defense and space technology programs hit their peaks in the late 1960s and then leveled off for the better part of the next decade.[1]

[1] A. Hunter Dupree, "National Security and the Post-War Science Establishment in the United States," *Nature* 323, September 18, 1986, 213–16; Jeffrey G. Stine, *A History of Science Policy in the U.S., 1940–1985,* background report no. 1, House of Representatives, Committee on Science and Technology, Task Force on Science Policy, 99th C., 2d s., 1986, 41–46; John G. Welles and

President John F. Kennedy's effort to get the country "moving again" also inspired reform liberal and Keynesian entrepreneurship in science and technology policy, including proposals for active labor market policies to facilitate adjustment to technological change, investment tax breaks, and more aggressive antitrust enforcement. Assistant Secretary of Commerce Herbert Holloman spearheaded an effort to spend federal R&D dollars in support of older industries, such as textiles and construction. Holloman chose to try to get his Civilian Industrial Technology Program (CITP) funded under existing authority but was rejected by the House Appropriations Committee. Among the fiercest foes of the measure were spokesmen of the very industries that the program aimed to aid, who claimed that it would duplicate and then supplant private sector R&D. In the context of such conservative opposition, Keynesian initiatives supported by other members of the administration, such as the consumption-oriented tax cut that was enacted in 1964, appeared as moderate economic policy alternatives, much as they had in the late 1940s. The Nixon White House's effort to identify "domestic Apollos" had a similar result. William Magruder, former director of the ill-fated supersonic transport (SST) program, quickly ran into conservative opposition and a macroeconomic budget constraint. The "major initiatives" promised by the president in his 1972 State of the Union address were whittled down to two inconsequential experimental programs before the package was even offered to Congress.[2]

In the 1950s, 1960s, and 1970s, public health and environmental protection emerged as objectives for federal science and technology policy of comparable significance to national security and economic growth. Although a modest fed-

---

Robert H. Waterman, Jr., "Space Technology: The Payoff from Spinoff," *Harvard Business Review* (November–December 1963): 106–18; Thomas L. McNaugher, *New Weapons, Old Politics: America's Military Procurement Muddle* (Washington: Brookings, 1989); James Kurth, "The Follow-On Imperative in American Weapons Procurement, 1960–1990," paper presented to the conference on Economic Issues of Disarmament, South Bend, Indiana, November 30, 1990; Linda Cohen and Roger Noll, *The Technology Pork Barrel* (Washington: Brookings, 1991); National Science Board, *Science Indicators 1972* (Washington: GPO, 1973), 111; David C. Mowery and Nathan Rosenberg, *Technology and the Pursuit of Economic Growth* (New York: Cambridge University Press, 1989), 138–39. Although Cohen and Noll claim that their work can be generalized to all federal commercialization programs, their cases are drawn exclusively from the aerospace and energy industries and are typically motivated more by national security or national prestige considerations than by economics.

[2] Dorothy Nelkin, *The Politics of Housing Innovation* (Ithaca: Cornell University Press, 1971); Gary Mucciaroni, *The Political Failure of Employment Policy* (Pittsburgh: University of Pittsburgh Press, 1990), 47–53; Herbert Stein, *Presidential Economics* (New York: Simon and Schuster, 1984), 101–13; *Economic Report of the President, 1972* (Washington: GPO, 1972), 125–30; "State of the Union Address," *Public Papers of the President, 1972* (Washington: GPO, 1974), 37; Harvey Averch, *A Strategic Analysis of Science and Technology Policy* (Baltimore: Johns Hopkins University Press, 1985), 62–63; John M. Logsdon, "Toward a New Federal Policy for Technology: The Outline Emerges," staff discussion paper no. 408, Program of Policy Studies in Science and Technology, George Washington University, August 1972.

eral program for funding biomedical research predated World War II and the war stimulated its growth, it did not really take off until the mid-1950s. Pushed forward by policy entrepreneurs such as James Shannon, director of the National Institutes of Health, and supported by key members of Congress over the objections of the White House, the federal biomedical R&D budget grew at double-digit rates through the next decade, crossing the $1 billion mark (three times the size of NSF) in 1968. NIH funded academic medical centers not only in areas in which such centers had traditionally been strong, but throughout the nation. "Disease groups" provided a vocal and broadly distributed social constituency to complement the universities. In the late 1960s the federal government began to exert itself in environmental policy as well. Rather than directly fund R&D, policy-makers responded to environmental concerns primarily by imposing regulations. Although some have interpreted this policy as an expression of public disenchantment with new technology, Harvey Brooks notes that Congress and the president were guided more by a naive faith in technological innovation to mitigate environmental damage than by an impulse to control technology. Science and technology policy for public health and environmental protection are not easy to incorporate into the theoretical framework that I have developed, although there are intriguing parallels between the "military-industrial" and "medical-industrial" complexes and between national security and health security. The NIH is a particularly ripe subject for historical research.[3]

The oil shock of 1973 at first provoked a policy response similar to that of Sputnik; with the nation's security perceived to be at stake, President Richard Nixon appointed an energy "czar" and initiated ambitious technology development programs. This approach reached its climax after the second oil shock in 1979 with the establishment of a Federal Synthetic Fuels Corporation at the behest of President Jimmy Carter. The economic difficulties of the 1970s, however, went beyond energy dependence. Perplexed by stagnation in productivity growth that was unprecedented in the postwar period, Carter advanced a set of proposals in 1979 that included accelerated depreciation of investment, stronger patent incentives, relaxed antitrust enforcement, and deregulation. The package reflected the moderate brand of Keynesianism endorsed by the CED and championed within the administration by science advisor Frank Press. However, as policy analyst Claude Barfield points out, the Carter team by no means spoke with one voice. The president also proposed new R&D programs for "generic technology" to support industry in the reform liberal mold as well as a high-level, tripartite Economic Revitalization Board to coordinate and syn-

---

[3] Harvey Brooks, "Lessons of History: Successive Challenges to Science Policy," in S. E. Cozzens et al., eds., *The Research System in Transition* (Dordrecht: Kluwer, 1990), 15; Richard Rettig, *The Cancer Crusade* (Princeton: Princeton University Press, 1977); Harvey Brooks, "National Science Policy and Technological Innovation," in Ralph Landau and Nathan Rosenberg, eds., *Positive Sum Society* (Washington: National Academy Press, 1986), 130.

thesize federal economic development policies. Proposed in the final year of Carter's term, most of these initiatives were soon swept away.[4]

Ronald Reagan was elected president in 1980 in an atmosphere of economic confusion. "Stagflation," in which inflation and unemployment moved upward together, baffled and disturbed Keynesians. As economist Paul Krugman puts it, "The establishment had no answers." Reagan offered a conservative causal story for the mess: he blamed the state. Social welfare policies that had their roots in the New Deal, Reagan claimed, gutted the incentives to work and invest that made capitalism dynamic, while placing an enormous tax burden on private output. Technological innovation figured centrally in the conservative account; without incentives for risk taking, the economy was wanting for "intellectual capital" (to use the phrase of budget director David Stockman). George Gilder, the conservative intellectual who was most enamored of technology, stated baldly that "the U.S. was taxing and harassing successful businesses more than any other capitalist country, regulating them as if they were dangerous conspirators against the public interest." Conservative policy entrepreneurs, such as Stockman and Representative Jack Kemp, accused Keynesians of tinkering while the system collapsed around them. Rather than the targeted tax incentives for investment and R&D that the CED preferred, they advocated across-the-board cuts in marginal rates for individuals and corporations. President Reagan made Kemp's bill the highest priority of his first year and pushed it through Congress, although he had to to concede targeted tax breaks to a wide range of interests (including an R&D credit and accelerated depreciation schedules) along the way. On the spending side, the Reagan administration successfully slashed technology demonstration programs, but far too little else to make up the revenue shortfall brought about by the tax cut, setting in train budget deficits that were to play a very large role in ensuing policy debates.[5]

In addition to the economic crisis, President Reagan perceived a military crisis that demanded equally dramatic departures. His call for a vast expansion of the military budget, the armed forces, and the defense industries echoed that of

[4] Bruce L. R. Smith, *American Science Policy since World War II* (Washington: Brookings, 1990), 92–96; Cohen and Noll (above, n. 1), 270–98; Claude Barfield, *Science Policy from Ford to Reagan: Change and Continuity* (Washington: American Enterprise Institute, 1982), 30–36; Frank Press, "Science and Technology in the White House, 1977–80, Part I," *Science* 211, January 9, 1981, 139–45; Committee for Economic Development, *Stimulating Technological Progress* (New York: CED, 1981), 1–9; "Industrial Innovation Initiatives," *Public Papers of the President, 1979*, vol. 2 (Washington: GPO, 1980), 2070–74; "Economic Renewal Program," *Public Papers of the President, 1980*, vol. 2 (Washington: GPO, 1982), 1585–91.

[5] Paul Krugman, *Peddling Prosperity: Economic Sense and Nonsense in the Age of Diminished Expectations* (New York: Norton, 1994), 100; David Stockman, *The Triumph of Politics: How the Reagan Revolution Failed* (New York: Harper and Row, 1986), 236, 253; George Gilder, *Wealth and Poverty* (New York: Basic Books, 1981), 84; Barfield (above, n. 4), 39–46, 53–57; Smith (above, n. 4), 133, 136–38.

NSC-68 in 1950. Indeed, a prominent group in the campaign for this program, the Committee on the Present Danger (CPD), had originally been formed to promote the ideas of NSC-68 and counted that document's author, Paul Nitze, among its leading members. These advocates of a reinvigorated national security state mainly wanted an acceleration of existing programs, like the modernization of strategic forces, including the Trident submarine and the MX and cruise missiles. Within this camp, however, a small minority, drawn from right-wing think tanks and the nuclear weapons laboratories, devised an even more radical program. By pressing its advantage in high technology, such as lasers, computers, and communications, they claimed, the United States would become able to defend itself against a Soviet missile strike and gain an enormous edge. Unlike the devotees of supply side economics, who won Reagan's support for their tax-cut program while he was still a candidate, strategic defense policy entrepreneurs, such as weapons scientist Edward Teller, retired army general Daniel Graham, and former Undersecretary of the Army Karl Bendetsen, had to wait a couple of years before their moment arrived. In the winter of 1982–83, as modernization stalled and the nuclear freeze movement gathered momentum, key White House staff members saw in strategic defense a way to outflank both the Soviet Union and the domestic opposition. Sidestepping the military bureaucracy and the science advisory apparatus, they engineered the president's extraordinary public commitment to "rendering these nuclear weapons impotent and obsolete" on March 23, 1983. While the Secretaries of Defense and State were blindsided by the speech, Teller was invited to the White House to enjoy his victory.[6]

A small cadre of activists inspired the Strategic Defense Initiative (SDI), but once the president announced it and whipped up public support, a bandwagon on its behalf swept the administration, the military services, and defense contractors. SDI, with a projected ultimate cost of up to $1 trillion and a 10-year budget of $69 billion, promised patronage to the aerospace and electronics industries for the foreseeable future. Despite intense opposition within the scientific community, Democratic control of Congress (including the Senate after 1986), and perestroika in the Soviet Union, the administration secured $16.2 billion of the $25 billion it requested to fund SDI between fiscal 1985 and fiscal 1989. Overall military R&D spending rose from 50 percent to 70 percent of federal R&D spending and totaled nearly $40 billion annually at the end of Reagan's second term. This expansion of the national security state's technological

---

[6] Fred Block, "Economic Instability and Military Strength: The Paradoxes of the 1950 Rearmament Decision," *Politics and Society* 10: (1980): 35–58; Jerry Sanders, *Peddlers of Crisis* (Boston: South End Press, 1983), 241–67; Donald R. Baucom, *The Origins of SDI, 1944–1983* (Lawrence: University of Kansas Press, 1992); Sanford Lakoff and Herbert York, *A Shield in Space? Technology, Politics and the Strategic Defense Initiative* (Berkeley: University of California Press, 1989), 252–60; William J. Broad, *Teller's War: The Top-Secret Story behind the Star Wars Deception* (New York: Simon and Schuster, 1992), 99–132; Stockman (above, n. 5), 277–99.

capabilities threatened the institutional authority of Congress, in the view of leading SDI opponents. They also argued that SDI would be bad for the economy, draining scientific and technological resources from academic and civilian industrial R&D.[7]

The paradox of an avowedly conservative president promoting such an expansion of federal power was not lost on advocates of an explicit civilian "industrial policy," a new version of reform liberalism advanced as an alternative to "Reaganomics." Industrial policy was the product of a highly publicized search for "new ideas" in the Democratic Party that was supposed to shrug off the legacy of the failed policies of the Carter period. Its enthusiasts, such as MIT's Lester Thurow and Harvard's Robert Reich, claimed that U.S. economic problems stemmed from domestic industry's failure to modernize as effectively as its Japanese competitors. Some sectors, they argued, were complacent and collusive; in others, management was locked in fruitless conflict with labor; in still others, firms failed to solve collective action problems that foreign governments solved for their national industries. The federal government could overcome these problems by developing the capacity to identify and subsidize promising investments and by providing fora to promote cooperation. The reform liberals pointed to New Deal agencies like the Reconstruction Finance Corporation and the Tennessee Valley Authority as well as the Japanese Ministry of International Trade and Industry (MITI) and even DOD as evidence that their approach was plausible. Technological innovation, whether to upgrade old sectors or to create new ones, was an essential goal of industrial policy.[8]

As unemployment shot past 10 percent for the first time in decades and the trade deficit soared in the early years of the Reagan presidency, industrial policy entrepreneurs captured the fancy of Senator Gary Hart of Colorado, a Democratic presidential hopeful for 1984, and other "Atari Democrats" in Congress. They came under harsh attack, however, not only from conservatives in the administration, but from Keynesians like Charles Schultze, who had chaired the Council of Economic Advisors (CEA) under Carter. Schultze argued that the nation's problems had macroeconomic solutions and that government channeling of investment would distort the market rather than enhance it. The leading Democratic presidential candidates backed away from industrial policy during the primary season in 1984, and the eventual nominee, former Vice-President Walter Mondale, built his losing campaign around the Keynesian theme of deficit reduction. Mondale's defeat banished industrial policy from the po-

[7] Edward Reiss, *The Strategic Defense Initiative* (New York: Cambridge University Press, 1992), 60–111; Lakoff and York, (above, n. 6), 263–89; David C. Mowery and Nathan Rosenberg, "The U.S. National Innovation System," in Richard R. Nelson, ed., *National Innovation Systems* (New York: Oxford University Press, 1993), 42; Smith, (above, n. 4), 133.

[8] James Shoch, "Party Competition, Divided Government, and the Politics of Economic Nationalism" (Ph.D. diss., MIT, 1993); Otis Graham, *Losing Time: The Industrial Policy Debate* (Cambridge: Harvard University Press, 1992).

litical agenda. Within the executive branch under Presidents Reagan and Bush, the idea became a demon with a life of its own. Officials accused of conducting "industrial policy" faced severe sanctions, as Defense Advanced Research Projects Agency (DARPA, the successor to ARPA) Director Craig Fields, who was fired in 1990, discovered. Among Democrats, industrial policy was perceived as out of temper with the conservative times and unappealing to key constituencies, particularly in business, even though it was never tested in practice.[9]

The opposition during the second Reagan administration thus embarked on a renewed search for new ideas and hit on public-private technology "partnerships." Rather than pulling the state out of the economy altogether (as the conservatives argued) or giving it a larger say (as industrial policy advocates wanted), partnership advocates, such as Hewlett-Packard CEO John Young, sought business-government cooperation to achieve national economic goals, much as associationalists had earlier in the century. While MITI helped Japanese auto firms by promoting exports and supporting technological innovation, they argued, the Big Three automakers and federal agencies spent their time squabbling over environmental and labor regulations. This causal story placed the blame for economic woes not on business alone or government alone, but on foreigners and on the American political-economic system as a whole. The associative vision appealed especially to the Democratic Leadership Council (DLC), which aimed to broaden the party's appeal to business and moderates. The DLC's membership included a number of governors like Arkansas's Bill Clinton (the organization's chair for several years) who saw public-private technology partnerships working already at the state level. With the waning of the Cold War in the late 1980s, partnerships also appealed to politicians like Senators Jeff Bingaman of New Mexico and Ernest Hollings of South Carolina, whose states faced the loss of the nuclear weapons laboratories and production sites that were their major industrial facilities. The extensive technological capabilities of the national security state, which no longer needed to be as tightly held in the absence of a Soviet threat, were put on the table as a government contribution to partnerships for competitiveness.[10]

Ironically, the new associative vision made its first prominent appearance on the national agenda in the 1985 report of the Reagan Administration's Commission on Industrial Competitiveness, chaired by Young. The report was ignored, and a piqued Young formed a nonprofit organization to continue to press the case from the outside. Congress, led by Bingaman, Hollings, and others,

---

[9] Shoch (above, n. 8); "Beheaded," *Economist,* April 28, 1990, 27–28; D. Allen Bromley, *The President's Scientists: Reminiscences of a White House Science Advisor* (New Haven: Yale University Press, 1994), 124.

[10] Shoch (above, n. 8), 594–603; Carnegie Commission on Science, Technology and Government, *Science, Technology, and the States in America's Third Century* (New York: Carnegie Commission, 1992).

then took the initiative, broadening the scope of Cooperative Research and Development Agreements (CRADAs) between government laboratories and private firms, expanding the mission of the National Bureau of Standards (changing its name in the process to the National Institute of Standards and Technology [NIST]), and giving it a new Advanced Technology Program (ATP). The Pentagon also took steps to establish partnerships, notably SEMATECH, a consortium for the development of semiconductor manufacturing equipment. Under President George Bush, partnerships gained a stronger foothold in the executive branch, despite resistance from those who equated any government-business cooperation with industrial policy. D. Allan Bromley, the president's science advisor, was able to win more funds for Sematech, ATP, and related programs. The Clinton administration made "stimulate partnerships" a central tenet of its science and technology policy, dramatically expanding funding for NIST and defense technology conversion in its first two years.[11]

The associative idea of partnerships, like the reform liberal concept of industrial policy, ran into trouble with Keynesians as well as conservatives. For Keynesians, the federal deficit, rather than any institutional defect, was the fundamental economic problem. The deficit undermined public confidence, they argued, and it raised interest rates, crowding out private investments, particularly those that take a long time to mature, such as investments in new technologies. The conservative successes of the early 1980s and their continuing powerful presence in the 1990s made tax increases substantial enough to close the deficit politically infeasible. With revenue off limits, Keynesian attention was riveted on the approximately one-third of the federal budget considered to be "discretionary," excluding interest payments and politically untouchable entitlement programs. All federal R&D spending falls in this discretionary budget, accounting for about one-seventh of it. (About half of both discretionary spending and federal R&D are defense-related.) Although deficit reduction was but a battering ram against the state for some conservatives, just as David Stockman once hoped, Keynesian "deficit hawks," backed by many mainstream economists, saw it as an essential first step that ought to be given a chance to work before more interventionist experiments were undertaken.

The Mondale campaign of 1984 interpreted the Keynesian vision to require a tax increase, a politically unpalatable message that failed miserably at the bal-

---

[11] Shoch (above, n. 8), 658–62, 679–80; John A. Alic et al., *Beyond Spinoff: Military and Commercial Technologies in a Changing World* (Boston: Harvard Business School Press, 1992), 79–80; Bromley (above, n. 9), 122–41; "Industrial R&D Wins Political Favor," *Science* 255, March 20, 1992, 1500–1502; Eliot Marshall, "R&D Policy That Emphasizes the 'D,'" *Science* 259, March 26, 1993, 1816–19; Michael E. Davey, *CRS Issue Brief: Research and Development Funding: Fiscal Year 1995* (Washington: Congressional Research Service, 1994); John D. Moteff, *CRS Issue Brief: Defense Technology Base Programs and Defense Conversion* (Washington: Congressional Research Service, 1994); William J. Clinton and Albert Gore, Jr., *Science in the National Interest* (Washington: Executive Office of the President, 1994), 9, 21.

lot box. The recession that began in 1990 contributed to a resurgence of both the deficit and concern about it. Deficit reduction was a major theme of the surprisingly successful 1992 presidential campaigns of Paul Tsongas and Ross Perot. In the first Clinton administration, Leon Panetta (initially OMB director and then White House chief of staff) and Robert Rubin (assistant to the president for economic policy and then Secretary of the Treasury) were the chief advocates of deficit reduction. The influence of this faction substantially reduced the scale of the "investments," including investments in joint public/private R&D, that the president asked for in his first two budgets. The administration's hand was forced, too, by deficit hawks in Congress, particularly members elected for the first time in 1992. For example, many Democratic "freshmen" voted against the administration-backed Superconducting Supercollider (SSC) project in 1993 out of concern about the deficit, prompting one House veteran to comment, "This new generation of leaders doesn't understand the difference between an expenditure and an investment." Although the SSC was hardly the sort of government-business partnership championed by administration "investment hawks" like Robert Reich (Secretary of Labor) and Laura Tyson (CEA chair and then director of the National Economic Council), the deficit-reduction fervor of the Congress was a substantial brake on their entrepreneurship.[12]

The election of 1994 brought the recent science and technology policy debate around full circle. The new Republican congressional majority added a strong dash of conservatism to the deficit reduction stew, attacking every technology policy initiative of the first two years of the Clinton presidency. Conservative members of the Republican congressional leadership, backed by an even more conservative freshman class, called for the abolition of the Departments of Energy and Commerce, two of the main technology partnership agencies. Representative Robert Walker, the first Republican chairman of the House Science Committee ever, targeted Commerce's ATP, Energy's Partnership for a New Generation of Vehicles, and other partnership programs for elimination. The White House dug in its heels and managed to keep most of these programs going, but some, like ATP, sustained deep cuts. On the other hand, conservative defense hawks (although not necessarily all conservatives) pressed for and won increases in the funding of the Ballistic Missile Defense Organization, the successor to SDI.[13]

[12] Bob Woodward, *The Agenda: Inside the Clinton White House* (New York: Simon & Schuster, 1994), 154–56, 161–62, 324; Jeffrey Mervis, Christopher Anderson, and Eliot Marshall, "Better for Science Than Expected," *Science* 262, November 5, 1993, 836–38; "R&D Budget: Growth in Hard Times," *Science* 263, February 11, 1994, 744–46; "The Hand on Your Purse Strings," *Science* 264, April 8, 1994, 192–94; Gary Taubes, "The Supercollider: How Big Science Lost Favor and Fell," *New York Times,* October 26, 1993, D1; Clifford Krauss, "Knocked Out by the Freshmen," *New York Times,* October 26, 1993, D12.

[13] "Committee Clamor Illustrates Extent of Partisan Divide," *Congressional Quarterly Weekly Report* 54, May 11, 1996, 1291–92; Kei Koizumi et al., *Congressional Action on Research and Development in the FY 1997 Budget* (Washington: American Association for the Advancement of Science, 1996).

One can no more easily declare an absolute victor in science and technology policy in the post-Cold War era than one could in the Depression, World War II, or the early Cold War. Just as associationalism survived the Crash, conservatism survived the New Deal, and Keynesianism survived stagflation, reform liberalism seems likely to survive the Republican revolution, and the national security state, the collapse of the Soviet Union. These are durable ideas. One reason for their durability is that policy entrepreneurship often leads to their institutionalization, leaving a reservoir of people and organizations, as well as ideas, for later entrepreneurs. The Bureau of Standards and the nuclear weapons laboratories have played this role for associationalists and national security advocates, respectively, in the past decade. Another reason is that there is usually some new venue in which policy entrepreneurs can continue to fight, even if the first skirmishes go against them. John Young and Robert Reich, for instance, have worked both the executive and legislative sides of the fence in recent years. Finally, in a diverse and rapidly changing society, there is no shortage of interests and there is always some ambiguity about them. Should U.S. auto companies expect technology partnerships to be a profitable investment of money, expertise, and political capital? Compared to what? These questions have no certain answers.

My analysis of the 1980s and 1990s adds value to the existing literature and suggests some interesting possibilities for the future. The stalemate shaping up between the president and Congress is reminiscent of the late 1940s. Partisan control of the branches is divided, and the parties seem to be drifting further apart. Rigid budget caps constrain programmatic innovation. One might expect policy entrepreneurs to be drawn to other venues, such as the courts, regulatory agencies (and deregulation), and state governments. At least for the moment, conservatives might find the judicial arena particularly appealing, while the influence of Presidents Reagan and Bush still lingers. The adaptation of the national security state to the new international and fiscal environment brings to mind another interesting scenario. An increasing proportion of conservatives might renounce the alliance with military high technology enthusiasts and their big budgets forged in the late 1940s. Whether the associative vision can successfully be adapted to incorporate national security interests fully into a political partnership is an open question. (So is whether a science and technology policy produced by such a coalition would do enough for the military or the economy to warrant the expense.) If such a coalition is formed, it might, ironically, bring Vannevar Bush's original postwar vision closer to reality than the "postwar consensus" ever did.[14]

[14] Smith (above, n. 4), 135–45; Lewis M. Branscomb, "Empowering Technology Policy," in Branscomb, ed., *Empowering Technology* (Cambridge: MIT Press, 1993), 266–94; Evan Berman, "The Politics of Federal Technology Policy: 1980–1988," *Policy Studies Review* 10 (1992): 28–42. Of recent work on technology policy, Jay Stowsky, "America's Technical Fix," Berkeley Roundtable on the International Economy Research Paper, University of California, Berkeley 1996, comes closest to my approach.

IN CONCLUSION

However fascinating the analogies between, say, the 80th Congress of 1947–48 and the 104th Congress of 1995–96, the late 1940s are not going to be replayed. Nor will they be run in reverse, with the United States demobilizing fully from the Cold War. These analogies and the historical analysis on which they are built should be used as aids to the political imagination, rather than pose as attempts at prediction. They should be used, too, to understand differences between the past and the present. Federal biomedical research funding may now play roles analogous to military R&D spending, including sustaining academic researchers who care not a whit for practical applications and spinning off new economic sectors, but the underlying mission and public appeal is not the same. As long as members of Congress and their constituents keep getting sick and pray that science can provide cures, it seems likely that the NIH budget juggernaut will continue to roll on. The global economic context of the contemporary debate also has no exact parallel in the past. Technological competence has diffused widely, and macroeconomic independence has eroded. As a result, the structure and consequences of associative or Keynesian policies, for instance, are likely to be quite different than in the past. Conditions placed on the access of foreign firms to publicly funded technology development consortia and concerns about foreign direct investments in U.S. high-technology industries are among the new issues that perplex today's science and technology policy entrepreneurs.

The fundamental questions and processes, however, remain the same. In what ways does the market fail to generate scientific research and technological innovations? Can the federal government make markets work better in this regard? How? Policy-makers answer these questions by integrating what they understand about science and technology with what they understand about the state and the market. Science and technology policy entrepreneurs provide the intellectual links between the grand visions of the political economy and the nitty-gritty of proposals for government action. They execute political as well as intellectual strategies, targeting particular institutions and interests. They cannot, however, choose their opposition, nor insulate their efforts from wars, depressions, realignments, and other cataclysms that shuffle the Washington scene. As much as they make their own destinies, they are at the mercy of events too large to be controlled.

Public policy has a similar relationship with science and technology. States cannot determine what nature will permit, what geniuses can devise, or what other states decide to do. They must react. But they may also act, facilitating or obstructing the creation and diffusion of new knowledge and products, tempering or reinforcing their effects on people and places. The United States has been the preeminent actor in this regard for most of this century. Its science and technology policy has changed the way its people and the people of the rest of the world live, work, and fight. A deeper understanding of the decision-making processes that led to these consequences holds the promise not necessarily of a world transformed, but perhaps of a world made a little better. This modest hope ought to be the lodestone of citizens, policy-makers, and scholars alike.

Bibliography

1. Manuscript Collections

American Research and Development Corporation corporate reports, Harvard Business School Archives.
Wendell Berge papers, Library of Congress, Manuscripts Division.
Francis Biddle papers, Franklin D. Roosevelt Library (FDRL).
Vannevar Bush papers, Library of Congress, Manuscripts Division.
Gerhard Colm papers, Harry S. Truman Library (HSTL).
Karl Compton-James Killian papers (MIT Office of the President, Collection AC4), MIT Archives.
Lammot Dupont papers (Accession 1662), Hagley Museum and Library.
Pierre S. Dupont papers (Longwood Manuscripts 10), Hagley Museum and Library.
Ralph E. Flanders papers, Syracuse University Archives.
William T. Golden papers, HSTL.
Alvin H. Hansen papers, Harvard University Archives.
Willis F. Harrington papers (Accession 1813), Hagley Museum and Library.
Herbert Hoover papers, Herbert Hoover Presidential Library (HHPL).
Dugald C. Jackson papers, MIT Archives.
Leon H. Keyserling papers, HSTL.
Simon B. Kuznets papers, Harvard University Archives.
Frederick J. Lawton papers, HSTL.
Robert A. Millikan papers, California Institute of Technology Archives.
National Academy of Sciences Archives.
National Industrial Conference Board papers (Accession 1057), Hagley Museum and Library.
Edwin G. Nourse papers, HSTL.
Franklin D. Roosevelt papers, FDRL.
Samuel I. Rosenman papers, FDRL.
Harold D. Smith papers, FDRL.
Stephen J. Spingarn papers, HSTL.
Stuart L. Symington papers, HSTL.
James S. Taylor papers, HHPL.
Harry S. Truman papers, HSTL.
Henry A. Wallace papers, University of Iowa collection, microfilm edition.
James E. Webb papers, HSTL.

2. National Archives Record Groups

RG40, Records of the Department of Commerce.
RG51, Records of the Bureau of the Budget.
RG144, Records of the Temporary National Economic Committee.
RG167, Records of the National Bureau of Standards.
RG179, Records of the War Production Board.

RG207, Records of the Housing and Home Finance Administration.
RG227, Records of the Office of Scientific Research and Development.
RG250, Records of the Office of War Mobilization and Reconversion.
RG330, Records of the Secretary of Defense.

3. Contemporary Periodicals

American Bankers Association Journal
American Federationist
Annals of the American Academy of Political and Social Sciences
Architectural Forum
Atlantic
Bulletin of the National Research Council
Business Week
Circular and Reprint Series of the National Research Council
Congressional Digest
Editorial Research Reports
Fortune
Housing Progress
Housing Research
Industrial and Engineering Chemistry
Industrial Management
Iron Age
Journal of Commerce
Journal of the Patent Office Society
Mill and Factory
Monthly Labor Review
Nation
New Republic
New York Law Journal
New York Times
Newsweek
Reader's Digest
Review of Scientific Instruments
Saturday Evening Post
Science
Scribner's
Survey Graphic
Technology Review
Time
U.S. News and World Report
Vital Speeches of the Day
Washington Post

4. Government Documents

Annual Report of the Attorney General (Washington, D.C.: GPO, various years).
Annual Report of the Secretary of Commerce (Washington, D.C.: GPO, various years).

Annual Report of the Secretary of Defense (Washington, D.C.: GPO, various years).

Budget of the United States Government (Washington, D.C.: GPO, various years).

Building Research Advisory Board. *A Survey of Housing Research* (Washington, D.C.: HHFA, 1952).

Bureau of Labor Statistics. *New Housing and Its Methods, 1940–1956*. Bulletin no. 1231. August 1958.

Bureau of Labor Statistics. *Structure of the Residential Building Industry in 1949*. Bulletin no. 1170. November 1954.

Bush, Vannevar. *Science, the Endless Frontier* (Washington, D.C.: GPO, 1945).

Byrnes, James F. *Reconversion: A Report to the President*. 78th C., 2nd s., 1944, S. doc. 237.

———. "War Production and VE Day." Office of War Mobilization and Reconversion pamphlet. April 1, 1945.

Civilian Production Administration, Bureau of Demobilization. *Industrial Mobilization for War. Volume I, Program and Administration* (Washington, D.C.: GPO, 1947).

Clinton, William J., and Albert Gore, Jr. *Science in the National Interest* (Washington, D.C.: Executive Office of the President, 1994).

Cochrane, Rexmond C. *Measures for Progress* (Washington, D.C.: U.S. Department of Commerce, 1966).

Colean, Miles L. *The Role of the Housebuilding Industry* (Washington, D.C.: NRPB, July, 1942).

Committee on Recent Economic Changes. *Recent Economic Changes in the United States* (New York: McGraw-Hill, 1929).

Davey, Michael E. *CRS Issue Brief: Research and Development Funding: Fiscal Year 1995* (Washington, D.C.: Congressional Research Service, 1994).

Economic Report of the President (Washington, D.C.: GPO, various years).

England, J. Merton. *A Patron for Pure Science* (Washington, D.C.: National Science Foundation, 1982).

Federal Trade Commission. *Report to the President with Respect to the Basing-Point System in the Iron and Steel Industry* (Washington, D.C.: GPO, 1935).

Flanders, Ralph. *The High Cost of Housing*. Report for the Joint Housing Committee. 80th C., 2d s., 1948.

Green, Constance, Harry C. Thomson, and Peter C. Roots. *The Ordnance Department: Planning Munitions for War* (Washington, D.C.: Department of the Army, 1955).

Hamilton, Walton. *Patents and Free Enterprise* (Washington, D.C.: GPO, 1941).

Hansen, Alvin H. *After the War—Full Employment* (Washington, D.C.: NRPB, 1942).

Hewes, James E., Jr. *From Root to McNamara: Army Organization and Administration, 1900–1963* (Washington, D.C.: Center for Military History, 1975).

Housing and Home Finance Administration. *Annual Report* (Washington, D.C.: GPO, various years).

———. *A Handbook of Information on Provisions of the Housing Act of 1949* (Washington, D.C.: HHFA, 1950).

Joint Committee on the Economic Report. *Volume and Stability of Private Investment*. 81st C., 1st s., 1950.

Joint Housing Committee. *Housing Study and Investigation: Final Majority Report*. 80th C., 2d s., 1948, H. Rept. 1564.

Komons, Nick A. *Science and the Air Force* (Arlington, VA: Office of Aerospace Research, 1966).

Mid-Year Economic Report of the President (Washington, D.C.: GPO, various years).

Moody, Walter S. *Building a Strategic Air Force* (Washington, D.C.: Center for Air Force History, 1996).

Moteff, John D. *CRS Issue Brief: Defense Technology Base Programs and Defense Conversion* (Washington: Congressional Research Service, 1994).

National Housing Agency. *Annual Report* (Washington, D.C.: GPO, various years).

———. "Housing Costs and Cost Reduction." December 1944. Mimeo.

National Recovery Administration. *Machine and Allied Products.* Code Hearings, no. 277 (Washington, D.C.: Recordak Corp, 1934).

National Resources Committee. *Technological Trends and National Policy* (Washington, D.C.: GPO, 1937).

National Resources Planning Board. *Research—A National Resource.* 3 vols. (Washington, D.C.: GPO, 1938, 1940, and 1942).

———. *Housing: The Continuing Problem* (Washington, D.C.: NRPB, June 1940).

———. *National Resources Development Report for 1943. Part I: Post-War Plan and Program* (Washington, D.C.: GPO, 1943).

National Science Board. *Science Indicators 1972* (Washington, D.C.: GPO, 1973).

Neufeld, Jacob, ed. *Research and Development in the U.S. Air Force* (Washington: Center for Air Force History, 1993).

Office of Alien Property Custodian. *Annual Report* (Washington, D.C.: APC, various years).

Office of the Secretary of Defense. "The Growth of Scientific Research and Development." RDB 114/34, July 27, 1953.

Perazich, George, and Philip M. Field. *Industrial Research and Changing Technology* (Philadelphia: Works Progress Administration, 1940).

President's Research Committee on Recent Social Trends. *Recent Social Trends in the United States* (New York: McGraw-Hill, 1933).

President's Scientific Research Board. *Science and Public Policy, Volume I: A Program for the Nation* (Washington, D.C.: GPO, 1947).

Public Papers of the President (Washington, D.C.: GPO, various years).

Rearden, Steven L. *History of the Office of the Secretary of Defense. Volume I: The Formative Years, 1947–1950* (Washington, D.C.: Historical Office, Office of the Secretary of Defense, 1984).

Roland, Alex. *Model Research: The National Advisory Committee for Aeronautics, 1915–1958* (Washington, D.C.: NASA, 1985).

Science Advisory Board. *Report* (Washington, D.C.: National Research Council, various years).

Shapley, Willis H. "Problems of Definition, Concept, and Interpretation of R&D Statistics." In *Methodology of Statistics on R&D* (Washington, D.C.: NSF, 1959), 8–15.

Smaller War Plants Corporation. "Technical Advisory Service." March 1945. Mimeo.

———. *Economic Concentration and World War II* (Washington, D.C.: GPO, 1946).

Snyder, John W. *Battle for Production* (Washington, D.C.: GPO, 1946).

Solo, Robert A. *Synthetic Rubber: A Case Study in Technological Development under Government Direction.* Study no. 18. Prepared for U.S. Senate, Committee on the Judiciary, 85th C., 2d s., 1959.

Stine, Jeffrey K. *A History of Science Policy in the United States, 1940–1985.* Science

Policy Study Background Report No. 1. U.S. House of Representatives, Committee on Science and Technology, 99th C., 2d s., 1986.

Stone, Peter J., and R. Harold Denton. *Toward More Housing,* TNEC monograph no. 8, 76th C., 3d s., 1940.

Tennessee Valley Authority. *Annual Report of the Tennessee Valley Authority for Fiscal Year 1934.* 74th C., 1st s., 1935, H. doc. 82.

———. *TVA—1933–1937* (Washington: GPO, 1937).

———. "Soil . . . People, and Fertilizer Technology." 1949. Mimeo.

———. "Fertilizer Science and the American Farmer." 1958. Mimeo.

U.S. Department of Commerce. "Simplified Practice: What It Is and What It Offers." 1924. Mimeo.

———. *Trade Association Activities* (Washington: GPO, 1923).

U.S. House of Representatives. Committee on Appropriations. *Appropriations, Department of Commerce, 1929.* 70th C., 1st s., 1928.

———. *Department of Commerce Appropriation Bill, 1934.* 73d C., 1st s., 1933.

———. *Department of Justice Appropriation Bill for 1941.* 76th C., 3d s., 1940.

———. *First Supplemental Appropriation Rescission Bill, 1946.* 79th C., 1st s., 1945.

———. *Department of Commerce Appropriation Bill for 1947.* 79th C., 2d s., 1946.

———. *Department of Commerce Appropriation Bill for 1948.* 80th C., 1st s., 1947.

———. *Department of Commerce Appropriation Bill for 1949.* 80th C., 2d s., 1948.

U.S. House of Representatives. Committee on Banking and Currency. *General Housing,* 80th C., 2d s., 1948.

U.S. House of Representatives. Committee on Labor. *Six Hour Day—Five Day Week.* 72d C., 2d s., 1933.

U.S. House of Representatives. Committee on Military Affairs. *Muscle Shoals.* 73rd C., 1st s., 1933.

———. *Research and Development.* 79th C., 1st s., 1945.

U.S. House of Representatives. Committee on Patents. *Pooling of Patents.* 74th C., 1st s., 1935.

———. *Compulsory Licensing of Patents.* 75th C., 3d s., 1938.

U.S. House of Representatives. Committee on Ways and Means. *Revenue Revisions, 1947–1948.* 80th C., 1st s., 1948.

U.S. House of Representatives. Select Committee on Small Business. *Problems of Small Business Related to the National Emergency.* 82d C., 1st s., 1951.

———. *General Revenue Revision.* 83rd C., 2nd s., 1954.

United States Patent Law Sesquicentennial Celebration, April 10, 1940 (Washington: GPO, 1940).

U.S. President. "Muscle Shoals Development." 73rd C., 1st s., 1933, H. doc. 15.

———. "Strengthening and Enforcement of Antitrust Laws." 75th C., 3d s., 1938, S. doc. 173.

U.S. Senate. Committee on Appropriations. *Independent Offices Appropriations for 1952.* 82d C., 1st s., 1951.

U.S. Senate. Committee on Banking and Currency. *Full Employment Act of 1945.* 79th C., 1st s., 1945.

———. *General Housing Act of 1945.* 79th C., 1st s., 1946.

———. *Veterans' Emergency Housing Act of 1946.* 79th C., 2d s., 1946.

U.S. Senate. Committee on Commerce. *To Establish an Office of Technical Services in the Department of Commerce.* 79th C., 1st s., 1945.

U.S. Senate. Committee on Expenditures in Executive Departments. *Technical Information and Services Act.* 80th C., 1st s., 1947.

U.S. Senate. Committee on the Judiciary. Subcommittee on Patents, Trademarks, and Copyrights. *Compulsory Patent Licensing under Antitrust Judgments.* 86th C., 2d s., 1960.

U.S. Senate. Committee on Military Affairs. *Technological Mobilization.* 77th C., 2d s., 1943.

———. *Scientific and Technological Mobilization.* 78th C., 1st and 2d s., 1943–44.

———. *Government's Wartime Research and Development, 1940–1944. Part II—Findings and Recommendations.* 79th C., 1st s., 1945.

U.S. Senate. Committee on Patents. *Forfeiture of Patent Rights on Conviction under Laws Prohibiting Monopoly.* 70th C., 1st s., 1928.

———. *Patents.* 77th C., 2d s., 1942.

U.S. Senate. Special Committee on Postwar Economic Policy and Planning. *Postwar Economic Policy and Planning.* 79th C., 1st s., 1945.

———. *Postwar Housing,* 79th C., 1st s., 1945.

———. *Postwar Tax Plans for the Federal Goverment.* 79th C., 1st s., 1945.

U.S. Senate, Special Subcommittee on HR 9659. *Housing Act of 1948.* 80th C., 2d s., 1948, S. doc. 202.

Watson, George M., Jr. *The Office of the Secretary of the Air Force, 1947–1965* (Washington, D.C.: Center for Air Force History, 1993).

Watson, Mark S. *Chief of Staff: Prewar Plans and Preparations* (Washington, D.C.: Department of the Army, 1950).

Youtz, Philip N. "Programs for Regional Development of Industry." July 4, 1944. Mimeo.

5. Unpublished Dissertations, Conference Papers, and Working Papers

Branyan, Robert L. "Anti-Monopoly Activities during the Truman Administration" (Ph.D. diss., University of Oklahoma, 1961).

David, Paul A., and Gavin Wright. "Resource Abundance and American Economic Leadership." Pub. no. 267. Center for Economic Policy Research. Stanford University, 1991.

Dennis, Michael A. "A Change of State: The Political Cultures of Technical Practice at the MIT Instrumentation Laboratory and the Johns Hopkins University Applied Physics Laboratory, 1930–1945" (Ph.D. diss., Johns Hopkins University, 1991).

Eden, Lynn Rachele. "The Diplomacy of Force: Interests, the State, and the Making of American Military Policy in 1948" (Ph.D. diss., University of Michigan, 1985).

Ferleger, Louis, and William Lazonick. "The Managerial Revolution and the Developmental State: The Case of U.S. Agriculture" (paper presented at the Business History Conference, Boston, March 19–21, 1993).

Florida, Richard, and Mark Samber. "Capital and Creative Destruction: Venture Capital, Technological Change and Economic Development." Carnegie-Mellon University, May 1994.

Genuth, Joel. "The Local Origins of National Science Policy" (Ph.D. diss., MIT, 1996).

Hill, William S., Jr. "The Business Community and National Defense: Corporate Leaders and the Military, 1943–1950" (Ph.D. diss., Stanford University, 1979).

Hutchinson, Janet Anne. "American Housing, Gender, and the Better Homes Movement, 1922–1935" (Ph.D. diss., University of Delaware, 1989).

Kaufman, Allen. "In the Procurement Officer We Trust: Constitutional Norms, Air Force Procurement and Industrial Organization, 1938–1947" (paper presented at the Hagley Museum and Library, October 1995).

Kellogg, Nelson R., and Stuart W. Leslie. "Civilian Technology at the National Bureau of Standards." Johns Hopkins University, 1990.

Kurth, James. "The Follow-On Imperative in American Weapons Procurement, 1960–1990" (paper presented to the conference on Economic Issues of Disarmament, South Bend, Indiana, November 30, 1990).

Liles, Patrick R. "Sustaining the Venture Capital Firm." Management Analysis Center, Cambridge, MA, 1977.

Logsdon, John M. "Toward a New Federal Policy for Technology: The Outline Emerges." Staff discussion paper no. 408. Program of Policy Studies in Science and Technology. George Washington University, August 1972.

Mindell, David A. "'Datum for Its Own Annihilation': Feedback, Control, and Computing, 1916–1945" (Ph.D. diss., MIT, 1996).

Nelson, Richard R. "What Is Public and What Is Private about Technology?" Consortium on Competition and Cooperation. Working paper 90–9. Center for Research in Management. University of California, Berkeley, 1990.

Neushul, Peter. "Science, Technology, and the Arsenal of Democracy" (Ph.D. diss., University of California, Santa Barbara, 1993).

Rowan, Carl. "Politics and Pure Research: The Origins of the National Science Foundation, 1942–1954" (Ph.D. diss., University of Miami, Ohio, 1985).

Shoch, James. "Party Competition, Divided Government, and the Politics of Economic Nationalism" (Ph.D. diss., MIT, 1993).

Stowsky, Jay. "America's Technical Fix." Berkeley Roundtable on the International Economy Research Paper. University of California, Berkeley, 1996.

Wagnon, William O., Jr. "The Politics of Economic Growth: The Truman Administration and the 1949 Recession" (Ph.D. diss., University of Missouri, 1970).

Wang, Jessica. "American Science in an Age of Anxiety: Scientists, Civil Liberties, and the Cold War, 1945–1950" (Ph.D. diss., MIT, 1994).

6. Books, Articles in Books, and Pamphlets

Abrams, Duff B., "The Contributions of Scientific Research to the Development of the Portland Cement Industry in the United States." Pub. no. 1886. American Academy of Political and Social Sciences. May 1925.

Aitken, Hugh G. J. *The Continuous Wave: Technology and American Radio, 1900–1932* (Princeton: Princeton University Press, 1986).

Akin, William E. *Technocracy and the American Dream* (Berkeley: University of California Press, 1977).

Alchon, Guy. *The Invisible Hand of Planning: Capitalism, Social Science and the State in the 1920s* (Princeton: Princeton University Press, 1985).

Alic, John A., et al. *Beyond Spinoff: Military and Commercial Technologies in a Changing World* (Boston: Harvard Business School Press, 1992).

Appleby, Joyce. *Liberalism and Republicanism in the Historical Imagination* (Cambridge: Harvard University Press, 1992).

Arnold, Peri. "Ambivalent Leviathan: Herbert Hoover and the Positive State." In J. David Greenstone, ed., *Public Values and Private Power in American Politics* (Chicago: University of Chicago Press, 1982), 109–36.

Arnold, Thurman. *The Folklore of Capitalism* (Garden City, NY: Blue Ribbon Books, 1937).

———. *The Bottlenecks of Business* (New York: Reynal and Hitchcock, 1940).

———. *Fair Fights and Foul: A Dissenting Lawyer's Life* (New York: Harcourt, Brace and World, 1965).

Averch, Harvey. *A Strategic Analysis of Science and Technology Policy* (Baltimore: Johns Hopkins University Press, 1985).

Bailey, Stephen K. *Congress Makes a Law: The Story behind the Employment Act of 1946* (New York: Columbia University Press, 1950).

Balogh, Brian. *Chain Reaction: Expert Debate and Public Participation in American Commercial Nuclear Power, 1945–1975* (New York: Cambridge University Press, 1991).

Barber, William J. *From New Era to New Deal: Herbert Hoover, the Economists and American Economic Policy, 1921–1933* (New York: Cambridge University Press, 1985).

———. "Government as a Laboratory for Economic Learning in the Years of the Democratic Roosevelt." In Furner and Supple, eds., 103–37.

Barfield, Claude. *Science Policy from Ford to Reagan: Change and Continuity* (Washington: American Enterprise Institute, 1982).

Baucom, Donald R. *The Origins of SDI, 1944–1983* (Lawrence: University of Kansas Press, 1992).

Baxter, James P., III. *Scientists against Time* (Boston: Little, Brown, 1946).

Beard, Edmund. *Developing the ICBM: A Study in Bureaucratic Politics* (New York: Columbia University Press, 1976).

Bensel, Richard F. *Yankee Leviathan: The Origins of Central State Authority in America, 1859–1877* (New York: Cambridge University Press, 1990).

Bernal, J. D. *The Social Function of Science* (London: George Routledge and Sons, 1939).

Beyer, Glenn H. *Housing and Society* (New York: Macmillan, 1965).

Birr, Kendall. "Industrial Research Laboratories." In Reingold, ed., 193–207.

Blair, John M. *Economic Concentration: Structure, Behavior, and Public Policy* (New York: Harcourt Brace, 1972).

Blanpied, William, ed. *Impacts of the Early Cold War on the Formulation of U.S. Science Policy* (Washington: American Association to the Advancement of Science, 1995).

Blum, John Morton, ed. *The Price of Vision: The Diary of Henry A. Wallace, 1942–1946* (Boston: Houghton-Mifflin Co., 1973).

———. *V Was for Victory: Politics and American Culture during World War II* (New York: Harcourt, Brace, and Jovanovich, 1976).

Bogen, Jules. "The Market for Risk Capital." American Enterprise Association. Washington D.C., August 1946. Pamphlet.

Brand, Donald R. *Corporatism and the Rule of Law* (Ithaca: Cornell University Press, 1988).

Branscomb, Lewis M., ed. *Empowering Technology* (Cambridge: MIT Press, 1993).

Bright, Charles D. *The Jet Makers: The Aerospace Industry from 1945 to 1972* (Lawrence: Regents Press of Kansas, 1978).

Brinkley, Alan. "The New Deal Order and the Idea of the State." In Steve Fraser and Gary Gerstle, eds., *The Rise and Fall of the New Deal Order* (Princeton: Princeton University Press, 1989), 85–121.

———. *The End of Reform: New Deal Liberalism in Recession and War* (New York: Knopf, 1995).

Broad, William J. *Teller's War: The Top-Secret Story behind the Star Wars Deception* (New York: Simon and Schuster, 1992).

Brody, David. "The New Deal and World War II." In John Braeman, Robert Bremner, and David Brody, eds., *The New Deal: The National Level* (Columbus: Ohio State University Press, 1975), 267–306.

Bromley, D. Allen. *The President's Scientists: Reminiscences of a White House Science Advisor* (New Haven: Yale University Press, 1994).

Brooks, Harvey. "National Science Policy and Technological Innovation." In Ralph Landau and Nathan Rosenberg, eds., *Positive Sum Society* (Washington: National Academy Press, 1986), 119–67.

———. "Lessons of History: Successive Challenges to Science Policy." In S. E. Cozzens et al., eds., *The Research System in Transition* (Dordrecht: Kluwer, 1990), 11–22.

Brown, Michael E. *Flying Blind: The Politics of the U.S. Strategic Bomber Program* (Ithaca: Cornell University Press, 1992).

Bureau of National Affairs (BNA). *Verbatim Record of the Proceedings of the Temporary National Economic Committee,* 14 vols. (Washington: BNA, 1940).

———. *Patents and the Antitrust Law: Analyses from BNA's Antitrust Trade Regulation Report* (Washington: BNA, 1966).

Burns, Arthur R. *The Decline of Competition: A Study of the Evolution of American Industry* (New York: McGraw-Hill, 1936).

Bush, Vannevar. *Modern Arms and Free Men* (New York: Simon and Schuster, 1949).

———. *Pieces of the Action* (Cambridge: MIT Press, 1970).

Butler, William F. *Business Needs for Venture Capital* (New York: McGraw-Hill, 1949).

Cantril, Hadley, ed. *Public Opinion, 1935–1946* (Westport, CT: Greenwood, 1978).

Carnegie Commission on Science, Technology and Government. *Science, Technology, and the States in America's Third Century* (New York: Carnegie Commission, 1992).

Catton, Bruce. *The Warlords of Washington* (New York: Harcourt, Brace, 1948).

Caves, Richard. *American Industry: Structure, Conduct, Performance.* 5th ed. (Englewood Cliffs: Prentice-Hall, 1982).

Chalmers, W. Ellison. "The Automobile Industry." In Galloway, ed., 301–10.

Chandler, Alfred D. *Scale and Scope: The Dynamics of Industrial Capitalism* (Cambridge: Harvard University Press, Belknap Press, 1990).

Chapman, Keith. *The International Petrochemical Industry* (Cambridge: Blackwell, 1991).

Chapman, Richard N. *The Contours of Public Policy, 1939–1945* (New York: Garland, 1981).

Chase, Stuart. *Men and Machines* (New York: Macmillan, 1929).

Coffey, Thomas M. *Iron Eagle: The Turbulent Life of General Curtis LeMay* (New York: Crown, 1986).

Cohen, Linda R., and Roger G. Noll. *The Technology Pork Barrel* (Washington: Brookings Institution, 1991).

Colean, Miles L. *American Housing: Problems and Prospects* (1944; reprint, New York: Twentieth Century Fund, 1949).

Collins, Robert M. "The Emergence of Economic Growthmanship in the United States: Federal Policy and Economic Knowledge in the Truman Years." In Furner and Supple, eds., 138–70.

Colvin, Fred. "The Machine Tool Industry." In Galloway, ed., 311–20.

Committee for Economic Development. "Meeting the Special Problems of Small Business." 1947. Pamphlet.

———. "Monetary and Fiscal Policy for Greater Economic Stability," 1948. Pamphlet.

———. "Economic Policy for Rearmament." September 1950. Pamphlet.

———. *Stimulating Technological Progress* (New York: CED, 1981).

Committee on Elimination of Waste in Industry of the FAES. *Waste in Industry* (Washington: FAES, 1921).

Conant, James B. *My Several Lives: Memoirs of a Social Inventor* (New York: Harper and Row, 1970).

Cormier, Frank, and William J. Eaton. *Reuther* (Englewood Cliffs: Prentice-Hall, 1970).

Coughlin, Charles E. *Eight Lectures on Labor, Capital, and Justice* (Royal Oak, MI: Radio League of the Little Flower, 1934).

Coyle, David Cushman. *The American Way* (New York: Harper and Bros., 1938).

Cuff, Robert D. *The War Industries Board: Business-Government Relations during World War I* (Baltimore: Johns Hopkins University Press, 1973).

Dahlberg, Arthur. *Jobs, Machines, and Capitalism* (New York: Macmillan, 1932).

Dallek, Robert. *Franklin D. Roosevelt and American Foreign Policy, 1932–1945* (New York: Oxford University Press, 1979).

Davies, Richard O. *Housing Reform during the Truman Administration* (Columbia: University of Missouri Press, 1966).

DeChazeau, Melvin G., et al. *Jobs and Markets: How to Prevent Inflation and Depression in the Transition* (New York: McGraw-Hill, 1946).

Dennison, Henry S., Lincoln Filene, Ralph E. Flanders, and Morris E. Leeds. *Toward Full Employment* (New York: Whittlesey House, 1938).

Dewhurst, J. Frederic, and Associates. *America's Needs and Resources* (New York: Twentieth Century Fund, 1947).

———. *America's Needs and Resources: A New Survey* (New York: Twentieth Century Fund, 1955).

Dominguez, John. *Venture Capital* (Lexington, MA: D. C. Heath, 1974).

Dorwart, Jeffrey M. *Eberstadt and Forrestal: A National Security Partnership, 1909–1949* (College Station: Texas A&M University Press, 1991).

Dupree, A. Hunter. *Science in the Federal Government.* 2d ed. (Baltimore: Johns Hopkins University Press, 1987).

Dyer, Davis, and David Sicilia. *Labors of a Modern Hercules: The Evolution of a Chemical Company* (Boston: Harvard Business School Press, 1990).

Eden, Lynn. "Capitalist Conflict and the State: The Making of U.S. Military Policy in 1948." In Charles Bright and Susan Harding, eds., *Statemaking and Social Movements: Essays in History and Theory* (Ann Arbor: University of Michigan Press, 1984), 233–61.

Eisner, Marc A. *Antitrust and the Triumph of Economics* (Chapel Hill: University of North Carolina Press, 1991).

Fabricant, Solomon. "Armament Production Potential." In Jules Backman, ed., *War and Defense Economics* (New York: Rhinehart, 1951), 19–45.

Flamm, Kenneth. *Creating the Computer* (Washington: Brookings Institution, 1988).

Flanders, Ralph E. *Senator from Vermont* (Boston: Little, Brown, 1961).

Flash, Edward S., Jr. *Economic Advice and Presidential Leadership* (New York: Columbia University Press, 1965).

Foster, Mark S. "Henry John Kaiser." In *Encyclopedia of American Business History and Biography: The Automobile Industry, 1920–1980.*

Fraser, Steve. *Labor Will Rule* (New York: Free Press, 1991).

Frederick, J. George. "What Are Technocracy's Assertions?" In Frederick, ed., *For and Against Technocracy.* New York: Business Bourse, 1933, 10–13.

Freeman, Christopher, and Carlota Perez. "Structural Crises of Adjustment, Business Cycles, and Investment Behavior." In Giovanni Dosi et al., eds., *Technical Change and Economic Theory* (London: Pinter, 1988), 38–66.

Fuller, Douglas R. *Government Financing of Private Enterprise* (Stanford: Stanford University Press, 1948).

Furner, Mary O., and Barry Supple, eds. *The State and Economic Knowledge: The American and British Experiences.* (New York: Cambridge University Press, 1990).

Fusfeld, Daniel R. *The Economic Thought of Franklin D. Roosevelt and the Origins of the New Deal,* 2d ed. (New York: AMS Press, 1970).

Gaddis, John L. *Strategies of Containment* (New York: Oxford University Press, 1982).

Galambos, Louis. *Competition and Cooperation: The Emergence of a National Trade Association* (Baltimore: Johns Hopkins University Press, 1966).

Galbraith, John Kenneth. *American Capitalism: The Concept of Countervailing Power* (Cambridge: Riverside Press, 1952).

Galloway, George B., ed. *Industrial Planning under Codes* (New York: Harper and Bros., 1935).

Geiger, Roger L. *To Advance Knowledge: The Growth of American Research Universities, 1900–1940* (New York: Oxford University Press, 1986).

Gellman, Aaron J. "Surface Freight Transportation." In William M. Capron, ed., *Technological Change in Regulated Industries* (Washington: Brookings Institution, 1970), 166–196.

Gilbert, Richard V., et al. *An Economic Program for American Democracy* (New York: Vanguard, 1938).

Gilder, George. *Wealth and Poverty* (New York: Basic Books, 1981).

Gimbel, John. *Science, Technology, and Reparations* (Stanford: Stanford University Press, 1990).

Goodwin, Craufurd D. "Attitudes toward Industry in the Truman Administration: The Macroeconomic Origins of Microeconomic Policy." In Michael J. Lacey, ed., *The Truman Presidency* (New York: Woodrow Wilson International Center for Scholars and Cambridge University Press, 1989), 89–127.

Goodwin, Craufurd D., and R. Stanley Herren. "The Truman Administration: Problems and Policies Unfold." In Goodwin, ed., *Exhortation and Controls: The Search for a Wage-Price Policy, 1945–1971* (Washington: Brookings Institution, 1975), 9–93.

Graham, Margaret B.W., and Bettye H. Pruitt. *R&D for Industry: A Century of Technical Innovation at Alcoa* (New York: Cambridge University Press, 1990).

Graham, Otis. *Losing Time: The Industrial Policy Debate* (Cambridge: Harvard University Press, 1992).

Graham, Otis L., and Meghan Robinson Wander, eds. *Franklin D. Roosevelt—His Life and Times: An Encyclopedic View* (Boston: G. K. Hall, 1985).

Greenstone, J. David. *The Lincoln Persuasion: Remaking American Liberalism* (Princeton: Princeton University Press, 1992).

Gressley, Gene, ed. *Voltaire and the Cowboy: The Letters of Thurman Arnold* (Boulder: Colorado Associated University Press, 1977).

Gries, John M., and James Ford, eds. *Housing Objectives and Programs* (Washington: National Capitol Press, 1932).

Hamby, Alonzo. *Beyond the New Deal: Harry S. Truman and American Liberalism* (New York: Columbia University Press, 1973).

Hamby, Alonzo. *Man of the People: A Life of Harry S. Truman* (New York: Oxford University Press, 1995).

Hammond, Paul Y. "NSC-68: Prologue to Rearmament." In Schilling, ed., 267–378.

Hansen, Alvin H. *Full Recovery or Stagnation?* (New York: Norton, 1938).

Harris, Seymour E., ed. *Saving American Capitalism* (New York: Knopf, 1948).

Hartz, Louis. *The Liberal Tradition in America* (1955; reprint, San Diego: Harcourt, Brace, Jovanovich, 1991).

Hawley, Ellis W. *The New Deal and the Problem of Monopoly: A Study in Economic Ambivalence* (Princeton: Princeton University Press, 1966).

———. "Three Facets of Hooverian Associationalism: Lumber, Aviation, and Movies, 1921–1930." In Thomas K. McCraw, ed., *Regulation in Perspective* (Cambridge: Harvard University Press, 1981), 95–124.

———. "'Industrial Policy' in the 1920s and 1930s." In Claude Barfield and William Schambra, eds., *The Politics of Industrial Policy* (Washington: American Enterprise Institute Press, 1986), 63–86.

Herbert, Vernon, and Attilio Bisio. *Synthetic Rubber: A Project That Had to Succeed* (Westport, CT: Greenwood, 1985).

Herken, Gregg. *The Winning Weapon: The Atomic Bomb in the Cold War, 1945–1950* (New York: Knopf, 1980).

Hershberg, James G. *James B. Conant: Harvard to Hiroshima and the Making of the Nuclear Age* (Stanford: Stanford University Press, 1993).

Hewlett, Richard G., and Oscar E. Anderson, Jr. *The New World, 1939/1946* (University Park, PA: Pennsylvania State University Press, 1962).

Hewlett, Richard G., and Francis Duncan. *Atomic Shield: A History of the U.S. Atomic Energy Commission. Volume II, 1947–1952*. Paperback ed. (Berkeley: University of California Press, 1990).

Hicks, John D. *Republican Ascendancy, 1921–1933* (New York: Harper & Bros., 1960).

Himmelberg, Robert F. *The Origins of the National Recovery Administration: Business, Government and the Trade Association Issue, 1921–1933* (New York: Fordham University Press, 1976).

Hirsh, Richard F. *Technology and Transformation in the American Electric Utility Industry* (New York: Cambridge University Press, 1989).

Hodge, Clarence L. *The Tennessee Valley Authority: A National Experiment in Regionalism.* (1938; reissue, New York: Russell and Russell, 1968).

Hooks, Gregory. *Forging the Military-Industrial Complex: World War II's Battle of the Potomac* (Urbana: University of Illinois Press, 1991).

Hoover, Herbert. *The New Day: Campaign Speeches of Herbert Hoover, 1928* (Stanford: Stanford University Press, 1928).

———. *Memoirs* (New York: Macmillan, 1952).

Hounshell, David. *From the American System to Mass Production, 1800–1932: The Development of Manufacturing Technology in the U.S.* (Baltimore: Johns Hopkins University Press, 1984).

Hounshell, David, and John K. Smith. *Science and Corporate Strategy: DuPont R&D, 1902–1980* (New York: Cambridge University Press, 1990).

Huntington, Samuel P. *The Soldier and the State: The Theory and Politics of Civil-Military Relations* (Cambridge: Belknap Press, 1957).

———. *The Common Defense: Strategic Programs in National Politics* (New York: Columbia University Press, 1961).

Investment Bankers Association of America. "Capital for Small Business," April 5, 1945. Pamphlet.

Israel, Fred, ed. *State of the Union Messages of the Presidents,* 3 vols. (New York: Chelsea House, 1966).

Jerome, Harry. *Mechanization in Industry,* Pub. 27 (New York: National Bureau of Economic Research, 1934).

Jones, Franklin D. *Trade Association Activities and the Law* (New York: McGraw-Hill, 1922).

Jones, Jesse. *Fifty Billion Dollars* (New York: Macmillan, 1951).

Jungk, Robert. *Brighter Than a Thousand Suns: A Personal History of the Atomic Scientists.* Trans. James Cleugh (New York: Harcourt, Brace, Jovanovich, 1958).

Kaplan, Fred. *The Wizards of Armageddon* (New York: Simon and Schuster, 1983).

Karl, Barry D. *The Uneasy State: The U.S. from 1915 to 1945* (Chicago: University of Chicago Press, 1983).

Keck, Otto. "The National System for Technological Innovation in Germany." In Nelson, ed., 1993, 115–57.

Keith, Nathaniel S. *Politics and the Housing Crisis since 1930* (New York: Universe Books, 1973).

Kevles, Daniel J. *The Physicists* (New York: Knopf, 1977).

———. "K_1S_2: Korea, Science, and the State." In Peter Galison and Bruce Hevly, eds., *Big Science* (Stanford: Stanford University Press, 1992), 312–33.

Keynes, John Maynard. *The General Theory of Employment, Interest, and Money* (1936; San Diego: Harvest/HBJ edition, 1964).

King, Ronald F. *Money, Time, and Politics: Investment Tax Subsidies and American Politics* (New Haven: Yale University Press, 1993).

Kingdon, John W. *Agendas, Alternatives, and Public Policies*, 2d ed. (New York: HarperCollins, 1995).

Kirsh, Benjamin S. *Trade Associations in Law and Business* (New York: Central Book Co., 1938).

Kleinman, Daniel Lee. *Politics on the Endless Frontier* (Durham: Duke University Press, 1995).

Kofsky, Frank. *Harry S. Truman and the War Scare of 1948* (New York: St. Martin's, paperback ed., 1995).

Kohler, Robert E. *Partners in Science: Foundations and Natural Scientists, 1900–1945* (Chicago: University of Chicago Press, 1991).

Koizumi, Kei, et al. *Congressional Action on Research and Development in the FY 1997 Budget* (Washington: American Association for the Advancement of Science, 1996).

Kolodziej, Edward A. *The Uncommon Defense and Congress, 1945–1963* (Columbus: Ohio State University Press, 1966).

Krog, Carl E., and William R. Tanner, eds. *Herbert Hoover and the Republican Era* (Lanham, MD: University Press of America, 1984).

Krugman, Paul. *Peddling Prosperity: Economic Sense and Nonsense in the Age of Diminished Expectations* (New York: Norton, 1994).

Lakoff, Sanford, and Herbert York. *A Shield in Space? Technology, Politics and the Strategic Defense Initiative* (Berkeley: University of California Press, 1989).

Lasch, Robert. *Breaking the Building Blockade* (Chicago: University of Chicago Press, 1946).

Latham, Earl. *The Politics of Railroad Coordination* (Cambridge: Harvard University Press, 1959).

Layton, Edwin T., Jr. *The Revolt of the Engineers: Social Responsibility and the American Engineering Profession* (Cleveland: Press of Case Western Reserve University, 1971).

Lee, Bradford. "The Miscarriage of Necessity and Invention: Proto-Keynesianism and Democratic States in the 1930s." In Peter A. Hall, ed., *The Political Power of Economic Ideas: Keynesianism across Nations* (Princeton: Princeton University Press, 1989), 129–70.

Lee, David D. "Herbert Hoover and the Development of Commercial Aviation, 1921–1926." In Krog and Tanner, eds., 36–65.

Leffler, Melvyn P. *A Preponderance of Power: National Security, the Truman Administration, and the Cold War* (Stanford: Stanford University Press, 1992).

Lekachman, Robert. *The Age of Keynes* (New York: Random House, 1966).

Leslie, Stuart W. *The Cold War and American Science: The Military-Academic Complex at MIT and Stanford* (New York: Columbia University Press, 1993).

Leuchtenburg, William E. *The Perils of Prosperity*, 2d ed. (Chicago: University of Chicago Press, 1993).

Levin, Richard. "The Semiconductor Industry." In Nelson, ed., 1982, 9–100.

Lewis, Kevin N. *The U.S. Air Force Budget and Posture over Time* (Santa Monica: RAND Corporation, 1990).

Lewis, W. Arthur. *The Theory of Economic Growth* (Homewood, IL: Richard Irwin, 1955).

Lichtenstein, Nelson. *Labor's War at Home: The CIO in World War II* (New York: Cambridge University Press, 1982).

Lichtenstein, Nelson. *The Most Dangerous Man in Detroit: Walter Reuther and the Fate of American Labor* (New York: Basic, 1995).

Lilienthal, David E. *TVA: Democracy on the March* (New York: Harper and Bros., 1944).

Lincoln, George A. *Economics of National Security,* 2d ed. (New York: Prentice-Hall, 1954).

Lincoln and Therese Filene Foundation. "Memorandum on Semi-Fixed and Permanent Capital for Small Business." December, 1939. Pamphlet.

Lynch, David. *The Concentration of Economic Power* (New York: Columbia University Press, 1946).

Lyon, Leverett S., et al. *The National Recovery Administration: An Analysis and Appraisal.* 2d ed. (New York: Da Capo Press, 1972).

Machlup, Fritz. "The Nature of the International Cartel Problem." In Corwin Edwards et al., *A Cartel Policy for the United Nations* (New York: Columbia University Press, 1945), 1–24.

MacLaurin, W. Rupert. *Invention and Innovation in the Radio Industry* (New York: Macmillan, 1949).

Markowitz, Norman D. *The Rise and Fall of the People's Century: Henry A. Wallace and American Liberalism, 1941–1948* (New York: The Free Press, 1973).

Mason, Edward S. "Controlling Industry." In *The Economics of the Recovery Program* (New York: Whittlesey House, 1934), 38–63.

McCraw, Thomas K. *TVA and the Power Fight, 1933–1939* (Philadelphia: J. B. Lippincott, 1971).

McCullough, David. *Truman* (New York: Simon and Schuster, 1992).

McDougall, Walter A. . . . *the Heavens and the Earth: A Political History of the Space Age* (New York: Basic, 1986).

McFarland, Stephen L. *America's Pursuit of Precision Bombing, 1910–1945* (Washington: Smithsonian Institution Press, 1995).

McNaugher, Thomas L. *New Weapons, Old Politics: America's Military Procurement Muddle* (Washington: Brookings Institution, 1989).

Mehrens, Edward. "Concrete: Yesterday, Today, Tomorrow." American Concrete Institute, February 1935. Pamphlet.

Mellon, Andrew W. *Taxation: The People's Business* (New York: Macmillan, 1924).

Millard, Andre. *Edison and the Business of Invention* (Baltimore: Johns Hopkins University Press, 1990).

Millis, Walter. *Arms and Men: A Study in American Military History* (New York: G. P. Putnam, 1956).

Milward, Alan S. *War, Economy, and Society* (Berkeley: University of California Press, 1977).

Moggridge, Donald, ed. *The Collected Writings of John Maynard Keynes,* 30 vols. (London: MacMillan, 1973).

Morone, James A. *The Democratic Wish* (New York: Basic, 1990).

Morris, Peter J. T. *The American Synthetic Rubber Research Program* (Philadelphia: University of Pennsylvania Press, 1989).

Mowery, David C., and Nathan Rosenberg. *Technology and the Pursuit of Economic Growth* (New York: Cambridge University Press, 1989).

———. "The U.S. National Innovation System." In Nelson, ed., *National Innovation Systems,* 29–75.

Mucciaroni, Gary. *The Political Failure of Employment Policy, 1945–1982* (Pittsburgh: University of Pittsburgh Press, 1990).

Mumford, Lewis. *Technics and Civilization* (1934; reprint with a new introduction, San Diego: Harvest/Harcourt, Brace, and Jovanovich, 1963).

Meyers, W. S., ed. *State Papers of Herbert Hoover* (New York: Doubleday, 1934).

Nagle, James F. *A History of Government Contracting* (Washington: George Washington University, 1992).

National Planning Association. "Can We Afford Additional Programs for National Security?" October, 1953. Pamphlet no. 84.

Nelkin, Dorothy. *The Politics of Housing Innovation* (Ithaca: Cornell University Press, 1971).

Nelson, Richard R., ed. *Government and Technical Progress* (New York: Pergamon, 1982).

———. *National Innovation Systems.* (New York: Oxford University Press, 1993.)

Newman, James R., and Byron S. Miller. *The Control of Atomic Energy: A Study of Its Social, Economic, and Political Implications* (New York: Whittlesey House, 1948).

Noble, David. *America by Design* (New York: Knopf, 1977).

Odagiri, Hiroyuki, and Akira Goto. "The Japanese System of Innovation: Past, Present, and Future." In Nelson, ed., 1993, 76–114.

Ogburn, William F. "You and Machines." American Council on Education, 1934. Pamphlet.

Olson, James S. *Herbert Hoover and the Reconstruction Finance Corporation, 1931–1933* (Ames: Iowa State University Press, 1977).

———. *Saving Capitalism: The Reconstruction Finance Corporation and the New Deal, 1933–1940* (Princeton: Princeton University Press, 1988).

Parris, Addison W. *The Small Business Administration* (New York: Praeger, 1968).

Parrish, Michael E. *Anxious Decades: America in Prosperity and Depression, 1920–1941* (New York: Norton, 1992).

Patterson, James T. *Congressional Conservatism and the New Deal: The Growth of the Conservative Coalition in Congress, 1933–1939* (Lexington: University of Kentucky Press, 1967).

Peck, Merton J., and Frederic M. Scherer. *The Weapons Acquisition Process: An Economic Analysis* (Boston: Harvard Business School, 1962).

Proceedings of the Constitutional Convention of the CIO (n.p., various years).

Prothro, James W. *The Dollar Decade: Business Ideas in the 1920s* (Baton Rouge: Louisiana State University Press, 1954).

Pursell, Carroll W., Jr. "Science Agencies in World War II: The OSRD and Its Challengers." In Reingold, ed., 359–78.

Quigley, John M. "Residential Construction." In Nelson, ed., 1982, 361–410.

Rae, John B. *Climb to Greatness: The American Aircraft Industry, 1920–1960* (Cambridge: MIT Press, 1968).

Reich, Leonard. *The Making of American Industrial Research* (New York: Cambridge University Press, 1985).

Reingold, Nathan, ed. *The Sciences in the American Context: New Perspectives* (Washington, D.C.: Smithsonian Institution Press, 1979).

Reiss, Edward. *The Strategic Defense Initiative* (New York: Cambridge University Press, 1992).

Rettig, Richard. *The Cancer Crusade* (Princeton: Princeton University Press, 1977).

Rhodes, Richard. *The Making of the Atomic Bomb* (New York: Simon and Schuster, 1986).

———. *Dark Sun: The Making of the Hydrogen Bomb* (New York: Simon and Schuster, 1995).

Roberts, Edward B. *Entrepreneurs in High Technology* (New York: Oxford University Press, 1991).

Roos, Charles F. *NRA Economic Planning* (Bloomington, IN: Principia Press, 1937).

Rosegrant, Susan, and David Lampe. *Route 128: Lessons from Boston's High-Tech Community* (New York: Basic, 1992).

Rosen, Philip T. *The Modern Stentors: Radio Broadcasting and the Federal Government, 1920–1934.* (Westport, CT: Greenwood Press, 1980).

Rosenman, Samuel, ed. *Public Papers and Addresses of Franklin D. Roosevelt,* 13 vols. (New York: Random House, 1938).

Ross, Dorothy. "Liberalism." In Jack P. Greene, ed., *Encyclopedia of American Political History.* Vol. II (New York: Scribner's, 1984).

Ross, Malcolm, ed. *Profitable Practice in Industrial Research* (New York: Harper and Brothers, 1932).

Sachs, Alexander. "NRA Policies and the Problem of Economic Planning." In *America's Recovery Program* (New York: Oxford University Press, 1934), 107–92.

Samuels, Richard J. *Rich Nation, Strong Army: National Security and the Technological Transformation of Japan* (Ithaca: Cornell University Press, 1994).

Samuelson, Paul A. *Economics: An Introductory Analysis,* 2d ed. (New York: McGraw-Hill, 1951).

Sanders, Jerry. *Peddlers of Crisis* (Boston: South End Press, 1983).

Sapolsky, Harvey M. *The Polaris System Development: Bureaucratic and Programmatic Success in Government* (Cambridge: Harvard University Press, 1972).

———. *Science and the Navy* (Princeton: Princeton University Press, 1990).

Scherer, F. M., et al. *Patents and the Corporation,* 2d ed. (Boston: Patents and the Corporation, 1959).

Schilling, Warner R. "The Politics of National Defense: Fiscal 1950." In Schilling, ed., *Strategy, Politics, and Defense Budgets* (New York: Columbia University Press, 1962), 1–266.

Schlesinger, Arthur M., Jr. *The Crisis of the Old Order, 1919–1933* (Boston: Houghton-Mifflin, 1957).

———. *The Coming of the New Deal* (Cambridge: Riverside Press, 1958).

Schulman, Bruce J. *From Cotton Belt to Sunbelt: Federal Policy, Economic Development, and the Transformation of the South, 1938–1990* (New York: Oxford University Press, 1991).

Schumpeter, Joseph A. *Capitalism, Socialism, and Democracy* (1942; New York: Harper & Row [colophon ed.], 1975).

Schwarz, Jordan A. *The Speculator: Bernard Baruch in Washington, 1917–1965* (Chapel Hill: University of North Carolina Press, 1981).

———. "Baruch, the New Deal, and the Origins of the Military-Industrial Complex." In Robert Higgs, ed., *Arms, Politics, and the Economy: Historical and Contemporary Perspectives* (New York: Holmes and Meier, 1990), 1–21.

————. *The New Dealers: Power Politics in the Age of Roosevelt* (New York: Knopf, 1993).

Scott, Howard. *Introduction to Technocracy* (New York: John Day, 1933).

Sherry, Michael S. *Preparing for the Next War: American Plans for Postwar Defense, 1941–1945* (New Haven: Yale University Press, 1977).

————. *The Rise of American Air Power* (New Haven: Yale University Press, 1987).

Skocpol, Theda. *Protecting Soldiers and Mothers: The Political Origins of Social Policy in the United States* (Cambridge: Harvard University Press, 1993).

Skowronek, Stephen. *Building a New American State* (New York: Cambridge University Press, 1982).

————. *The Politics Presidents Make: Leadership from John Adams to George Bush* (Cambridge: Harvard University Press, 1993).

Slichter, Sumner. *Union Policies and Industrial Management* (Washington: Brookings Institution, 1941).

Smith, Bruce A. *Technological Innovation in Electric Power Generation, 1950–1970* (East Lansing: Michigan State University Public Utility Papers, 1977).

Smith, Bruce L. R. *American Science Policy since World War II* (Washington: Brookings Institution, 1990).

Smith, John K., Jr. "World War II and the Transformation of the American Chemical Industry." In E. Mendelsohn, M. R. Smith, and P. Weingart, eds., *Science, Technology, and the Military* (Dordrecht: Kluwer, 1988), 307–22.

Smith, Merritt Roe. "Army Ordnance and the 'American System' of Manufacturing, 1815–1861." In Smith, ed., *Military Enterprise and Technological Change* (Cambridge: MIT Press, 1985), 39–86.

Snyder, Glenn H. "The 'New Look' of 1953." In Schilling, ed., 379–524.

Soule, George. "A Critique of Technocracy's Five Main Points." In Frederick, ed., 95–108.

Speece, Glenn Harrison. *After Roosevelt* (New York: Alliance Press, 1936).

Stein, Harold. "Disposal Of The Aluminum Plants." In Stein, ed., *Public Administration and Policy Development,* (New York: Harcourt, Brace & World, 1952), 313–63.

Stein, Herbert. *The Fiscal Revolution in America* (Chicago: University of Chicago Press, 1969); rev ed. (Washington: American Enterprise Institute, 1990).

————. *Presidential Economics* (New York: Simon and Schuster, 1984).

Stewart, Irvin. *Organizing Scientific Research for War* (Boston: Little Brown, 1948).

Stockman, David. *The Triumph of Politics: How the Reagan Revolution Failed* (New York: Harper and Row, 1986).

Striner, Herbert, et al. *Defense Spending and the U.S. Economy.* 2d ed. (Baltimore: The Johns Hopkins University, 1959).

Sweezy, Alan. "Declining Investment Opportunity." In Seymour E. Harris, ed., *The New Economics* (New York: Knopf, 1947), 425–35.

Tanner, William R. "Secretary Hoover's War on Waste, 1921–1928." In Krog and Tanner, eds., 1–35.

Terborgh, George. *The Bogey of Economic Maturity* (Chicago: Machinery and Allied Products Institute, 1945).

Tomlins, Christopher L. *The State and the Unions: Labor Relations, Law and the Organized Labor Movement in America, 1880–1960* (New York: Cambridge University Press, 1985).

Tugwell, Rexford Guy. *The Industrial Discipline and the Governmental Arts* (New York: Columbia University Press, 1933).

Vagtborg, Harold. *Research in American Industrial Development* (New York: Pergamon, 1976).

Vander Meulen, Jacob. *The Politics of Aircraft* (Lawrence: University of Kansas Press, 1991).

Vatter, Harold G. *The U.S. Economy in World War II* (New York: Columbia University Press, 1985).

Wallace, Henry. *Sixty Million Jobs* (New York: Reynal and Hitchcock, Simon and Schuster, 1945).

Weart, Spencer. "The Physics Business in America, 1919–1940: A Statistical Reconnaissance." In Reingold, ed., 295–358.

Weidlein, Edward R., and William A. Hamor. *Science in Action* (New York: McGraw-Hill, 1931).

Weiss, Marc A. *The Rise of the Community Builders: The American Real Estate Industry and Urban Land Planning* (New York: Columbia University Press, 1987).

Weissman, Rudolph. *Small Business and Venture Capital* (New York: Harper and Bros, 1945).

White, Gerald T. *Billions for Defense: Government Financing by the Defense Plant Corporation during World War II* (University, AL: University of Alabama Press, 1980).

Whitney, Simon N. *Antitrust Policies: American Experience in Twenty Industries* (New York: Twentieth Century Fund, 1958).

Williamson, Samuel R., Jr., and Steven L. Rearden. *The Origins of U.S. Nuclear Strategy, 1945–1953* (New York: St. Martin's, 1993).

Wilson, Joan Hoff. *Herbert Hoover: Forgotten Progressive* (Boston: Little-Brown, 1975).

"The Winning Plans in the Pabst Postwar Employment Awards," Pabst Brewing Company, 1944. Pamphlet.

Wise, George. *Willis R. Whitney, General Electric, and the Origins of U.S. Industrial Research* (New York: Columbia University Press, 1985).

Wood, Laurence I. *Patents and Antitrust Law* (New York: Commerce Clearing House, 1942).

Woodward, Bob. *The Agenda: Inside the Clinton White House* (New York: Simon and Schuster, 1994).

Yergin, Daniel. *Shattered Peace: The Origins of the Cold War and the National Security State* (Boston: Houghton-Mifflin, 1977).

York, Herbert. *The Advisors: Oppenheimer, Teller, and the Superbomb,* 2d ed. (Stanford: Stanford University Press, 1989).

Ziegler, Harmon. *The Politics of Small Business in America* (New York: Public Affairs Press, 1961).

7. Periodical Articles

Bean, Jonathan J. "World War II and the 'Crisis' of Small Business: The Smaller War Plants Corporation, 1942–1946." *Journal of Policy History* 6 (1994): 215–43.

Berle, A. A., Jr. "High Finance: Master or Servant?" *Yale Review* 23 (1933): 20–42.

Berman, Evan. "The Politics of Federal Technology Policy: 1980–1988." *Policy Studies Review* 10 (1992): 28–42.

Bernstein, Barton J. "The Automobile Industry and the Coming of the Second World War." *Southwestern Social Sciences Quarterly* 47 (1966): 22–33.

Biles, Roger. "Nathan Straus and the Failure of U.S. Public Housing, 1937–1942." *Historian* 52 (1990): 33–46.

Bittlingmayer, George. "Property Rights, Progress, and the Aircraft Patents Agreement." *Journal of Law and Economics* 31 (1988): 227–48.

Block, Fred. "Economic Instability and Military Strength: The Paradoxes of the 1950 Rearmament Decision." *Politics and Society* 10 (1980): 35–58.

Bright, Arthur A., Jr., and John Exter. "War, Radar, and the Radio Industry." *Harvard Business Review* (Winter 1947): 256–65.

Bright, Arthur A., Jr., and W. Rupert MacLaurin. "Economic Factors Influencing the Development and Introduction of the Fluorescent Lamp." *Journal of Political Economy* 51 (1943): 429–50.

Brinkley, Alan. "The Antimonopoly Ideal and the Liberal State: The Case of Thurman Arnold." *Journal of American History* 80 (1993): 557–79.

Butters, J. Keith. "Taxation and New Product Development." *Harvard Business Review* (Summer 1945): 451–60.

Clark, Mark. "Suppressing Innovation: Bell Laboratories and Magnetic Recording." *Technology and Culture* 34 (1993): 516–38.

Davis, Lance E., and Daniel J. Kevles. "The National Research Fund: A Case Study in the Industrial Support of Academic Science." *Minerva* 12 (1974): 207–20.

Douglas, Paul H., and Joseph Hackman. "The Fair Labor Standards Act of 1938 I." *Political Science Quarterly* 53 (1938): 491–515.

Dupree, A. Hunter. "National Security and the Post-War Science Establishment in the United States." *Nature* 323, September 18, 1986, 213–16.

Edwards, Corwin. "The New Antitrust Procedures as Illustrated in the Construction Industry." *Public Policy* 2 (1941): 321–40.

———. "Thurman Arnold and the Antitrust Laws." *Political Science Quarterly* 58 (1943): 338–55.

Ellis, Richard J. "Radical Lockeanism in American Political Culture." *Western Political Quarterly* 45 (1992): 825–49.

Etzkowitz, Henry. "Enterprises from Science: The Origins of Science-Based Regional Economic Development." *Minerva* 31 (1993): 326–60.

Feuer, Mortimer. "The Patent Monopoly and the Anti-Trust Laws." *Columbia Law Review* 38 (1938): 1145–78.

Field, Gregory B. "'Electricity for All': The Electric Home and Farm Authority and the Politics of Mass Consumption, 1932–1935." *Business History Review* 64 (1990): 32–60.

Forman, Paul. "Beyond Quantum Electronics: National Security as a Basis for Physical Research in the United States, 1940–1960." *Historical Studies in the Physical and Biological Sciences* 17 (1987): 150–229.

Fox, Daniel M. "The Politics of the NIH Extramural Program, 1937–1950." *Journal of the History of Medicine and Allied Sciences* 42 (1987): 447–66.

Friedberg, Aaron. "Why Didn't the U.S. Become a Garrison State?" *International Security* 16 (1992): 109–42.

Genuth, Joel. "Groping towards Science Policy in the United States in the 1930s." *Minerva* 25 (1987): 238–68.

———. "Microwave Radar, the Atomic Bomb, and the Background to U.S. Research Priorities in World War II." *Science, Technology, and Human Values* 13 (1988): 276–89.

Gerstle, Gary. "The Protean Quality of American Liberalism." *American Historical Review* 99 (1994): 1043–73.

Goldberg, Stanley. "Inventing a Climate of Opinion: Vannevar Bush and the Decision to Build the Bomb." *Isis* 83 (1992): 429–52.

Gordon, Robert J. "$45 Billion of U.S. Private Investment Has Been Mislaid." *American Economic Review* 59 (1969): 221–38.

Gough, Terrence J. "Soldiers, Businessmen, and U.S. Industrial Mobilization Planning between the World Wars." *War and Society* 9 (1991): 63–99.

Graham, Margaret. "Industrial Research in the Age of Big Science." *Research on Technological Innovation, Management, and Policy* 2 (1985): 47–79.

Gulick, Luther. "War Organization of the Federal Government." *American Political Science Review* 38 (1944): 1166–79.

Hansen, Alvin H. "Economic Progress and Declining Population Growth." *American Economic Review* 29 (1939): 1–15.

Harris, Seymour. "Should the Scientists Resist Military Intrusion?" *American Scholar* (April 1947): 223–25.

Hawley, Ellis W. "Herbert Hoover, the Commerce Secretariat, and the Vision of an 'Associative State,' 1921–1928." *Journal of American History* 61 (1974): 116–40.

———. "Herbert Hoover and the Sherman Act, 1921–1933: An Early Phase of a Continuing Issue," *Iowa Law Review* 74 (1989): 1067–1103.

Jones, Byrd L. "The Role of Keynesians in Wartime and Postwar Planning, 1940–1946." *American Economic Review Papers and Proceedings* 62 (1972): 125–41.

Kargon, Robert, and Elizabeth Hodes. "Karl Compton, Isaiah Bowman, and the Politics of Science in the Great Depression." *Isis* 76 (1985): 301–18.

Karl, Barry D. "Presidential Planning and Social Science Research: Mr. Hoover's Experts." *Perspectives in American History* 3 (1969): 347–409.

Katznelson, Ira, and Bruce Pietrykowski. "Rebuilding the American State: Evidence from the 1940s." *Studies in American Political Development* 5 (1991): 301–39.

Kevles, Daniel J. "Federal Legislation for Engineering Experiment Stations: The Episode of World War I." *Technology and Culture* 12 (1971): 182–89.

———. "FDR's Science Policy." *Science* 183, March 1, 1974, 798–800.

———. "The National Science Foundation and the Debate over Postwar Research Policy, 1942–1945." *Isis* 68 (1977): 5–27.

———. "Foundations, Universities, and Trends in Support for the Physical and Biological Sciences, 1900–1992." *Daedalus* 121 (1992): 195–235.

Kitschelt, Herbert. "Industrial Governance Structures, Innovation Strategies, and the Case of Japan: Sectoral or Cross-National Comparative Analysis?" *International Organization* 45 (1991): 453–94.

Kline, Stephen J. "Innovation Is Not a Linear Process." *Research Management* (July/August 1985): 36–45.

Kohler, Robert E. "Science, Foundations, and American Universities in the 1920s." *Osiris,* second series, 3 (1987): 135–64.

Lasswell, Harold D. "The Garrison State." *American Journal of Sociology* 46 (1941): 455–68.

LeCuyer, Christophe. "The Making of a Science-Based Technological University: Karl Compton, James Killian, and the Reform of MIT, 1930–1957." *Historical Studies in the Physical and Biological Sciences* 23 (1992): 158–80.

Lowen, Rebecca. "Entering the Atomic Power Race: Science, Industry, and Government." *Political Science Quarterly* 102 (1987): 459–79.

Mowery, David C. "The Relationship between Intrafirm and Contractual Forms of Industrial Research in American Manufacturing, 1900–1940." *Explorations in Economic History* 20 (1983): 351–74.

———. "Firm Structure, Government Policy, and the Organization of Industrial Research, 1900–1950." *Business History Review* 58 (1984): 504–31.

Nelson, Richard R., and Gavin Wright. "The Rise and Fall of American Technological Leadership: The Postwar Era in Historical Perspective." *Journal of Economic Literature* 30 (1992): 1931–64.

Owens, Larry, "MIT and the Federal 'Angel': Academic R&D and Federal-Private Cooperation Before World War II." *Isis* 81 (1990): 189–213.

———. "The Counterproductive Management of Science in the Second World War: Vannevar Bush and the Office of Scientific Research and Development." *Business History Review* 68 (1994): 515–76.

Parsons, Talcott. "National Science Legislation, Part 1: An Historical Review." *Bulletin of the Atomic Scientists* (November 1946): 3–5.

Pursell, Carroll W., Jr. "The Anatomy of a Failure: The Science Advisory Board, 1933–1935." *Proceedings of the American Philosophical Society* 109 (1965): 342–51.

———. "The Administration of Science in the Department of Agriculture, 1933–1940." *Agricultural History* 42 (1968): 231–40.

———. "A Preface to Government Support of Research and Development: Research Legislation and the National Bureau of Standards, 1935–1941." *Technology and Culture* 9 (1968): 145–64.

———. "'A Savage Struck by Lightning': The Idea of a Research Moratorium, 1927–1937." *Lex et Scientia* 10 (1974): 146–58.

"The RCA Consent Decree." *George Washington Law Review* 1 (1933): 513–16.

Reich, Leonard S. "Lighting the Path to Profit: GE's Control of the Electric Lamp Industry, 1892–1941." *Business History Review* 66 (1992): 305–34.

Reingold, Nathan. "Vannevar Bush's New Deal for Research, or the Triumph of the Old Order." *Historical Studies in the Physical and Biological Sciences* 17 (1987): 299–344.

Rosenberg, David Alan. "US Nuclear Stockpile, 1945–1950." *Bulletin of Atomic Scientists* (May 1982): 25–30.

———. "The Origins of Overkill: Nuclear Weapons in American Strategy." *International Security* 7(4) (1983): 3–71.

Rosenberg, Nathan, and Richard R. Nelson. "American Universities and Technical Advance in Industry." *Research Policy* 23 (1993): 323–48.

Ruggie, John Gerard. "International Regimes, Transactions, and Change: Embedded Liberalism in the Postwar Economic Order." *International Organization* 36 (1982): 379–416.

Scherer, F. M. "Antitrust, Efficiency, and Progress." *New York University Law Review* 62 (1987): 998–1019.

Schumpeter, Joseph A. "John Maynard Keynes, 1883–1946." *American Economic Review* 36 (1946): 496–518.

Seely, Bruce. "Research, Engineering, and Science in American Engineering Colleges." *Technology and Culture* 34 (1993): 344–86.

Servos, John W. "The Industrial Relations of Science: Chemical Engineering at MIT, 1900–1939." *Isis* 71 (1980): 531–49.

Smith, Arthur M. "Recent Developments in Patent Law." *Michigan Law Review* 44 (1946): 899–932.

Solo, Carolyn Shaw. "Innovation in the Capitalist Process: A Critique of Schumpeterian Theory." *Quarterly Journal of Economics* 65 (1951): 417–28.

Solow, Robert. "Technical Change and the Aggregate Production Function." *Review of Economics and Statistics* 39 (1957): 312–20.

Spaatz, Carl. "Strategic Air Power: Fulfillment of a Concept." *Foreign Affairs* (April 1946): 385–96.

Stewart, Robert K. "The Office of Technical Services: A New Deal Idea in the Cold War." *Knowledge* 15 (1993): 44–77.

Stone, Deborah A. "Causal Stories and the Formation of Policy Agendas." *Political Science Quarterly* 104 (1989): 281–300.

Tuttle, William M., Jr. "The Birth of an Industry: The Synthetic Rubber 'Mess' in World War II." *Technology and Culture* 22 (1981): 35–67.

Van Keuren, David K. "Science, Progressivism, and Military Preparedness: The Case of the Naval Research Laboratory, 1915–1923." *Technology and Culture* 33 (1992): 710–32.

Wang, Jessica. "Science, Security, and the Cold War: The Case of E. U. Condon." *Isis* 83 (1992): 238–69.

Weiss, Stuart L. "Maury Maverick and the Liberal Bloc." *Journal of American History* 57 (1971): 880–95.

Welles, John G., and Robert H. Waterman, Jr. "Space Technology: The Payoff from Spinoff." *Harvard Business Review* (November–December 1963): 106–18.

Wells, Samuel F. "Sounding the Tocsin: NSC 68 and the Soviet Threat." *International Security* 4 (1979): 116–58.

Wolfman, Bernard. "Federal Tax Policy and the Support of Science." *University of Pennsylvania Law Review* 114 (1965): 171–86.

Zeitlin, Jonathan. "Flexibility and Mass Production at War: Aircraft Manufacture in Britain, the U.S., and Germany, 1939–1945." *Technology and Culture* 36 (1995): 46–79.

Index

Acheson, Dean, 193
"adaptation," 66, 85, 210
Advanced Research Projects Agency (ARPA), 222, 228
Advanced Technology Program (ATP) 229–30
Aeronautical Chamber of Commerce, 52
aircraft carriers, 121, 176–77, 179–80, 186, 188, 193, 194, 212
aircraft industry, 52–53, 119–21, 126–27, 176, 186, 221
air defense, 188, 195, 200, 201, 204, 214
air force. *See* United States Air Force
Air Policy Commission. *See* Finletter Commission
Alcoa, 81, 90, 91, 92, 95, 136, 153. *See also* aluminum industry
Alien Property Custodian (APC), 94, 138, 139
"all-outers," 116, 149, 197
aluminum industry, 37, 93, 95, 136. *See also* Alcoa
American Construction Council (ACC), 50
American Federation of Labor (AF of L), 59, 60, 64, 101, 106, 109–14
American Research and Development Corporation (ARD), 168–70, 173, 202
antitrust division, Department of Justice, 85–86, 89, 90–96, 100, 109–13, 115, 135, 139, 153, 210
antitrust policy: and corporate research, 38, 153, 206; in housing industry 109–16, 210–11; and patent reform, 21, 54, 81–82, 85–96, 99–100, 210–11
Army. *See* U.S. Army
Army Air Corps. *See* U.S. Air Force
Army Air Forces (AAF). *See* U.S. Air Force
Army Corps of Engineers. *See* U.S. Army
Army Ordnance Department. *See* U.S. Army
Arnold, H. H., 176
Arnold, Thurman, 4, 82, 132, 160; antitrust offensive of, 83–86, 149, 216; and housing industry, 109–15; and patent reform, 89–96, 100, 210–11, 217; and reform liberalism, 20–21, 210–11
associationalism: Bureau of Standards and, 19,

30; and Clinton administration, 228–29; and commercial Keynesians, 147; defined, 18–20; and "hybrid," 25–28, 209–12; in the first Roosevelt administration, 71–78, 78–80, in the housing industry, 104–8; and NRA, 20, 25, 63, 136, 147, 209–10, 218, 220; and NSF, 158–64; in the 1920s, 30–31, 39–60, 61; in World War II mobilization, 119, 129–36. *See also under* Hoover, Herbert
AT&T, 18, 35, 53, 87, 96
atomic (all subjects). *See* nuclear power; nuclear weapons
Atomic Energy Act (AEA), 184, 189–90, 191
Atomic Energy Commission (AEC), 162, 177, 189–93, 195, 196, 202, 206, 212, 213
"automatic stabilizers," 147, 154, 170

B-52 bomber, 119, 121, 176, 186, 195, 221
Baruch, Bernard, 42, 119, 123, 135, 137, 147, 176
Bausch and Lomb Company, 81, 93
Beard, Charles, 43
Bell Telephone Laboratories, 18, 35, 45, 75, 87, 122, 135, 161, 219–20
Berge, Wendell, 86, 91, 94–96, 110, 210
Bingaman, Jeff, 228
Black, Hugo, 67, 94
Blandford, John, 105, 106, 108
Boeing Corporation, 180, 192
bombers, strategic, 119, 121, 127, 176, 178–80, 186–88, 195, 221
Bowles, Edward, 128, 178
Bowman, Isaiah, 72–73
Brandeis, Louis D., 54, 85
Brinkley, Alan, 84
Bromley, D. Allan, 229
Brooks, Harvey, 224
Building Research Advisory Board (BRAB), 108,114
building trade unions, 109–13
Bureau of the Budget (BOB) (U.S. Treasury Dept.): under Andrew Mellon, 45; antitrust division and, 86; and defense budget, 179,

ABOUT THE AUTHOR

DAVID M. HART is Assistant Professor of Public Policy at the Kennedy
School of Government, Harvard University, and the author of numerous
articles and book chapters. He received his Ph.D. in Political Science
from the Massachusetts Institute of Technology in 1995.